The Digital Double Bind

D1602411

Oxford Studies in Digital Politics

Founder and Series Editor: Andrew Chadwick, Professor of Political Communication and Director of the Online
Civic Culture Centre (O3C) in the Department of Communication and Media, Loughborough University

The Digital Double Bind

CHANGE AND STASIS IN THE MIDDLE EAST

MOHAMED ZAYANI AND JOE F. KHALIL

OXFORD
UNIVERSITY PRESS

Oxford University Press is a department of the University of Oxford. It furthers
the University's objective of excellence in research, scholarship, and education
by publishing worldwide. Oxford is a registered trade mark of Oxford University
Press in the UK and certain other countries.

Published in the United States of America by Oxford University Press
198 Madison Avenue, New York, NY 10016, United States of America.

Library of Congress Cataloging-in-Publication Data
Names: Zayani, Mohamed, 1965- author. | Khalil, Joe F., author.
Title: The digital double bind : change and stasis in the Middle East /
Mohamed Zayani & Joe F. Khalil.
Description: New York, NY : Oxford University Press, [2024] |
Series: Oxford studies digital politics series |
Includes bibliographical references and index.
Identifiers: LCCN 2023040393 (print) | LCCN 2023040394 (ebook) |
ISBN 9780197508626 (hardback) | ISBN 9780197508633 (paperback) |
ISBN 9780197508657 (epub)
Subjects: LCSH: Information technology—Economic aspects—Middle East. |
Information technology—Social aspects—Middle East. |
Technology and civilization—Middle East.
Classification: LCC HC415.15.Z9 I559 2023 (print) | LCC HC415.15.Z9 (ebook) |
DDC 303.48/330956—dc23/eng/20231010
LC record available at https://lccn.loc.gov/2023040393
LC ebook record available at https://lccn.loc.gov/2023040394

DOI: 10.1093/oso/9780197508626.001.0001

Paperback printed by Marquis Book Printing, Canada
Hardback printed by Bridgeport National Bindery, Inc., United States of America

To Aymen, Chris, Malek, Mia, and Yasmine

Contents

Acknowledgments

Shortly after we embarked on this book project, the COVID-19 pandemic hit hard, disrupting our lives, breaking our routines, and resetting our priorities. Recurrent coronavirus waves, protracted lockdowns, lasting travel restrictions, and mandated social-distancing measures all meant that our collaboration was confined to the online sphere and carried out on social-media platforms. We recognize that it was a privilege to be able to continue our work, even if digitally. What started as a project about the digital became itself an intense digital experience. Countless evening Zoom conversations and passionate discussions kept us connected, engaged, and focused on our work. We found solace in the knowledge that our discussions were breaking our social isolation, even as we navigated the challenges of the pandemic.

This project has been long in the making. Over the past two decades, we have been consumed by the study of media and communication developments in the Middle East. That journey brought us face-to-face with subtle changes that have been further complicated by the advent of the digital, the understanding of which calls for deeper engagement with theory and closer examination of lived experiences. In this book, we attempt to make sense of changes adumbrated by the digital turn. As participant observers, living through these changes and writing from within the region, our interest in how the Middle East experiences its gestations and navigates its challenges is as much a personal reflection on our lived reality as it is an intellectual pursuit. Though our perspectives have not always been fully aligned, the convergences and divergences that emerged helped us challenge our own ways of thinking about the digital Middle East and opened our eyes to new lines of analysis, enabling us to connect our knowledge to broader understandings of change. It is our hope that *The Digital Double Bind* will not only contribute to ongoing academic conversations but also inspire others to engage in critical discussions about the digital turn in the Middle East region and, more broadly, throughout the Global South.

We owe a special debt to a number of scholars and colleagues who read earlier drafts of the manuscript and provided invaluable critical commentary and insightful feedback: Patrick Burkart, Andrew Chadwick, Nick Couldry, John D. H. Downing, Tarek El-Ariss, Marwan Kraidy, Betsy Lancefield Lane, Rory Miller, Anto Mohsin, Paul Musgrave, Zarqa Parvez, Tarik Sabry, and Karin Gwinn Wilkins. Their comments and feedback have improved this work tremendously. Needless to say, the book's shortcomings are entirely our own.

We are also grateful to Rogaia Abusharaf, Omar Al-Ghazzi, George Anghelcev, Hatim El Hibri, Amira El Zein, Tourya Guaaybess, Sami Hermez, Shakir Hussein, Elizabeth Kassab, Patrick Laude, Torsten Menge, Suzi Mirgani, Gerd Nonneman, Firat Oruc, J. R. Osborn, Aswin Punathambekar, Sofiane Sahraoui, Christine Schiwietz, Amira Sonbol, Helga Tawil-Souri, Clyde Wilcox, Bilge Yesil, and William Youmans for their intellectual engagement with various aspects of the project and to Nino Kader, Yuri Tamer, and Asma Ajroudi for sharing their industry insights and experiences. We wish also to extend our thanks to Fatma Oueslati, Maha Essid, Abdullah Imran, Tayyaba Imran, Ngoc Nguyen, and Shiza Abbasi for their research assistance.

Thanks also go to our dedicated colleagues at the Research Office, who facilitated our work: Vabona Zenku, Jihene Chebby Ghannay, Reina Rosales, and Bianca Simon. From the library, we wish to thank Mark Paul, Iman Khamis, Victoria Ng'eno, Mel Aquino, Robert Laws, Paschalia Terzi, Mirta Lendić, Arwa El Kahlout, and Tatiana Usova. Deborah McKee, Ute Kraidy, Hanan Bou Akl, Andrew Henley, André Hajjar, Mohamed Adel, Alessandro Di Muro, Ghazanfer Ansari, and Bob Vance helped in other ways. We are also thankful for the assistance we received from Safwan Masri, Kathleen Hewett-Smith, Adel Iskandar, S. Venus Jin, Gholam Khiabani, Gregory Lowe, Dina Matar, and Tamir Mustapha.

Many of the ideas developed in this book were discussed in the context of three seminars we offered at our institutions: Global Culture and Communication; Media, Culture, and Politics in the Middle East; and Alternative Media in the Middle East. We especially thank our students for their critical engagement with our formulations. A note of thanks goes to the anonymous readers who provided useful commentary and constructive readings of the manuscript and grateful acknowledgment goes to Qatar Foundation for its support of research and scholarly endeavors.

We are also deeply grateful to our editor at Oxford University Press, Angela Chnapko, and our series editor, Andrew Chadwick, who believed in this project and saw it through to its completion. We are equally thankful to Alexcee Bechthold, the senior project editor at OUP; Wendy Keebler, the book's meticulous copyeditor; and Vinothini Thiruvannamalai, the book project manager, for all their work and great assistance throughout the production stage.

Last but not least, we would like to express our gratitude and thanks to Sonia and Kareen for their forbearance and unwavering support, without which we would not have been able to complete this project.

Part I

CONJUNCTURES AND DISJUNCTURES

Chapter 1

The Digital Middle East

Even for the casual observer of the Middle East, the digital has been a driving force of change. More countries are converting to e-government, embracing artificial intelligence, building smart cities, and experimenting with the next-generation networks. Consider Dubai's One Million Arab Coders, an initiative to help youth play a greater role in the knowledge economy by building their skills; Saudi Arabia's Neom, a high-tech mega development project that seeks to reorient the kingdom's economy; Red2Med, a multimillion-dollar submarine cable expansion connecting the East and the West through Egypt's Internet Corridor; and MoroccoTech, a private-public partnership designed to develop a globally competitive digital ecosystem. For those seeking to reinvigorate their economies, the digital has become synonymous with technology-driven innovation and glitzy regional startups playing on the world stage, from the ride-hailing app Careem to the music-streaming service Anghami. Fortuitously, the COVID-19 pandemic accelerated the digitization of sectors once deemed either unlikely or unfit to change, leading to unexpected transformations such as the adoption of e-courts, the licensing of digital payment services, and the promotion of telehealth solutions. Accompanying these developments are sociotechnical reconfigurations of lived reality itself. For most people, the digital has become simply a way of life, made pervasive by the prosaic nature of social media. More users follow global innovations and immerse themselves in digital cultures, participating in recreational activities that range from TikTok dances to online gaming communities. Others are reinventing themselves around constantly evolving economic trends (e.g., cryptocurrencies) and political practices (e.g., Twitter diplomacy). Taken at face value, these verdant developments in the Middle East point to a digital turn that is avowedly transformative.

Yet embracing the digital has not turned Middle Eastern societies into smoothly gliding network societies any more than the persistence of particular forms of social relations, cultural values, and systems of governance makes them thoroughly "traditional." In the accepted image of network societies (typically

The Digital Double Bind. Mohamed Zayani and Joe F. Khalil, Oxford University Press. © Oxford University Press 2024.
DOI: 10.1093/oso/9780197508626.003.0001

associated with technologically advanced Western nations), key social structures and activities are effortlessly intertwined with information and communication technologies (ICTs) and seamlessly organized around flows and networks that define international polities, knowledge economies, and social change.[1] Despite globalization forces and transnational flows, the network society is not an all-encompassing development.[2] Regional discrepancies defy glib prognostications about the Middle East's digital transformation. With so much publicity around the ascent of a handful of predominantly Gulf countries to advanced scales of digital readiness, it is increasingly difficult for media commentators to imagine the much less favorable conditions in other parts of the region. Unequal access and con-strained affordances, limited digital literacies, and disparate deployment of tech-nologies mean that techno-cultural geographies are asymmetrical, even if those asymmetries are often overlooked. The flagrant digital inequalities the COVID-19 pandemic exposed are a stark reminder that the region has yet to achieve over-hyped technology-driven transformation. Even where it has been heavily adopted, the digital has ushered in complex and at times contradictory dynamics that require careful attention.

The Middle East did not experience digital transformation uniformly, unilat-erally, and systematically. That observation, simple as it is, undermines sweeping claims about the transformative potential of the digital. It raises questions about the nature of digital transformation given the region's propensity for, or resistance to, change in the face of entrenched political structures, established economic sys-tems, and ingrained sociocultural norms. For example, one could ask: Why do the uses of certain information technologies in the region remain restricted despite political and financial investments in their deployment and popular interest in their prospects? What does it mean that some Middle Eastern countries have acquired 5G networks ahead of the most developed nations yet periodically ban basic services such as Voice over Internet Protocol (VoIP), popular social-media apps, and the use of virtual private networks (VPNs)? Why do many people decry censorship but at the same time demand greater governmental control over the production and distribution of digital content? What does it mean for states to leverage ICTs in pursuit of a knowledge economy premised on unlocking human potential, while simultaneously constraining freedoms, controlling media, and censoring the internet? What happens when Middle Eastern societies promote collectivist identities constructed around humility, modesty, and restraint, while social-media practices and online socialization promote individualistic identities fashioned around self-promotion and commodification? Finally, what kind of dis-junctures emerge when state and society embrace the affordances of the informa-tion era but remain apprehensive about its disruptive potential?

Current conceptualizations of the digital Middle East do not fully capture these complexities. Such articulations are often constructed around normative benchmarks (such as speed, access, and affordances) and anchored in prescriptive models of human, economic, and political (eco)systems rooted in Western paradigms. Others are defined through assumed binaries (such as utopia/dystopia, development/underdevelopment, progression/regression) that project a Middle East either pursuing the network society at a breakneck pace or that is pinioned and unable to change. These conventional accounts either invoke the transformative power of technology or affirm the inherent and inhibitive nature of the region. As such, they run the risk of either universalizing the digital or orientalizing the Middle East. They flatten complex dynamics that require deeper engagement to arrive at an understanding of the digital Middle East rather than the application of an inappropriate model. A probing study needs to go beyond presentism and determinism and, at the very least, avoid the temptation to invoke convenient explanations for evolving and complex dynamics.

The digital Middle East we depict is not a static condition or the product of a fully enacted transformation. The region's encounter with the digital can best be understood as an ongoing process that manifests itself as a multilayered transition interlinked with technological dimensions but riven with conflicts and contradictions. Embracing the digital is thus fraught with seemingly irreconcilable tensions. Whatever new possibilities the digital turn heralds must be examined in relation to inherent technological challenges as well as in the context of enduring sociocultural norms and economic and political systems. As such, the Middle East's immersion in the digital turn unfolds along a course that simultaneously extends and delimits, animates and inhibits, drives and disrupts ongoing transformations.

We argue that the logics that underpin these layered, fluid, and mutating dimensions engender a double bind that represents the salient feature of the Middle East's digital turn. The theory of the double bind is credited to British anthropologist Gregory Batson, who, along with his team, set out to study the relationship between behavior and communication. In its original formulation in social psychology, the double bind posits a communicative situation that involves contradictory messages. A successful response to one message would require failing to respond to the other, which necessarily entails a breakdown in communication, leading to the entrapment of the receiver in a no-win situation.[3] When such a breakdown is constantly and unavoidably present, it often becomes accepted as a fact of life, even if it could be loosened should the pattern of relations change. Importantly, the double bind is not a simple contradiction or mere opposition between two conflictual realities, nor is it even a paradox. Whereas a paradox is characterized by the incomprehensibility of a contradictory state,[4] a double bind designates an insoluble complexity. As such, the double bind depicts a range of everyday situations we learn to navigate, accept, overcome, or simply ignore. In recent years, the theory has gained some traction in women's studies[5] and gender studies[6] but more so in cultural studies[7] and postcolonial studies,[8] generally centering on the question of what Stuart Hall calls "the power-ideology nexus,"[9] namely how power structures are articulated and how power is constituted.[10] Here what we retain from the concept of the double bind is not only the coexistence of competing and seemingly incongruous logics but their irreducibility to a mere paradox. What is of interest is not only how a digital double bind emerges but also how the ensuing complexities become embedded, how they are navigated, and how they are accommodated.

The attention to the digital double bind is also an invitation to revisit the question of change and stasis.[11]

The Digital Turn

An inquiry into the intricacies of the digital turn requires attention to the uneven pace of technological change as well as the multiple sociopolitical and historical entry points into the adoption of digital technologies. Ever since the global commercialization of the internet, discourses developed in policy circles around the economic prospects of ICTs in what promised to be a renewed opportunity for modernization. Further highlighting the potential of the digital is the plethora of business analyses, industry reports, and regional outlooks that extoll the Middle East's potential as an emerging digital economy. These are outdone only by popular media accounts and mainstream journalistic reports whose enthusiasm for technology-driven sociopolitical change has often been projected onto waves of protest movements that raged across much of the region, making the Arab uprisings indissociable from the power of information technologies. The appeal of these interpretations often comes at the expense of a deeper and more encompassing engagement with the digital Middle East.

Typically, when technology and change are discussed in industry reports, policy documents, or the trade press, the invocation of the digital Middle East is accompanied by tired and tiresome clichés: "rapid," "unprecedented," and "unique" changes that could "produce" global tech hubs, economies, or markets.[12] Making sense of these developments has been an elusive endeavor. That access to the internet has become near ubiquitous throughout the region and that the affordances of digital tools have accelerated should not obscure the fact that change had been under way for some time. To say that the changes the region is witnessing are more transitional than transformative is also to affirm that the binary distinction between a digital and a nondigital Middle East is superficial. The continuum binding the two makes the digital increasingly indissociable from the predigital. This recognition is key to understanding how the digital actually unfolds in the region and what tensions it engenders.

Accordingly, the analysis developed in this book establishes a historical grounding[13] and theoretical foundation for understanding what we call the *digital turn*. This turn designates a process of incremental societal changes associated with the digital yet irreducible to a straightforward technological transformation.

The qualifier "digital" is more than simply a technical attribute referring to technological and media systems dependent on electronic configurations and complex computations that are in essence a binary code in the form of digits. It also goes beyond particular manifestations of digital technologies, whether systems (computers and networks), devices (game consoles and smartphones), services (banking and streaming), or applications (browsers and apps). We use "digital" to refer to information technologies, digital tools, and creative uses, as well as to the knowledge required to develop them. Such definition is anchored in the notion of *techne* (or *tekhne*),[14] which positions digital systems, services, and applications as part of broader sociotechnical practices.[15] Commonly translated as "craft," "art," or "technical knowledge," the Greek term *techne* has also come to refer to the transformation of knowledge into some form of practice or a practical application. Conceiving the digital more broadly as *techne* allows us to consider both the contexts and processes in which ICTs are developed and transformed as well as the various ways in which knowledge is embodied. Phenomenologically, the digital as *techne* becomes a "know-how" embedded in specific environments (whether technological or social).[16] The interest in the digital as *techne* is an interest in "how it is done and performed, rather than how it is thought."[17]

The term "turn"—which designates the unfolding of an era—underscores both the scope and scale of this digital change. By signaling a temporal shift, the turn underscores the importance of time in discussions of technology and change. The digital turn, then, captures both sociotechnical dimensions and temporal configurations. Whereas time is usually seen as universal, temporality refers to experiences of "lived time."[18] Our analysis of the turn heeds two temporalities: gradual changes in the region as it endeavors to transition to the digital and the fast-paced changes resulting from the processes of technological invention, innovation, and diffusion. Time often manifests intensely as multiple temporalities—time that is associated with the lived, the ephemeral, and the instantaneous but also time that endures; time that is associated with colonialism and independence, revolutionary fervor and autocratic rule, war and peace, to name a few. The ensuing tensions and aporias are characterized by interwoven interactions. Such overlapping temporalities complicate the Orientalist binary premodern/modern,[19] which often describes the region's reluctance to change. At the same time, technologies emerge, endure, and disappear or figure alongside "older" infrastructure, tools, and services. The deployment of technologies has different histories, varying speeds, and divergent trajectories.[20] Such temporal variations are evident in references to countries as either "getting ahead" or "falling behind," which is premised on a linear development trajectory associated with the adoption of certain technologies.

The Middle East's digital turn designates a transition process whereby various technological imaginaries are interwoven with multiple temporalities. The changes that are adumbrated by the digital reflect broader economic, political, and sociocultural shifts that predate the digital as we know it and have become more pronounced over time. The turn we depict is also deeply intertwined with specific conditions, from changing expectations of digital natives to the challenges of information dissemination and control.[21] These pressures are inseparable from the forces of globalization[22] and also from the logics of digital capitalism.[23] Understanding this historical process and its implications for the region requires more than highlighting spikes of change and flatlines of stasis; it calls for grounded analysis of the way the digital double bind manifests itself.

The Digital Double Bind

How the region is engaging with the digital turn is not simply a question of strategies of hegemonic power play in the hands of the state actors, market forces, or social players. It is not enough to ascertain that the digital turn unfolds as a series of contradictions and paradoxes. It is not especially analytically productive to label the region's fraught relationship with technology as a "predicament"[24] or to see it from the perspective of culturally essentialist or technologically deterministic accounts. It is equally unproductive to either extol achievements, rankings, and milestones or to bemoan social ailments, moral panics, and cultural lapses assumed to have been triggered by the digital turn. Instead, a more nuanced approach to the Middle East's digital turn demands a careful consideration of the conjunctures and disjunctures that constitute the digital double bind's logics and structure its dynamics—how specific logics (and illogics) persist while competing ones emerge within particular spatiotemporal configurations and how the ensuing dynamics influence the unfolding of the digital Middle East. Such an approach highlights a productive tension between the growing impetus for change and complex dynamics that impede such change. This reframing of the region's digital turn contrasts its aspirations for technologically induced sociocultural change and its anchoring in sociocultural, political, and economic systems that perpetuate stasis.

Accounting for contradictory tendencies illuminates the double bind that characterizes the Middle East's digital turn. States embrace the digital while walling off the internet from their citizens. They seek to develop knowledge economies that thrive on innovation and creativity while refusing to relinquish clientelistic economic systems based on privileges and entitlements. They promote a startup culture while remaining protective of hierarchal, risk-averse, and family-oriented business culture. To preserve their power and privileges, the region's elites must reckon with the digital, leveraging its promises and limiting its undesired effects. Whichever path they choose is bound to unsettle key elements of the system that upholds them.

These tensions also manifest themselves in sociocultural practices. Supported through far-flung networks and promoted as the pathway for social change, digital technologies have been restructuring social relations. Yet much of what digitally enabled individuals and communities do disrupts long-established traditional relationships predicated on national, religious, or kinship affiliations (e.g., ethno-religious, political, or interest groups developing transnational digital networks). With the prominence of digital-content creators, the process of identity formation is negotiated within the context of encroaching media representations and ineluctable networks. Adding to these complexities is the extent to which certain self-produced images and particular types of behavior are legitimated and accepted through routine online and offline public engagements. Once a novel phenomenon, social-media influencers are bound by the platform's algorithmic logic and are ultimately subjected to state-mandated social norms. On another level, the adoption of digital technologies can fuel movements toward either re- or de-traditionalization. Many conservatives who advocate a return to traditions use the same social-media tools that have been accused of disrupting social norms. Extremist groups that espouse retrograde or ultraconservative discourses routinely appropriate the most sophisticated digital technologies to promulgate the most reactionary visions to a wide public.[25] Whence the double bind: in the process of states, markets, and societies adopting new practices and forging new structures, they empower different actors and unleash different processes that undermine the foundation of existing systems—be it political, cultural, social, economic, or otherwise.

The Middle East is in a "hybrid state," reckoning with modernity that has not entirely arrived and negotiating its relation to traditions that have not yet disappeared.[26] Contemplating the ensuing tensions provides insights into the logics that characterize the Middle East's digital turn. The conditions, situations, or circumstances in which the state's embracing of, the market's alignment with, and the public's immersion in the digital create conflictual pulls that constitute a digital double bind. Whereas a paradox, for example, occurs when activists take to social media to call for street protests but choose not to take part in public demonstrations, a digital double bind occurs when the activists' use of social media recalls the state security's ruthless retaliation or the platform's deletion of content or profiles. The digital double bind requires accounting for the fundamental interdependencies and cycles of interactions between and within states, markets, and publics whether national, regional or international. Similarly, the Middle East's complex engagement with development cannot be understood without recognizing that the digital double bind presents a situation where the choice of a particular technological path promotes change while at the same time undermining its ultimate objectives—regardless of which choice is made. The incommensurability of this double bind defies the teleological conceptions of change through which the region is often perceived.

In highlighting the digital double bind, we eschew the question of how consequential the digital turn may be. Our endeavor shifts the analysis away from the digital turn's close ties with linear progression of change and its assumed effects on state, market, and society and onto the conflictual pulls and mutating dynamics it generates. In so doing, we move the debate away from generic affordances of digital technologies and toward the uneven productive tensions that give the digital Middle East its defining character. A deep understanding of the digital double bind clarifies how the digital manifests within particular spheres while also highlighting its intersectionality. The digital double bind cannot be understood in isolation. Choices about change are made in complex and intertwined contexts tied to lived temporalities and constructed imaginaries of both the region and the digital. The forces of urbanization, modernization, and globalization are promoting change within each society and across the Middle East. These forces operate along different temporalities and move at different speeds. For example, Libya and Sudan are subject to an enduring legacy of revolutionary regimes, state-socialist economic policies, and intractable conflicts, all of which limit their development despite their oil riches and abundance of natural resources. By contrast, other parts of the region have oriented themselves toward the digital, such as the UAE's city-state of Dubai—an ultramodern cosmopolitan center where a combination of political will, financial clout, human talent, and technological affordances is driving change. These conditions are not exclusive. The region lives in multiple temporalities where manifestations of tradition and (post)modernity, stasis and change, also coexist, be it at the level of the nation-state, city, or neighborhood.

Similarly, although change is typically associated with progress, it does not preclude regression. The same Middle East that embraces the digital turn and orients itself toward the knowledge economy is also the Middle East that gave rise to ultraconservative currents and extremist groups that decry modernity. Both those who welcome change and those who seek to reverse it have been affected by the speed with which new, constantly evolving forms of information technologies are adopted. As it transpires, the digital Middle East unfolds along a double bind. In one respect, digital imaginaries[27] are associated with logics and dynamics and ultimately configure tools, practices, and services that set forth a specific pathway for change. Yet the very same digital imaginaries, conceived and deployed with different logics and dynamics, either resist or undermine that pathway for change. What ensue are imperfect, even false choices: whatever actors choose as a path for change alters their own proclaimed objectives.

The double bind does not necessarily entail stasis. The discordances we pinpoint are not perpetually immutable, nor does their unfolding follow a predictable path. Apparently irresolvable conflicts do not have a predetermined ending. The dynamics produced by interactions between the constitutive elements proliferate openings and forestall closures.[28] As will become clear, incremental changes are likely to happen when the double bind arises from asynchrony between different temporalities and imaginaries. When it happens, this very same change reinforces the dynamics that ultimately constrain the possibility of effecting long-lasting, radical change. Hence the semblance of stasis. What this means is that the complex and uneven dynamics engendered by the digital turn are shaping the Middle East in peculiar ways, compelling it to change at varying paces and according to different logics. Considered from a *longue durée* perspective, these antagonisms have manifested themselves variably in relationship to the question of technology and change but have become more acute with the digital turn.

While the book considers various manifestations of the digital Middle East, it does so within appropriately micro and macro levels of analysis. Such inquiry into the lived experiences of the digital is grounded in empirical analyses of a wide range of issues relating to social structures, political economy, techno-cultural geographies, and beyond. The formulations we put forth open the analysis beyond media-centered approaches or infrastructural and economic models.[29] Pertinently, while the digital is no longer confined to "new media," neither can it be considered "old."[30] It occupies liminal spaces constituted by the digital turn, allowing us to juxtapose multiple experiences of digitality.

Throughout this book, we trace histories of the digital Middle East, identifying its roots and routes and analyzing how the digital bears on political, economic, and cultural questions. The arguments, issues, and ideas outlined here should remain relevant beyond the immediacy of the latest "unicorn deal" or crossing a new digital-readiness milestone and beyond controversies surrounding a backlash against a particular social-media fad or an egregious cyberlaw that institutionalizes censorship. To these ends, we foreground connections between different historical moments, which span decades going back to the predigital era as a rejoinder to ahistorical accounts of the digital Middle East. We also focus on logics and dynamics that connect with long-running concerns about technology, change, and stasis that exist well beyond the Middle East. For communities of the Global South, the temporalities and imaginaries of the Middle East must appear as a familiar series of junctions and disjunctions that are associated with the question of technology and change.

Chapter 2

Reckoning with Change

At the turn of the twenty-first century, a number of media observers affirmed that although not everyone in the Middle East was wired, the region was not beyond the reach of the "information revolution."[1] One impetus for these pronouncements was the influx of satellite channels, which ushered in an era of "information plenty."[2] Web 2.0 heralded "a new media revolution"[3] favoring different modes of media consumption and participation among "networked publics."[4] Captivated by the events of the Arab uprisings, a wave of scholars confidently declared the "crucially important" role digital social-networking tools played in the street protests that swept the region.[5] Even more nuanced accounts still saw a "socio-technical revolution" in these developments.[6] For others, emerging tech trends in the region incarnated what they effusively described as "the Middle East's other revolution."[7] If anything, these proclamations about sweeping revolutionizing transformations that break away from the past and herald the new point to the complexities of the digital turn. Understanding these evolving dynamics and their logics requires a *longue-durée* approach that reveals what the Middle East designates and how its relationship with technology is constructed. This chapter delves into particular histories of the region, probes its technological imaginaries, and chronicles specific encounters with modernity. It provides a historical engagement with the question of change and stasis associated with the digital double bind.

Whither the Middle East?

The Middle East is a territorially vast, economically diverse, and geopolitically significant region.[8] A relatively more homogeneous subset of the region is the Arab Middle East—a grouping of twenty-two sovereign states with a combined population of more than 400 million, representing just more than 5% of the global population. Geographically, the Arab Middle East addressed in this book extends

The Digital Double Bind. Mohamed Zayani and Joe F. Khalil, Oxford University Press. © Oxford University Press 2024.
DOI: 10.1093/oso/9780197508626.003.0002

over two continents and spans four distinct subregions: the Arabian Peninsula, the Mashriq (Eastern Mediterranean countries, including the Levant, or Bilad al-Sham, and Iraq), the Nile River region, and North Africa. These four subregions are marked by geographical contiguity but also defined by sociocultural affinities. Such proximities have led some subregions to form intergovernmental, political, and social unions, such as the Gulf Cooperation Council and the Arab Maghreb Union, fragile as these organizations may be. Even more prominent and still more unwieldy is the Arab League, founded in 1945. The League comprises all Arab states and serves as an umbrella organization for political, cultural, and economic policies, though its status and dynamics reflect the geopolitical priorities of its member states.[9]

Despite the appearance of strong commonalities and affinities across many Middle Eastern societies, including shared cultural histories and demographic challenges, the region's components are distinct and its pluralism complex.[10] The region includes a mosaic of ethnicities, multiple languages, and diverse socio-political systems. Linguistically, although standard Arabic is a common shared language, its spoken dialects are so distinct as to nearly form different languages. These dialects coexist with Western languages that endured as colonial legacies (French and English, for example) and community or indigenous languages that continue to be defining elements of identity politics (Kurdish, Syriac, Tamazight, and Coptic, among others). Politically, while some states are republics that foster a degree of political pluralism, others are absolute monarchies. Economic divisions are equally stark. Many of the region's states are classified as moderate-income countries, but some (such as Qatar and Kuwait) are among the richest in the world, and others (such as Yemen and Sudan) rank among the poorest.

The colonial experience of the region's society varied, with effects that continue to differ. For example, North Africa's direct and prolonged experience with French colonialism was unlike the legacy of the French mandate in parts of the Levant as far as their postindependence relationship to the French language is concerned. Similarly, while the smaller Gulf monarchies derive their existence as territorial states in part from Britain's agreement with particular coastal sheikhs, Saudi Arabia stands out as having been spared a formal imperial presence. Such distinctive historical trajectories produced different experiences with modernization and manifestations of statehood.[11] For many, today's Middle East continues to reckon with neocolonialism in the form of enduring geopolitical, economic, and cultural influences which are compounded with persisting ideological divides and Islamic revivalism.[12] More relevantly, the colonial legacy bears on how these states have come to view, appropriate, or contest Western technologies.

Two additional considerations that arise from colonial legacies and geopolitical rivalries further complicate any understanding of the Middle East. First, the region is arguably one of the most unstable parts of the world, politically and otherwise. Wars have endured over the decades, most notably the Israeli-Palestinian conflict.

Even geographic subregions that share history and culture are characterized by tension. Historical animosities and shifting state interests are constantly changing the region's sense of interconnectedness. Second, the Arab Middle East also borders some countries that are significant both historically and geopolitically but can be considered distinct subregions in themselves. These include Turkey, with its Ottoman legacy; Iran, the region's non-Arab theocracy; and Israel, which positions itself as a major regional non-Arab power. Relevantly, Israel is a leading digital actor whose growing relations with some Arab countries is partly framed around mutually beneficial technological investments.[13] Further, there are other actors (such as the Kurds, the Amazighs, and the Palestinians) that constitute nations without states.

The region's historical ties to other areas through geographical proximity and trade activities form a set of relations that have shaped and continue to shape the region's geographical contours, geopolitical realities, and international economic position. Home to strategic waterways, the region long constituted a market and meeting ground for peoples, cultures, religions, interests, and goods across the vast continents of Asia, Africa, and Europe. Today those same facts—as well as the presence of substantial natural resources—mean that the region continues to be a contested area between external powers.

The Middle East continues to defy geographical teleologies for reasons ranging from globalization forces and diasporic communities to regional crises and shifting geopolitical interests.[14] As Edward Said's seminal work on Orientalism reveals,[15] the Middle East is defined as much by colonial discourses about the region as by its geographical location. The Middle East cannot be easily disentangled from Western essentializing conceptions of "the Orient" premised on discourses of "othering" and projections of power.[16] Cultural (mis)representations do more than create self-images that demarcate the "superior" Occident from the "inferior" Orient; they legitimize relations of domination. Accordingly, Western media and policy circles often cast the Middle East as static, lacking development, resistant to change, and incompatible with modernity. Equally important are the self-perceptions that Arab-produced discourses reveal. Compared with the notion of "Arabness" or "Arabism" (urubah), which emphasizes a common language and identity, for instance, the more political designation "Arab nationalism" (al qawmiya al arabiya) refers to a projected unity of Arabs who share a common economic future and political destiny. Although an Arab political union has failed to materialize politically or economically, the rallying collective cultural identity of Arabness has endured.

Seen from this perspective, the Middle East can be usefully understood as an "imagined community"[17] with mediated interactions around political ideologies, economic interests, cultural practices, and postcolonial legacies. In the latter part of the twentieth century, this community was primarily formed around state-sponsored transnational mass media (the press and radio) and ideologies that cross borders and transcend individual nation-states, including Arab nationalism, Baathism, and leftist ideologies.[18] As these secular ideologies receded after the Cold War and economic liberalism became more widely adopted, political Islam emerged as a sociopolitical force. While religious heritage continues to be a defining element of the region, Islam as an identity marker is constantly challenged by sectarian, nationalistic, and ethnic considerations.[19] In contrast to the failure of secular and religious ideologies to produce a pan-Arab project, the rise of pan-Arab satellite television in the 1990s helped energize a renewed sense of shared Arab identity. Subsequently, the internet and social media promoted an expanding "digital Arabness."[20]

Beyond Technology and Modernization

A discussion of technology and change necessitates a sociohistorical perspective on the question of modernity as a condition of social existence with its contested histories, diverse processes, and divergent pathways. The motivation for this analysis is not a search for prescriptive answers that are informed by either manifestly Western conceptions of development or postcolonial critiques that decry the development project altogether.[21] Instead, this analysis is motivated by the belief that a critical account of competing visions of what is otherwise a fraught relationship among modernity, technology, and change can help grasp the intricacies of the digital Middle East.

The condition of modernity preoccupied Arab thinkers, intellectuals, and reformers long before the digital. With the intrusion of Western colonial powers in the region, such engagements became more pressing as contending projects of modernization emerged. As early as the mid-nineteenth century, an Arab modernization movement known as Al Nahda ("Awakening" or "Renaissance") crystallized.[22] Al Nahda's project encompassed distinct but intersecting religious, secular, and nationalist modernization currents. It aimed to rejuvenate the region's cultural norms, attitudes, and practices. That ambition precluded a Western approach that sought to transform Middle Eastern societies from "traditional" to "modern," a project that manifested itself as a modernization paradigm in the middle of the twentieth century.

Though not coterminous, these two movements reveal the extent to which preoccupations with what it means to be "modern" are rooted in divergent conceptions of the Middle East. Al Nahda's modernity project, born partly in response to the colonial experience, had envisioned avant-garde approaches in the arts and culture and promoted progressive forms of governance, education, and even lifestyle.[23] A contending modernization project, which gained prominence during the Cold War, provided a rationale for the West to adopt it as an interventionist foreign policy and for the Middle East to become a receiver of foreign aid and expertise.

As articulated by American social scientists, modernization envisaged shaping the consciousness of traditional societies and promoting an entrepreneurial model of society, conceivably a continuation of the colonial project.[24] One influential text, Daniel Lerner's *The Passing of Traditional Society* (1958), exhibited assumptions that continue to underlie currents of scholarship about the Middle East, namely that traditional values, antiquated practices, and premodern structures restrain "progress."[25]

Technology formed an essential element for both projects. Western technologies and concepts proved to be a source of inspiration for many reformers and thinkers, while technocratic elites and modernization adherents viewed communication technologies (especially mass media and communication) as a catalyst. The two camps approached these influences in strikingly different ways and envisioned them being used in distinctive fashions. Al Nahda's adoption of Western technologies was driven by the desire to renew the East. By contrast, Lerner and his advocates viewed mass communication as a conveyor belt carrying ideas from technologically advanced nations to the developing world, where they would help people shed their traditional ways of life and adopt putatively Western values, systems, and practices that champion liberal democracy and free market economies.

Neither project fully succeeded. In the case of Al Nahda, its efforts, although enlightened, did not amount to modernizing the philosophical, religious, and political conception of the state or society. Nor did they produce critical discourses in the natural and social sciences,[26] although their contributions in the fields of humanities and the arts shaped a new generation of Arab intellectuals and policymakers.[27] Similarly, although the modernization paradigm continues to have a certain resonance,[28] it relegates endemic issues of development to intrinsic conditions, which downplays exogenous forces.[29] Issues such as income disparities, gender inequalities, educational reform, chronic unemployment, and weak governance loom large in the international development agenda. Although modernization, within this manifest agenda, amounted largely to the westernization of postcolonial societies,[30] it nonetheless resonated with a number of political elites and social reformers who adopted Euro-American models, systems, and technologies in pursuit of their nations' development goals.[31] In some cases, the promises of modernization and the desire to rank highly in international "league tables" impelled Arab states to acquire and adopt Western technologies.[32]

Disillusionment with Al Nahda and skepticism toward modernization gave way to a new momentum, particularly with newly independent Arab states and revolutionary regimes embarking on large national development projects. By the 1970s, new, critical intellectual and activist currents brought questions of dependency and cultural imperialism to the fore, which found an outlet in sociopolitical movements that advocated participation, empowerment, and resistance.[33] Adherents of these anti-hegemonic philosophies, which originated primarily in Latin America and echoed throughout the developing world, argued that modernization theory ignored both structural barriers to development and the weight of the colonial legacy.[34] They decried modernization theory's lack of understanding of local cultures and unquestioned faith in the ability of Western technology to effect worthwhile change. Instead, they advocated a conception of socioeconomic development that could lead to lasting social change embedded in local communities.[35] Just as modernization theorists pitted modernity against tradition, proponents of these newer theories set the non-Western "periphery" against the "core."[36] In the words of Samir Amin, a vocal critic of global inequality and a dependency theorist, rich world development and global underdevelopment are inextricably linked.[37]

As more non-Western countries gained political clout, they advocated for economic and cultural change on a global scale. The weight of the Global South manifested through the rapid ascension of newly decolonized countries into the United Nations (UN) during the 1970s and 1980s (and the emergence of the political Non-Aligned Movement [NAM] and the economic Group of 77). As a key Arab state, Egypt was one vocal advocate of a New International Economic Order (NIEO) in which the dependency of developing countries on foreign aid would be replaced by fair trade with developed countries.[38] These non-Western countries also decried structural inequalities in international communication, challenged media's one-way flow and communication technology imbalances, and advocated a New World Information and Communication Order (NWICO).[39]

While the impact of these efforts is debatable, they signaled a shift in the global discourse regarding development and technology. Communication for Development (C4D) emerged as a participatory model that recognizes local knowledge and engages with local stakeholders in pursuit of relevant and enduring change.[40] This grounded approach to technology found many local expressions. In the Middle East, an interest in inter-Arab collaborations in science and technology led to the development of the region's first shared satellite communication initiative, the Arab-funded and Western-manufactured ArabSat.[41] Rather than dismiss the satellite as yet another manifestation of Western hegemony, proponents of change in the Middle East came to consider the acquisition of technology as an enabler of transnational cooperation—as well as a marker of independence and an indicator of a nation's standing.[42] To be sure, this conception of development was (and is) constrained by dominant state institutions' restrictions on technology, internal regional inequalities, the politics of inter-Arab cooperation, and the exigencies of a hegemonic international system of foreign aid that controls funding[43]—all of which preclude a dialogic approach for social change that incorporates participatory communication and meshes local needs and policy considerations.[44]

Even a brief discussion of modernization in the region is incomplete without reference to the appeal of another modernization project, this one inspired by state socialism, anchored in reformist ideologies and populist projects, and carried out through central planning and dirigiste policies.[45] At the peak of US-Soviet

Cold War rivalry, revolutionary regimes in the Arab world (particularly in Algeria, Libya, Syria, Iraq, and Yemen) that sought to distance themselves from their former Western colonizers saw hybrid Soviet-style socialism as providing both a model and a means for an alternative modernization project. This project foregrounded institutional practices that gave the state a central (and monopolistic) role in economic planning and management. Emulating the Soviet Union's five-year plans for national development, a series of state educational policies and industrialization projects was instrumental in developing local technological capabilities, including military industries. In the long run, however, the interests of the ruling classes and their business allies paved the way for a reorientation toward state-dependent capitalism.

Despite various experiments, the prospects for Arab modernization soon dissipated. As the Arab world emerged out of the 1970s, it became clear that promised socioeconomic progress was not within reach.[46] The 1980s brought additional challenges. Many countries in the global periphery, the Middle East included, experienced an economic downturn and fell into debt crises, largely the result of profligate lending by Western banks and heavy borrowing by kleptocracies.[47] Foreign assistance designed to address the debt crisis became predicated on fulfilling international organizations' expectations that countries receiving such assistance would follow prescribed macroeconomic reforms, which included adopting structural adjustment policies, promoting neoliberal policies, and deepening integration into a global economy.[48] The Western push for neoliberal policies broadened such neocolonial practices. Western experts and leaders proclaimed that a free market, rather than the state, would serve as the engine for socioeconomic development. Those calls came at a time when reformers in a number of Middle East states—already frustrated by state-led programs that had vitiated rather than accelerated development—became open to different approaches. At the same time, the retreat of socialist powers removed a counterweight to Western discursive and economic power. These policies, coupled with persistent underdevelopment, led to further reliance on the West for technology even as multinational corporations grew stronger at the expense of local- or state-owned companies.

By the 1990s, innovations in ICTs consolidated the state-private nexus. The relevant advances included a broad range of innovations, from commercial satellite television broadcasting to email services and internet browsers, which ushered in digital capitalism. In the telecommunications sector, local elites and international companies forged new partnerships across the region at the expense of state monopolies. Notably, national and foreign investment in ICTs was considered not only essential to economic growth but also a potent instrument for social change.[49] The unrelenting process of globalization further enshrined the premise that economic liberalization moved in tandem with political liberalization. As these expectations extended to the Middle East, a new discourse emerged in which democratization was promoted as the path to development. That idea took hold even though economic development at the time also occurred under autocratic regimes (e.g., Singapore and Taiwan). Several Arab countries (e.g., Iraq and Egypt) stalled political reform in the name of development.[50]

Since the mid-twentieth century, the democratization agenda has been tightly connected to US political and economic hegemony.[51] Through much of the decade following the terror attacks of September 11, 2001, democracy promotion was deemed essential to enhancing US security and to maintaining influence in the Middle East.[52] In this endeavor, democracy promoters placed considerable faith in communication technologies and the mass media. The appropriation of state-sponsored international broadcasting, including radio, is hardly new; it stretches back to the colonial era. What is noteworthy, though, is how communication technologies, from satellite television to the internet, became part of a widely adopted discourse for change and, in fact, integral to the US public diplomacy strategy.[53] Over time, a slew of state-sponsored international broadcasters—from America's Al Hurra to France 24 and from Russia Today to China Global Television Network—vied for the hearts and minds of audiences in the Middle East and elsewhere. For many foreign-policy strategists and technology enthusiasts alike, the alleged role that social media played in the 2011 Arab uprisings was nothing less than a vindication of democracy promoters' faith. Although the illusion of technological triumph proved hollow, these discourses about democracy and freedom remain seductive even today, subsumed in the activities of various international development organizations (e.g., USAID)[54] and forming the unstated assumptions of state policy choices and planning.[55]

Whereas these theories maintain the West as a referent, Arab intellectual historiographies tend to focus on Arab culture as a strong determinant for what came to be known as the "Arab predicament": what observers claimed to be the region's inability to change.[56] Largely driven by a sense of fatalism, this predicament frames endogenous variables as the root cause of Arab societies' seeming stasis. Various articulations of the Arab predicament drew from reactions to defining historical moments in the region (most notably the 1967 Arab-Israeli war) and generated critical reflections on the Arab condition as such.[57] These intellectual debates oscillated between cultural impediments and sociohistorical determinants. Individually, the Arab self is perceived as emulating the Western other who innovates and is therefore bound by an uneven relationship characterized by a "civilizational gap."[58] Collectively, this discourse disparages Arab societies as trapped by nostalgia, keener on preserving the past than on embracing the future.[59] Where elites, intellectuals, and artists offered alternatives to cultural dependency on the West, these movements struggled to challenge the dialectics of tradition, as the source of collective authority, and modernity, as a form of autonomy.[60] Further impeding efforts to overcome this predicament is the assumed need for Arab societies to replicate the ways Western societies evolved when they developed these technologies.[61] At the core, the understanding of the Arab predicament largely rests on the view that Arab societies are at an impasse, resulting in intellectual inertia and sociopolitical malaise.[62] To those who subscribed to such views, the information era offered the hope for change.

Discourses and Imaginaries of the Digital

Exploring the intricacies of the digital Middle East starts with the recognition that technology has its own myths. The globalization of the digital has created discourses and imaginaries that sustain myths[63] about how nations, markets, and individuals around the world are connected through technological properties—flows of data, information, and ideas that make the everyday increasingly indissoluble from the digital. Addressing perceptions about technology leads to revelations as important as those to be drawn by addressing conceptions about the region.

The "digital" part of the digital Middle East is not simply about technology. The digital is, of course, typically associated with a complex array of material technologies and related information and communication infrastructure. Yet the digital cannot be reduced to a purely technical dimension or conflated with computer-related functions. Experientially, the digital is encountered as a disembodied reality articulated in intangibles (the internet, cyberspace, and the cloud) and permeated by incessant flows.[64] But the digital is also experienced as "imaginaries" that summon its potential, its affordances, and its power. "Social imaginaries"[65] or "social myths"[66] are beliefs and values that are internalized and, as such, usually unchallenged. These imaginaries manifest as a set of ordering conceptions and visions that people embrace. They advance certain interpretations, define particular expectations, and generate specific meanings that are collectively shared and even institutionally adopted. The more deeply embedded these imaginaries are, the more they structure forms of social life, shape perceptions of power, circumscribe public debate, and delimit future possibilities. An examination of common sociotechnical imaginaries[67] reveals how both aspirations and apprehensions about a digital transformation remain amorphous in its configuration and uneven in its deployment.

Imaginaries constructed around digital technologies are produced through a complex process involving a range of stakeholders (including states, markets, publics institutions, interest groups, and individuals) who operate at the intersection of local, regional, or global levels. Digital imaginaries are intimately connected with history, political economy, and sociality.[68] These can take any form. They could be articulated in neoliberal digital policies that reflect the encroachment of digital capitalism, as evinced in the region's startup culture. Alternatively, they could be evident in the way marginalized groups (such as youth, women, and minorities) have placed digital tools at the service of their cultural politics. The ways in which particular imaginaries take hold strongly influence how the digital Middle East unfolds and, in some ways, order the very configurations that animate it.

This vantage point allows us to illuminate a prevailing imaginary regarding how the digital drives sociocultural, political, and economic change in the Middle East. The digital is often sought out as a convenient solution to ongoing challenges—as a "technological fix" to societal problems. A technological elixir proves appealing. Such a cure does not necessarily require unsettling institutional norms, altering cultural dispositions, or changing personal behaviors. Thus fetishized, the digital induces ever-expanding desires that are matched only by the technologies' promises. The self-perpetuating nature of technological application and the promise of techno-futures facilitate the integration of digital technologies into different spheres of societal activities. For businesses, a growing array of e-commerce platforms premised on user engagement are promoted as sustaining an ever-expanding consumerism. For individuals, growing platforms and enhanced e-services are adopted because of their convenience, time savings, cost effectiveness, and other benefits. For the state, e-government is depicted as a means for curbing public spending, increasing efficiency, and monitoring crime. In all these spheres, the adoption of new technologies is inscribed within an imaginary that considers the digital as a panacea. The ultimate promise is that a leap into the digital will rid the Middle East of its perceived ills.

The digital also emerged as the antidote to autocracy and repressive political cultures.[69] During and after the 2011 Arab uprisings, digital technologies came to be perceived as effective tools for political change. Many commentators, journalists, and pundits effusively described the events in Tunisia, Egypt, and beyond as social-media revolutions, portraying Facebook and Twitter as engines of regime change and conduits for political transformation.[70] The media turned Wael Ghonim, a Google techie, into the face of the 2011 Egyptian revolution. Ghonim was hurriedly proclaimed a catalyst for what was dubbed "revolution 2.0."[71] Media discourses such as these, which characterize the uprisings as digitally enabled revolutions, reflect a fervent belief in the power of technology to effect sociopolitical change even in entrenched, clientelistic autocracies.[72] Despite revisionist accounts aiming to rebut such fanfare,[73] the digital acquired a manifest political dimension beyond the momentous events of the uprisings. Whether used by social movement actors as "liberation technology,"[74] adopted by government surveillance agencies in the form of "digital authoritarianism,"[75] or deployed by extremist groups and radical organizations as "nefarious technology,"[76] the digital has reconfigured how politics are imagined and contested. Irrespective of whether these technologies are liberating or hegemonic (a weighty question in itself), the multiple and incongruous constructs that underpin such discourses are inevitably entangled with digital imaginaries.[77]

Considerable faith has also been placed in the ability of the digital to energize the development of the region. The recursive nature of the technology means that newer apps constantly replace existing ones, which often amounts to planned obsolescence. That trait seems to make plausible a "digital sublime"[78] fantasy of seamless technological progress. One such digital imaginary fueled discourses about individual assertion and group empowerment rooted in the ability of the digital to create private and public spaces where women, young people, and other marginalized communities could express themselves. Another involved economic growth. Governments promote the digital as a harbinger of development and economic diversification. In this vision, the market fosters digital innovations that create value, while individuals orient their education and careers toward the digital in pursuit of a better future, thus producing a cycle.

For many enthusiasts, the region's observable digital successes provide evidence of how the Global South is replicating Silicon Valley. Venture capital and sovereign wealth funds have encouraged private and state investments in the digital economy, including supporting an incipient startup culture. Across the region, economic free zones for digital sectors have fostered an ecosystem resulting in a steady stream of deals, investments, and exits. Consider the rise of Careem (Generous), the region's largest ride-hailing company. Barely seven years after its modest launch in 2012, Careem boasted the creation of more than one million employment opportunities,[79] luring the San Francisco–based Uber to acquire it in a multibillion-dollar deal. However, such dramatic successes are not common for startups in the Arab Middle East. Most of them are largely concentrated in the UAE, Saudi Arabia, and Egypt. Even there, these companies often face regulatory challenges that inhibit cross-border investments, ownership, and operations. Similarly, the ecosystem that supports them lacks sociocultural, political, and economic embeddedness. The Arab Silicon Valley is more easily envisioned than achieved.

Whether constructed as a technological fix, an empowering tool, or an equalizing force, the digital is ingrained in everyday practices and popular culture[80] and sustained in political and economic discourses to such a degree that it has become indissociable from the way it is conceived, lived, and experienced. These imaginaries are not fixed in space or time. They are constantly reinvented, readapted, and reappropriated. Acknowledging these imaginaries as interpretative processes through which discourses about the digital are constructed and internalized is another step toward grasping the complexities of the digital Middle East.

Part II

ASPIRATIONS AND HINDRANCES

Technological Foundations and Trajectories

No account of the Middle East's digital turn is complete without reference to the infrastructures of information and communications technologies (ICTs). Exploring the many facets of the region's infrastructure provides an initial understanding of the complexity of the digital turn. What the term "infrastructure" designates is often distinct from what are perceived as the benefits of infrastructure. This analytical distinction can be pointed out in a growing body of literature on infrastructure in media studies, internet studies, and science and technology studies (STS), as well as in cognate fields such as cultural anthropology and human geography. Recognizing that distinction has turned the attention of researchers from focusing on the technological properties of a particular medium to analyzing the sociotechnical dimensions and embedded practices that define and structure the production, circulation, and use of various technologies.[1] A focus on the digital's infrastructural underpinning conjures visions of its hard dimensions: physical networks, data centers, cloud systems, and other equipment necessary for the operation of digital connections and the transfer of data. The fuller view also incorporates the soft dimensions of digital infrastructure: the institutions, processes, and environments needed to maintain the economic, political, and sociocultural functioning of the hardware. Examining how both dimensions coexist and mutually define each other is essential for any critical discussion of infrastructure.

Research in infrastructure studies that examines these dimensions tends to fall into two broad categories: the first, anchored in political economy, highlights dynamics ranging from power relations to value extraction; the second, influenced by sociological and phenomenological interpretations, privileges infrastructure's inherently relational dimensions. The complex and multidimensional nature of infrastructure requires scholars to distinguish the material from the immaterial, the conspicuously technical from the characteristically relational.[2] Increased digitization has made these pursuits even more pressing. In particular, ongoing research on the "infrastructuralization" of digital platforms highlights the need for an infrastructural optic that encompasses a range of issues, including scale of operation, technical labor, industry logics, government regulations, state power, and sociocultural practices.[3] This multidimensional perspective also recognizes that infrastructure is inherent in the process of digital transformation and that it operates in an increasingly integrated global arena.

This part of the book draws on insights from infrastructure studies to unravel the lineaments of a digital Middle East that is shaped by the material deployment of technologies as much as it is premised on a set of imaginaries, relations, and practices. Examining change beyond conceptions of information technologies as exogenous forces with defined characteristics helps illuminate the extent to which infrastructural systems are embedded in sociopolitical and economic relations,[4] as well as how they are associated with earlier technologies (e.g., telephony), entrenched practices (e.g., internet control), and forms of access (e.g., piracy).[5]

This analysis goes beyond facile accounts that reduce the region's digital turn to the inevitability and exigency of technological change. Highlighting the "blurred materiality of infrastructure"[6] illuminates complex relationships and connections that underpin the development of ICT infrastructure and in doing so complicates conventional understandings of the digital turn as a simple result of the region's adoption of information technologies. While technological infrastructures have facilitated the Middle East's digital turn, global discourses accompanying the Information Revolution (such as the "right to communicate" for the Global South)[7] and forces of globalization (dynamics of international collaboration, transnational networks, and information flows)[8] have also played pivotal roles. The logics and imperatives that shaped the region's digital turn encompass the technological but are intimately connected with national agendas, regional contexts, and historical conditions as well.

Chapter 3

The Digital as Infrastructure

The digital turn is the latest phase in an ongoing process of modernization enabled by ICT infrastructure. In the postindependence era, an "interventionist-redistributive" development model led states in the region to invest massive resources in such infrastructure in pursuit of development and nation-building.[1] Broadening the analytical focus beyond the enabling role of technology, the agenda of state actors, and the interests of local and international markets permits an examination of more complex dynamics that impel the region's drive for technology-centered modernization. Recognizing the full complexity and significance of the region's pursuit of modern ICTs requires paying attention to historical junctures (postindependence state formation and state building), geopolitical dynamics (cold war rivalries, interstate political strife, and regional wars), supranationalist ideologies (Arab nationalism and anti-imperialism movements), and strategic (inter)national interests (state power, security, and foreign investments). The pursuit of ICT infrastructure has also been shaped by various actors (Arab states, foreign powers, investment groups, satellite operators, transnational broadcasters), a constellation of enabling factors (oil wealth, strategic sectors, human capital), and legal structures and international policies (telecommunication ownership, licensing, and regulation).[2] Significantly, a historical *longue-durée* approach reveals a tenuous balance between sets of different poles: the local and the global, competition and cooperation, national agendas and regional dynamics.

Technological Roots and Routes

The development of communication infrastructure in the Middle East and North Africa (MENA) region has been closely connected to the evolution and adoption of mass media. Three factors played a particularly significant role: the development

The Digital Double Bind. Mohamed Zayani and Joe F. Khalil, Oxford University Press. © Oxford University Press 2024.
DOI: 10.1093/oso/9780197508626.003.0003

of the press during the colonial period, the introduction of radio in the 1930s, and the advent of television in the second half of the twentieth century.[3]

As Arab states emerged from the colonial period, their newly independent governments recognized the role of media in state propaganda. At the same time, they also realized the importance of achieving communication independence, developing a communication strategy, and enhancing inter-Arab communication. Consequently, Arab states sought to acquire modern technologies as part of their nation-building endeavors. A key moment leading up to the digital turn was the establishment of a regional infrastructure of satellite technology. The growing use of Earth-orbiting satellites, which began in the late 1950s, shifted attention away from undersea coaxial cables, which previously constituted the backbone of the world's communication infrastructure. By integrating the region into global networks, satellites enhanced connectivity, improved telecommunication services, and advanced national media. Initially, Arab states depended on foreign ICT infrastructure, as they leased transponders on Western satellites and largely relied on Intelsat[4] for their domestic networks. The motivation to acquire independent satellite technology, then, was partly rooted in geopolitical considerations ranging from curbing cultural imperialism and achieving infrastructure independence to promoting intraregional collaboration and contesting regional rivalries.

Political events spurred the adoption of satellite technology for hard and soft reasons. By the 1967 Six-Day Arab-Israeli War, newly independent Arab states began contemplating satellite technology as a way to enhance Arab cooperation and unity in meeting regional threats. Some blamed the Arab retreat in part on the inadequacies of a retrograde medium (the radio) for modern mass communication, particularly Egypt's Voice of the Arabs.[5] One of the recommendations of the 1967 Arab information ministers' postwar meeting in Tunisia was "to use modern technology associated with satellites to develop Arab media."[6] The Arab states' objective was to restore the Arab collective morale following the defeat of Arab armies while simultaneously developing a media presence that could better serve the Arab world's political agendas and sociocultural development objectives.

Under Gamal Abdel Nasser, Egypt played a leading role in establishing the Arab States Broadcasting Union (ASBU) in 1969 to promote the exchange of Arab production expertise and programs and coordinate Arab states' broadcasting activities. In this professional organization's founding meeting, held in Khartoum, participants entertained the idea of launching an Arab satellite.[7] Despite a shared enthusiasm for a regional television network, the project quickly became mired in regional rivalries. Nasser's vision of a united Arab nation entailed a political struggle with the Gulf monarchies. Most notably, Saudi Arabia bristled at Egypt's bid for regional leadership and the ideological appeal of the secular Arab nationalism it advocated. Initially, Riyadh did not join the ASBU, as the Saudis and the Egyptians were fighting a proxy war in Yemen (1962–1970). Even after it nominally joined the union in 1974, Saudi Arabia contemplated creating a rival communication organization focused on satellite communication.

An enormous influx of revenues following the 1973 oil crisis gave the Saudis the financial strength to become a central player in the region's satellite systems. In 1976, they took the lead in establishing a multination Arab Satellite Communication Organization (ArabSat) headquartered in Riyadh. This ambitious undertaking evolved out of earlier efforts by the Arab League to develop a regional communications network.[8] ArabSat's aim was to promote an Arab satellite network, put communication satellites in orbit, and facilitate the sharing of infrastructure and technical knowledge to benefit Arab states.[9] The Saudi state was the main funder of—and continues to have the largest share in—ArabSat, an investment that proved both strategically and politically important for the kingdom.[10] The project took nearly a decade to move from conception to implementation and involved difficult negotiations and agreements to stringent conditions (including assurances that the technology would not be used for military purposes).[11] With help from the French, the first generation of ArabSat was launched from French Guiana in 1985. This provided a transnational infrastructure of satellite technology that would profoundly influence the development of the Arab communication sphere in general and the Arab media industries in particular.[12]

Nevertheless, in the first few years of its launch, a combination of technical disincentives, financial factors, and political considerations resulted in ArabSat remaining an underutilized telecommunication infrastructure.[13] Arab states were slow to construct Earth stations. Many continued to use Intelsat because it had a more predictable future, better services, and more competitive rates. Similarly, some states feared that satellite broadcasts could circumvent national controls[14] and that the ArabSat's shared community channel could be used to their rivals' political advantage.[15] It was not until Saddam Hussein (who himself had developed a fleeting, experimental satellite program in the late 1980s)[16] invaded Kuwait in 1990 that the potential of satellite infrastructure started to become clear. For Arab states, satellite signals became a battleground. Wary of the effect of Iraqi television propaganda on Arab troops stationed in Saudi Arabia, Egypt leased an ArabSat transponder aimed at community service broadcasting to air programs on what eventually became the Egyptian Space Channel (ESC).[17] Taking advantage of ArabSat's footprint, which covered the MENA region, Europe, and parts of Asia, Saudi entrepreneurs launched the first private transnational Arab channel—the Middle East Broadcasting Center (MBC)—from London in 1991. MBC's successful introduction ushered in a decade of unprecedented development in Arab satellite broadcasting. Gradually, the telecommunication technology energized predominantly private media corporations, attracted media moguls, and fueled the proliferation of private satellite channels.

Arab cooperation in developing a regional satellite organization did not ease rivalries between key member states. If anything, the communication sphere became a crucial battlefield for regional power struggles. Following its Camp David Accords with Israel in 1978, Egypt was ostracized by the Arab League and suspended from the ArabSat project (even though Cairo was one of ArabSat's principal financial backers). This regional realignment and isolation heightened Cairo's desire to achieve technological sovereignty. Egypt's need for satellite capabilities also became pressing for security considerations, especially after Israel's 1988 launch of its satellite, Ofeq, which had a wide footprint and was equipped with developed imaging capacities.[18] Launched in 1998, NileSat was the culmination of a decade-long plan under the cosponsorship of the Egyptian state and the private sector.[19]

Investing in satellite infrastructure, whether ArabSat or NileSat, unleashed new dynamics. As will become clear, satellites did more than enable cross-border broadcasting and the restructuring of the region's communicative space; they signaled a digital turn. Egypt's investment in satellite communication infrastructure issued a challenge to competing regional players. To keep its technological edge, ArabSat launched a new generation of satellites in 1999 with more capacity, a longer life span, and a larger footprint. The third generation of ArabSat used Ku-band and was endowed with higher frequencies that could accommodate smaller, less expensive Earth stations. This encouraged the large-scale adoption of Earth stations by Arab countries. The enhanced ability to offer multiple channels per carrier, smaller dish requirements to receive signals, and more affordable receivers favored the explosion of satellite channels.[20] These satellites also offered digital telephony, data transmission, and internet services, which paved the way for the region's acclimation to the digital era.[21] Other Gulf states later acquired their own space technology with substantial assistance from international partners and foreign agencies. Considerations of national sovereignty, communication infrastructure independence, and commercial interests—all tightly connected to the region's complex geopolitical reality[22]—motivated these investments.[23]

Satellite technology remains part of the region's digital infrastructure. Saudi Arabia continues to invest in satellite technology. In 2019, the kingdom expanded its satellite communication fleet[24] by launching SaudiGeoSat-1 to provide advanced telecommunications capabilities, including internet, secure communication, and defense applications.[25] Other Gulf states, such as the UAE, have also developed satellite communication technology since the late 1990s, in pursuit of national prestige, economic diversification, and a knowledge-based economy.[26] In 2000, the government of Abu Dhabi tested its Thuraya 1 satellite and followed up with the launch of Thuraya 2 in 2003 and Thuraya 3 in 2008 as a mobile satellite service (MSS) delivering voice and data in more than 161 countries. Qatar has also entered the fray by launching Es'hail1 in 2013 and Es'hail2 in 2018.[27] These satellites provide television, voice, and data services across the region,[28] with the aim of achieving broadcasting independence[29] and meeting growing communications needs in the region.[30] Beyond the Gulf region, NileSat continued to expand its fleet while ArabSat developed new services and forged new partnerships. In 2019, ArabSat partnered with the Sudanese satellite communication company SudaSat to launch ArabSat 6A and provide broadband communication and internet services in Sudan and across the region,[31] and in 2021, Tunisia's Telnet launched its first homebuilt satellite, Challenge, specializing in the Internet of Things (IoT).

Significantly, it is not the availability of satellite technology but the advent of fiber optic networks that has done the most for the region's digital transformation. Just as the adoption of satellites was expedited by the interest in television broadcasting,[32] the fiber optic cable boom was tied to the commercialization of the internet.[33] While the signal transmission capabilities of satellites made them ideal for broadcasting, the technical properties and increased capacity of fiber optic cables (which use light to encode information, thereby transmitting data faster) made them the backbone of the global internet. During the first decade of the twenty-first century, submarine telecom cable networks became the preferred means of communication for a number of reasons: their cables' increased capacity compared with coaxial copper cables, their lower cost compared with satellite links, and the fact that telecommunication carriers can own fiber optic cables instead of leasing transponder capacity. Initially used for voice services, fiber optic cables were later adopted for video transmission. As demand for teleconferencing and streaming media grew, fiber optic networks offered a more affordable and popular option to provide bigger broadband capacity for high-definition video transmission. Local characteristics also mattered. The deployment of digital technologies for gas and oil exploration in natural-resource-rich countries further spurred the adoption of high-capacity undersea fiber optic cables.[34]

The expansion of the global network of subsea cables was particularly beneficial for a region with the unique geographical advantage of being located on China's "digital silk road" connecting Asia to Europe. Because of its proximity to those corridors, the region could construct multiple cable landing stations. All MENA countries except Palestine connect to international undersea cables, with the highest concentration in Egypt and the UAE and the lowest in Yemen.[35] Both Egypt and the UAE have become regional and international internet hubs. Egypt's location at the crossroads of three continents made it a main route for East-West connectivity, with the Alexandria-Suez landings being preferred transit points for interregional connectivity. The fact that nearly half of the thirty-nine cables serving the region land in the UAE, Saudi Arabia, and Oman[36] enabled the Gulf region to develop a regional connectivity hub. These subsea cable networks were then augmented with terrestrial cross-border connectivity systems, providing an increased broadband regional network with built-in redundancy.

The emergence of these networks signaled yet another shift. Initially, infrastructure development was the purview of the state. Over time, deregulation policies, growing demand on information services, and market exigencies placed privatized telecommunication companies at the forefront of infrastructure building and expansion.[37] This reorientation did not make the state irrelevant, as leading regional telecommunication companies that inherited state-built infrastructure continue to have significant stakes in the sector.

The Intricacies of Internet Penetration

The 1990s saw the introduction of the internet to the Arab world, though internet presence was segmented and took the entire decade to materialize on a broad scale. Early adopters developed international connectivity through BITNET and experimented with competing systems, such as Minitel in North Africa.[38] Initially, the internet was limited to government research centers and educational institutions.[39] Slowly, states started licensing providers to offer commercial internet service. Tunisia was the first country in the region to connect to the internet; information networking was introduced in the country as early as 1987 through ERN/BITNET, and in 1991, it started to interface with the internet.[40] Other early adopters of the internet included Kuwait, in 1992, followed in 1993 by Egypt and the UAE. Algeria, Jordan, Lebanon, and Morocco linked to the internet in 1994. Yemen followed suit in 1996, and Syria and Libya adopted the internet in 1998. Saudi Arabia (in 1999) and Iraq (in 2000) were the last Arab states to provide public internet access.

Initially, internet growth in the Middle East was slow. In 2000, barely 1% of the Arab region's population was online.[41] In 2002, just 2.6% of the population had access to the internet.[42] Internet adoption was stunted both by political concerns about the uncontrollable flow of information and by sociocultural concerns about the effect of unmediated information on local values.[43] Diverse factors affected internet access and use: (computer) literacy rates; the low penetration rate for fixed-line telephony (restricting dial-up and modem internet); the low ownership rate of relatively expensive imported computers,[44] considering the region's nascent computer hardware industry; and limited international bandwidth capacity.[45] Although many states signaled their commitment to deregulation, key aspects of telecommunication—such as fiber optic connectivity and broadband offerings—were still government-owned and -regulated. As monopolies, national telecommunication operators had little incentive to promote internet connectivity voluntarily.[46]

Over time, the internet expanded from a narrow research and academic network used primarily by the highly educated and relatively wealthy to a network used by a broader public for a wide range of purposes.[47] Until the mid-1990s, internet access was still more common at institutions than at home,[48] and public access was largely through community internet telecenters and cafés that sprang up throughout the region.[49] These institutions provided affordable access, which lowered the barrier for internet adoption and increased the number of users. Still, the challenges of Arabic-language adaptation inhibited internet growth. Even when browsers started to support Arabic content, English was the language of the web, which limited non-English-literate users' ability to access material online. Noticeably, Arab users in the diaspora helped bridge this divide by bringing the Arab world into an emerging cyberspace.[50]

While the spread of the internet accelerated with the turn of the century, both access and use remained limited compared with many other global regions. Initially, the internet was used to spread information more often than to search for it.[51] The commercial sector, in particular, was among the earliest exploiters of the internet, and business demands drove improvements in communication services (e.g., the banking sector and multinational corporations).[52] Some within official policy circles also pushed for better and wider access to the internet.[53] Gradually, access to the internet highlighted the importance of adequate information and communication infrastructure for economic development. These factors pushed states in the region, even reluctant ones,[54] to increasingly support internet expansion even while they attempted to limit the effects of the technology and attenuate its impact on both cultural values and political systems, which they sought to accomplish primarily by monitoring internet connectivity. Many governments took an active role in promoting ICTs and strengthening their technical capabilities. Demand for faster internet and the profitability of the state-dominated telecommunications sector provided additional incentives for developing the internet. In turn, higher internet penetration and steady decline in the cost of broadband increased demand on telecommunications systems, calling for further upgrades of these systems and expansion of internet capacity.

Greater access to personal computers (PCs) also helped promote internet adoption. In the early 2000s, several Arab countries set up different initiatives to promote PC ownership, including implementing computer literacy programs, subsidizing PCs, and authorizing multiple internet access points.[55] Tunisia devised plans to provide internet access to schools, universities, and research centers.[56] Egypt sought to modernize and develop its information and communication industry, providing training programs to enhance its information technology (IT) workforce, contracting with international IT companies, and promoting IT education.[57] Saudi Arabia launched the Home Computer Initiative and set up a National Committee for Information Society to increase ICT awareness and usage.[58] Jordan established the National Information System to develop the sector and enhance data communication and information services to promote socioeconomic development.

To further promote internet adoption, many countries sought to modernize their technical infrastructure. To ensure wider internet access, improve internet speed, and provide high-quality ICT services, Arab countries started the conversion to fiber optic networks, invested in satellite access, deployed broadband technology, and rolled out mobile networks. They also enacted multiple national network upgrades. Accompanying these technical improvements were adjustments that ranged from restructuring the communication sector to implementing liberalization plans. Partly because of how these initiatives improved national and international connectivity and lowered prices, internet use grew. In the mid-2000s, internet diffusion in the Arab world increased exponentially, and by the end of the decade, the number of users had more than tripled, from 8 million to 26 million.[59]

With more users and new forms of usage, the internet took on new importance. Infrastructure development became tightly connected to individual countries' social development policies. Telecommunication companies were not only technology actors but also socioeconomic and political instruments. Pursuing and implementing different ICT development strategies yielded "specific types of internet."[60] Thus, whereas Jordan favored private investment in telecommunication that supported an export-oriented ICT sector, Syria favored a centralized model with the state as the dominant player, and the Egyptian state assumed the role of a catalyst, promoting private investment without relinquishing control over the sector. In oil-rich Gulf states, telecommunication companies led the charge with massive investments in internet infrastructure capable of producing excess capacity and expanding beyond national borders.[61] Such investment facilitated these states' insertion into globalization processes in ways that were essential for their national development plans and strategies. This was the case with Qatar and the UAE, two emerging Gulf states with the financial clout to position themselves at the forefront of ICT-energized change in the region. Both countries pursued vigorous digital transformation agendas as part of national visions aimed at achieving economic diversification. Policymakers hoped that such a transformation could eventually help Qatar and the UAE move away from their predominantly hydrocarbon-dependent economies in favor of sustainable growth.[62]

This does not preclude other forms of cooperation, most notably the region's increased reliance on China for digital infrastructure. Economic diversification includes opting for different sources of technologies. Instead of relying predominantly on Western companies, for example, the region has been increasingly open to working with Asian providers, such as those from China, Singapore, and South Korea. China's bid for cyberspace influence in emerging markets is evident in its Digital Silk Road, the technological arm of the broader Belt and Road Initiative, which encompasses the Middle East and where it has been building its influence.[63] From artificial intelligence to smart cities, the digital is where Beijing's technological ambitions and economic interests meet the Gulf region's technology-supported national development visions.[64] Chinese tech giants such as Huawei have been instrumental in the deployment of next-generation infrastructure, placing ambitious Gulf countries striving to consolidate their digital capacity ahead of developed nations in 5G technologies.[65] China's involvement in multilateral technology standards-setting efforts further places countries adopting China's technologies in its orbit of influence, economically, strategically, and otherwise.[66]

Forging digital partnerships with China did not preclude states from tapping into regional non-Arab cyber powers to further develop technological capabilities. A case in point is the tech alliance between the UAE and Israel following the signing of the Abraham Accords in 2020. For Abu Dhabi, this geopolitical realignment would accelerate technology transfer not only in the areas of cybersecurity and artificial intelligence but also in financial technology, agrifood tech, and cleantech education. For Tel Aviv, the new alliance draws investments to its capital-intensive technology sector and offers a gateway to the regional tech market.[67] In other instances, Gulf states have turned to large internet companies to consolidate their digital infrastructure. Saudi Arabia has capitalized on Google's planned Blue-Raman undersea fiber optic cable to lay a new corridor for internet traffic across the Arabian Peninsula that would link India to Europe while bypassing the default regional choke point of Egypt.[68] Whereas such partnerships may help these countries overcome their infrastructural challenges, reliance on foreign-supplied technologies and companies nonetheless undermines their ability to achieve technological independence and cyber sovereignty.

Despite collaborative efforts to solidify regional communication networks (such as the jointly owned Fiber Optic Gulf Network),[69] by and large infrastructure continues to be defined nationally rather than regionally. The lack of a concerted regional digital strategy has resulted in wide variations in telecommunication capacities. In this respect, country size and resources matter. Impoverished nations such as Yemen have undeveloped systems and substandard infrastructure, while wealthy countries such as Qatar have state-of-the-art telecommunication systems and ultramodern infrastructure. Whereas Algeria is stuck with ICT modernization promises, Dubai devised a futuristic vision that enabled it to be fully immersed in the information era and acquire financial clout in the information economy.

Beyond resources, internet infrastructure development has been shaped by state policies impelled by political and economic considerations. Controlling access to information within autocratic or authoritarian systems, protecting the profits of quasi-state telecommunication companies, and maintaining the privileges of monopolies in patronage-based systems have shaped how the internet developed in the region.[70] In some instances, a lack of telecommunications infrastructure has impeded internet access. In others, states have intentionally limited internet infrastructure to exert structural control over access. Saudi Arabia was initially reluctant to offer wide public access to the internet and opted for older, more centralized—and therefore more controllable—systems, such as intranet, before finally introducing the internet.[71] Even early adopters, such as Tunisia, did so only to the extent that they were able to maintain physical and regulatory control over internet infrastructure.[72] In the Levant, ICT infrastructure is inscribed within dynamics shaped either by neocolonial practices (the state's purposeful appropriation of ICTs as technologies of power) or by public resistance (the determination of publics to defy state monopoly and reclaim the right to communicate). For example, in Palestine, where infrastructure must rely on the Israeli backbone, the network is not independently operated. Instead, Israel doles out cellular frequencies and restricts where telecommunications infrastructure can be built and which equipment can be used.[73] In practice, Israel-imposed spectrum restrictions render advanced mobile broadband network coverage outside the reach of Palestinians.[74] Conversely, the lack of a developed telecommunication infrastructure and competitive services in Lebanon did not prevent widespread internet access. Confronted with a government monopoly over communication, unreliable internet services, and overpriced internet connections, Lebanese users were essentially forced to resort to a sprawling network of illegal internet providers that rely on microwave towers to acquire bandwidth from nearby Cyprus.[75]

Leapfrogging into the Digital Era

For developed economies, reaching the current era of the Fourth Industrial Revolution took decades of technological innovation, moving from standard technology (railways, automobiles, electricity) to high technology (digital communications, microelectronics, biotechnology). For some less developed economies, education programs, economic policy, and technology transfer helped tap into foreign knowledge to build advanced industrial capacity more quickly. Neither took place in the Middle East. The domestic orientation of the region's economies resulted in a lack of competitiveness and insufficient openness to external technological knowledge.[76] Thus, technology inflows did not necessarily lead to knowledge transfer, nor did attempts to assimilate foreign technology lead to technological advances. Although the digital turn offers countries in the region a valuable opportunity to leapfrog to higher-level technologies and relaunch their economies, efforts to provide adequate ICT infrastructure have been stymied by many obstacles.

Technological "leapfrogging" describes how countries can bypass intermediate stages—moving from relative technological underdevelopment to a more developed stage—and achieve rapid development by adopting the latest technological solutions.[77] Mobile phone leapfrogging is one such example. The relatively limited wired infrastructure and low penetration of fixed telephone lines in many Arab countries prompted them to take advantage of mobile technology and launch mobile communication networks, which grew rapidly. Thus, while fixed telephone lines remained low in the region (ten subscriptions per one hundred inhabitants in 2021),[78] mobile cellular penetration rates grew significantly, from 62% in 2008 to 98% in 2021. In turn, changes in mobile technology and the adoption of smartphones helped bring more people online.

The transition from standard technology to superior, highly modern technology is usually made in response to a time-sensitive need to overcome infrastructure deficiencies, find an alternative solution, or fix a situation that would otherwise hinder the adoption of new approaches and systems.[79] Yet leapfrogging also offers advantages, such as blazing new paths and benefiting from new technological advances. For example, the Egyptian telecommunication infrastructure benefited from the latecomer advantage. Developing NileSat a decade after the launch of ArabSat enabled Egypt to implement a digital data compression system its competitor lacked.[80] Equally noteworthy is the case of Lebanon, an early mobile technology leapfrogger. Having endured the destruction of its traditional telecommunication infrastructure during its devastating civil war (1975–1990), the country nearly abandoned fixed-line technology and moved straight into the mobile and wireless era. By the mid-1990s, when wireless communication was still a novelty in the West and pay phones were the most common way of making calls on the run, mobile phones became common among Lebanese people, many of whom had cell phones but never had a fixed-line phone.

Yemen is another example. Unable to expand its landline infrastructure beyond cities and urban centers because of its mountainous geography and scattered population, the country laid out wireless communication systems to benefit rural areas.[81] Significantly, the Yemeni case also demonstrates that the same technologies that allow states to leapfrog from traditional to alternative communication technologies also enable nonstate actors and terrorist organizations to overcome the limits of existing communication infrastructure and enhance their networks. As early as the 1990s, Osama Bin Laden was using a satellite phone from remote areas in Yemen to communicate with and coordinate the activities of Al Qaeda's operatives.[82] When it became evident his satellite communication was tapped, he started using encryption[83]—all when basic telecommunication services in Yemen were unreliable and nearly half of the population did not have access to electricity.[84] Yemen also shows that leapfrogging is not irreversible. The conflict in Yemen, which began in 2014, halted progress in the telecommunications sector. With parts of the infrastructure no longer functional, portable satellite phones and ham radio emerged as default communication technologies.[85]

The value of leapfrogging includes its potential spillover effects to other sectors. For example, digitally enabled wireless connectivity on mobile devices enables greater communication while also facilitating economic connectivity and providing value-added services (e.g., SMS and data). In the MENA region, where 86% of adults do not have a bank account, cash culture is deeply embedded, and the use of credit cards is not widespread,[86] financial technologies (fintechs) that combine banking services with mobile technology create innovative financial solutions to fill a service-area gap within formal banking. Fintechs help bridge the gap between people who participate in formal banking activities and those who do not, by providing financial services that are more convenient, accessible, and mobile, as well as offering more affordable payment systems for acquiring goods and services and facilitating financial inclusion. For instance, Egypt's adoption of the simple mobile money-transfer service M-Pesa (developed in Kenya) points to the potential of ICTs to improve people's lives across the Global South. The UAE's promotion of digital wallets, which require a bank account, is another such initiative aimed at increasing financial inclusion while reducing overreliance on cash. In places such as Sudan, where mobile money service is not available, beneficiaries receive payments as credit on their mobile, which they can convert into cash at local stores.[87] The innovative uses of tools and services are contingent on supporting physical infrastructure (broadband networks, data centers, cloud computing, etc.), enacting data protection policies, and developing flexible regulatory frameworks that would sanction mobile money providers offering electronic transactions within the legal financial system.[88]

Several Arab countries are taking advantage of digital opportunities in various sectors to achieve their national visions. Oil-rich Gulf countries are witnessing rapid technological leapfrogging in certain key sectors. In the field of healthcare, some states are absorbing the latest innovations in the field and investing in state-of-the art technologies, including artificial intelligence (AI) and advanced robotics. For governments, the primary motivation for investing in AI and adopting digital medical platforms and solutions (including remote diagnosis) is improving healthcare and ensuring the delivery of better, more accessible, more responsive health services. For end users, the uptake of AI-enabled services and robotic solutions means quicker access to more accurate and potentially more effective healthcare.[89] The effect of this was noticeable during the COVID-19 pandemic. Investing in advanced digital infrastructure helped these Gulf states have a better crisis response and ensure a degree of digital resilience.[90] Significantly, the successful adoption of these digital technologies requires more than simply investing in advanced technology. Supporting the use of AI and robotics requires an entire ecosystem that spans the healthcare sector and includes prevention, early detection of diseases, diagnosis, treatment, research, and training. Fostering this ecosystem requires highly specialized skills as well as efficiency in both operation and administration, none of which is uniformly attainable.

The key to successful leapfrogging is building absorptive local capacity, acquiring the necessary know-how, and leveraging innovation to develop a range of complementary capabilities.[91] This is not evident across the region, which lacks some of the necessary conditions to harness ICT-related development.[92] According to the 2021 Global Innovation Index (GII), innovation is not the region's strength (except for Israel, which ranks among the top fifteen worldwide), and many Arab countries rank low on the list.[93] Typically, states that develop knowledge-economy status go through the path of industrialization first. This is not the case for oil-based Gulf economies, with the exception of Saudi Arabia, which has previously pursued intermediate industrialization in some sectors. Nevertheless, more ambitious and faster-growing Gulf economies have leapfrogged into the service-oriented, knowledge-based economy. Exploring why they have succeeded, even partly, is instructive.

Developing local human capacity and harnessing technical innovation are important considerations if leapfrogging is to evolve beyond dependency on foreign technologies. Short of that, implementing the newest technologies amounts to being caught in an endless endeavor to catch up.[94] As the top-ranked Arab country on the GII, the UAE (ranked 33rd globally) has attempted to develop a few high-tech, ICT-driven, knowledge-intensive industries, including semiconductors, AI, and aerospace. Even this relatively successful attempt, however, shows the difficulties inherent in such an approach. It remains to be seen whether the UAE can build capacity and innovate when it comes to these skill-intensive technologies—especially considering some of its ambitions depend on the deep pockets and foreign acquisitions of Mubadala, a state-owned investment company with a mandate to create sustainable financial returns. The country's semiconductor industry is largely dependent on foreign expertise, imported labor, and technology acquisition[95] and therefore is more of a standalone industry than part of a larger, more integrated ecosystem. Similarly, in the aerospace industry and satellite-technology sector, the UAE relies on foreign support to develop, maintain, and service these technologies. Finally, and despite efforts to promote STEM education,[96] the UAE's technological innovation and knowledge creation have yet to be widely shared and absorbed in order to enable broad-based development.

While the Gulf states' wealth helps them acquire state-of-the-art technology, hire talent from a global talent pool, and engage in local capacity-building activities, financial resources alone are insufficient for innovation.[97] Creating a competitive environment conducive to innovation may prove difficult in sheltered economies that strive to build global expatriate-based hubs for talent even as they attempt to nurture local labor. For one thing, although the Gulf region has attracted international talent and built clusters of innovation, a local culture of competitiveness and innovation has not taken hold.[98] Similarly, the research capacity in much of the region is not adequately developed, which undermines the prospects for innovative learning and entrepreneurship.

Beyond these challenges, technological leapfrogging depends on the ability to develop enabling conditions. It requires devising proper regulatory environments, institutional frameworks, and ICT policies. It also calls for institutional capacity building, from developing an attractive investment environment to fostering social, economic, and political stability to having a proper and flexible regulatory environment and enabling frameworks in place. While some Gulf countries are moving in that direction (as evinced in Qatar's Science and Technology Park and Dubai's Techno Park and Silicon Oasis), it remains to be seen whether the effect of such initiatives can trickle down to the rest of their societies or to other countries in the region.

Multiple Geographies of ICT Infrastructure

Making sense of these divergent histories calls for a better understanding of the role various actors, structures, and processes played in shaping the deployment of ICTs in the region.[99] The diverging and converging routes to the digital in the Middle East have resulted in multiple geographies of ICT infrastructure. The notion of geographies does not refer to particular territories or "spaces generated by digital networks"[100] but designates competing and complementary activities affecting technological development within a given context. The geographies of ICT infrastructure can best be conceived as a multilayered map of national and subregional dynamics that facilitate or hinder the development of capacities as part of the digital turn. These layers encompass political and economic systems, social institutions, and cultural norms that affect the breadth of digital transformation, which in the case of the Middle East has been shaped by the heterogeneity of the adopted strategies.

Three cases deserve particular attention as models of ICT infrastructure development in the Middle East: (1) the UAE, a rentier state that adopted a free-market orientation and a corporate model premised on strong ties between the state and private multinational sectors; (2) Jordan, a liberalizing kingdom that thrives on a state-supported ICT development led by the private sector; and (3) Syria, an autocratic state with a nominally socialist (but in practice mixed) economy that operates through centralized planning. These three cases reflect the range of geographies of ICT infrastructure that are widely adopted by policy experts. For example, Arab countries are typically clustered into three groups according to their digital readiness.[101] In the first cluster, the UAE tops the six Gulf Cooperation Council countries as digital leaders. Jordan is in the second cluster as a digital accelerator, along with Egypt, Lebanon, Morocco, and Tunisia. Cluster three, the largest group, includes Arab countries suffering from economic and political issues, such as Syria, Iraq, Libya, Yemen, Algeria, Mauritania, Palestine, Somalia, and Sudan.

The UAE has made ICT development a critical priority, aided partly by its state-corporate model, abundant wealth, and global orientation. As early as 1999, the city-state of Dubai, which has a unique development record and an ambitious vision for its future, launched its first ICT strategy, which aimed to turn Dubai into a key ICT hub for the region. Inspired by convergence in the telecommunications sector and the success of its "free zone" economic model, Dubai established Internet City in 2000 as an IT hub for international and regional hardware, software, and service companies.[102] The success of Internet City was soon replicated through a number of specialized "cities" across media and communications industries. Over the next twenty years, Dubai's strategies and initiatives inspired a national overhaul of state efforts toward economic diversification. These sweeping changes affected nearly all activities. From e-government to "smart government," and from the Smart Dubai initiative (2014) to the Dubai Metaverse Strategy (2022), Dubai built state-of-the-art infrastructure, acquired technologies, deregulated sectors, and provided legal frameworks for digital transformation. The ICT infrastructure included localized projects such as Dubai Internet City as well as broader initiatives from fiber optic networks to satellite connectivity systems. Nationally, these initiatives feed into the UAE Strategy for the Fourth Industrial Revolution (2017). In addition to becoming an important node for the European IP Network Coordination Centre, the UAE is also a global player in mobile satellite services through the Thuraya Telecommunications company.[103] The federation's capital, Abu Dhabi, is positioning itself as a player in the global semiconductor industry, while Dubai has become a center for venture capital investments in the technology sector, as epitomized by the acquisitions of Careem and Souq by Uber and Amazon, respectively. The UAE stands out as a prime example of productive synergies between state investment, business interests, and consumer adoption that placed the country at the center of the region's digital transformation. Notably, though, the velocity of such transformation depends on local vision and leadership.

The strategy of hiring foreign expertise while developing local talent distinguishes the Gulf ICT development model from other models in the region. Less wealthy states such as Jordan have made investments in human capital their focus. Since the 1980s, Jordan has sought to develop a significant IT talent pool to address unemployment and attract foreign investments in the National Information System, the National Information Center, educational institutions, and training centers to build ICT human capacity. As a result, Jordan became a center for "Arabizing" foreign software and computer programs, reexporting and servicing them across the region. Jordan's geopolitical relationships have affected its development. The kingdom's status as a Western ally in the Middle East made it a prime recipient of foreign direct investments. As the host of Palestinian, Iraqi, and Syrian refugees, Jordan benefited from additional foreign aid to bolster its infrastructure. Since the 1990s, the government has developed initiatives toward the business community and sought to increase consumer access to cheaper computers and internet connections.[104] In 2010, King Abdullah II initiated his Oasis500 business accelerator, a seed investment company targeting tech and creative startups, complemented in 2016 by Reach 2025 as a comprehensive digital economy strategy.[105] Significantly, and unlike that in Dubai, the ICT infrastructure strategy in Jordan revolves less around developing hard infrastructure than soft infrastructure. This strategy fits Jordan's economic strengths and limitations well and represents a symbiotic relationship between a government eager to develop its economy and a local, technologically oriented entrepreneurial community keen on expanding its business across the region. As a result of this relationship, Jordan developed an ecosystem—including incubators and accelerators for digital startups—that has nurtured successful home-grown enterprises. For example, the online services company Maktoob emerged as a regional success story in 2005, when the Dubai-based Abraaj Capital purchased 40% of its shares for USD 5.2 million. By 2009, Maktoob was sold to Yahoo! for USD 164 million.[106] Maktoob's success created a ripple effect throughout the next decade, with more than 128 Jordanian startups listed in 2022 on Crunchbase, a database for tech firms.[107] Significantly, the inter-dependence between Jordan's ICT infrastructure and its economic growth means that any disruption to investments is likely to have dire consequences for employ-ment, prosperity, and stability in a country with limited material resources and modest physical infrastructure.

By contrast, government control, state monopoly, and ambivalence toward the internet hampered ICT development in neighboring Syria. The internet did not appear in Syria until around 1997. During the rule of Hafez Al-Assad, it was largely restricted to educational and government organs.[108] Upon coming to power in 2000, Bashar Al-Assad (a self-proclaimed internet advocate who previously helmed the Syrian Computer Society) made digital transformation a cornerstone of his new vision for Syria. Al-Assad pushed for increasing internet literacy, expand-ing connectivity, and liberalizing the telecommunications sector to attract neces-sary funding. Through internet cafés and mobile access, internet users expanded from 0.2% of the population in 2000 to 7.83% in 2006, 29.6% by 2016, and 44.6% in 2022 despite the country's decade-long conflict.[109] Following the short-lived liberalizing movement of the Damascus Spring (2000–2001), mounting pressure for Syrian forces to withdraw from Lebanon and increasing regional tensions led the regime to tighten its grip. Whatever economic benefits the internet held for the country were outweighed by the political risks that the free flow of informa-tion posed for the regime. Starting in 2006, the initial political backing for internet freedom was curbed with frequent internet blackouts and growing restrictions on websites. In 2007, Reporters Without Borders noted that Syria imprisoned more cyber dissidents than any other country in the Arab world.[110] Significantly, at that time, Syria did not roll back state support for the development of ICT capabilities, because the regime understood its importance for economic growth.[111]

The Arab uprisings of 2011 represented a turning point. With the outbreak of the Syrian revolution and subsequent civil war, the ICT infrastructure (human and physical) became integral to the conflict. Both the regime and its opponents leveraged ICTs to "contest the political space."[112] Online, regime opponents chal-lenged Al-Assad's narrative, exposed state repression, and organized digital dis-tribution of filmed protests and documentaries to bypass state censorship. These opponents have in turn been opposed by the Syrian Electronic Army, a group of tech-savvy activists widely believed to have tacit regime support and known for launching cyberattacks on the regime's challengers and critics. Benefiting from the state's infrastructure, this virtual army was responsible for hacking the websites of international news organizations and human rights organizations. The case of Syria stands out as an example of the precariousness of ICT infrastructure, particularly when the state is the main financier and regulator and where this infrastructure is considered a matter of national security.

As reflected in the foregoing analysis, the multiple geographies that transpire are marked by sociocultural, political, and economic structures tied to specific national, regional, and global interactions. In the cases at hand, the development of ICT infrastructure resulted from factors and considerations that both hinder and accelerate progress. In Dubai, infrastructure development depends heavily on geo-economic factors and is tied to conditions including the regulatory role of the state and its geographical location (especially its proximity, cultural ties, and trade routes to the Indian Ocean). In Jordan, different geopolitical considerations influenced the development of its ICT infrastructure. Positioning itself as a trusted Western ally in a conflict-riddled Middle East, Jordan leveraged its involvement in refugee crises and peace initiatives, which made it a "deserving" recipient of foreign aid, to develop its infrastructure. Unlike Jordan, Syria has neither robust technological support nor ICT momentum. Yet to dismiss Syria as merely lagging and war-ridden is to obscure how its ICT infrastructure evolved and became instrumental for the state and its opponents. Defining its endeavors are geo-cultural considerations stemming from long-standing aversion to dependency on foreign support and a pronounced resistance to Western hegemony; consequently, Syria's ICT infrastructure was beholden to a nationalist ideology, a socialist orientation, and a do-it-yourself culture. In each of these cases, the immersion in the digital turn reveals how in the process of adopting particular technologies and promoting specific practices, multiple actors are empowered to unleash different processes that undermine the foundation of existing systems. Whether the adoption of satellites or the leapfrogging to mobile phones, the geographies of the digital are ridden with discordances. As the next chapter reveals, the proclamation of change is also subject to refutations of stasis.

Chapter 4

Technologies of Center and Periphery

Most assessments of the extent and potential of a region's digital transformation use quantitative indicators. Typically, these include performance indices and data-centered classifications tied to standardized targets and performance indicators. Such macro analyses identify current market and user trends, compare performances across regions and industries, and predict future trajectories. Notable for their comparative design, thematic diversity, geographic inclusiveness, and, in some cases, longitudinal data, these reports and indices are a key source of information about the MENA region because of the lack of reliable, verifiable, accessible, and current national ICT data. For policymakers and business leaders, these indices describe the digital transformation in a region where official statistics are often guarded as state secrets and infrastructural data tend to be treated as sensitive information.[1] The indices also provide insights into the region's inclination, or lack thereof, to align its ICT infrastructure development with international standards and development expectations for global economic integration. For international organizations, global consulting firms, leading tech companies, and niche regional consortia alike, benchmarking the Middle East's digital transformation constitutes an important first step for the region's transition into the digital era.

For all their merits, these indices offer only snapshots of a continuously changing phenomenon. Digital competitiveness is avowedly "a moving target."[2] Methodologically, composite indices produced by international organizations tend to apply uniform categories and normative evaluation rubrics to facilitate comparative analyses at the expense of local specificities. The resulting descriptions homogenize experiences and obscure the sociopolitical constructions of technologies. Anchored in research instruments designed for predominantly Western contexts that privilege specific pathways for digital transformation and universalized criteria for development, these analyses tend to offer circumscribed, and at times misguided, understandings of the digital Middle East. If anything, the comparative models that inform these metrics are more reflective of the status—and positionality—of technologically advanced nations than the

The Digital Double Bind. Mohamed Zayani and Joe F. Khalil, Oxford University Press. © Oxford University Press 2024.
DOI: 10.1093/oso/9780197508626.003.0004

conditions of other, less advanced regions. Commonly adopted within policy circles and disseminated by the mainstream press, these metrics serve more as instruments for justifying and advancing political, economic, and cultural agendas than as tools for informing policy and monitoring economies. Similar issues emerge when considering other aspects of data collection and use. There is an inherent conflict of interest and lack of objectivity when international consulting firms that are engaged in both digital capacity-building and transformation activities also produce assessments and analyses. Importantly, analyses that take their cues from such data limit the discussion of the digital to descriptions of the present and predictions of the future, thereby obscuring important dynamics at play. Such presentism overshadows critical engagement with how these dynamics manifest themselves.

These shortcomings notwithstanding, exploring what the indices and reports tell us about the digital Middle East is useful. It offers a qualified perspective on the region's digital status relative to other countries around the world and also clarifies which questions the data leave unanswered.

ICT Leaders, Aspirers, and Laggards

One widely cited index, the World Economic Forum's Network Readiness Index (NRI), assesses digital transformation in 130 countries around the world based on four pillars: technology, people, governance, and impact. In 2022, the leading Arab countries are the UAE (with a global rank of 28) and Saudi Arabia (35), followed by Qatar (42) and Oman (53).[3] In the bottom half of the ranking are Jordan (70), Egypt (73), Morocco (79), Tunisia (84), Lebanon (91), and Algeria (100). Overall, the MENA region performs better in ICT infrastructure, access, and usage of technology than in areas of governance, regulation, inclusion, or overall impact of technological adoption. Significantly, performance in each of the NRI's four pillars varies even within countries. Whereas the UAE is ranked in the top quartile across all categories, its strongest subindex pertains to the ability of individuals, governments, and businesses to have the access, resources, and skills to use technology productively. Lebanon, in contrast, is at the low end of the second quartile in terms of access to and usage of ICTs but has a worse score when it comes to regulation, trust, inclusion, and governance, and its national environment is hardly conducive to participation in the knowledge economy. Based on the NRI index, digital transformation is linked to the quality of the technologies and the novelty of the infrastructure but also to good governance and management of human resources.

These findings are echoed by Economist Impact's Inclusive Internet Index, which is commissioned by Meta (formerly known as Facebook) and which measures internet inclusion across the combined categories of availability, affordability, relevance, and readiness in 100 countries, including 11 Arab economies. The 2022 index ranks the Gulf states among the higher-performing countries. The UAE tops the regional ranking (at position 26), followed by Qatar (27), Kuwait (33), Oman (38), Saudi Arabia (39), and Bahrain (40). The third quartile includes Morocco (52), Egypt (57), Jordan (60), Tunisia (66), Algeria (71), and Lebanon (74), while Sudan (at 90 internationally) ranks last at the regional level.[4] Across three of the four categories, the Gulf countries are ahead of other MENA countries, most of which are ranked in the lower half of the index. The UAE (at 5 internationally) ranks first regionally in terms of available infrastructure, Kuwait (at 31 internationally) ranks first regionally in affordability and the cost of access, and Qatar ranks first both regionally and internationally in readiness and the capacity to access the internet.[5] Regionally, Sudan has the lowest score for availability (95), Algeria has the lowest score for affordability (86), Lebanon has the lowest score for readiness (97), and Tunisia has the lowest score for relevance (79). The above figures underscore both inequalities of access and the unevenness of the digital turn. In prosperous economies, the internet is reaching saturation levels, while in developing countries, internet access remains a privilege.

Another frequently used index, the International Telecommunication Union's (ITU) ICT Development Index (IDI), published from 2009 to 2017,[6] monitors progress and measures development toward the information society over time. The IDI is based on indicators in three categories: ICT access and readiness, ICT intensity and usage, and ICT capabilities and skills.[7] In the 2017 IDI, which includes 176 economies, the Arab countries that rank highest are Bahrain (at 31 globally), Qatar (39), and the UAE (40), all slightly above the global average. MENA countries in the upper-middle quartile include Saudi Arabia (54), Oman (62), Lebanon (64), Jordan (70), and Kuwait (71), while in the lower-middle quartile are Tunisia (99), Morocco (100), Algeria (102), and Egypt (103). The lowest-ranked Arab countries are Syria (126) and Sudan (145). The index highlights not only the state of ICT for individual countries but also their efforts to improve their performance. Significantly, although the economies that lead in terms of ICTs have already achieved high levels of internet use and access (and therefore have less room for growth than low-performing countries), the regional rankings have remained relatively consistent overall compared with previous IDI indices (conflict-affected Syria being an exception). Notably, while the top-performing countries in the region are on the heels of the IDI's best global performers, low-performing Arab countries at the bottom of the regional rankings—such as Sudan, Yemen, and Syria—have not kept up with technological developments, upgraded their infrastructure, or increased their ICT capabilities.

The findings of international organizations generally align with the evaluations of industry reports and market research by international and regional firms. McKinsey's Digitization Index, which compares the degree and status of digitization across nine Middle Eastern countries, ranks the UAE, Qatar, and Bahrain high, followed by Saudi Arabia, Jordan, and Oman, whereas Kuwait, Egypt, and Lebanon are ranked low.[8] The Arab Advisors Group's own 2018 ranking of regional digitization levels also shows the UAE and Qatar as regional leaders, followed by the remaining Gulf countries, though slightly lower in the first quartile, while Jordan leads the second quartile, distantly followed by Tunisia, Morocco, Lebanon, and Egypt.[9] Similarly, Cisco's 2019 Global Digital Readiness Index places the UAE at the top (the "amplify" stage), while most other Arab countries rank in the middle (the "accelerate" stage), with the remaining Gulf countries leading the region by a considerable margin and Yemen relegated to a low rank (the "activate" stage). To quantify these stage labels for the region's highest and lowest performers, out of a total possible score of 25 points, the UAE ("amplify") scores 16.42, approaching the UK's 17.86, the US's 19.03, and Singapore's 20.26 (the highest ranking in the index). Yemen ("activate"), one of the world's least-developed countries, scores just 5.48.[10]

What is evident from the various metrics and classifications these reports offer is that some high-income countries in the MENA region have demonstrated strong enough performances to count as globally competitive. Indeed, in categories such as ICT access and usage, regional leaders are also global leaders. Comparatively, the Middle East's overall performance in the various indicators places the region ahead of the African continent and slightly above the Asia and Pacific region.[11] Yet the data also clearly show a highly unevenly developed digital Middle East. The disparity between different countries' digitization efforts is clearly captured in the Arab Federation for Digital Economy report, which identifies three categories of countries (leaders, aspirers, and laggards) based on their performance in five dimensions (digital infrastructure, policies, and regulations; digital innovation; digital government and service delivery; digital business; and digital adoption, accessibility, and affordability).[12] Leading the charge is cluster 1, digital leaders, which is populated by the six Gulf economies. Cluster 2, digital accelerators, consists of countries at a middle stage of digital readiness, including Egypt, Jordan, Lebanon, Morocco, and Tunisia. Cluster 3, digital activators, is for countries at a modest or low stage of digital readiness and includes Iraq, Libya, Syria, and Yemen, in addition to Algeria, Mauritania, Palestine, Somalia, and Sudan. Even among the top-ranked countries in the region, the digital turn is anything but uniform. Professional-services firm Deloitte reports that although the Gulf countries have leveraged technologies in a range of areas aimed at diversifying their economies and transforming their public sector, they are at different stages of growth and maturity.[13]

Although such indices convey some important insights, they do not tell the whole story. These reports say little about the lasting social, economic, and political implications of the digital turn, nor do they provide a deep understanding of the nature of the challenges the region faces with regard to the digital turn.

Network Readiness and ICT Development

Digital inclusion, or universal and affordable access to the internet, figures prominently in the UN's Sustainable Development Goals (SDGs).[14] Since about 2010, the region has witnessed remarkable growth in quantifiable aspects of digital transformation, especially ICT access and internet penetration. In 2008, the average internet user penetration level in the Arab world was a mere 16%.[15] In 2010, the region had nearly 25 internet users per 100 inhabitants, slightly above the developing countries' average (21%) but below the world average (30%).[16] By 2015, internet penetration did not exceed 37%, and in 2016, only 41.6% of the Arab world's population was using the internet.[17] It was not until 2019 that more than half of the region's population (51.6%) was using the internet.[18] In 2021, this figure went up to 66%, which is above the average for developing countries (57%) but almost on a par with the world average (63%).[19] Contributing to this increase are a number of factors, including the rise of digital natives, decreasing subscription costs, advanced mobile infrastructure, and commercial applications.

Rates of internet penetration vary strikingly by country: while some have reached saturation, others continue to have some of the lowest internet penetration rates in the world. World Bank data[20] on internet usage in 2020–2021 confirm wealthy Gulf Cooperation Council (GCC) countries' standing at the top of the rankings. Qatar, Bahrain, Saudi Arabia, Kuwait, and the UAE all have penetration rates of 100%—all of which exceed those of developed nations. Oman (95%) is not far behind. Internet use in Levantine countries (such as Lebanon at 84% and Palestine at 75%) compares to that in North African countries (such as Morocco at 88%, Tunisia at 72%, and Algeria at 63%). With 72% of its population using the internet, Egypt stands slightly above the regional average (68%), while Iraq's 44% penetration rate places it below the average. Lagging behind in terms of internet usage are Syria (36%), Sudan (28%), and Yemen (27%). Trailing the chart is conflict-ridden Libya (18%).[21] These wide variations result from economic considerations as well as geographical characteristics. In particular, wealthy Arab states have better ICT infrastructure and internet access than poorer ones, while small countries with compact urban settlements (such as Jordan and Lebanon) have higher penetration rates than larger countries with low population density and challenging geographical conditions (such as Sudan and Yemen).[22]

In earlier phases of ICT development, low landline penetration and limited access to computers hindered internet connectivity. By 2008, only Gulf states had household computer penetration rates above 30%. Fixed broadband uptake has been consistently low, with just 2.5 fixed broadband subscriptions per 100 inhabitants in 2010—below average penetration levels in developing countries (with an average of 4.4 subscriptions per 100 inhabitants) and even further below the world average of 7.5 subscriptions per 100 inhabitants.[23] In 2015, fixed broadband penetration stood at 3.7% subscriptions, about a third of the global average of 10.8%.[24]

Figures from 2021 show that the regional rate of fixed broadband subscriptions remains low, with a subscription rate of only 9%.[25] Contemporary stagnation is due partly to the high cost of landline implementation and the deficient fixed-line infrastructure and partly to leapfrogging directly to mobile telephony.

In recent years, mobile telephony has grown considerably. This development has provided added connectivity, albeit with variation from country to country. In high-income Gulf countries, mobile ownership either is at or exceeds 100% (as some people own multiple devices), while in the rest of the region, it ranges from 75% in Palestine to 80% in Tunisia, and from 95.6% in Morocco to 99.5% in Egypt.[26] Compared with 2008, when mobile cellular penetration stood at 62%, these rates represent significant growth. The number of mobile cellular subscriptions in 2021 stood at 98 per 100 inhabitants, while the active mobile broadband subscriptions stood at 67 per 100 inhabitants.[27] Smartphone adoption in the MENA region has increased noticeably, as devices became more affordable, users demanded advanced applications and data services, and telecommunication companies deployed faster mobile broadband networks that supported the users' needs. In 2022, smartphones accounted for 77% of all connections across the region, compared with 62% in 2019, 33% in 2015, and just 3% in 2008.[28] Despite this rapid growth, the region's average smartphone adoption rate remains below the global average.[29] Furthermore, connectivity in the region is far from uniform, with notable discrepancies between the subregions: the Gulf countries boast 91% smartphone adoption, while the adoption rate in the Levant is 82% and in North Africa is 79%.[30]

The Middle East has also witnessed significant, if uneven, advances in ICT capabilities and usage. International bandwidth usage grew from 6 Tbit/s in 2015 to 55 Tbit/s in 2022.[31] This increase in traffic should come as no surprise with the internet's reinvention of traditional forms of communication, entertainment, education, and shopping. On the individual level, international bandwidth usage per internet user stood at 172 kbit/s in 2021, significantly above the average for the developing world (143 kbit/s), though below the global average (190 kbit/s) and far below what is available in Europe (340 kbit/s).[32] Similarly, 2021 ITU data show that more than 95% of the region's population has access to mobile broadband network coverage (3G and above). By contrast, at 70%, 4G network coverage in the Arab world falls behind the world average (88%). In fact, a quarter (25%) of the region's population relies on 3G coverage, compared with the world average of just 7%.[33] Though revealing, these figures are fluid and will likely change with the incipient deployment of next-generation wireless networks. Gulf countries in particular have been early adopters of the 5G mobile network, promoting it more aggressively than some of the world's most technologically advanced countries.[34] The more digitally ambitious Gulf countries are even playing a role in the development of the next generation of mobile communication networks.[35] The advent of advanced networks, however, still demonstrates the inequalities of ICT within the region. The footprint of 5G may be expanding, but the spread of this technology across the region have been slow to materialize. The looming "5G divide" could exacerbate existing disparities that have marked the region's digital turn.[36]

The inconsistencies in internet access across the region and within its individual countries are compounded by a persistent gender gap. In 2013, 15.5% fewer women in the region used the internet than men. In 2022, ITU statistics indicate a large internet user gender gap in the Arab world, where 74.9% of males and 65.4% of females are internet users, which translates to a gender parity score of 0.87 (compared with the global gender parity score of 0.92, where full equality would be scored as 1).[37] Comparatively, the internet user gap (the percentage difference between internet penetration rates for males and females) has increased from 19.2% in 2013 to 24.4% in 2019, compared with a global internet user gender gap of 11% in 2013 and 17% in 2019.[38] No less significant is the rural/urban gap. Although mobile broadband coverage in urban areas is nearly universal, many rural areas remain underserved. ITU statistics from 2021 indicate that 82% of the region's urban population has access to 4G networks, compared with just 51% in rural areas, and all users served by 2G coverage (2%) are based in rural areas.[39] The 2022 ITU data on individuals using the internet reveal a narrowing of the rural/urban gap, as access in rural areas (56%) now accounts for nearly three-quarters of that in urban areas (80%).[40] These discrepancies highlight the unevenness of digital opportunities within the region as well as within individual countries.[41]

Discrepancies in ICT development track economic development closely, and differences in internet user uptake and ICT services reflect income disparities in the region (see table 4.1). While Gulf countries have high per-capita GDPs, the remaining Arab countries are middle- or low-income economies with considerably lower per-capita GDPs. The strong correlation between income level and ICT development is evident not only in network coverage and the quality and speed of broadband connections but also in the affordability of and access to the internet. In fact, cost is a key factor impeding internet access, as connectivity remains expensive for many people when expressed as a percentage of median income. Although ICT services in the Arab world are becoming more affordable, the average cost of mobile data in the region in 2020 is 3.1% of the monthly gross national income (GNI) per capita—which falls short of the 2% affordability target set by the UN Broadband Commission for Sustainable Development.[42]

Adjusted for purchasing-power parity, high-income countries have more affordable connection costs than low-income countries. According to 2021 ITU statistics, for a high-income country such as Qatar, basic internet access (data-only mobile broadband basket) costs 0.31% of GNI per capita, compared with 3.54% in Jordan and 10.06% in Yemen. Similarly, while in the UAE, the cost of a fixed mobile broadband basket is 0.55% of GNI per capita, in Algeria, it is nearly eight times as high as a share of per-capita national income (4.18%) and more than twenty times higher in Jordan (12.08%).[43] A 2021 report by the Alliance

Table 4.1 **Population, internet usage, and GDP per capita (current USD), Middle East and North Africa.**

Country	Population (2022)	Internet usage (2021)	GDP per capita (2022)	Income group
Algeria	44,903,225	71%	$4,273	Lower middle
Bahrain	1,472,233	100%	$30,152	High
Egypt	110,990, 103	72%	$4,295	Lower middle
Iraq	44,496, 122	49%	$5,937	Upper middle
Jordan	11,285,869	83%	$4,204	Lower middle
Kuwait	4,268,873	100%	$43,233	High
Lebanon	5,489,739	87%	$4,136	Lower middle
Libya	6,812,341	46%	$6,716	Upper middle
Mauritania	4,736,139	59%	$2,190	Lower middle
Morocco	37,457,971	88%	$3,527	Lower middle
Oman	4,576,298	96%	$25,056	High
Palestine	5,043,612	75%	$3,789	Lower middle
Qatar	2,695,122	100%	$88,046	High
Saudi Arabia	36,408,820	100%	$30,436	High
Sudan	46,874,204	28%	$1,102	Low
Syria	22,125,249	36%	$537	Low
Tunisia	12,356,117	79%	$3,776	Lower middle
UAE	9,441,129	100%	$53,757	High
Yemen	33,696,614	27%	$676	Low

Source: World Bank and OECD national accounts data.

for Affordable Internet shows notable national differences between the low- and middle-income countries in the region. Morocco ranks high on the affordability list (number 9 of 72 global countries surveyed), followed by Jordan (26), and Tunisia (24). Egypt (34) and Algeria (40) are less affordable, and Sudan (63) and Yemen (72) are at the bottom of the affordability index.[44] Naturally, elevated costs limit access, and service affordability is a key factor in ICT uptake, which tends to be higher for mobile voice than mobile data.

Another barrier to internet uptake, particularly in the region's less developed countries, is literacy, both basic and digital. According to the World Bank, the adult literacy rate in the MENA region in 2020 stood at 80%.[45] In many countries, less than half the population has the basic e-skills needed to use services and access content. According to 2019 ITU data, in Iraq, only 30% of the population possesses basic computer skills, compared with Egypt (54%) or Oman (75%).[46] Similarly, 2020 data show that the percentage of the population with advanced ICT skills in Saudi Arabia (21%) and UAE (17%) is more than double the percentage in Morocco (10%) and Algeria (7%), respectively.[47] The percentage of people with sufficient ICT skills bears strongly on the region's ability to move toward a knowledge economy, as well as on citizens' ability to avail themselves of ICT-enabled products and services.

Opportunities and Challenges

Several trends characterize the Middle East's digital turn. Some countries consistently meet or exceed international standards and benchmarks, while others trail behind. Similarly, we find obvious discrepancies when we consider digital readiness and ICT development markers within the broader Middle East region. Notably, most Arab countries perform at a lower level than Israel, with its global reputation in technology, and Turkey, with the region's largest economy and an expanding ICT sector. Overall, most countries have made only moderate to modest progress, and a few remain mired in a low state of digital transformation. When considering the individual countries of the region, however, a more nuanced picture emerges. For example, in the case of high-income Gulf countries, the UAE outperforms Kuwait in nearly every indicator. Similarly, in the Levant, there are notable disparities between the digital readiness of Jordan and Lebanon. The variations among states from comparable income categories point to the complexities of the digital turn and its irreducibility to financial resources or technical considerations.

From a macro perspective, the foregoing data-driven performance analysis reveals that the road to digital transformation requires an integrated approach and an enabling environment. Harnessing the power of the digital calls for a comprehensive, interconnected, and highly functional ecosystem including infrastructure (technology, policies, regulations, human capital skills), digital participation (accessibility, affordability, inclusion), digital government, and robust financial structures. It is here, however, that a major limitation of quantitative indicators and indices stands out. These indices tend to be informed by conventional orthodoxies that view digital transformation as linear and unidirectional. Considering that the region is not easily classified, treating MENA states as separate entities or clusters based on shared (linear) progress smacks of classical technological diffusion theory (with its attention to innovators, aspirers, and laggards). On the other hand, a country-specific focus risks missing the larger context of the region as a whole and the level of interaction of individual countries within subregions, such as human expertise movement, capital flows, and infrastructure interdependencies. Conceiving of the Middle East in terms of leaders and laggards overlooks the extent of the region's technological interdependency (e.g., telecommunication operators) even as regional integration continues to be impeded by geopolitical rivalries.

Although useful in many ways, the data leave unanswered questions such as why countries' performance varies across different indicators, why some can forge ahead with ICT development while others stagnate, and why countries with the most advanced infrastructure are not necessarily the ones ranked as the best performers. Furthermore, the data do not explain why ICT diffusion differs considerably across countries in the region, under what conditions these countries develop digital capabilities, what path(s) lead to better digital readiness, what hinders ICT development, or what factors leave some countries effectively sidelined in their digital transformations. Finally, beyond indicating which countries are ICT leaders, aspirants, or laggards, the intricacies of the intraregional dimension of these digital transformations and the effect of the region's interconnectedness and interdependence on their digital outlook remain unexplored.

National Strategies and Digital Manifestos

The successful introduction of new technologies requires the development of adequate frameworks for their acquisition and deployment, their governance and regulation, and their public acceptance and access. Often, these frameworks are referred to as national digital strategies. They articulate state visions about digital transformation and project a road map and a timeline for realizing them. These documents feature infrastructural and technological targets, including specific steps to develop regulatory, organizational, and technical digital environments. To implement those strategies, governments usually partner with stakeholders, from national bureaucrats, policymakers, and local business communities to global technology players, international NGOs, and leading consulting firms.

Although these are called "national" strategies, in many cases international assistance plays a pivotal role in their formulation. For example, Egypt's strategy was developed by the UN Conference on Trade and Development (UNCTAD) at the request of the Egyptian government.[48] More generally, several UN agencies (such as ITU and UNESCO) play a crucial role in orienting such grand strategies as part of their goal of ensuring that all UN member states meet the SDGs (e.g., for innovation and infrastructure). In addition, devising and promoting such strategies offer the international donors and investors signs of determination and commitment to participate in the global digital economy.[49]

A brief overview of the development and status of national digital strategies in the region reveals disparate levels of digital planning and execution.

The shared objectives and breadth of these strategies can be broadly captured in a three-tiered typology. First, the strategies reflect the political leadership's vision of national identity, culture, and security and its ideas for socioeconomic reforms and state-citizen relationships. Thus, they mirror the leadership's concerns about the effect of increasingly decentralized systems in which access and exchange of information take place outside the purview of the state. Second, these national strategies represent ambitions toward sustainable economic and social development that place faith in technological affordances. In many cases, such promises result in states rushing to pursue goals with little consideration of socioeconomic dynamics and overall suitability to existing infrastructure. Third, the objectives tend to follow predetermined "templates" from international organizations (e.g., UNCTAD, ITU) or international funding agencies (e.g., World Bank, USAID), with little attention paid to the sociocultural embeddedness of the adopted strategies. For example, while offering e-government services is considered a key indicator of transparency, the implementation of these services tends to disregard both the informal economy developed around traditional bureaucracies and the limited access and lack of basic literacies that prevent wider participation.

By and large, national digital strategies across the region lack differentiation and tend to outline a set of standard tasks and milestones viewed as requisite for digital transformation. Under catchy themes (e.g., the digital transformation of government services into e-government, the digital transformation of education and healthcare, or the digital participation and engagement of citizens), some objectives remain constant. These include open data (for transparency), legal framework (for state and businesses), connectivity (for advanced infrastructure), inclusion and digital skills (for bridging gaps), and interoperability (for international collaboration).[50] Yet these objectives do not necessarily meet with local realities, and their pursuit is often at the expense of other contextual changes needed to adapt to the digital turn.

The history of national digital strategies is intertwined with economic interests, political ambitions, international goals, and local considerations. Early digital strategies were folded into state bureaucracies' modernization plans. Often they were purely technical; sometimes they formed part of other plans related to telecommunications. After all, the early infrastructure for the internet relied on modems to modulate internet signals using telephone connectivity. Throughout the 1980s and 1990s, digital infrastructure was treated as an adjunct to, or a minor upgrade of, existing telecommunications infrastructure. Even then, however, digital transformation was ushering in a new era of governance and, as such, was subject to each country's system. In politically and economically liberal countries such as Lebanon, the technology was rolled out long before the development of institutional frameworks, leading to a speedy but disorderly diffusion of digital innovations.[51] By contrast, in politically autocratic and economically dirigiste countries such as neighboring Syria, the development of infrastructure was halted awaiting the political will and blessing of the country's leaders.

As the twentieth century came to a close, countries needed a comprehensive approach to existing and emerging digital technologies. After all, the internet expanded, and the public's modes of usage changed, requiring additional resources and higher capabilities.[52] In response to the internet's increased global integration, Arab states realized the value of building local capacities for organizing, governing, and regulating technical infrastructure, motivated by a desire to harness the internet's socioeconomic promises while ensuring some level of state control. ITU's World Summit for the Information Society (WSIS) Plan of Action (adopted in Geneva in 2003 and amended in Tunis in 2005), along with the UN Millennium Development Goals (MDGs, 2000–2015), created an international framework, support, and impetus for serious long-term engagements with digital strategies. As a result, several country-based initiatives emerged in the region centered on digital transformation in specific sectors (e-government, e-education, e-health) and empowering specific groups (youth, women, individuals with disabilities).

The current state of national digital strategies is a far cry from these modest beginnings. Over time, the development of national digital strategies has become a cornerstone of government planning and is increasingly recognized as a process requiring regular assessment, reevaluation, and adaptation. These national digital strategies have been revised and updated regularly to remain relevant in an era of rapid changes. Prepared by dedicated teams from specialized authorities and relevant ministries, with input and collaborations across government bodies and nonstate stakeholders, these documents became an arena for policy formulation where international organizations assess local political commitment to developmental goals, domestic and global business communities partner in building digital infrastructure, and the state reaffirms its role in regulating digital transformation.

A review of publicly available national strategies points to multiple models that can be schematically charted as limited, modest, or sophisticated. The first (limited) model, which is prevalent in conflict-ridden countries such as Libya, Yemen, Palestine, and Syria, reflects a stalled or inadequate national digital strategy that is often a response to foreign requests or developed with the support of international organizations. For example, Palestine introduced its National Information Technology Strategy in 2017, while Syria's Digital Transformation Strategy 2030 is still under development with assistance from the UN Economic and Social Commission for Western Asia (ESCWA).[53] Typically, such plans lack both national political will and funding commitment, rely on foreign support, and are affected by volatile security conditions. International aid agencies often advocate for these strategies as gateways for better governance and transparency, making foreign aid contingent on the national government's commitment to such strategies. Without centralized national plans, digital infrastructure depends on civil-society groups, entrepreneurs, and self-taught enthusiasts.

The second (modest) model reflects national digital strategies characterized by restricted political, economic, or other resources and often serves short-term, instrumentalist objectives. These national strategies may also reflect political tensions, competing priorities, a constrained business community, or controlled civil society. As a result, the road maps for these modest national digital strategies are not amenable to robust transformation. For example, the national strategy plan Digital Tunisia 2020 was introduced in 2016 but curbed by competing supervisory ministries and agencies.[54] Similarly, Digital Jordan Strategy (2018–2025) was hindered by a multitude of competing initiatives and plans—including Digital Opportunity Trust Incubators (2019) and Startup Pitch (2019)—and struggled to captivate a vibrant and entrepreneurial Jordanian ICT community.[55]

Conversely, the third (sophisticated) model takes a comprehensive approach, features a multisectoral ambit (encompassing traditional and emerging business activities from agriculture to climate), and often presents detailed long-term goals and implementation plans. The Gulf countries lead the region in offering elaborate and ambitious national digital strategies that encompass wide-ranging efforts toward digital transformation, including AI, blockchains, big data, smart cities, IoT, and virtual reality.[56] These multipurpose, multisectoral strategies set economic goals while also taking into account regulatory issues regarding information privacy, cybersecurity, and state sovereignty. Some of these strategies are not consolidated into a master plan or document but are instead innovative additions to, or revisions of, existing documents. This is the case with UAE Vision 2021, which was originally adopted in 2014, supplemented in 2021, and then supplemented again to add a sector-specific strategy called the UAE Smart Government National Plan—all of which feed into the UAE's national strategy, Centennial 2071.[57]

This typology of national digital strategies illuminates the uneven approaches to digital transformation planning in the region. That heterogeneity translates into disparate levels of infrastructure, governance, and funding. While international and regional organizations offer assistance in planning, developing, and executing national strategies, these efforts remain subject to the individual states' interest in and control over digital transformation. State officials' natural impulse toward centralization conflicts with the natural tendency of digitization toward decentralization. Competing local and international stakeholders also complicate the development and, more critically, implementation of these national digital strategies. Nevertheless, these strategy documents remain valuable not merely as road maps but as a set of important milestones toward digital transformation. In this regard, national digital strategies help articulate policies, establish governance, encourage investments, and create public awareness.

Chapter 5

The Digital as Digitality

Digital infrastructure increasingly shapes how our planet is organized into hubs, nodes, and networks that channel constant transborder exchanges of immaterial flows. With expanded reach, capacity, and performance, digital infrastructure has become integrated into nearly every facet of economic, political, and sociocultural life. In this sense, digitality impels us to go beyond the materiality of digital infrastructure to examine the economic, political, and cultural conditions that organize (among other things) investment, governance, and public access to technology.[1] Such endeavor calls for attention to "convergence culture"[2] as a process at the core of the digital turn.

Convergence is not only a technological process but also an economic, cultural, and territorial one, insofar as it is associated with processes such as globalization. The confluence of computers, traditional media, and telecommunications into compact technological tools (such as the smartphone) allowed companies to develop several products and services in the same industry, thereby facilitating horizontal integration. This convergence also paved the way for the development of a digital participatory media culture characterized by an expansion of content types and genres as well as specific user behaviors (e.g., sharing, remixing). More important, convergence is global, bringing geographically distant places together via shared media practices and uses. Seen from this perspective, convergence entails the digital configuration of media production and distribution and the refocusing of consumption and culture around digitality. These media dynamics are not mutually exclusive. The boundaries between traditional media types and processes become increasingly blurred as new categories and roles emerge, thus favoring the rise of "produsers"[3] (a mixture of "producers" and "users") who use the digital to perform digitality. In short, digital media have become both extensively pervasive and increasingly invisible in today's everyday life.[4] Their uneven, conditional, and elusive deployment in the Middle East has consequences for the user, the state, and the market.

Starting in the mid-1990s, the "Information Revolution" epithet became nearly synonymous with change in the region.[5] Satellite technology became cheaper and

The Digital Double Bind. Mohamed Zayani and Joe F. Khalil, Oxford University Press. © Oxford University Press 2024.
DOI: 10.1093/oso/9780197508626.003.0005

more accessible, with Arab states and businesses racing to develop free-to-air or pay-television channels, which energized the media scene and changed audience habits. In the early phases of this "Information Revolution," Arabs in the diaspora and foreign-based regional media ventures played significant roles as users and producers, respectively. European capitals such as London provided the fertile ground for various transnational satellite television channels to emerge before relocating to the Middle East once the technology, talent, political will, and funding became available. The diffusion of regional satellite further benefited from the technological, sociocultural, political, and economic infrastructure of Western cities. At the time, the internet was a nascent technology that aimed to integrate the region into a global network—a move that proved to be technologically challenging, financially taxing, and politically risky.

As the culmination of decades of modernization efforts, this Information Revolution represents the triumph of the modernizing state. In their pioneering Arab Information Project, Jon Anderson and Michael Hudson observe that a Western-trained bureaucratic cadre in the region had advocated for continuous engagement with technology since the 1970s and introduced computer technologies to modernize the administration of the state.[6] In other ways, though, the Information Revolution reflected the efforts of more than the state alone. Some members of the business community also had an interest in developing the computer software sector as part of the economic liberalization policies of the 1980s.[7] ICTs became even more important, with a growing disposition toward privatization that echoed changes in international political economy. The 1990s saw the emergence of different groups of consultants and influential political figures motivated by neoliberal ideas. They sought to effect change and steer transformation efforts from outside the bounds of state bureaucracy. Working to integrate the MENA region into the global economy, these groups became instrumental in expediting the adoption of new technologies in the region.[8] Similarly, international organizations and investors pushed for an overhaul of the legal framework that recognized the digital as a business sector, and local entrepreneurs requested local legal protection and strategic policy initiatives. As part of their globalization policies and practices, international organizations supported efforts to develop state and private partnerships related to infrastructural issues. One early indication of such support was a resolution adopted by the ITU's Arab Regional Television Development Conference, held in Cairo in 1992, which aimed to restructure the telecommunications sector. The resolution urged Arab states to introduce appropriate national policies regarding information and telecommunications that focused on the sector's regulation and operation.

Significantly, the Information Revolution has come to be as much about what technologies are being consumed as it is about how these technologies are appropriated (whether by the public, state, civil society, business communities, particular demographic groups, or oppositional parties). Over the past three decades, observers have drawn attention to the "social life" of technology, questioning the impact of satellite television and the internet on the public sphere, popular culture, political activism, radicalization, and gender equity.[9] The legacy of the Information Revolution will be discussed throughout this chapter. The analysis explores conti- nuities and changes from the predigital to the digital era and highlights persistent tensions in the application, governance, and funding of digital developments.

The Legacy of the Predigital

Although computer technologies were first introduced to the region in the 1950s, their usage was largely limited to state agencies, large companies, and the mili- tary.[10] In subsequent years, the introduction of digital infrastructure was entwined with the political economy of independent states and sociocultural changes in the Middle East. These associations have been examined in detail by media and communication scholars,[11] many of whom consider satellite technologies and the internet as either "transformative" or "revolutionary" because of their ability to disseminate information and provide economic opportunities, as well as in the potential empowerment they offer for political dissent, social engagement, or religious activism. Despite such revolutionary connotations, these technologies are better understood as part of longer processes related to the region's modern- ization efforts, processes that began in an earlier era of predigital communication technologies.

The predigital and the digital we invoke in our discussion delineate two fluid and overlapping eras: the digital has begun, while the predigital remains. The predigital stands for specific economic, cultural, and political realities associ- ated with the modern, while the digital heralds a postmodern era with its chal- lenges to established ideologies, norms, and practices. Although these two eras are difficult to disentangle, a number of signposts clearly point to a digital turn, from national telecommunication infrastructure projects to modest technology manufacturing undertakings and from the adoption of multichannel multipoint distribution service (MMDS, a wireless cable technology) to the pursuit of the knowledge economy. In the predigital era, infrastructure projects, including tele- communications, were associated with large development projects that were, even if often executed with foreign technical support, centrally planned, developed, and financed by Middle Eastern states. Policies toward technological infrastruc- ture were governed by an interventionist, state-led approach geared toward pro- tecting the regimes against internal and external threats as part of state-building processes.[12] Historically, every Arab state exerted its authority over technologi- cal infrastructure by regulating usage, controlling access, and enforcing censor- ship. With the emergence of nation-states throughout the region, governments developed monopolies over national means of communication, particularly radio and television, while seeking to limit the onslaught of transborder broadcasting through various means.

The advent of market liberalization signaled a shift in this paradigm. In Egypt, for example, this economic transition started with the *infitah* (open-door) policies of the 1970s and became more pronounced by the end of the Cold War. Egypt's Telemisr was established in 1962 as a state-owned media company to support state broadcasting expansions with locally produced affordable television sets. Unable to keep up with competition, Telemisr was privatized in 1996. The company then entered into joint ventures with leading international technology manufacturers, which boosted its production capacity and facilitated the export of its products. Conversely, in countries such as Algeria where reform of the telecommunications sector has been slow, monopolistic practices and state intervention continue to define and dominate the sector.

Despite potential gains from liberalization, governments throughout the region generally have been reluctant to relinquish control of all sorts of infrastructure, from power plants to broadband. This would change only gradually. For one thing, just a few Arab countries could fund large infrastructure projects, and even those that do are bound by international agreements, particularly with the World Trade Organization (WTO), that mandate a competitive environment. Starting in the late 1980s, private Arab investors in Saudi Arabia, Bahrain, Morocco, and Egypt made numerous attempts to break state monopolies over broadcasting by adopting MMDS. For example, after three years of negotiations, Cable Network Egypt (CNE) started its operations in 1991, targeting wealthy Egyptians and foreign elites.[13] Yet, hobbled by government restrictions and weak demand for pay-TV services, cable failed to take off in the region until additional political, economic, and infrastructural conditions made the project viable. The emergence of satellite technologies in the 1990s slowed the prospects for local cable distribution outside the GCC countries, which were able to harness such technology to slow the spread of satellite receivers and retain control over access to content.

By the mid-1990s, satellite television channels presented governments with a control challenge. Arab channels based in Europe and elsewhere were not under direct state jurisdiction, nor could they be subject to traditional jamming techniques. States first resorted to controlling channels' access to advertisers and users' access to satellite receivers. By restricting funding and limiting distribution, states sought to reassert their authority over an emerging digital media based around a transborder satellite technology infrastructure. For example, Saudi Arabia initially banned access to satellite receivers (which were often smuggled into the country) and later levied a tax on installing satellite dishes, which proved difficult to enforce.[14] The Saudis also attempted to circumscribe the Qatari news channel Al Jazeera, an outlet that challenged the kingdom's media hegemony, by restricting the channel's access to its viewers and advertising market.[15] Through direct and indirect control of infrastructure, the state attempted to regulate how technologies were used and accessed with hopes of influencing content selection and distribution. With satellite technology making transnational channels available at the click of a button, it was hard for the state to enforce controls. Nor could the state offer competing content of its own. In short, neither regulating nor limiting access proved sustainable.

In the postindependence era, media infrastructure was the purview of the state, partly because providing it called for resources that only states possessed and also because media was a key aspect of the national development agenda. Over the years, technology investments continued to rely on the state, developing only limited collaboration with a "subservient" private sector. As a result, infrastructure spending relied on budget allocations from relevant state agencies, generally the telecommunications and information ministries. Inevitably, multiple competing power centers emerged, producing power struggles that focused less on technological efficiency and more on control over the means of communication. With a few exceptions (e.g., Dubai and Jordan), this resulted in layers of bureaucracy that limited the planning, investment, acquisition, and implementation of technological infrastructure. Today, while the state remains the main financier of ICT infrastructure, its pursuit of economic liberalization is undermined by its ambivalence toward adopting commercial practices that could unsettle the established forms of control upon which the system thrives. As a result, the state is able to neither maintain the existing system nor reinvent it.

These two patterns of state involvement are exemplified by the cases of Lebanon and the UAE. Although Lebanon established the first privately owned television channel in the region, the Lebanese government limited its investments in satellite and internet infrastructure. In 1972, it established Organisme de Gestion et d'Exploitation de l'ex Radio Orient (Ogero), a government agency that manages radio assets on behalf of the Ministry of Telecommunications. Gradually, Ogero became the operator for voice, data, and broadband services in Lebanon. As a government agency, Ogero was subject to the country's rampant corruption and security challenges. Consequently, it was incapable of developing, expanding, or upgrading services, while its collaboration with the private sector was limited to offering local ISP providers licenses for internet distribution. Ogero is a prime example of the limiting role of the state, which left Lebanon with one of the slowest and most expensive internet services in the region.

By contrast, state intervention enabled the UAE to establish itself as a regional leader in ICT development. Five years after its independence in 1971, the UAE combined all its telecommunications infrastructure under Emirtel (rebranded as Etisalat in 1984). With deep pockets and long-term planning, the country began expanding its networks and prepared for digital transformation as early as 1982, boasting the first mobile network in the Middle East. By 1997, the UAE established Al Thuraya to provide MSS as part of the country's strategic investments.

These ventures reveal the enabling role of the Emirati state through planning, developing, and upgrading ICT infrastructure.

The technologically foundational years of the 1970s and 1980s set the stage for different approaches to infrastructure, with the state taking a leading role in the process that varied across the Arab countries in the region. The levels of investment reflected each state's economy, with the Gulf countries making strategic investment and planning in infrastructure. To be sure, infrastructure development remains subject to national and regional political and economic interests that influence how the ICT sector is planned, financed, and executed. Despite that continuity, throughout the 1990s, there have been significant changes in the nature, scope, and geography of ICT development, with the state gradually relinquishing its hold on the process.

An Emerging Digital Environment

The Middle East entered the new millennium facing particular infrastructural challenges. The 2003 WSIS initiated a national and regional process to address the growing digital divide and create action plans to build information societies. During the second WSIS, held in Tunis in 2005, a new phase was launched. The focus was on carrying out concrete steps, identifying funding mechanisms, and addressing governance issues. Discourses about the "information society," "knowledge economy," and "Fourth Industrial Revolution" abounded with promises that the creation, management, and exchange of information through digital networks and tools would yield economic and social development. These discourses did not go unchallenged. As a 2019 report on the Arab League's digital plans warned, "there is a significant risk that any digital strategy encourages the introduction of technologies in search of a problem, instead of beginning with a problem and finding the right solution."[16]

Even before WSIS, Middle East states were beginning to consider ways to increase regional and international cooperation, foster partnerships with the private sector, and develop digital strategies. Transformation efforts, however, were an inconsistent mix of enthusiasm and apprehension. As the first Arab state to introduce the internet in 1991, Tunisia had developed a multilayered architecture to manage, promote, and control internet access. By 1996, it established its Internet Agency (known as ATI) to sell access to all internet service providers (ISPs) and control the increasing access to the internet, especially through "publinets" (internet cafés). In a trend that swept the region, many countries signaled the importance of ICT by rebranding government ministries to convey a focus on digital transformation and creating councils or special authorities to develop national strategies and plans. For example, in 1999, Egypt created the Ministry of Communications and Information Technology to establish research centers and industrial clusters. Some states moved more slowly. Security concerns and cultural protectionism delayed the connection of the locally restricted Saudi intranet to the global internet until 1999. Other states focused on developing frameworks for private-public partnerships while balancing local political and economic interests. For example, mobile communications in Sudan were made possible by that country's Economic Salvation Program (1990–1993), which attracted essential foreign investment from the Kuwait-owned telecommunications company Zain. Sudan's first mobile license was granted in 1996 to Zain Sudan (a local subsidiary), but it took another six years to attract a second licensee, MTN Sudan. In changing economic and political environments, each state's digital plans for broadband and mobile infrastructure became a matter of national economic and political security. The pace of digital transformation was calibrated against each state's ability to support and control it.

With the advent of the digital era, the state continued to play a significant role in the telecommunications sector but ceased to be its main broker. Whether prompted by international agreements or motivated by the need for foreign expertise and investments, Arab states opened their telecommunication markets to major global players. There was also a perceived need to formulate national strategies for ICT, which called for a multi-stakeholder approach to integrating a globally interlinked infrastructure with deep economic, social, and political ramifications. In the Levant, for instance, the Information and Communications Technology Association of Jordan (int@j) was formed in 2000 as an industry advocacy group representing the kingdom's vibrant and internationally active computer programming sector.[17] In 2002, int@j proposed the country's national ICT strategy, which was then adopted by the government. Similarly, other governments sought to lead by example with plans for digital transformation of government services that promised less bureaucracy and more efficiency and transparency. In particular, in the late 1990s and early 2000s, several states launched initiatives to harness ICT and slowly adopted deregulation and privatization policies, which allowed for certain forms of competition through licensing ISPs and mobile operators and nurturing technology parks. Nevertheless, in all these cases, including Jordan, ICT infrastructure remained under the direct purview of the state, which convenes discussions, develops plans, and coordinates implementation with predominantly Western-educated public officials championing the push for ICT adoption and neoliberal orientations.

State involvement complicates even seemingly straightforward assessments and implementations of decisions. When the state is involved, its logics of control clash with the logics of diffused and open digital networks. In Saudi Arabia, for instance, domestic internet connections did not arrive until January 1999, almost two years after the decision to allow access and four years after the issue was first considered.[18] When internet access finally arrived, it was limited by outdated regulation. Without a clear definition of its role, the internet became subject to

restrictions similar to those imposed on print and broadcast media, rules that targeted unsanctioned religious discourses, sexual content, or nonconformist views.
By and large, governments used state ownership or oversight over infrastructure
to retain control over internet communication. In some instances, they resorted to
regulations and bans; in others, they attempted to localize data or offer substitute
applications. Such restrictions often draw negative publicity and breed discontent
among a large group of avid users of digital communication.

Despite their strong control over various aspects of the digital turn, Arab states
were bound by global agreements to upgrade existing infrastructure, introduce
new policies and regulations, and provide support to develop their digital capacities. To finance the requisite investments, the region's governments nurtured
partnerships with local and transnational stakeholders, enhanced their financing
environments, and developed initiatives and spaces for innovations. For instance,
to develop mobile networks, states were encouraged to break up their monopolies
over the sector and license their spectra to local consortia or international groups.
In the Gulf region, state-owned telecom companies such as UAE's Etisalat or the
Saudi Telecommunication Company (STC) were the first beneficiaries and recipi-
ents of these licenses. Elsewhere, international companies such as France's Orange
Telecom and Germany's Vodafone bid for licenses to bring foreign investment and
expertise to emerging markets. Regional companies partnered with state proxy
sponsors or other investors to develop local companies, such as Kuwait's Zain in
Iraq and Egypt's Orascom (now the Amsterdam-based Global Telecom Holding)
in Algeria.

In addition to introducing digital policies, plans, and infrastructure, the region's
governments sought to develop both home-grown talent and technology in the
ICT sector. Throughout the past two decades, they introduced many initiatives,
such as providing innovation hubs, establishing business incubators and accelerators, and creating international partnerships, conferences, and exhibits that
foster the exchange of expertise. From Dubai's Internet City (1999) to Riyadh's
Digital City (2018), the Gulf countries have aggressively pursued the development of tech clusters. Such clusters have political, economic, and cultural goals.
In an attempt to diversify its economy, Saudi Arabia has attracted global companies such as Google to establish one of the largest innovation hubs in the region.[19]
Capitalizing on its leadership in the regional banking sector, Bahrain launched
Fintech Bay to serve the Middle East and Africa. The case of Palestine, especially
Ramallah, illustrates how a thriving tech community can emerge even in the
absence of favorable conditions, solid infrastructure, or established educational
institutions. From identifying digital security vulnerabilities to developing Arabic
games and apps, a generation of do-it-yourself tech tinkerers has thrived independently of any institution.[20]

While the private sector's entrepreneurial ethos seems to drive such ventures,
the state has remained a key player by establishing goals and priorities, facilitating

collaborations, cutting through its own red tape, and (at times) offering financial incentives. A frequently cited example is that of Abu Dhabi's state investor,
Mubadala Investment Company, which established its own technology hub. As an
incentive for talent and companies to relocate to the UAE, Mubadala has committed direct investment in projects developed in the country with its USD 250 million MENA tech funds.[21] It is within the emerging digital environment fostered by
these sites that an ecosystem is consolidating, with different sectors, stakeholders,
and centers playing a leading role in the digital turn.

Old Media and New Information Technologies

When discussing the digital turn, it is important to recognize inherent disjunctures between the predigital and the digital: between "old" media that clings to
print publications, radio stations, and satellite television and "new" media that
embraces and promotes the use of news portals, social media, and streaming services. Yet all of these media share overlapping dynamics, varying by specific sectors, demographics, and infrastructure. As the digital turn unfolds, the predigital
and the digital continue to overlap and blur rigid demarcations, often creating tensions stretching into everyday life. We analyze manifestations of these tensions
within three categories: national and regional infrastructure, governance and
investments, and publics and users.

The role of the state is central to any discussion of the predigital era. From water
and electricity to digital infrastructure, state control structured national development and international collaboration. In many countries, digital infrastructure for
broadband access remains slow, expensive, and with caps on traffic. Disparities
in internet access often mirror disparities in access to fixed telephones, with pronounced differences between rural and urban areas, limited competition, and
excessive bureaucracy. The Gulf countries are a notable exception to these tendencies,[22] with the UAE and Qatar being world leaders in fiber to the home (FTTH)
or to the building (FTTB). The differences among Arab countries in high-speed
broadband access are significant.[23] With the exception (again) of the Gulf countries, state control over ISPs and access to the global network slows development,
leading to limited national internet backbone and inadequate involvement of the
private sector in infrastructure.

Recall that the main digital infrastructure in the Middle East includes major
international submarine cables. Partly because of its dispersed geography, the
region favors connections through submarine cables that link the Indian subcontinent, East Africa, and the Mediterranean for both economic and logistical reasons.
Ironically, those same factors initially hindered the connection between Arab
countries. With a limited number of national internet exchange points (IXPs) to
route traffic between different networks, internet infrastructure linking the Arab

world suffers from backhauling and "tromboning."[24] Closely related, the national networks' dependency on long-distance networks to connect between IXPs negatively affects the speed and reliability of data transfer, driving the cost of service up and its quality down. Thus, whereas the centralized organization of telecommunication remains under the state's purview, national infrastructure is increasingly moving toward a decentralized, open model that includes the state and other parties. Whereas satellites could not offer inclusive and viable solutions to link neighboring Arab countries together, emerging digital technologies have yet to create the momentum and structures necessary to launch enterprising satellite programs. The uniting promises of the ArabSat project have given way to a national approach in which individual states launch their own satellites to address national communication needs and meet growing security demands. Since the first ArabSat satellite went into orbit in 1985, the Arab world has developed six space agencies (from Morocco in 1989 to the UAE in 2014) and more than a dozen state-owned satellites.

If the state can control infrastructure, the international community and local publics are able to exercise some pressure on digital uses. An explosion of citizen journalism in the form of blogging started to take shape by 2005. Online voices of political dissent, coupled with Western political discourses about internet freedom and democracy promotion, particularly under US presidents George W. Bush and Barack Obama,[25] alerted Middle Eastern regimes to the disruptive potential of the internet. The latter henceforth came to be seen as a threatening public space rather than a tamed private one. These apprehensions took on a new dimension when social media facilitated social movements. In response, states acted swiftly to monitor and control the digital world, mostly by leveraging their control of infrastructure, moves that civil-society actors and cyber activists resisted.

Unlike the organic and sometimes messy development of satellite television governance, three developments seemed to push for a controlled and more orderly articulation of internet policies. First, disenchantment with the "internet freedom fallacy"—the false belief that the internet can provide absolute freedom of expression, which ignores the role of the state and the market in regulating and constraining free speech—prompted cyber activists to call for independent, grassroots-based financial, logistical, and moral support of Arab digital activism and for a ban on sales of Western cyber surveillance equipment and software to Arab regimes.[26] Second, the WSIS (especially the 2005 Tunis meeting) and the WTO agreements pushed for a global harmonization of state policies toward the internet. These international forums and agreements provided a road map for digital transformation that included the business community and civil society as active stakeholders. Third, the regional alignment of digital infrastructure with economic diversification (e.g., in the Gulf) and sustainability (e.g., in North Africa) and the UN MDGs (e.g., in the Levant) offered long-term goals for state policies. As a result, states began to see the ICT sector as complementing the communications sector in its potential for socioeconomic development.

Starting in the 2010s, there has been considerable, widespread interest in digital governance as a gateway for balancing state security interests with economic prosperity. Digital governance is a state's effort to oversee digital networks and operation through drafting terms for legal and normative processes related to the country's economic and political systems. States approach digital governance differently, depending on their security, political, and economic interests. Long before the Arab uprisings, researchers could foresee that in their effort to maintain control, authoritarian regimes would likely suppress digital opposition.[27] At one extreme stand countries such as Syria where, after a brief opening in the early 2000s, state security superseded any perceived economic benefits from digitalization. In the most striking example, the Syrian Ministry of Communications and Technology failed to deliver on its e-government plans and instead diverted state resources to equip a special security unit (Branch 225) with sophisticated filtering, tracking, and mapping systems.[28] At the other end of the spectrum, the UAE serves as an example of a state in which enhanced security goes hand in hand with a strong commitment to economic diversification. The UAE developed a robust cybersecurity and surveillance program, including cutting-edge security camera systems on city streets and advanced systems for monitoring social-media activity. In 2020, the government established a national cybersecurity council to develop policies and regulatory frameworks and collaborated with the state-owned defense conglomerate Edge and relevant research institutes such as the Mohamed bin Zayed University of Artificial Intelligence.[29] Despite such security measures, the UAE is a pioneer in e-government and e-commerce. As early as 2001, most UAE government services were conducted electronically, while the country's e-commerce market is expected to double by 2025, reaching USD 17 billion annually.[30]

Beyond questions of governance, another tension arises from approaches toward investments in digital infrastructure. While the predigital era was state-centered, the digital era introduced multi-stakeholder approaches in response to political expediency, financial exigence, and market requirements. Whereas such arrangements can create ways for multiple actors—primarily the state, the market, and civil society—to work together, digital investments in the Middle East tend to adopt modified approaches. In one situation, the state continues to license companies that often include in their ownership leading government officials or ruling elites. Such opaque arrangements are prone to corruption, thus limiting infrastructural development at the expense of siphoning profits.

Consider the establishment of the mobile network in Syria. In 2001, state-owned Syria Telecom launched the BOT (build, operate, transfer) bidding processes to build the mobile network. In 2002, it restricted licenses to two operators, Syria Telecom and MTN-Syria. In theory, Syria Telecom and MTN-Syria are competitors; in practice, they offer identical pricing and packages. At the center of both companies are cronies who represent the regime's most powerful circles. In another approach representative of the predigital era, state-owned enterprises grew out of public utility companies or ministries that are privatized but in which the government retains significant control. The Gulf states have been leaders in converting these state entities into enterprising international players in the telecom industry. For example, the Qatar-owned Ooredoo has mobile, wireless, wireline, and wire services, with subsidiaries in the Gulf region, North Africa, and Asia.

Marking a departure from the predigital era, a community of digital entrepreneurs has emerged clearly distinguished from the media moguls whose empires stretched across multiple sectors and whose connections to power circles were essential for their success. From the modest operations of software localization (particularly into the Arabic language) to game and app developers, this digital business community is increasingly visible on the national, regional, and international stage. It flourishes in the technology and internet hubs that have mushroomed across the region, including King Abdulaziz City for Science and Technology (1977), Dubai Internet City (1999), Qatar Science and Technology Park (QSTP, 2009), and Egypt's Maadi Technology Park (2016). With varying degrees of success, these economic free zones spurred foreign direct investment inflows, technology transfer, and innovation and favored the emergence of startup tech companies. The fact that the contribution of the ICT sector to GDP in many Arab countries amounts to a modest 1% thus far should not obscure the sector's potential.[31] From Maktoob to Careem, Middle East–based innovations offer clear evidence of new approaches to investment in which governments develop infrastructural frameworks for digital innovations while the business community develops digital content, services, and applications.

Unlike the capital-intensive and regulation-restricted predigital model, the digital model is characterized by a lower investment barrier and evolving regulatory frameworks. This approach has allowed a number of groups, primarily young people, to enter the digital era as early users and producers. During the successive series of COVID-19 pandemic lockdowns, young people used digital infrastructure to seek, produce, or share information and entertainment, from health tips to cooking recipes and from TikTok videos to Zoom parties—thus becoming both the subject and the object of the story.

Everyday life, including business, education, and government, has been impacted by technological infrastructure. With more than 80% mobile penetration in most Arab countries and the popularization of smartphones, the demand for over-the-top communication services provided on the internet (such as video streaming) is increasing. Even before the pandemic, voice messages and texts were replacing private conversations and casual face-to-face meetings. Such transformations involve local particularities. Just as the language of satellite channels (with the exception of news) slowly moved away from classical Arabic to accommodate local dialects, the language of the internet moved from the domain of the written word to vernacular speech. For youth (ages fifteen to twenty-four), currently the largest demographic group in the region, dependency on ICT infrastructure for communication, socialization, and entertainment is unprecedented. These changes pose barriers as well as opportunities. In a region with high unemployment, there is often a poor match between the educational system and the job market. Even in Tunisia and Syria, where the educational system produces technologically competent youth, low-tech industries still dominate the economy. Addressing the problems of digital literacy, access, and inclusion remains complex and multifaceted. Whereas the early 2000s were marked by a dearth of Arabic-language internet content and applications, today's challenges also include quality of participation, level of engagement, and breadth of inclusion.

The significance of these changes extends even to dissent. Contentious politics remains a significant driver for how dissident groups based outside the region use technological infrastructure. In the predigital era, Saudi dissidents in London relied on facsimile transmissions to sabotage satellite television talk shows or compile and send news into the kingdom.[32] Under Zine El Abedine Ben Ali, Tunisian diasporic dissidents developed websites to compile and record human rights violations. Under Hosni Mubarak, Egyptian activists posted videos of abuses by security forces in their country. Today politics in its broadest sense remains a defining element in how infrastructure is monitored and controlled and how tools are used to communicate dissenting opinions. Consider social media. Just as Twitter became a platform for some of the region's leaders to address the public, the identity politics of marginalized or radical groups also played out with practices ranging from activists' support groups such as Telecomix to extremists' use of relatively more secure apps such as Telegram.

Toward a Digital Foundation

Based on the analysis thus far, several observations can be ventured. First, digital infrastructure in the region reflects individual countries' structural positions. The relevant factors include economics, politics, demographics, society, geography, and other areas of symbolic and practical relevance. The six affluent Gulf countries possess hydrocarbon wealth, stable political systems, large expatriate groups, small populations, homogeneous societies, and modern urban geographies. Those factors have contributed to high fixed and mobile internet penetration, advanced e-government and e-commerce adoption, digital entrepreneurship, and innovation. In contrast, countries such as Sudan, Syria, Libya, and Iraq have large and diverse populations, unstable political regimes, enduring conflicts, and dispersed or rough geographies—factors that have influenced low fixed and mobile internet penetration, near absence of reliable e-government and e-commerce, and limited access to digital development funding. Interestingly, the future may bring challenges even for countries in the former, more fortunate category.[33]

Second, there is a shift in the current dominant logic of communication infrastructure and its associated technologies, services, and practices from mass-targeted regional technologies to individually targeted "local" digital networks. Whereas satellite technologies offered the possibility to develop regional access, use, and production, differences in access to technological and other resources complicate the digital turn. As noted earlier, the digital prominently figures in government strategic plans and is of paramount importance for national and international investments. This shift is closely associated with the growing enclosure of those technologies by global market and state security interests. Writing in the early days of the internet, some scholars challenged the hasty but common (especially in Western circles) verdict that "the coming of the internet and the mushrooming of satellite dishes on Arab rooftops [are] signs of the retreating Arab state, the rise of civil society, the emergence of the public sphere, and maybe a dawn of new politics."[34] Even today, states continue to play a significant role in regulating and funding digital infrastructure and therefore are able to curb civil society, limit the public sphere, and counter constantly reinvented contentious politics.

Third, the digital turn's infrastructure and associated services, practices, and institutional arrangements are becoming increasingly intertwined with everyday life. This manifests itself in its most prominent guises in unabashed Instagram self-expressions and consuming video-gaming habits.[35] But behind the dizzying proliferation of photos and videos, regional apps, e-government, and e-commerce platforms lie physical, computational, and organizational technologies of communication that divide countries, and populations within countries, along lines of access, skills, and relevance. While in recent years there has been tremendous commitment to bridging the digital divide, more than one-third of the region's population is not regularly able to use the internet.[36] When disaggregated, regional averages reveal high rates of internet use in the Gulf countries and low levels in North Africa, and the gender gap remains significant, with 25% more men than women going online.[37] More importantly, perhaps, the ability and preparedness to engage in digital development and e-readiness are challenged by what Payal Arora calls the "leisure divide."[38] The utilization of digital infrastructure and internet access among a predominantly youthful population sheds light on their ability to navigate economic, political, and cultural systems that may lack relevance to them. However, this understanding does not inherently offer a straightforward trajectory toward modernization as envisioned by international organizations and endorsed by political and economic elites.

Finally, the overlapping values, goals, and organizational structures and their associated political, economic, and cultural activities reveal that digital infrastructure in the Middle East, as elsewhere, is not a neutral ground. The infrastructural dimension facilitates certain developments while inhibiting others; it also shapes how the digital turn is unfolding and determines both its intensity and its potential. Grasping the significance of infrastructure beyond material artifacts and organizational structures requires attention to the relational characteristics of digital foundation, which necessarily entails a critical engagement with the digital turn in politics, economics, and culture.

Part III

EXPRESSION AND SUPPRESSION

The Entangled Web of Politics

In a region where the state has traditionally exerted control over public discourse, the digital Middle East stands out as a contested space for the iteration of the political. The same tools that continue to control public discourse through monitoring and surveillance are also used to mobilize and promote anti-hegemonic discourses. Initially, Middle Eastern states perceived the internet as a development on the fringes of the lives of most people. Some even embraced digital technologies as a token of modernity. With more people acquiring digital tools and partaking in communication practices that facilitated access to unsanctioned information and enhanced self-expression, states were faced with three intractable dilemmas: how to capitalize on the opportunities the digital era affords while limiting its undesired effects; how to transform their economies while ensuring such technologies did not undermine their own power; and how to acknowledge difference while managing hegemonic representations of various groups and maintaining a culture of deference to authority. The desire to adopt yet control the technologies led states to take an ambivalent approach toward the digital. These dynamics took hold within an evolving context that transcends the state in its symbolic role and territorial capacity. The proliferation of networks, digital convergence, improved technological infrastructure, and increasing fluidity of advanced transborder communication have made power more diffuse, control more elusive, and contention more dynamic. In the ensuing web of expression and suppression, a power play has impelled digitally networked publics to continuously break the limits of political action and compelled regimes to perpetually redefine such boundaries and reposition themselves. In this regard, citizens and states alike have appropriated digital tools and developed digital strategies that could enable them to reassert themselves.

Of particular interest is how the digital is reconfiguring "the political" and, conversely, how politics shapes the digital. We use "the political" not in the narrow sense of government and party institutions, policies, and actions but in the more diffuse sense of ordinary acts and forms of engagement between states and publics. We situate the latter within dynamics similar to what Michel de Certeau calls "the practice of everyday life."[1] These formulations recognize that subjects negotiate their positions of power within a particular social system through everyday practices, using various tactics to claim spaces and reappropriate discourses. The most relevant set of practices involves everyday digital communications that articulate personal subjectivities and shared politics. For those with digital access, browsing, posting, liking, and sharing on social media are everyday practices. They can be appropriated for subversion and mobilization while being subject to state co-optation and corporate manipulation. This assembly of "subject positions" reconstitutes individual political interests as collective interests and markers of a renegotiated sense of citizenship.[2] Within today's context of increased digital engagement, citizenship is a condition that goes beyond judicial, political, and affective formulations to include a "quotidian politics."[3] Such a formulation draws attention to individuals, social groups, and communities whose everyday practices redefine citizenship and expand the sphere of politics.

Chapter 6

The Enticement of Digital Citizenship

Normative approaches to citizenship typically center on legal, political, and affective categories.[1] Legal or judicial citizenship is anchored in specific rights, such as claiming a nationality or acquiring status as a legal resident; political citizenship revolves around participating in the public sphere by accessing information, deliberating on issues of general interest, and influencing policies; and affective citizenship relates to the mobilization of "feelings of civil belonging, loyalty, and solidarity."[2] These perspectives are premised on individualistic conceptions of citizenship that are specific to predominantly Western societies. A different conception highlights a consensual citizenship that reflects processes such as political socialization that reinforce prevailing notions of identity and induce conformity among young people.[3] An even more dynamic conception of citizenship associates social subjects with contingent and heterogeneous positions. For example, enticed by the notion of "digital citizenship," various groups use the internet to project alternative identities and advocate their vision of society. The conceptions of citizenship that emerge from these fluid and dynamic conditions create oppositional and mutable venues for self-expression.

The digital promotes aspects of citizenship that are both overlapping and contentious and, in the process, creates different political narratives. For marginalized groups, information technologies provide alternative venues for debate—spaces that, historically, either did not exist or were exclusionary. The widespread use of digital tools favors the emergence of various online communities from chat room participants to bloggers and from YouTubers to Facebook groups. Digital spaces enhance the ability of marginalized populations, oppositional groups, and diasporic communities, among others, to associate and advance their visions. The potential and viability of these spaces depend on people's ability to afford, access, and use digital tools, as well as the state's appropriation of these same tools for surveillance, censorship, and criminalization of unsanctioned forms of participation.

Everyday articulations of citizenship merit attention. Particularly important are how communities deploy digital tools to create sites of contention and reorder

The Digital Double Bind. Mohamed Zayani and Joe F. Khalil, Oxford University Press. © Oxford University Press 2024.
DOI: 10.1093/oso/9780197508626.003.0006

public debate, thereby continuing a long-standing tradition of communication technologies opening up spaces for political civic engagement.

Sprawling Diasporas Online

Traditionally, the diasporic communities and ICT use have been examined in relation to the "networked public sphere,"[4] "transnational public sphere,"[5] or "global network society."[6] With the advent of the internet, the public sphere has migrated online and expanded globally, creating both synchronous and asynchronous communication. In the same vein, "diasporic public sphere" is used to describe "the realm of social interaction, discourse, identity and imagination associated with living as part of a diaspora."[7] It draws attention to how people's lives are increasingly reconstituted through images, ideas, and opportunities that originate elsewhere and circulate through global media.[8] The term "digital diasporas" has been used to describe forms of virtual social networks and technologically mediated coexistence.[9] As a result, increased levels of civic engagement;[10] opportunities for the expression, promotion, and consolidation of dissenting voices;[11] and alternative political visions have developed outside the purview of the state.[12]

All along, media, broadly defined, has been essential to diasporic identity construction and formative in the development of sociopolitical life in the diaspora.[13] Long before the introduction of ICTs, the Middle East diaspora capitalized on multiple tools to develop alternative political identities. In the nineteenth century, the Arab intelligentsia from the Levant mobilized against Ottoman rule through newspapers and chronicles. The 1920s were marked by the works of émigré men of letters who were inspired by the Arab awakening (*Al Nahda*). Banding together under the New York Pen League and coalescing around Kahlil Gibran, a group of diasporic (*mahjar*) writers contributed to the renewal of Arabic literature and created political awareness.[14] These publications, serving as print media, were primarily accessible to the literate population; however, they were usually slow in reaching the homeland and remained susceptible to censorship. In later decades, advanced telephony and satellite television allowed fast, relatively unfettered communication between the diaspora and the homeland. When the Algerian diaspora in France mobilized against the civil war of the 1990s, new information technologies allowed easier, faster access to information, and events occurring in one nation were rapidly communicated to the other.[15] Today, online diasporic media have become an important platform for minority and underprivileged groups voicing their opinions, arguing for their rights, and expressing their distinct identities.[16] Similarly, social interaction is no longer limited to being in the same place at the same time, unsettling the "neat equation between culture and community and geography" and affording new possibilities for envisioning oneself as being present both "here" and "elsewhere."[17]

Despite such widespread diasporic engagement, there are structural, personal, and practical limits to diasporas' ability to participate politically in their homelands. On a structural level, diasporas operate within multiple political contexts that might stretch or limit their ability to imagine different politics. Consider the difference in restrictions and protections between political refugees in Western countries and those in Arab countries. At the personal level, individuals' degrees of embeddedness in the host community influence the level of their commitment to political engagement with the host countries. Immigrants may want to invest in adopting the political practices of their new country, while expatriates' connections with the homeland are organically maintained. Practically, political organization and mobilization in the diaspora include online engagements but also physical links. Thus, online forms of organization such as participation in online forums or signing online petitions are often maintained and reinforced through physical community-building activities such as religious gatherings, conventions, associations, and professional communities.

Two cases illuminate how Arab diasporas have used ICTs to maintain transnational diasporic connections with the homeland while simultaneously claiming a voice in their host countries. In both cases, diasporas have engaged, mobilized, and connected with each other horizontally, inclusively, and openly. Although the tools and groups have changed over time, the trends illustrated by these cases serve as a useful lens for examining how digital technology enticed the diaspora.

The first trend is inward-looking and characterized by the development of intercommunity relations and making the diasporic presence felt among host communities. This trend evolved with the development of digital technology, increased accessibility, and acquired digital competency. In the 1980s, early use of computer networks was limited to professionals and university students who used networks to connect and share research resources.[18] In the 1990s, diaspora communities in the United States and Europe used LISTSERVs to follow and disseminate news and joined Usenet groups to exchange information or create a space for entertainment. Internet forums were a collection of web-based discussions that allowed users to create discussion threads or contribute to one or more topic categories, known as newsgroups. Diaspora communities used several hierarchies to organize their electronic interactions. For example, the hierarchy "soc." was designated for social discussions and enabled many users in the diaspora to congregate under the soc.culture.arabic or soc.religion.islam categories. Another such group was soc.culture.lebanon, letting Lebanese users from around the world engage with an emerging group of Lebanon-based users. As Lebanon was reassembling its fractured communities after a civil war (1975–1990), the group acted as a forum for reflection on postwar social, economic, and political projects. These online encounters could catalyze physical network building. Invoking a memorable line from Gibran's *The Madman*—"we know each other's minds; now we will know each other's faces"—members of soc.culture.lebanon organized a mini-conference in Boston in 1995 on how Lebanon could move forward in the postwar era.[19]

Practices changed as new tools appeared and different generations of users started to seek connection with one another and claim their own digital spaces, including using the then-new World Wide Web. As websites became easier to develop, the Arab diaspora in Europe capitalized on the internet to respond to the systemic marginalization to which they were subjected, developing platforms to expose social injustices and model inclusive practices. Many of these websites came to light as anti-Arab and anti-Muslim sentiments increased, particularly after the 9/11 attacks, the 2003 war on Iraq, and the terrorist attacks in Europe. These websites fostered a strong sense of diasporic community. They included refugee sites forging alliances and facilitating inclusion[20] as well as diasporic media cultures seeking to negotiate identity, sustain transnational ties, and build inter- and extra-diasporic connections.[21] These communicative practices operate within diasporic communities and across generations of immigrants, from second-generation British Muslims expressing their views on religious issues to Dutch-Moroccan youth sharing their experiences of exclusion in their native Dutch language.[22] Although the nature of online tools changed over time, these digital spaces served a similar purpose: building solidarity across diasporic communities and enabling reflections on the experiences of individuals living in them.

The second trend looks outward to how users in diasporas harness the potential of ICTs for developing, maintaining, and supporting transborder connections between their adopted homes and their homeland. Some seek to reconnect with the homeland, while others strive to echo and magnify the plight of the homeland. A case in point is Electronic Intifada (EI), one of the longest-running Middle East–centered digital media sites. The brainchild of four Palestinian activists, EI is "an independent online news publication and educational resource focusing on Palestine, its people, politics, culture and place in the world."[23] Established in 2001, EI draws its name from the second Palestinian Intifada but is more encompassing geographically and temporally. EI is based in Chicago and publishes content in English, but its contributors and followers live around the world. As a portal, EI offers a "Palestinian perspective of the news,"[24] often with more immediacy than the established media. It adopts an activist approach, as epitomized in its advocacy for the Palestinian-led Boycott, Divestment, and Sanctions (BDS) movement.[25] After more than twenty years in operation, the EI website integrated social media. Beyond activism, EI serves as a forum for Palestinians everywhere to come together as digital citizens with tools for information, education, debate, and participation.

Another example of this second, outward-looking trend is Elaph, a news portal launched in London in 2001 and founded by Saudi entrepreneur Othman Al Omeir with the aim of offering uncensored, liberal Saudi viewpoints. Al Omeir saw the internet as uncharted territory with unbounded potential, considering that it was not yet regulated.[26] For years, Elaph acted as a progressive voice from the diaspora across the Arab world, reaching more than a million global users. In many ways, Elaph is a digital variant of private, foreign-based, transnational media projects by Saudi moguls harnessing technologies to create spaces in the diaspora that focus on the homeland. The growing potential of digital media motivated Elaph's founder to maintain and expand its portal despite financial and techno-logical hurdles. In this sense, Elaph represents the digital liberalism of Gulf states, where business elites' interests overlap with their social and political aspirations.

The introduction of social media further expanded the scope of user engage-ment in diasporic communities. Facebook and Twitter became new spaces where members of the Arab diaspora discussed issues of common concern, includ-ing issues of identity. Many studies note the internet's impact on the develop-ment of Arab identity politics, particularly with multigenerational communities in Europe.[27] The public nature of emerging digital tools is more subjective and less restricted as "the links between networks and flows that surpass geographi-cal restrictions are reaffirmed as central to the process of identity construction."[28] Sprawling online diasporas have developed open, accessible, and egalitarian sites to discuss their dual citizenship and hybrid identities in communicative spaces that transcend borders.

These online communities have also helped develop shared political subjec-tivities that are not bound by space but nonetheless affect nationally defined sub-jectivities within the region. The term "subjectivities" is commonly associated with philosophical concepts that extol truth, agency, and consciousness, whereas some thinkers associate the term with power.[29] Political subjectivities are perspec-tives, feelings, thoughts, identities, and narratives, not just about relations with elite power but more broadly regarding everyday sociocultural and economic acts. The evolution of digital tools and the resulting expansion of virtual communities have increased the ability of people in the region to express political subjectivities related to their everyday lives. Significantly, however, these spaces have not been unbounded or void of restrictions. For example, although Syrians in the diaspora actively communicated news of the protests in 2011 and served as liaisons with local mainstream media offering their access and expertise,[30] fear of retribution against families in the homeland deterred many activists from challenging Syria's political regime online.[31]

Vibrant Virtual Communities

The advent of the internet favored the emergence of what Howard Rheingold calls "virtual communities," new techno-social systems in which groups of people form networks of social relations as a result of public discussions sustained over a period of time in cyberspace.[32] Virtual communities promoted different interests, including education, religion, entertainment, politics, and countless others. For those with the ability and inclination to participate, virtual communities offered spaces and resources that substituted or complemented restricted sociocultural and political spaces offline. In Multi-User Dimensions (MUDs), MUD Object-Oriented (MOO), and Internet Relay Chats (IRCs), virtual communities became ideal, placeless substitutes for traditional, geographically based communities such as tribes, clubs, and political associations.

Many scholars maintain that virtual communities offer safe spaces for free and independent discussions.[33] Some scholars even suggest connections between the adoption of technologies and democratization, although others have noted a lack of empirical evidence supporting this claim.[34] Despite such differences, most scholars would agree that these virtual communities enable users to imagine sociopolitical alternatives. At the peak of globalization and the disintegration of unifying Arab projects, these virtual communities (just like those formed around satellites) favored the emergence of international (Arab included) spaces for political imaginations. They allowed Middle East digital citizens to revisit their histories and reconstruct oppositional narratives that diverged from those sanctioned by the state. They renewed a shared sense of purpose and a desire for sociopolitical reconfiguration and helped challenge traditional gender relations, religious dogmas, and deference to authority. Virtual communities created their own rituals, protocols, and norms to guide member interactions, often with aspirations toward democratic practices. Virtual community moderators were entrusted with maintaining rules, calling out abusers, and ensuring that online communities remained inclusive spaces.

It would be misleading, however, to characterize virtual communities as utopian agoras cut off from the physical worlds in which their users lived. Ethnographic work on internet cafés in Kuwait suggests that "online behavior is in part shaped by offline variables."[35] The number of participants, the variety of contributions, and the novelty of these communication platforms, combined with political, cultural, and religious factors, often limited these virtual communities in realizing their potential. The digital citizenship that developed rested largely on passive subjectivities, meaning users relied on facilitators to produce knowledge. Considering the nature of their agency, users largely deferred to authorities, as is common in Arab societies. Participation in these virtual communities, with users often adopting pseudonyms for anonymity, mirrored the collectivist society from which users migrated. In these spaces, individuals found solidarity and support in the form of predetermined spaces with identifiable themes.

Yet even where offline factors persisted in influencing users' behaviors and expectations, virtual communities remained potential sites of activism and contestation that could, in turn, seek to transform the physical communities in which their users participated. Although virtual communities often mirrored existing social constructs and hierarchies, they broke with the state monopoly on information and with religious and political authorities' control over public opinion. Virtual communities increased participation and self-representation of diverse voices while maintaining some level of privacy and anonymity. Access to virtual communities was limited, but it provided members with the opportunity to share information, articulate plights, debate positions, and argue cases—though not all those individuals were politically motivated. Importantly, while the transborder nature of these communities created dynamics at the intersection of the local, the regional, and the global, the ensuing effects were not technological in essence; they were broad in nature and part of the dynamics of Middle Eastern societies themselves.

The emergence of Saudi forums illustrates how virtual communities constituted spaces for disrupting certain traditions and norms while imagining new ones. Even after the advent of social-networking media, these online communities continued to attract high rates of participation.[36] At first, these forums developed on the intranet, allowing the government the possibility to monitor and control speech.[37] As with older communication technologies, the authorities feared that these forums could attract regime dissidents and antiestablishment voices. Dissident groups based in the diaspora, such as the Committee for the Defense of Legitimate Rights (CDLR) and later the Movement for Islamic Reform in Arabia (MIRA), had long proved adept at using new technologies to develop a following. Having repeatedly intervened during live call-in shows on satellite television, Saad Al-Faqih, MIRA's London-based leader, resorted to using the widespread network of fax machines in Saudi Arabia to disseminate news digests and political manifestos from his office. He even sought to build a community around the organization's website. In reaction, the Saudi authorities curbed access to the website, waged legal battles against MIRA in the British courts, and unsuccessfully lobbied the British government to take legal action against the group. Although MIRA failed to "raise any groundswell of support,"[38] it demonstrated the ability of online communities to develop political subjectivities and push the limits of political activism that relies solely on virtual organizations.

The trajectory of Islamic groups online reveals how their virtual communities were adept at exploiting technological affordances. In the early days of the internet, Muslim students in North America and Europe used electronic mailing lists to inform and build community awareness of various issues of religious doctrine and social practices, as well as to build solidarity around conflicts from Kashmir to Palestine. The need to maintain virtual communities to seek and spread religious knowledge became the focal point of dedicated sites such as Islam Online, while some radical groups exploited the membership structure of online discussion boards such as Yahoo! Groups to develop a closed virtual community. Since the early 2000s, such groups have migrated to highly encrypted online networks with content that animates the "dark web."

Across the region, virtual communities such as Alsaha.com (1998), Swalif.net (1999),[39] and Arabsgate.com (2000) became spaces for members to explore the potential of digital citizenship. Among these communities, Al Saha al Arabiya (The Arab Scene)[40] merits attention as a transborder, Gulf-based community offering alternative imaginaries, practices, and outcomes at a time of tremendous political, economic, cultural, and social change. Developed by a group of Emirati youth, including the brothers Fares and Jaber Mohamed, the site primarily targeted youth in the Gulf. In existence between 1997 and 2012, Al Saha was the oldest and most diverse space in which ordinary people voiced their concerns. Noticeably, religious clerics, intellectuals, and political figures also regularly interjected their opinions on this forum. To create a neutral space for dialogue, the founding team carefully managed the commercialization of the site, thereby controlling how ads were selected. Gradually, Al Saha grew popular in neighboring Saudi Arabia, offering alternative venues for self-expression and, after 9/11, opening debates regarding contentious issues including democratization, the 2003 war on Iraq, and terrorism. As it evolved, Al Saha became a "forum for serious discussion and live debate"[41] and a place where people with various interests, backgrounds, and political leanings came together, as audiences and participants, to read and comment on wide-ranging issues, many of which had a political aspect. In some respect, Al Saha also acted as a de facto news and information site. It was the first to break the news about the deadly 2003 Riyadh compound bombings, even before official word was out, when one prominent contributor, Abu Lujain, probingly posted: "Oh people of Riyadh, what's happening out there?" Such fast, unfiltered flow of information would have been unthinkable only a decade earlier, when news that Saddam Hussein had invaded Kuwait was not announced on Saudi state media until three days after the fact.[42]

While Al Saha grew to be an engaging space that attracted ordinary users and other participants from both ends of the cultural spectrum, it was far from inclusive. Almost all conversations were moderated by site administrators and believed to be monitored by the state. Some discussions were for women only. The forum's popularity, the intensity of its users' debates, and its retransmission of controversial videotaped messages from Osama Bin Laden drew further scrutiny from Saudi authorities, who blocked the site even after its founders visited Saudi Arabia to make amends. While Saudi users could use VPNs to circumvent this block, such measures made it difficult to attract the advertising necessary to sustain the site.

Moderation, surveillance, and other difficulties left spaces such as Al Saha vulnerable to copycats and competing alternatives. With the introduction of Twitter, users began to shift from a desktop-based platform to a mobile-instant tool that was neither moderated nor controlled. Yet the advent of social media, particularly Twitter, atomized communities even as they offered new prerogatives to individual users. The eclipsing of spaces such as Al Saha brought to a close one of the most dynamic experiences of digital citizenship. Forums nurtured the development of online communities that mirrored traditional interactions in cultural clubs and *diwaniyas* or *majlises* (councils or assemblies) where various community debates and discussions were held. Occasionally, they allowed the intermingling of traditionally segregated groups based on gender, national origin, religious convictions, or other affiliations, as they participated in politically charged online discussions.

While the appeal and functionality of social-media features have made these forums obsolete, the enthusiasm and conviviality of virtual communities formed around Al Saha were unique. Interestingly, the massive growth of Clubhouse during the COVID-19 pandemic briefly reenergized virtual communities. The platform's real-time voice chats appealed to users in the diaspora and young people in the region. These "rooms" (similar to topics or threads) range from serious discussions about the normalization of relations with Israel and the political future of the region to town hall meetings and conversations with activists, opinion leaders, and intellectuals. The vibrancy of these virtual communities suggests that online and offline communities increasingly co-construct each other.

Toward a Claimed Subjectivity

Whereas web forums reflected the collectivist aspect of Arab societies, blogging and social media put the spotlight on the interests of individuals. The ensuing articulations of politics can be described as constructing digital citizenship and a move toward claimed subjectivities. As digital tools moved from web pages (which were simply repositories of information) to blogs, YouTube channels, and other platforms offering more dynamic user-engaged and -generated content, the possibilities for self-expression increased. Tim O'Reilly, who coined the term "Web 2.0," describes its emphasis as "harnessing collective intelligence."[43] But unlike the collective discussions of web forums, Web 2.0 centers individual subjectivities.

The Web 2.0 environment effaces demarcations between producers and audiences. This fundamental change reveals sociocultural shifts in collectivist societies away from individuals as state subjects (particularly under autocratic regimes) to individuals thinking and acting as independent citizens. Through digital tools and other means, a predominantly young generation was able to advance its oppositional politics in public. For example, one young Iraqi started blogging with the 2003 invasion of Iraq under the pseudonym Salam Pax. At one point, he was labeled the "most famous blogger in the world"[44] due to the large following his "Where Is Raed?" blog generated. Originally created to remind his friend, Raed, to answer emails, the blog evolved to chronicle the US invasion as experienced by an Iraqi. Salam Pax's detailed accounts of daily life in Baghdad contrasted with the sanitized, prepackaged perspective the mainstream Western media's journalists offered while embedded with the occupying forces. Beyond these chronicles, Salam Pax expressed the subjectivities of a young, Western-educated,

English-speaking, and gay Arab.[45] Expressing such intersectional identities was in itself a political statement. The perspectives Salam Pax offered differed markedly from the stereotypes of both Western and Arab mainstream media, whose reporting was framed in binaries of "terrorist" versus "resistance" and whose stories conspicuously ignored or blatantly misrepresented gay communities. The curiosity around Salam Pax led the *Guardian* to investigate him and reveal his true identity as a twenty-nine-year-old Iraqi named Salam Abdulmunem, an architect by training and a translator for foreign journalists.[46]

Local blogs revealed another level of engagement with political issues. Three years after Salam Pax became popular, Samer Karam, writing as Fink Ployd, started bloggingbeirut.com as a blog celebrating tourism in Lebanon. In July 2006, a border skirmish between Hezbollah and Israel turned into a thirty-three-day war that included a blockade and land invasion. The blog immediately pivoted to provide continuous documentation of the war from the perspective of those living in and around Beirut. Equipped with a digital camera, Fink Ployd uploaded images ranging from street life to empty supermarket shelves. At a time when mainstream media was featuring military activities, diplomatic negotiations, and political pundits, bloggingbeirut.com offered the perspective of a young professional who had just returned to Lebanon after completing his studies in the United States and wanted to share the charm of his country with his international friends. These subjectivities were quickly set aside to prioritize content actively raising consciousness about the war and catalyzing collective action. The blog became an instant resource for the diaspora, offering alternative perspectives and drawing solidarity with the country through the "I (heart) Beirut" campaign.[47] With war being blogged live, digital citizens found spaces to voice perspectives, share feelings, and build solidarity.

The difference between Salam Pax's and Fink Ployd's blogs are indicative of how technological advances and developments have reconfigured the nature of digital engagement. Whereas Salam Pax had illustrated his accounts with digital photographs, Fink Ployd went beyond that, making ingenious use of YouTube videos to produce eyewitness accounts of life in Beirut. The move from still photography to video marked a new era in digital participation. Following its acquisition by Google, YouTube became a regional sensation, with professionals and amateurs producing, remixing, uploading, and sharing content on and for the platform. While YouTube became instantly popular for enabling the dissemination of pirated content (both local and international), the platform also enabled activists to document their actions and circulate uncensored political content. In 2011, Egyptian activist Asma Mahfouz became famous after she posted a YouTube message urging fellow citizens to go to Tahrir Square on January 25. When a veiled Mahfouz looked confidently straight into the camera and, defying security forces, called for civil disobedience, it marked a turning point. The release of the Khalid Said Facebook video about the police corruption that had cost him his life a few months earlier was another powerful act of witnessing. Whether in blogs, YouTube videos, or social-media posts, these courageous acts of activism consolidated a digital citizen journalism movement, circumvented the state control over access, and claimed subjectivities that would prove consequential.

The convergence of the spread of mobile phones with powerful cameras and services such as YouTube turned citizens into eyewitnesses and investigators. The moniker of Egypt's "Facebook Revolution" came about because activists deftly employed Facebook to organize, mobilize, and share information by many means, including embedding YouTube videos. During the Syrian uprising, amateur videos on social media offered visual anchorage for news reporting. Some Syrian activists were recruited, equipped, and trained to act as field reporters—a by-product of the corporatization of citizen journalism. Initially, the Syrian uprising was labeled as the "YouTube Revolution" because it was communicated through YouTube videos documenting neighborhood demonstrations, protesters' plights, and the regime's brutality. Protesters became skilled at filming, editing, compressing videos, and evading online censors by smuggling the videos outside the country using flash drives to physically distribute their messages.

More than merely offering a place to store records of events, YouTube videos served as a living archive for political critiques that tested the limits of free speech. Young Saudis in particular were drawn to YouTube as a space where they could reveal their subjectivities while adhering to state rules. As early as 2008, Saudi YouTube multi-channels became harbingers of diverse collectives from U-Turn to Telefaz 11, producing everything from standup comedies to web series. These spurred the development of a collective consciousness around taboo sociopolitical topics such as unemployment, racism, and women's rights, as well as the use of comedy to push the limits of permissible speech. Often working in the gray zone of media regulation, authorities were baffled by the popularity of YouTube, being both an unthreatening venting place for youth and a tool for "creative insurgency."[48]

Contestations over Saudi women's right to drive illustrate the point. Saudi women have been campaigning for the right since at least 1990. In later years (2008, 2011, and 2014), they used YouTube to document videos of themselves driving.[49] Whether fueling testimonies or satirical critiques, the ban on women driving was a subject of poignant YouTube videos. In October 2013, satirical comedian Hisham Fageeh released a music video titled "No Woman No Drive" on the YouTube multi-channel Telefaz 11. This parody of Bob Marley's "No Woman No Cry," which Fageeh sang in English (with Arabic subtitles) while wearing a traditional thobe, attracted more than 17 million views on YouTube.[50] Consistent with the Saudi tradition of avoiding direct criticism of state policies, the video was a digital intervention poking fun at the arguments in support of the driving ban. Describing himself as an "artist and social activist," Fageeh told the BBC he made the video "not aiming to do anything political, just to entertain."[51] As an academic, he declared to *Arab News* that he was "interested [in] and fascinated by social politics."[52] Such articulations draw attention to the intersection between digital entertainment and the politics of everyday life, particularly considering that comedy attracts a diverse audience. Even after the driving ban was lifted in 2018, YouTube and other social-media platforms continued to circulate commentary, either with young women behind the wheel or female rappers celebrating their right to drive. Watching, sharing, or commenting on such videos is an articulation of claimed subjectivities. Such engagements favor a social heterogeneity that media often misses, and what might otherwise pass for apolitical takes on a political significance.

Across the Middle East, young people use social-media tools to express an understanding of citizenship that holds power accountable and stretches existing limits of free speech. In Jordan, a group of bloggers developed Arabic-language animated cartoons and music videos focused on local and regional sociopolitical issues. Kharabeesh (Scribbles) has been developing content since 2008 and distributing it on its own website as well as social-media platforms. The company's political cartoons and animated series have become part of the digital narrative of the Arab uprisings. Of particular interest are the company's satirical videos "Mubarak Is High," which were released less than a week after the start of the anti-regime demonstrations in 2011. Similar animated cartoons featured Syria's Bashar Al-Assad and Libya's Muammar Gaddafi. Over the years, Kharabeesh became home to various content developers with commercial and political interests.

In Egypt, although comedy was popular, political satire was largely censored, except when it served to ridicule regime opponents.[53] After assisting the wounded during the January 25 Revolution, surgeon Bassem Youssef launched a YouTube satirical show named the *B + Show*, which gathered more than 5 million viewers in less than three months.[54] Youssef's popularity drew the interest of ONTV, a private channel owned by Naguib Sawiris. ONTV rebranded the show into *Al Bernameg* (*The Show*), modeled it after the American satire *The Daily Show* (then hosted by Jon Stewart), and supported it with production and promotional resources. *Al Bernameg*'s pithy satirical comedy clashed with the station's ability to withstand political pressure; between 2011 and 2014, the show moved across three channels (ONTV, CBC, and MBC Masr) before it was discontinued and its host entered a self-imposed exile in the United States.[55] While Youssef was wrestling with the constraints of mainstream media, another Egyptian, Youssef Hussein, started a satirical YouTube show, *JoeTube*, in 2013, taking a dig at the new Egyptian regime and other autocratic regimes around the region, before it was rebranded as the *Joe Show* and relaunched on Al Araby TV.[56]

The various uses of Web 2.0 tools have opened up spaces for articulations of digital citizenship that could challenge the hegemony of the collective order. Creative practices—from blogging wars to sharing politically charged satire—point to increased realizations of agency among individuals and communities.

Such awareness of claimed subjectivities will gradually turn the seemingly discon-nected expressions of contestation into digital citizenship fomenting forms for activism.

Trans-Local Subjectivities

Today's digital citizenship is a complex web of subjectivities. It may be helpful in this context to recall the concept of trans-locality to understand the development of digital users' practices (both physical and virtual) of their subjectivities and their citizenship.[57] Trans-locality encompasses local-to-local exchanges that tran-scend physical, political, economic, social, and cultural borders. Trans-local sub-jectivities can shed light on phenomena such as how homelands are created and recreated using digital means and how digital interventions shape understandings of space. Examining manifestations of trans-local subjectivities allows us to better understand the mobility of actors, ideas, and practices, but it also complicates our understanding of sociopolitical identities in the Middle East and their association with various forms of communication, mobilization, and activism.

The borders of the modern Middle East states reflect internal ethno-religious groups and external colonial power imbalances. These geographical delineations denied many groups the possibility of citizenship in nation-states of their own. Consider North Africa's Amazighs, a group of an estimated 20 million to 30 mil-lion indigenous people. This non-Arab community's members, who live in an area ranging from the southern parts of Egypt through Niger and Mali, have been try-ing to develop political unity. Amazigh communities have demanded sovereignty across their motherlands, particularly in Kabylia (Algeria) and Tuareg (Saharan regions). Amazigh-based political movements have focused on their shared cul-ture and closely related Berber languages. Another example is the Kurds, who live divided along political boundaries in Iraq, Syria, Turkey, and Iran, with a sizable diaspora concentrated in European capitals. As a minority group, Kurds have been unable to reclaim the promised Kurdish state after the fall of the Ottoman Empire. Their quest for sovereignty has fueled military conflicts, yet they have only achieved the status of a self-administered region in Iraq. Similarly, the Armenian com-munities dislocated under Ottoman rule have suffered multiple waves of forced migration during Lebanon's civil war (1975–1990) and since the beginning of the Syrian civil war (2011). In the Gulf region, the Bedoon ("those without [national-ity]") are communities traditionally living in Kuwait, Iraq, and Saudi Arabia with-out being recognized as citizens of any of these states. To demand full citizenship, some Bedoon sought various forms of integration (joining the army, for example), while others attempted to plead their case via international organizations.[58]

With the digital turn, the Amazighs,[59] Kurds,[60] and Bedoon have developed vir-tual communities that maintain bonds, develop solidarity networks, and create imaginaries of their state. In this sense, the cultural, the social, and the symbolic are all political as they reflect a core attachment to a nation-state that, at least for now, exists only in a virtual world—a truly "imagined community." These digital forms of engagement, which enable communities to perform their citizenship, serve as a national archive for people's written, spoken, or visual expression of their identities, whether in the clandestine "mountain journalism" practiced by Kurds opposing Saddam Hussein's regime,[61] visual narratives from the Amazighs,[62] or the recited poetry of the Bedoon. In each of these cases, digital citizenship is pitted against under- or misrepresentation in their communities and the denial of self-determination. This phenomenon may be even more clearly observed in the virtual existence of the Palestinian state. Recognized by the UN and 138 UN member states, a Palestinian state has not yet fully materialized but has inspired poetry, songs, fiction and nonfiction publications, and broadcast and film artifacts. In the digital realm, this Palestinian state was quick to claim official and unofficial sites representing the Palestinian Authority and various diaspora or local groups to offer alternative subjectivities of Palestine and its people. The Palestinian National Internet Naming Authority operates the internet country code ".ps" and promotes it as a way to "communicate the Palestinian identity."[63] In the cultural realm, digital archiving is at the heart of the Palestinian Museum's endeavor to foster an affective citizenship.

Not all contestation is peaceful. Some actors use social-media platforms to manipulate digital discussions through suppression or distraction. These behaviors, however, also illustrate the characteristics of trans-local subjectivities. Saudi writer and Tweeter Abdullah Al-Ghathami cites Al Rahtawiya (Blitzkrieg), in which a group of Twitter followers who idolize someone's tweets descend en masse on critics to curb unfavorable views. These trans-local collective practices of subjectivities impact what Al-Ghathami calls "the freedom of expression and the responsibility of expression."[64] The line between the political activities of individuals and those of organized campaigns for disinformation is increasingly blurred. Today the spread of suppression, manipulation, and disinformation extends beyond messages on public social media to messages circulated on personal messaging systems such as WhatsApp. Although not unique to the Middle East, the numerous local, regional, and international state and nonstate actors there exponentially increase the volume, reach, and magnitude of these discussions. These messages carry trans-local subjectivities across borders, nationalities, and political agendas, reflecting an economic and cultural globalization characterized by the instantaneous interconnectivity of digital networks.

The digital turn has fostered multiple subjectivities from Middle Eastern communities around the world, reinvigorating aspirations for social belonging, cultural recognition, and political participation. Many of these aspirations existed before the digital era, but the digital turn has created venues and added momentum for reaffirming multiple subjectivities. Nevertheless, the enticement of digital citizenship remains largely unfulfilled. Many diasporic communities continue to struggle with discord between their native and acquired citizenships. Even where enhanced digital access exists, virtual communities are still monitored, censored, or banned—often in both the diaspora and the homeland. Digital citizens have, to varying degrees, recreated the physical world's structural hierarchies and limitations in terms of access and participation. Claimed subjectivities on social media have created political figures and digital opinion leaders who remain beholden to evolving regulatory systems and commercial interests that shape, limit, and sanction speech. The unfolding of trans-local subjectivities suggests that digital citizenships are constructed alongside affective forms of belonging to a homeland and a pragmatic need for political exclusion and affirmation.

Chapter 7

Collective Voices and Digital Contention

Animated by micro-political participation, the acquisition of digital citizenship overlaps with the rise of collective voices and forms of political empowerment. In an environment characterized by formal and informal controls, the appropriation and reappropriation by publics of information technologies, including social media, involves negotiation. This process is influenced by individuals' ability to overcome constraints such as cost, availability, and access, as well as by their motivation to engage and mobilize collectively using digital applications given the limits on speech. These considerations are particularly important when exploring how the digital turn has come to bear on collective action and political agency.

Online Voices

For users in the Middle East accustomed to restrictions on speech, the internet offered a freer space for communication. In the late 1990s and early 2000s, many users joined Usenet groups, forums, bulletin boards, and email lists (such as LISTSERV) that provided information about myriad topics and offered an opportunity to discuss them while avoiding limits on speech.[1] While much of the content of this online engagement centered around everyday issues, there was also a growing amount of political content online. Many users routinely consumed and shared political information among trusted circles, and some activists created alternative newscasts. Dissident groups started to use online platforms to circulate their ideas. Some oppositional political parties and individual actors were also active online. This online presence included websites and news portals managed by webmasters in the diaspora but also the activities of actors who straddled a social and political presence online.[2]

The Digital Double Bind. Mohamed Zayani and Joe F. Khalil, Oxford University Press. © Oxford University Press 2024.
DOI: 10.1093/oso/9780197508626.003.0007

These early genres of online discourse and participation were soon joined by weblogs (or blogs), which emerged in 2003. In the early days, blogs were marginal, and their readership was generally limited to technology professionals.[3] The 2003 US-led war on Iraq sparked intense political debate, catalyzing interest in blogs as vehicles for unsanctioned discussion.[4] Soft infrastructure further expanded access: in 2005, Jordan-based Maktoob, Jeeran, and Al Bawaba added a bilingual blog service; WordPress began hosting blogs in Arabic in 2006; and Google's blog publishing service, Blogger, began supporting right-to-left languages in 2008. Although blogging was common throughout the region, the Arab blogosphere was not monolithic. It was nationally defined, and local issues took precedence over transnational matters.[5] Despite its prominence, though, blogging was a limited phenomenon[6] involving a small segment of connected Arab publics in the region and across the diaspora.[7] Even in a sizable country such as Egypt, which had a lively blogsphere, limited access to the internet and low broadband penetration mitigated against its uptake there.[8]

To the extent that blogging was not a mass medium, it stood out less for its size than for its momentum. For some scholars, blogs manifested a "potential to change how citizens think or act, mitigate or exacerbate group conflict, facilitate collective action, spur a backlash among regimes, and garner international attention."[9] Many, perhaps even most, bloggers were not political activists, however. They encountered—and engaged with—politics only insofar as it affected their daily lives. For many users, blogging was about embracing the internet's culture of inclusivity, claiming a voice, interacting with others, and engaging in conversations. The development of the Arab blogsphere was a sociotechnical undertaking that grew from the need for self-expression. The blogosphere brought together people with shared interests, experiences, and anxieties. Blogging also helped loosen the strictly enforced prohibition on the right of public expression and afforded the opportunity to engage others around a range of issues, common and sensitive alike, and overcome a culture of conformity. Blog aggregators went a long way toward creating online communities and fostering a sense of group recognition.[10]

Yet the political significance of seemingly apolitical engagement should not be overlooked. To the extent that even everyday blogging entails the public contestation of views and ideas, it is as much a political expression as it is a social form of engagement. In an environment inimical to free speech, the blogsphere had a contentious dimension from its beginning. Considering that the state managed the public lives of its citizens, blog posts and commentaries inevitably addressed aspects of everyday life that had political dimensions. Over time, such forms of engagement meant that a wider range of citizen bloggers became more overtly political. In addition, blogs gained popular credibility when they became news sources for both the mainstream press and the public at large.

In Kuwait, for example, youth blogged to speak out against nepotism, political corruption, and voting irregularity. In 2006, a youth-led movement for political reform emerged. What came to be known as Kuwait's Orange Movement called for the redistricting of electoral constituencies to limit the government's ability to influence the political process. Blogs helped organizers promote the movement.[11] Such activism reflected Kuwaitis' disposition to express themselves on issues that matter to people and affect their daily lives—concerns that often involve the government. In essence, the Orange Movement[12] was more about mobilization against the broad issue of corruption than about the narrowly defined question of parliamentary seats and voting districts—just as Kuwait's 2005 Blue Revolution, in which women gained suffrage, was more about claiming citizenship and advocating for inclusiveness than about antiestablishment politics.[13]

Similar cases developed elsewhere in the region. In neighboring Bahrain, where mobilization is nothing new, blogging was used for more overtly political ends to mount human rights campaigns, initiate calls to free detainees, and demand democratic change. Yet lively discussion on wide-ranging issues typically shunned by traditional media also enlivened digital spaces.[14] Some issues—such as the controversy surrounding MBC's production of the show *Big Brother* (2004), which transgressed cultural sensitivities, in Bahrain—crossed the Shia-Sunni divide that characterized many aspects of the country's political life. The Bahraini blogosphere reflected a culture of critique, lobbying, and the assertion of rights—all of which favored a broad engagement with politics, transcending the narrow confines of party politics and religious or sectarian affiliations. Blogging thus helped foster an online community in an otherwise tightly controlled environment. In Morocco, bloggers took on local issues with a global resonance, ranging from the Western Sahara conflict to freedom of the press.[15] In Tunisia, disenchanted youth took to blogging to contest internet control and build momentum for the Sayyeb Salah anti-censorship campaign, which brought together young techies, lay users, and cyber activists. In the face of the aversion of the Ben Ali regime to internet freedom, the blogosphere helped heighten the sense of citizen entitlement, thereby recasting the problem of censorship from a technical issue of internet access into an issue of citizen rights, sowing the seeds for a social movement that subsequently gained broader significance.[16]

In Lebanon, an already overtly political blogosphere gained momentum with events that gripped the country, from mounting public opposition to the Syrian presence to the 2006 war between Hezbollah and Israel.[17] Subsequent developments in Lebanese blogging, however, led to the consolidation of a deeper counter-publicness. Bloggers provided social commentary and raised awareness about diverse issues, often using unconventional forms and content.[18] Bloggers were invested in discussions about sectarianism, power structures, and business corruption but more commonly dealt with wide-ranging topics such as foreign workers' rights, gender discrimination, and other sociocultural issues.[19]

Blogging in Egypt developed at the intersection of everyday-life forms of engagement and alternative forms of political activism. The advent of blogging coincided with the arrival of a popular movement named Kefaya (Enough). Initially a loose coalition of political players and actors united by deep resentment of Egyptian president Mubarak's long rule and adamant opposition to his son's presumed ambition for succession, Kefaya was energized by the mass protests that accompanied the 2003 US-led war on Iraq. The development of the movement was also assisted by increases in freedom of expression reluctantly ceded by Mubarak's regime when pressured to do so in response to proclaimed US efforts to promote democratization in the Middle East after the 9/11 attacks. For digital activism, Kefaya relied on mobile phones and the internet to circumvent government controls, to provide counternarratives to those of state-sponsored media, to nurture blogging, and to energize Egypt's nascent blogosphere.[20] The vibrancy of the blogosphere made it attractive as a community space for communication, an outlet for activism, and a site of protest.[21]

By 2006, increased state repression and crackdown on street protests largely confined Kefaya's activism to cyberspace. The Mubarak regime sought to eviscerate all street dissent and confine antiestablishment voices to an online space where it could monitor critical voices—which it then constrained. There was also a sense among the regime's members that by virtue of being restricted to digital spaces, with the limited access and affordances of those spaces, the Kefaya movement would eventually be marginalized. This proved to be a serious miscalculation. The regime failed to grasp the political potential of digital contention. As Kefaya faltered, a new wave of digitally adept youth energized the blogosphere. This cycle produced further repression, and the authorities began arresting outspoken bloggers, especially as members of the Muslim Brotherhood became more visibly active on the blogosphere. The government crackdown redirected digital activism from anti-regime, pro-democracy political discourses toward issues that touched people's lives.[22] Activists started posting about everyday injustices whether it was corruption, police torture, or sexual harassment. Wael Abbas, who ran the blog Misr Digital, epitomized this trend. Applying his media experience, he based his stories on testimonies, videos, photos taken on cell phones, and leaked documents—all of which helped publicize sexual assaults against women and denounce police abuse and injustices. By circulating alternative narratives to ordinary Egyptians, Abbas and other defiant bloggers made the public aware of controversial issues intentionally overlooked by the national press. Speaking out on such issues as corruption and mismanagement enabled these activist bloggers to engage in antiestablishment politics under the guise of social critique.

Beyond the case of Egypt, political blogging existed within a context of traditional media, which increasingly defied state control. It intensified trends sparked by the pervasiveness of transnational satellite television and the tenacity of some of the opposition press.[23] Blog posts about abuses of power and the plight of citizens, when supported with evidence, often get picked up by independent newspapers for their political significance and, from there, make their way to the foreign press and international NGOs, compelling the mainstream media to cover these stories—and, at times, forcing the state to acknowledge them in response to public outrage.[24]

In some respect, experienced bloggers developed a greater ability to shape the news by framing events and engendering conversation. The more influential Arab bloggers—such as Fouad Al-Farhan (known as the "Dean of Saudi Bloggers"), Tunisian blogger Sami Ben Gharbia (and, before him, Zouheir Yahyaoui, whose forum TUNeZINE [a pun on "Tunisian" and "Zine El Abedine Ben Ali"] was a precursor to activist blogs), and Alaa Abdel Fattah (known for serving multiple jail sentences)—cultivated networks that included local journalists and international internet-based freedom organizations.[25] As more activists started to use blogs, governments implemented measures aimed at stifling the blogosphere, from closing down blogs to altering data packages to limit users' ability to upload material.[26]

Yet silencing bloggers proved difficult. Although the expansion of blogging served more as a space for exchanging ideas publicly (particularly among youth) than as an instrument of cyber activism, it nonetheless lowered the barriers to public mobilization. Over time, the many discourses and deliberations that animated the blogosphere highlighted a disconnect between users' aspirations and regimes' instincts to control. That disconnect created a growing desire for change. Many bloggers who steered clear of politics came to be politically socialized by being part of "an opinion platform."[27] Political socialization associated with the blogging experience was an important precursor to the growing digital contention that ultimately came to capitalize on various sociopolitical dynamics and emerging platforms to fuel social movements and renegotiate the state-society relationship.

The Arab Uprisings as a Digital Awakening

The expansion of mobile web access and the rise of social media had a particularly profound effect on youth. Online activism often extended to offline organizing, and offline mobilization could carry its momentum online. The ensuing dynamics of mobilizing and organizing began to push the limits of dissent trans-locally and globally as movements of solidarity transcended national boundaries.[28]

Egypt's April 6 Movement demonstrates the processes well. In 2008, textile workers at Al Mahalla Al Kubra, an industrial town in the Delta Nile, planned a strike. Bloggers who had been active during the Kefaya movement created a Facebook group to support the workers' cause. With the group's call for a nationwide strike, what started as a local labor union's action burgeoned into a dynamic pro-democracy movement. Using blog posts, short message service (SMS) updates, and platforms such as Facebook and Flickr, activists and ordinary Egyptians coordinated action, reported events, and shared pictures.[29] Though the protest was met with a firm police response, the movement managed to attract a large number of followers on its Facebook page. The 2009 arrest of a core member of the movement, Esraa Abdel Fattah, popularized the movement even further, though with little effect on the streets.[30] Even government strategies to counter the movement could have ironic effects. In celebration of the strike's one-year anniversary, the April 6 Movement attempted to organize a general strike. Its efforts were thwarted by Egyptian authorities, who took decisive action to prevent mobilization and block text messages. Ironically, the fact that many people stayed off the streets due to newly imposed limits on movement and safety concerns brought several parts of Cairo to a standstill, thus turning nonaction into action.

Others in the region have also attempted to use social media for mobilization. In 2009, social-media networks became an important tool for energizing a massive protest movement in Iran. Mahmoud Ahmadinejad's declaration of victory in Iran's presidential election was met with skepticism among the supporters of the opposing candidate, Mir Hussein Mousavi. Protests erupted to contest the election results and call for real change in what came to be known as the Green Movement.[31] Mousavi's supporters used digital communication tools to mobilize protesters, record street protests, and disseminate information about what was taking place both locally and internationally. Social-media platforms such as the then-nascent microblogging site Twitter enabled protesters to circumvent government censors and bypass restrictions on text messaging. The death of Neda Agha-Soltan, captured on witnesses' mobile phones and circulated widely on the internet, catalyzed international support. Digital tools did not alter the outcome of the events, but they accentuated the political potential of social media just as the circulation of cassette tapes carrying anti-shah messages highlighted the political potential of small media before the Iranian revolution.[32] The absence of on-the-ground reporters pushed mainstream media such as CNN to establish a special "Twitter desk" to monitor, distill, cross-reference, and synthesize information in activists' and eyewitnesses' tweets—a practice that soon became essential for mainstream media reporting the impending uprisings.

The dynamics of contestation took on another dimension in 2011. In that year, the Arab world was shaken by widespread protests against socioeconomic adversity, neoliberal policies, and the excesses of an authoritarian political culture. Protest movements had historical precedents in a region marked by fragile stability and long-standing plights (from Egypt's "Bread Revolution" to Bahrain's Shia grievances) that have gone unaddressed for generations.[33] Nevertheless, two modern elements are often singled out as defining the 2011 uprisings: youth activism and the use of digital tools. Common treatments of these uprisings oscillate between technology enthusiasts who champion social media and emphasize the democratizing power of ICTs and technology skeptics who caution that undue faith in communication technologies' ability to drive sociopolitical change downplays agency.[34] Such framing underplays the social construction of the digital. Beyond their technological dimension, these social movements are enmeshed with the politics of everyday life, and as such, they reframe politics as an exercise of power that flows from the bottom up, rather than from the top down.

In Tunisia, where the initial uprisings broke out, digital media was a visible factor in social mobilization fostered through "local solidarities."[35] The circulation of news about Mohamed Bouazizi's self-immolation led to spontaneous outbursts of popular rage. Those outbursts were captured on mobile phones, and images of protests soon found their way to the internet, where the story became a matter of interest to the broader public. As the town of Sidi Bouzid came under siege, activists turned to social media to tell their stories. They recorded scenes of the confrontations on their phones and shared these images on social-media networks, capturing the attention of sympathetic audiences. The online mediatization of the unrest helped connect the local setting to the broader national context. Images and feeds of violence and police brutality were a stark reminder of the ruthlessness of a sclerotic regime. As the protests spread far and wide, what started as demands for social justice and cries for dignity transformed into pro-democracy protests. Here again, the digital connection between the diaspora and the homeland should not be underestimated. Some Tunisian bloggers in the diaspora and local activists aggregated, curated, and promoted protest videos posted on Facebook while others tweeted updates about the events, collaboratively spreading the words and images that led to an information cascade. Widely shared video footage on Facebook provided the fodder for reporting by pan-Arab satellite channels such as Al Jazeera, which helped weave the events into a powerful narrative of change. This narrative accentuated the power of the street and the political thrust of the events, thus framing the widening social protests into a popular uprising that ultimately toppled the ruler of what appeared then to be one of the most stable countries in the region.

The revolution in Tunisia had a spillover effect on Egypt, where digital infrastructure and social media were an important component of mobilization against the Mubarak regime. The launch of the Arabic version of Facebook had increased the number of users on this social-media platform,[36] which some exploited to speak out on issues and mobilize support for various causes. "We are All Khalid Said" was one of the popular Facebook groups that emerged a few months before the Egyptian January 25 Revolution. It started with a Facebook page created to protest police abuses in reaction to the circulation of gory pictures of the bruised face of a young Alexandrian, Khalid Said, who was apprehended at a cybercafe and beaten to death by security forces for exposing police corruption. What was initially a collective form of digital commiseration developed into an anti-Mubarak protest movement calling for regime change.[37] A mixture of shared grievance for the masses and savvy uses of digital tools by activists led to the world watching massive protests in Tahrir Square and elsewhere. The circulation of photos and videos of the protests on social media spurred the Mubarak regime to shut down the internet in a desperate attempt to regain control.[38] Following several days of massive protests, which took a violent turn as the regime pushed back, the Egyptian army took control, putting an end to three decades of autocratic rule. Images of jubilant protesters celebrating the resounding fall of Mubarak, and before it the undignified escape of Ben Ali, inspired publics from Bahrain to Algeria and from Yemen to Syria to protest.

As the use of digital tools became more widespread, new sociopolitical practices started to take shape. Initially, digital tools enabled users to share views and engage in debates and groups around certain issues, helping forge common and participatory identities and spread the sphere of activism and at times converging with existing networks of dissent and contention. During upheavals, digital tools offered users ways to agitate and organize with a speed and scale that made the revolutionary tide seemingly unstoppable. Yet the potential of social networks and digital media must not obscure the role of grassroots activism and traditional forms of political organizing or the link between the conventional (protesters and squares), the emerging (citizen reporting, digital tools, and social platforms), and the traditional (local and global mainstream media, the press, and live television broadcasts).[39] The three are constantly interacting with sites of conventional mobilization echoed on emerging platforms and magnified through traditional media.[40] What stands out is not so much the catalytic effect of digital technologies and the use of social media to challenge state power in authoritarian contexts (as history is rife with such uses of media) but how digital media and their environments have helped foster political identity, redefine the sphere of politics, and reconfigure political action over time. Whether it is a small, committed group of Egyptian cyber activists exposing police abuses and sexual harassment in public places or larger online campaigns to protest internet censorship in Tunisia, the digital turn is gradually expanding the sphere of politics that is enmeshed with the practice of everyday life, which in turn heightens its exposure to the digital double bind.

With the benefit of hindsight, it seems that in the process of developing a leaderless movement that escapes state surveillance, the use of digital tools created its own pseudo-leaders (e.g., Egyptian activist Wael Ghonim) and failed to protect its tech architects (e.g., Syrian activist Bassel Khartabil). Moreover, the very tools of the revolution became instruments of regime counter-operations to restore the previous order.

Negotiating Agency

Whatever hope the uprisings brought about was tinged with apprehension and curled into disappointment. Gradually, social movements started to wither and lose their momentum. The initial euphoria accompanying the 2011 revolts gave way to an Arab disenchantment marked by uneasy transitions and tumultuous developments. Some states sought to regain control through repression, while others attempted to placate the contenders and mollify the masses with conces-sions. By and large, counterrevolutionary forces, setbacks, and reversion to author-itarianism undermined the ability of peaceful social movements to effect change. The deployment of GCC forces put an end to the uprising in Bahrain. Egypt reverted to military rule. Elsewhere the prospects for change have been under-mined by turmoil. Libya became mired in prolonged armed conflict, Syria fell prey to a civil war, and Yemen was torn by violence and factionalism.[41] Even Tunisia's fledgling democracy is facing an uncertain future.[42]

Despite these setbacks, dignity, freedom, and change became widely shared aspirations across much of the Arab world, sowing the seeds for the consolida-tion of a wider space of citizen action and a more pronounced sense of agency. Just when people wrote off the Arab uprisings, a new wave of protests swept the region—from Beirut to Baghdad and from Khartoum to Algiers—demanding freedom and justice while also pressing for meaningful sociopolitical change and greater governmental accountability. Various socioeconomic and political factors motivated these movements, leading to protests on the streets and online. The use of communication technologies and digital tools for collective action is particu-larly noteworthy for increasing young protestors' ability to exert agency, reclaim political action, and effect change.

In 2019, Lebanon and Iraq witnessed their largest demonstrations in decades. Both countries have adopted sectarian political systems premised on fragile power-sharing arrangements that engendered weak states with no obvious or accountable central power. Unlike the protests that took place in Lebanon in 2005 (dubbed *Intifadat al Istiqlal* and known in the West as the Cedar Revolution)[43] where protesters found in SMS a convenient tool, the 2019 demonstrations were coordinated on WhatsApp, using live videos, with many reporting and mobiliz-ing initiatives such as Megaphone (digital journalism), Lebanonprotests.com (livestreaming), and Daleel Al Thawra (The Revolution's Guide) listing various activities related to the demonstrations.[44] In Iraq, the government took more pro-active measures to curb the use of social media for organizing demonstrations or reporting eyewitness accounts. Using advanced technologies, it compromised WhatsApp and Facebook accounts and occasionally shut down the internet. In response, demonstrators had to increase their digital cybersecurity through the use of VPNs, among other means.[45] Whether in Lebanon or Iraq, this second wave of social movements coincided with the pervasiveness of "fake news." In a region too familiar with propaganda, local and international social actors targeted these movements to discredit them, influence their followers, and sow discord among their members. In addition to various acts of hacking, these social movements also witnessed the rise of *al thoubab el electroni* (electronic flies) in reference to various bot accounts.

Lebanon's unrest was triggered by the government's proposal to levy addi-tional taxes as part of austerity measures. The protests condemned the country's deepening economic problems and the government's corruption, nepotism, and mismanagement. They evolved to call for a rejection of an entrenched sectarian and political system. A similar situation unfolded in Iraq, where popular protests sparked by mounting frustration with high unemployment, endemic corruption, and threadbare public services soon developed into demands to overthrow the government and overhaul an entire sectarian political system that thrives on patronage and is plagued by foreign interference. For months, large-scale demonstrations were organized in Baghdad as well as in Iraq's southern and central provinces, drawing momentum from a youth-led movement that included a cross section of society, only to be met with government suppression.

Elsewhere in the region, massive demonstrations were staged to demand change that eventually led to military intervention and the ousting of the sitting presidents. In 2018, Sudan was the scene of a popular uprising. Protests erupted in reaction to a hike in the price of bread. As these protests spread and intensified, they took on a political dimension and evolved into demands for regime change. Chanting *"tasgut bass"* ("just step down, that's it"), people called for an end to Omar Al-Bashir's rule. Once he was deposed, the civilian groups that took an active part in the protests pushed further. They began tough negotiations with the army to ensure that the change in power was not merely cosmetic. In 2019, Algeria also saw widespread and massive demonstrations in what came to be known as the Hirak (Movement)—a youth-led, nonviolent movement after years of political acquiescence following the Algerian civil war. The protests were sparked by Abdelaziz Bouteflika's decision to run for a fifth term in office. For twenty years, Algeria's incapacitated president served as front man for a country effectively controlled by a powerful military. His anti-constitutional bid for a new term did not mesh well with a young, disaffected generation. The swelling weekly demonstrations, which attracted people from across the social spectrum, rejected the government's system of clientelism, corruption, and mismanagement of the country's natural resources. The nation's growing unemployment added to the discontent. The protests demanded fundamental changes to the power structure, including overthrowing the political establishment.

What makes these movements stand out is less the protests themselves than the scope of mobilization and their steadfast demand for real reforms and deep changes that break from an entrenched system of governance they believe has repeatedly failed them. This is particularly evident in the resilience of the protesters and the common slogans they chanted, from *"kellun yaani kellun"* ("all of them means all of them") in Lebanon to *"yetnahaw gaa"* ("they should all go") in Algeria. The commonalities between these movements also suggest that activists are taking inspiration from one another, and their media (online and offline) operate like a rhizome creating networks of communities and organization across the region.[46]

Throughout these popular movements, social media was a constant. In Lebanon, the WhatsApp tax was the straw that broke the camel's back. Young people rejected a proposal to generate more revenue by levying a monthly charge on internet calls that use messaging services amid growing distrust of political elites. The government's retraction of its proposal failed to placate the protesters, who responded with greater demands and expanded protests across the country. In Iraq, the initial calls to demonstrate were circulated on social media. Online communication and social media helped the protesters organize, post on Facebook, and use hashtags to tweet about the events. The government responded by intermittently blocking social media and shutting down the internet, as did the Sudanese government when faced with mounting online and offline activism. In 2019, the Sudanese diaspora found in social media a conduit for showing solidarity and supporting the protesters who rose up against Al-Bashir's rule, with some activists translating Arabic tweets to English to give them an even wider reach and garner media attention.[47] In Algeria, the initial anonymous call to protest was circulated on various social-media platforms, which helped break the fear of protesting, draw massive participation, and coordinate efforts to keep demonstrations peaceful.[48] When the pro-change forces were faced with anti-protest maneuvers, social media helped combat fake news, misinformation, and government propaganda aimed at delegitimizing the protests.[49]

Despite the prominence of social media as an integral part of protest movements, these events were not a by-product of social-media activism. ICTs are neither a novelty to social movements nor a driver of change.[50] Rather, they have become naturalized tools for collective action because of the ubiquity of smartphones and the increasing role that social media plays in the daily lives of users. Digital contention reveals the agency of a counter-public whereby political demands are articulated using digital tools and conventional forms of activism— the two increasingly constitutive of each other. This is clearest for the youth, for whom digital tools are the preferred space and the common language and who are increasingly exposed to globalized forms of contention. The pressing question is not how social media empowers youth but how political agency manifests itself where activism on social media intersects with activism on the street.

This line of analysis diverges from analytical frames that tend to instrumentalize ICTs in general and social media in particular. The role that digital media played in the second wave of the Arab social movements calls into question celebratory accounts smacking of technological determinism. Consider Tunisia. Yes, the social web was rife with footage of widespread unrest and daily anti-regime protests, but the Tunisian revolution unfolded on social media largely unbeknownst to the rest of the world. This remained true even after footage of protests was picked up from social-networking sites and reported on a few Arabic-language satellite news channels.[51] These same digital tools were celebrated in subsequent uprisings as "liberation technology."[52] In Sudan, social-media activism helped spread the protests and mobilize people beyond Atbara (the city where the bread protest began), but the presence of the event on social media did not muster the kind of international media attention and Western support the Egyptian uprising received. In large part, this reflects how the Sudanese story did not "fit into a pre-existing [Western] narrative about Sudan as a country whose politics are defined by political Islam, civil war, and mass atrocities."[53] If anything, such frames smack of digital Orientalism.

Analyses focusing on the instrumentalization of ICTs similarly fail to capture diffuse forms of contention that develop over time. In some instances, the development of agency was not predicated on the use of ICTs. This is the case in countries where the digital turn was undermined by instability and turmoil. In Iraq, for instance, limits to infrastructure, accessibility, usage, and affordances led people to rely more on legacy media and traditional tools of communication and forms of mobilization. Similarly, in Libya, the country's incipient digital turn also led activists to rely more on traditional forms of communication—even though there were attempts to appropriate digital communication, as in the case of the Rebel Media Center, which used a livestream channel to communicate to the external world and bypass government restrictions at the inception of the revolution.[54] In other instances, usages that develop in one context take on a particular relevance in another context. One example is the Sudanese all-women group Minbar-Shat, which started in 2015 as a Facebook group for a community of women to help identify cheating husbands and hold men accountable for their behavior. The group then spearheaded a movement advocating for female equality and contesting the country's morality laws.[55] By 2018, the Forces of Freedom and Change coalition built on this movement's social-media tactics to mobilize and campaign against the regime.[56]

Significantly, portraying both waves of protests as being (digital) media-driven overlooks the complex nature of mobilization and the deep roots of popular discontent in the region. These social movements have been brewing for some time, with deepening crises, a wider involvement of different constituents, and a richer repertoire of contention. As Charles Tilly reminds us, repertoires of contention consist of various means and an array of tactics, ranging from associations to coalitions and from public meetings to rallies and strikes.[57] Digital technology is one among several tools at the disposal of protesters and activists. Most often, these technologies are intuitively and routinely used to witness, document, and/ or share. Under certain conditions, though, they become part of a "repertoire of innovation" at the disposal of actors in social movements and contenders staging action.[58]

In Sudan, the dynamics of the uprising point to significant linkages and a degree of coordination and collective efforts of professional associations, civil society organizations, youth groups and activists, trade unions, and opposition political parties, as well as solidarity across ethnic and class lines.[59] Similarly, what gave Algeria's Hirak momentum was the coming together of collectives, civil society, trade unions, an alliance of political parties, citizen groups, activist associations, opinion leaders, and political activists—though Hirak did not have nationwide support.[60] These synergies coalesced within a background of growing discontent with institutional inertia, increasing strikes, proliferating stories of corruption, and heightened digital contention. Everyday forms of activism that grew over time, the emergence of informal networks, and the development of critical opinions toward political authorities[61] all helped people exert agency, culminating in a determination to reclaim the public space, ultimately through peaceful youth street mobilization and collective action.[62] As one acute observer noted, "the movement advocates a vision of citizenship that seeks to transcend the political, social and regional divisions that have led to civil strife in the past. . . . The demonstrations allowed [protesting youth] to regain the status of political actors, something they felt the authorities had denied them."[63]

The affordances of the digital offered pathways among disaffected youth and marginalized citizens who used various forms of digital communication to speak out on issues and engage in contention—and even mobilization—though often bound by matters of everyday life that touched their freedoms, conditions, and aspirations. These forms of contention found their clearest manifestation in the 2011 uprisings, when mass streets demonstrations and heightened digital activism helped the Arab public reclaim agency. In subsequent waves of social movements, digital tools and platforms were deployed by aspiring publics to communicate, organize, and mobilize. For all their novelty, sophistication, and popularity, these digital tools and their use for sociopolitical activism have attracted the state's digital capabilities, from surveillance and cybersecurity to disinformation and propaganda. As these tools cease to be a novelty and become part of everyday life, the digital is no longer a space for recluse dissident politics or savvy cyber activists but an arena where the politics of everyday life manifest themselves. More than a technological exploit, the digital stands out as a techne through which people pointedly manifest their agency.

Chapter 8

Digital Adaptations and Disruptive Power

The proliferation of digital technologies has emboldened cyber activists, but it has also reinforced state power. States and their allies constantly strive to improve their digital capabilities to maintain a strong grip on power. Faced with globalized digital activism and challenged by networked publics, autocratic and hybrid regimes alike have resorted to criminalization laws, online censorship, and digital surveillance. Just as cyber activists have benefited from increased connectivity, digital literacy, networked social movements, and digital solidarities, states have relied on a global surveillance market for sophisticated, dual-use technologies and expertise to silence contentious voices with the fewest repercussions[1]—often with the approval, explicit or tacit, of advanced nations whose companies sell these technologies.[2]

Yet wielding digital power in the digital is not a straightforward endeavor. Evolving technological challenges and constraints require states to continually upgrade their digital capabilities and strategies, only to face new, more complex challenges that require further upgrades and adaptation. Having adapted to digital contention and "a perpetual culture of dissent,"[3] states now find themselves challenged by "disruptive power,"[4] emanating from unconventional digital actors as well as global digital platforms. This is not to underestimate the ability of regimes in the region to cope with these challenges. Far from eroding states' ability to control information, the digital turn has increased their adaptability and reinforced their resilience. At the same time, states are faced with a digital double bind. The same infrastructure deployed to transition toward the knowledge economy is often used to threaten the states' legitimacy, forcing them to choose between economic prosperity and political survival.

The Digital Double Bind. Mohamed Zayani and Joe F. Khalil, Oxford University Press. © Oxford University Press 2024.
DOI: 10.1093/oso/9780197508626.003.0008

Digital Criminalization

While access to ICTs has disrupted the state's ability to manage information flows, it has not lessened the state's resolve to do so, nor has it proved to be an insurmountable threat. Although control over the internet does not always correspond to the nature of the political system or depend on regime type, the impulse to constrain cyberspace is a constant in the Middle East.[5] Wary that the internet is increasingly used to challenge the status quo, states in the region have sought to attenuate the effects of digital technologies by any means at their disposal, including constricting digital access, limiting free speech, and devising legal and administrative frameworks that allow them to deploy advanced monitoring and surveillance tools. While protecting power, wealth, and influence are the motivations for controlling digital spaces and infrastructures, political elites usually frame such decisions as necessary for protecting sociocultural values, shoring up national security, and safeguarding economic interests.[6] Conveniently, invoking the obligation to conform to sociocultural norms and moral values often serves as a pretext for curbing internet freedom, just as it has always been used to suppress free speech and constrain political rights.[7] The advent of digitality did not eliminate blatant and arcane censorship practices—it made them more sophisticated.

Traditionally, states in the Middle East have controlled the communication sphere through their hold on communication infrastructure, whether that be printing presses or broadcasting facilities. With the internet, even when states pushed some of the controls to ISPs, they did not relinquish their authority over the network or the infrastructure that supports it. Those intermediaries are designated as regime proxies and enforcers of censorship as needed. For example, during the Egyptian revolution, the Mubarak regime instructed the ISPs to shut down the network, citing the 2003 Telecommunications Regulation Law as a legal justification. Monopolistic control of infrastructure also affords the state a convenient and effective way to censor content, control usage, and monitor users. Preventing citizen connectivity, denying access to certain websites and platforms, controlling information, blocking undesired content, and censoring unfavorable views all remain common practices throughout the region, although the method, degree, and intensity of control vary from country to country. While continuing to practice traditional forms of censorship, governments have intensified their use of sophisticated technology to monitor internet activities and enhance their ability to conduct pervasive communication surveillance and filter content. Such state-authorized filtering and communication surveillance are common throughout the region. Although users still devise ways to circumvent online censorship, the adoption of counter-technologies (such as VPNs, encryption, proxies, and anonymity software) to secure safe online access requires skills beyond most average users' reach, and even so, these activities are increasingly criminalized.

These forms of control are used alongside more coercive methods, such as heavy-handed measures to clamp down on online activism and scare tactics to make an example of cyber dissidents and underscore the perils of loose lips and reckless fingers. A Committee to Protect Journalists report, published on the eve of the Arab uprisings, singled out five MENA countries as being among the ten worst countries globally in which to be a blogger.[8] With digital surveillance, governments target activists almost anywhere in the world.

Going hand in hand with these practices are measures designed to expand censorship rules, legitimize control, and suppress freedom of expression online. Several governments in the Middle East have reinforced policies, tightened regulations, and passed laws pertaining to cyberspace in an effort to control online activities and information flows.[9] Social-media activists and online journalists now face many of the same restrictions on freedom of speech as traditional journalists do, such as requiring online publications and websites to be registered. For example, recognizing the expediency of regulation, in 2014, Egypt passed the Terrorist Entities Law, which allows the government to prosecute websites for "spreading lies" and "supporting terrorism."[10] This law increased the state's control over cyberspace by blocking numerous established foreign and local news websites, as well as websites that enable access to VPNs. By 2018, the Egyptian parliament passed legislation that classified and treated social-media accounts (such as Twitter and Facebook) with more than five thousand followers as "media outlets," which are governed by the same harsh regulations (including prosecution) that govern the press.[11] Under this bill, establishing a website requires a license. Similarly, anti-cybercrime laws in other countries are applied against the production and distribution of online content that the state declares disruptive to public order.[12] The vagueness and selective enforcement of laws governing cyberspace leave users in a precarious situation and give states free rein to prosecute and silence voices they deem unruly.

Further, ISPs and operators collect information on behalf of the government, often in the absence of clear or adequate legal frameworks that regulate privacy and data collection. Where they serve the state, these regulations are stern, as with the limits on telecom operators' use of encryption software. In some instances, cybercrime laws are used as a legal shield to control usage. In countries known for their heavy internet policing, enacting emergency laws that give the state sweeping powers and passing anti-terrorism legislation are sometimes "motivated more by the wish to further curb freedom of expression and strengthen controls over the media than by a fear of terrorism."[13]

States and Stakes

Whereas the exploits and promises of the Arab uprisings prompted some commentators to rave about the power of digital tools, the developments and setbacks that ensued led others to lament what they saw as the rise of "digital authoritarianism."[14] Adaptation to digital activism varied from state to state. On one end of the spectrum lies the use of pervasive surveillance technology; on the other is a recourse to harsh forms of control of both users and tools. A range of approaches exists between these two poles, which often results in a constantly evolving repertoire of tactics and countertactics that reveal mutual adaptations more than determined outcomes.

Most states have adopted selective censorship and informal controls to avert negative publicity and international criticism. They have also procured state-of-the-art surveillance technology and deployed high-tech solutions including equipment that allows mass surveillance, malicious software (malware) to gain remote access to telephones and computers, deep packet inspection (DPI) to monitor internet traffic, and surveillance centers to intercept communication. With no shortage of suppliers in a thriving market for surveillance tools, these dual-use technologies have legitimate applications (such as in law enforcement), but they can also be weaponized and used against ordinary citizens, among other targets.[15] The phone hacking of Saudi journalist Jamal Khashoggi and the deployment of Pegasus spyware to spy on his associates and infiltrate the phones of the *Washington Post*'s owner, Jeff Bezos, and Al Jazeera journalists are patent examples of the technology's nefarious application.[16]

Starting with Tunisia and Egypt, countries that faced social movements adopted familiar strategies, adapted to activists' tactics, and became adept at instigating network disruptions and periodic outages. In 2011, Libya shut down many popular networking sites before it temporarily inhibited internet access amid widespread protests. In 2012, the Syrian government resorted to blanket censorship, crippling phone networks nationwide and shutting down the internet at a critical stage of its civil war.[17] When protests flared up in Sudan in 2013 and again in 2019, the authorities blocked popular social-media platforms and then briefly took down the internet to prevent the spread of news about the suppression of the protests.[18] Similarly, during the social protests in Iraq in 2019, the government shut down the internet and blocked social media and messaging apps across much of the country, cutting nationwide connectivity by nearly two-thirds.

Yet even with such a blanket approach, activists found ways to communicate with each other and the public. When Mubarak restricted internet access, networked activists, supported by Twitter, Google, and digital startups (such as SayNow, Yamli, and Meedan), outwitted the censors by exploiting a loophole in the system that enabled defiant Egyptians to use voice to tweet about their situation. When Ben Ali went after cyber activists in Tunisia, the international hacktivist group Anonymous came to the rescue, sabotaging official websites in retaliation and solidarity. In Sudan, protesters worked around the intermittent availability of the internet to post footage of the crackdown there, inviting critical scrutiny of the regime's practices.

In instances where the state's intolerance of street mobilization pushed activism to cyberspace, activists grew even more tenacious. When Bahrain's short-lived uprising was silenced in 2011, a youth-driven coalition of activists used an "anonymous [and decentralized] organizational structure"[19] to evade state control, circumvent government censors, and communicate with supporters. This same organizational structure continued to be adopted in sporadic offline activism, with hybrid campaigns involving online mobilization and localized street action on a small scale.[20] Although these forms of contention were subject to a media blackout, they demonstrated the activists' resilience and their continued ability to exert agency despite the state's increasingly sophisticated attempts to stop them.

Morocco also had to reckon with digital activism. The February 20 protest movement (M20) emerged in 2011 against the backdrop of the Arab uprisings and in the face of widespread disillusionment with the ability of institutional politics to effect change. A collective of activist bloggers adopted the slogan "Mamfakinch" ("No Concession") to exert social and political pressure in support of a push for reforms. This blog-based platform for aggregating and circulating information developed into a popular political discussion space advocating increased state accountability, curating conversations, and circulating information outside mainstream channels. Mamfakinch is noteworthy not only for being the largest grassroots mobilization in the country's history but also for its use of innovative strategies to build a broad-based collective that encompassed diverse national subgroups (including Moroccans in the diaspora) and facilitated different modes of activism. Grounded primarily in local issues, Mamfakinch helped articulate expectations for political reform, advocated social justice, and pressured the government to reveal abuses of power. Mamfakinch exemplifies how networked publics construct "new processes of public formation and modes of publicness" that oscillate between online and offline spaces.[21] Although the movement failed to secure deep reforms, it energized the public to reclaim political and social agency and pressured the state to adopt a constitutional referendum that led to the recognition of the Amazigh's traditional language (Tamazight) as one of the kingdom's official languages. Importantly, the movement was tolerated as long as it heeded the kingdom's political culture. Despite frequent online monitoring and infrequent arrests of bloggers and activists,[22] Morocco has proven willing to accommodate public demands without unsettling existing power relations.

Where the state's response is rigid, digital contention is more intense but less conclusive. From the outset of the Syrian turmoil, the conflict played out on the street and online, with an abundance of digital media content shaped by the actions and motivations of various actors and defined by competing interests.[23] Here the state's tenacity and the activists' resilience have only perpetuated digital activism and counter-activism. All along, ordinary citizens, activists, and rebels used digital tools to advocate change. Equipped with cell phones, they recorded and circulated footage of spontaneous outbursts of popular discontent on social media. Throughout these acts of witnessing,[24] footage of rebellious communities chanting anti-regime slogans provided a counternarrative to the regime's official version of the events, which framed the protesters as outlaws and enemies of the state.[25] When Syria's peaceful revolution turned violent, cyber activism intensified. Activists infiltrated government systems,[26] hackers obtained government emails and fed them to WikiLeaks, and defecting members of the regime used thumb drives to copy incriminating pictures of citizens who died in detention centers.[27] Widely circulated videos documented state repression and exposed abuses of power, garnering support for the protesters locally and internationally. The activists' use of social media and livestreaming prompted the regime to ban iPhones and switch off internet connections. Activists responded by improvising ways to circumvent access restrictions, from smuggling satellite phones to using mobile SIM cards from neighboring Jordan (on the border with Daraa) and Turkey (on the border with Idlib).[28]

Notably, Syrian regime supporters, state agents, and soldiers have also used digital media to record retaliatory measures, violent acts, and scenes of torture to highlight the dire consequences of dissent, intimidate anti-regime protesters, and reaffirm the state's authority. These images were met with videotaped condemnations, as were the abuses committed by the rebels and circulated on the social web.[29] The online battle has been intensified further by a social-media cyber war between the Syrian Free Army and the Syrian Electronic Army.[30] Launched at the outbreak of the revolution, the Syrian Electronic Army is a group of technologically savvy hackers who support Al-Assad's regime. The group conducted malicious cyberattacks against various targets, taking control of the Twitter feeds of international news agencies, manipulating information about the civil war, and hacking private communication among dissidents.[31] On the online battlefield, the Syrian Free Army employed applications to locate and eliminate targets among the Syrian Electronic Army, while regime forces deployed their own cyber capabilities to gain tactical advantage and geolocate targets from the Syrian Free Army.[32] These tactics invited counterattacks by cyber activists within and outside Syria, such as when Anonymous doxxed some members of the Syrian Electronic Army. In a complex conflict that has broad geopolitical ramifications and involves international players, cyber activism has embroiled activists and regime supporters in a perpetual cycle of reactive adaptation.

The foregoing analysis points to the complexity of the digital turn. The affordances of digital technology enable horizontal, multiplatform, and multimodal forms of communication and favor networks that foster unencumbered communication.[33] Additionally, networked publics have grown savvy and adept at circumventing evolving forms of control, using anonymizers, proxies, and alternative platforms. These considerations make the question of how the digital undermines authoritarian inclinations and empowers publics less relevant than the question of how publics and states are subject to a digital double bind that simultaneously empowers and inhibits online activism and how the process of adaptation has spawned discordances that are perpetuated within a tenuous balance of power.

The fact that "the uprisings have led to authorities expanding surveillance to an unprecedented level"[34] illustrates the significance of this double bind. The more digital technologies are used by activists, the more determined governments are to constrain the online space, impose limitations on cyber activities, and curtail free-dom of expression. Activists avail themselves of digital tools and forms of com-munication to mobilize, disseminate antiestablishment messages, and advance causes, knowing full well that these essential digital tools of activism are closely monitored by state apparatuses determined to thwart their efforts. The same tools that allow activists to mobilize digital users are deployed to collect and filter data about the population, disseminate propaganda, and suppress dissenting voices. Activists' ingenuity sometimes compensates for their lack of resources, while state control is often accentuated by the ever-increasing breadth, depth, and signifi-cance of the digital turn.

From the state's perspective, despite apprehensions about digital contention, the digital not only has the prospect for better economic development but also has inescapably turned into a new modus operandi for the state itself. Throttling digi-tal technology is hardly an option, since the government itself is now online and its operations are, to varying degrees, dependent on such technology. Achieving digital sovereignty is an increasingly prioritized objective, as trailing in global indi-ces of digital readiness does not bode well in today's globalized economy for eco-nomic development in general or foreign direct investment in particular. In effect, states are open to the potential of the digital while remaining apprehensive about its unintended consequences.

The Shadow State of E-Government

Adamantly opposed to relinquishing control over the internet, governments throughout the Middle East are also committed to using new forms of digital com-munication to their advantage. Government communication is evolving to keep pace with changing messaging dynamics and the needs, preferences, and habits of digital citizens. Initially skeptical of digital tools, Arab leaders, savvy politicians, and government officials have themselves become active on social networks. The Facebook accounts of various presidents and rulers buzz with footage of activities and public statements. Dubai's ruler, Sheikh Mohammed bin Rashid Al Maktoum, ranks internationally among the top politicians on Twitter, with nearly 11 mil-lion followers—three times the population of his city-state.[35] Former Lebanese prime minister Saad Hariri, also known for his "selfie diplomacy,"[36] did not shy away from discussing politics on Twitter.[37] Even figures in advisory roles have taken to social media, using their personal Twitter accounts to write quasi-official tweets on various issues, often reflecting what their political patrons are inclined to think or taking controversial stands to boost their personal brand.[38] Several governments have launched online initiatives, state authorities have embraced digital forms of communication to engage citizens on public matters, and government departments have used digital platforms offering citizens online services and soliciting their feedback on various issues.[39] These online forms of engagement make government officials and decision-makers seem more accessible and transparent to their publics. In some instances, such as the 2017 Gulf crisis, social-media platforms have also been used for digital diplomacy, allowing various parties to share information and engage with global audiences.[40]

The extent to which adopting popular digital platforms—those that make states modern in form but not necessarily in substance—leads to real participation and the development of an engaged citizenry remains to be seen. In a region known for conformist traditions, the tendency of social media to enhance the publicness of the discourse has come with added challenges. In Saudi Arabia, for example, the diwan or informal council—whether with statesmen, tribal leaders, or religious authorities—is the conventional conduit to courting the public.[41] To build anticipation and muster support for its 2030 vision to move beyond an oil-dependent economy, the kingdom launched a social-media debate on Twitter.[42] It also enlisted the help of social-media influencers with huge followings to alter perceptions of the kingdom.[43]

The horizontal nature of social media should not obscure the top-down nature of these interventions. Significantly, the incipient culture of public expression introduced by social-media platforms has an effect on ingrained hierarchies and social norms. For women, taking to social media to voice their views eases (even if only symbolically) some of the cultural constraints that confine them to female-designated spaces and roles, even when such engagement triggers discrediting and harassment campaigns. As more users are able or willing to express their views, the potentially equalizing effect of social media increasingly undermines the ability of the political elite to uniformly shape the message. This is particularly evident during times of crisis, as in the case of the perennial Jeddah floods, when many social-media users were emboldened by human loss and material damage to express frustration, lash out at state bureaucracy, and denounce corruption.[44]

The digital turn has also impelled states to reckon with the question of e-governance. While the stated objective was to use ICTs to engage users on issues of government, such efforts tended to be limited to the digitization of certain services without any promise for engaging in "public consultation."[45] In an effort to harness ICTs to improve the functions and effectiveness of government processes, states have launched a range of platforms with the goal of delivering services to their citizens in more integrated and efficient ways while improving the business environment and standards in ways that stimulate private-sector development and attract foreign investment. The launch of government websites, portals, and apps that offer services around the clock and enable transactions through a single login has helped reduce red tape while increasing accessibility, enhancing transparency, and improving the delivery of public services. With the pervasiveness of mobile technology, many e-government efforts have transitioned to m-government, relocating the use of government agencies and centers onto users' mobile devices.

Like the eventual impact of states' adoption of popular platforms, the extent to which e-government initiatives could alter governance practices in the region also remains unknown. The reliability, efficiency, and transparency of e-services tend to improve trust in government, but concerns about privacy and intrusiveness tend to undermine them.[46] Despite increased efforts to use high encryption standards and secured microchips to make the online environment a safer and more reliable space for transferring sensitive personal and financial data, there is still resistance to these online transactions (particularly outside the Gulf states, which benefited from the early and gradual deployment of digital technologies).

Whether by design or by effect, the very seamlessness upon which the system of e-government is erected enables new forms of control.[47] As people become increasingly dependent on the system for government services, their private and personal information becomes data that are easily accessible, instantly retrievable, and conveniently shareable among government departments and units.[48] In the absence of established e-governance, e-government can itself be the basis for a de facto monitoring tool.

Accordingly, for many states, the transition toward integrated e-services and e-solutions—and more broadly, the drive to digitize—are impelled by security considerations as much as they are motivated by the urge to modernize. Some e-government initiatives are driven by international efforts to control the flow of funds to and from organizations suspected of illegal or terrorist activities, including the flow of funds through charitable organizations. In Jordan, for example, eFAWATEERcom, which was set up as part of the country's digital transformation plan, offers a range of payment services that also extend to state-approved e-donations.[49]

The flow of people can be an even greater threat than the flow of money. Consequently, states aimed other initiatives at targets including better managing unique population challenges, handling immigration, and addressing growing security concerns,[50] especially in Gulf countries with sizable expatriate populations.[51] In this regard, acquiring high-tech identity systems and adopting sophisticated biometric technologies formed part of a broader, digitally supported strategy to enhance "soft security" and "preventative surveillance."[52] Thus, the use of biometric e-gates at airports and the early adoption of smart chip-based ID cards containing biometric information ensured better identification, verification, and authentication than analog processes. Such innovations simultaneously facilitated cross-border travel while enhancing the ability of governments to manage immigration issues and track the flow of people. Similarly, the adoption of

advanced surveillance technology improves these states' ability to gather information and generate data that can increase their ability to track and monitor people's
movements.[53] These resources have also been used overtly for crisis management.
During the COVID-19 pandemic, some travelers to Abu Dhabi were required
to wear electronic wristbands that enabled authorities to track them and monitor compliance with quarantine rules to prevent the spread of the coronavirus.[54]
Similarly, the FIFA Fan ID that was introduced at the 2018 World Cup in Russia
proved to be a valuable innovation later used in Qatar's 2022 version. The system made it possible for the organizing authorities to recognize each spectator
digitally.[55] In addition to allowing its holders visa-free entrance to the country and
access to fan zones, events, stadiums, and transportation, Qatar's fan ID (dubbed
the Hayya card) helped with crowd management and security—a critical function, as the country hosted fans numbering nearly half its population.

The digital tools are a boon for states but also for global businesses that thrive
on monetizing the sale of digital technologies. These trends are not specific to the
region. What is particularly noteworthy about the Middle East is that the advent
of these dynamics was not accompanied by adequate legal frameworks to protect
citizens and prevent the abuse of power, and e-governance is premised on the very
transparency and openness that are anathema to the region's political culture.

Unconventional Digital Actors

Although states in the Middle East were quick to adapt to the digital era and consolidate their domestic control, they have also faced challenges posed by the uses
of disruptive power and challenged by unconventional uses of digital technologies. Increased access to the internet has lowered the threshold for cybercrime,
and identity theft and other malicious activities against users have become common problems. Phishing incidents, cyberattacks, malware attacks, and targeted
intrusions all challenge states in the region, particularly as such crimes become
more frequent and more harmful.[56] Despite the unprecedented growth of the
regional cybersecurity market,[57] organizations responsible for implementing
defense measures and reinforcing IT security systems struggle to keep up.[58] These
are global challenges, but the peculiarity of their regional manifestations and their
geopolitical implications make them particularly hard to confront effectively.[59]
Furthermore, these challenges reflect the cycles of attacks and counterattacks in
which digital tools and infrastructure are both the subject and the object.

Rising geopolitical tensions and prolonged proxy wars between regional rivals
have increased the risk of cyber threats. Cyberspace has become another battleground on which the region's key players and aspiring powers confront each other,
often using plausible deniability. Over the past decade, state and nonstate actors
have weaponized cyberspace, introducing new vulnerabilities and triggering a

race toward increased cyber defense in anticipation of an impending cyber war. States have been the target of damaging attacks and malicious online activities and cyberattacks, typically committed by unidentified perpetrators who infect computers with malware and severely damage the infrastructure of banks, telecommunications, and government services and agencies.[60] Some of these efforts sought to expose governments spying on their citizens, draw attention to Western-based companies and manufacturers that sell surveillance equipment to authoritarian regimes, or react to the repressive practices of Arab regimes. Groups such as Telecomix and Anonymous have caused disruption and damage through their hacking and cyberattacks. Over time, these operations intensified and took different forms, from targeted cyberattacks in support of causes, groups, and cyber activists to WikiLeaked documents and the revelation of classified materials undermining the credibility of states and giving legitimacy to public and popular dissent.[61]

Telling the scourge from the minister has become increasingly difficult, and the line between state actors (and their proxies) and nonstate actors has become thinner than ever. Similarly, the local and the global are inextricably linked in cyberspace. Some hacking attacks originate from within the region,[62] but other security intrusions come from elsewhere. In 2017, files released by the hacker group Shadow Brokers revealed that the US National Security Agency allegedly hacked a slew of banks in the Middle East by infiltrating EastNets, a Dubai-based service bureau that manages financial transactions for the global banking system SWIFT.[63] Such unauthorized access to the banks' computers and servers in the region is not unprecedented and is often motivated by the need to gather financial intelligence and other information related to suspected terrorist groups. Nevertheless, the timing of and motive for this hack (including escalating the war with Syria, Russia's ally) give these actions a political dimension. Espionage and data theft have always been a tool of war, and it is not surprising that in the digital age, cyber operations and attacks on critical information infrastructure have become more common.

States now engage in cyber warfare and digital weaponry on an unprecedented scale. In some instances, cyber warfare has enabled various nonstate actors to engage in asymmetrical wars. For example, cyber warfare has been used intensely between Israel and Hezbollah, in the form of distributed denial of service (DDOS) attacks, the acquisition of data and information, and the dissemination of propaganda and disinformation to influence public opinion.[64] The fact that it is not always possible to attribute responsibility for such cyberattacks complicates these developments. Destructive, indiscriminate attacks and malware spreading through computer networks are frequent. Often, these attacks are part of cyber warfare involving regional power holders and international actors in one of the most geopolitically complex and volatile regions of the world. In 2013, a virus targeting Saudi national oil company Aramco erased data and corrupted files on tens of thousands of computers, effectively destroying one-third of the company's terminals and forcing a temporary shutdown of its corporate network to prevent further damage.[65] Known as the Shamoon attack, it threw the oil giant into shambles and threatened to affect the oil-supply management operations of the world's largest oil producer.[66] The fact that responsibility for the attack was claimed by an unknown group called Cutting Sword of Justice, citing Aramco's support of the kingdom's retrograde policies in the region, did not dispel speculations about state-backed "hacktivism" by regional rivals. The Shamoon attack is widely believed to mimic Wiper or Flame, a 2012 data-destructive cyberattack that targeted Iran's critical petroleum industry.[67]

Shamoon was one of many attacks in an undeclared cyber war. In 2009, Iran suffered an even more destructive malware attack from a worm dubbed Stuxnet, which sabotaged its uranium enrichment efforts by temporarily crippling the Natanz nuclear facility.[68] Although the Stuxnet virus was designed to conceal its designers and no one claimed responsibility for it, only the cyber forces of technologically advanced states could possibly develop such a sophisticated attack, and indeed responsibility was eventually traced to experts in the United States and Israel.[69] In response to revelations about an American cyber plan designed to disable the Fordo uranium enrichment plant, a notoriously inaccessible facility built deep inside a mountain near Qum,[70] the Iranians devised their own protective system, launching a cyber army to bolster their defense against potential cyberattacks.[71]

The likelihood of cyber warfare in an unstable region such as the Middle East has heightened the need for detection, defense, and attack capabilities. Increasingly, cybersecurity is a key component of these states' national security and an important factor in their strategic geopolitical engagements. For example, the UAE integrated twenty-five state-owned and independent companies to form Edge, an advanced technology group centered on the defense industry.[72] Evidently, the growing arsenal of cyber weaponry could increase diplomatic tensions and potentially provoke kinetic attacks between states, potentially spinning the region's conflicts out of control.

Cyberspace has also empowered nonstate actors and increased the risk of cyber terrorism. Various violent or extremist groups have sought to use online spaces for radicalization. For Al Qaeda and its many branches, the internet was critical for communications outreach "for its pronounced, digitalized multiplier effects on jihadist consciousness-raising and operational activities."[73] Applauded during the 2011 Arab uprisings for toppling the region's authoritarian figures, social-media platforms emerged as a powerful tool in the hands of terrorist organizations. Social media became widely adopted in communication strategies, significantly enhancing the ability of various groups to reach global communities and maintain a digital connection with group members and supporters.[74] The Islamic State of Iraq and Al Sham (IS or ISIS) had a dedicated digital media operation (Al Hayat Media Center) and developed remarkable social-media capacity, which it used to recruit

new members, disseminate news, indoctrinate operatives, and foment radicalization, all of which cause serious concern.[75] ISIS's use of social media to engage in
psychological warfare and disseminate spectacles of terror by posting videos containing incendiary violence and gruesome scenes of beheading is shockingly brutal, inciting revulsion and stoking fear. Unfettered access to a global audience gave
(and still gives) these groups the ability to disseminate images and messages far
and wide.[76] Despite efforts to combat these tendencies, the appropriation of the
internet by extremist groups remains unabated, particularly as the root causes of
extremism itself persist in a region in turmoil. States and nonstate actors are caught
in a perpetual battle revolving around cyberattacks and cybersecurity, with each
group struggling to enhance capabilities in both areas simultaneously. In trying to
achieve proficiency in one area, actors increase their vulnerabilities in the other.

Intractable Cyber Challenges

The digital turn has accentuated the anachronistic nature of the Middle East's
political culture, particularly as it faces the natural inclination of ICT-enabled networks premised on openness and sharing. The liberal imaginaries of the internet
are tested against state practices that use digital tools to silence critical voices and
control the message. Whether it takes the form of online surveillance, manipulation, or propaganda, these forms of "digital authoritarianism," which coexist with
traditional forms of control, reinforce the state's resilience in the face of change.[77]
How various nonstate actors have reacted to these practices and how they navigated digital forms of repression merit attention.

    While digital influence campaigns and (dis)information operations are rela-
tively new, they follow the path blazed by traditional propaganda wars between
long-standing regional rivals. During the Algerian War of Independence (1954–
1962), both the French colonizers and the Algerian National Liberation Front
used radio to disseminate information and exercise influence.[78] Similarly, Egypt
used radio to influence Yemeni and Saudi populations during the North Yemeni
Civil War (1962–1970).[79] In the aftermath of September 11, the US set up Radio
Sawa and Al Hurra TV as part of a massive campaign to win the hearts and minds
of Arabs.[80] To take another example among many possible ones, the 2011 Libyan
uprising was rife with Gaddafi's broadcast and digital rumor mills.[81]

    Today these forms of influence are tied to digital campaigns that have been
commodified as part of an international market for tools and services. Several
states have harnessed the potential to influence publics digitally and garner fake
grassroots support for unpopular policies and political decisions. Oxford's 2020
ranking of the seventeen countries with the highest capacity for "cyber troops"
engaged in "computational propaganda" includes six countries in the Middle
East.[82] These countries' trans-local activities include hiring skilled operatives,

purchasing software, and developing dedicated state-sponsored facilities. Among those involved in disinformation activities are global private companies offering disinformation as a service. States in the Middle East are increasingly relying on seemingly legitimate organizations to spread disinformation, while maintaining deniability of their actions.[83] Commonly operating as public relations firms, data analytics providers, or social-media consultants, some companies have exploited the digital to increase message sophistication, audience reach, and political targeting. Particularly noteworthy are dubious activities, such as creating fake users, amplifying fake news against rival actors, pushing misleading stories, and engaging in diplomatic manipulation.[84] Between non-state and state actors, the region may be entering an era in which the ability to hack infrastructure is perhaps less critical than the ability to influence and sway public opinion.

At the center of cyber disinformation campaigns and digital manipulation are regional power struggles, geopolitical interests, and foreign interferences. The Gulf Crisis (2017–2021) was a stark reminder of how these dubious digital practices can stoke political tension in the region. In June 2017, a Saudi-led alliance (or quartet) that included Bahrain, the UAE, and Egypt alleged that Qatar was engaging in practices that could destabilize the region. They severed diplomatic, political, and economic ties with Doha and imposed a blockade on Qatar. While political tensions and diplomatic spats between the Gulf states are not new, this particular crisis began with the hacking of Qatar's state-run news agency and the posting of fake news villainizing Doha. The story was quickly picked up by the regional press and further propagated through bots, and it soon lit up the social web.[85] With Twitter emerging as a digital battleground, fake news, which sparked the whole incident, remained a constant feature of the crisis.[86]

The historical political tensions and regional rivalries between these countries came alive in posts or shared videos on small screens for everyday users. From the start, the crisis and its political ramifications needed to be channeled to tech-savvy, well-traveled, socially and economically integrated groups. Using disinformation clips from mainstream media outlets and carefully crafted short threads, governments and citizens offered interpretations of history and support for political positions. All parties were adamant in carving a following and advancing their narratives.[87] Social-media platforms were drawn into a crisis in which they could not take sides—not only because they would risk losing potential investments from some of the world's wealthiest countries but also because they claimed to stand for freedom of expression. After all, they partially built their regional fame with the triumphs of the Arab uprisings.

The cross flow of disinformation between traditional media and social media during the crisis was unprecedented. The content of television, press, and radio was almost instantly shared across Twitter, WhatsApp, and Snapchat. Similarly, social-media statements made by key political, religious, and cultural figures were widely covered and debated on mainstream media. Compounding these information flows were "electronic armies" or "electronic flies" which also used social-media platforms, particularly Twitter, to manipulate digital discussions through suppression, influence, or distraction. Trolls and fake accounts became favorite instruments of propaganda wars.[88] Some of these electronic armies were made up of "bots" (networks of purposefully created or repurposed accounts), real members of a particular group (paid or mobilized individuals), or passionate citizens; they also included a range of international firms offering influence as a service.

The battleground for the Gulf Crisis was not limited to posting; it involved more direct attacks on other forms of media as well, including an attack on the Qatari-based channel beIN Sports. The problem began when the blockading countries banned beIN, a media network that holds exclusive rights to broadcast international tournaments and matches to the Arab world. This situation left Saudi sports fans scrambling to view their favorite sports events. In August 2017, an online channel, beoutQ (with the Q presumably standing for Qatar), emerged, suspiciously using the same signal and content that beIN Sports transmitted.[89] Such ability to hijack digital satellite signals reflects a capacity combining a range of traditional spying techniques and sophisticated digital capabilities. For two years, beoutQ continued to transmit online (including IPTV) and even expanded to deliver content—including the highly valued 2018 FIFA World Cup—using a direct-to-home satellite and set-top box. In reaction to this bootlegging operation, beIN launched a far-reaching investigation to identify the source of the pirated signal and called on the Saudis to trace and curb these violations. The dispute involved multiple organizations, governments, and regulatory bodies, including the WTO and FIFA.[90] More than merely a commercial or political sanction, the piracy of beIN's signal demonstrates the region's deeply interconnected digital systems and their vulnerabilities.

These incidents illustrate the challenges that emerging state and nonstate cyber capabilities pose to even the most digitally advanced states in the region. While information and influence operations seem to offer regimes (and their proxies) the tools to block information flows and develop strong counternarratives, they also provide cyber activists (and foreign media) with tools and strategies to continue their engagement. The fact that both regimes and activists rely on Western-based corporations for technologies and access raises the question of how these corporations balance their commitments to freedom of expression, the right to privacy, and the security of their data against their corporate interests, financial pressures, and market access. For now, an occasional tracing of disinformation networks and the suspension of the most egregiously inappropriate accounts on Facebook and Twitter are as far as such global social-media giants seem willing to go to overcome these challenges.[91]

Digital Territoriality and the Nation-State

The digital turn has also raised the prospect that transnational digital corporations could change consumers' behavior and promote de-territorialized content in ways that could undermine state power. Powerful digital corporations are proliferating across national borders, attracting local audiences, and offering services that defy geographical boundaries and over which states have little or no control. Adumbrated by the advent of digital capitalism,[92] whereby an expanding array of digital technologies and networks are integrated into processes of economic value production and accumulation that are not bound by territoriality, these dynamics impinge on sociocultural contexts and disrupt political cultures.

Particularly problematic for states is secure digital communication. States were alarmed by the potentially disruptive effect of readily available services for encrypted communication even before the Arab uprisings made patent the potential of social-media platforms for contention and mobilization. In 2010, the UAE and Saudi Arabia announced they would ban BlackBerry mobile services for lack of compliance with national telecommunications regulations, citing national security concerns over the inability to access information and monitor encrypted messaged and traffic on BlackBerry devices. Research in Motion—the Canadian smartphone company that manufactured BlackBerry devices—provided a secure messenger service that encrypted data and routed communication through foreign-based servers, making it both unintelligible and out of reach. These configurations made BlackBerry communication "too secure."[93] The ban was eventually averted as the company reached an undisclosed agreement granting these Gulf states greater control over users' data. Nevertheless, the case highlights the dilemma that comes with recognizing both the value of encryption to the digital economy and the perils of uncontrollable information.

Growing demand for encrypted messaging services with new forms of communication has alarmed governments further. In 2017, Egypt blocked the encrypted messaging app Signal, which uses domain fronting to make it hard for a third party to access content.[94] Some Gulf countries have also disrupted VoIP services for users of popular messaging apps.[95] Others have devised comprehensive cyber strategies that include restricting or even criminalizing the use of VPNs,[96] localizing data servers inside the country, and developing alternative state-run applications (as with the controversial messaging app ToTok).[97] Although many restrictions on digital communication tools ostensibly are driven by security concerns, often they are also impelled by the need to safeguard economic interests. In some cases, states exerted pressure on outside firms that could jeopardize the financial interests of clientelistic networks and undermine the state's leverage over the telecommunications sector. In some Gulf countries, where there is a sizable expatriate workforce, restricting voice- and video-calling services shores up the demand for international calls, which plays into the hands of the leading communication service providers and, by extension, national governments and their local business allies who are stakeholders in the lucrative telecommunications market.[98]

When it comes to entertainment, the increased popularity of streaming services seeking a strong foothold in the region's market has further compounded the problem of state control, especially when cultural and political content are at stake. These complexities are particularly pronounced in the case of global content providers such as Netflix, which are committed to growth in the region. When Netflix's show *Patriot Act with Hasan Minhaj* satirized Saudi Arabia, the kingdom demanded the removal of the episode as it violated national anti-cybercrime laws that bar criticism of the monarchy's religious values and public morals. Notably, the outcome was determined less by the kingdom's stern cyber-content laws (which are unenforceable against foreign-based global tech companies) than by the voluntary withdrawal of the controversial content by Netflix itself.[99] Whether this global streaming company caved to the kingdom's request to remove "offensive" content or acted voluntarily in line with its own company strategy is irrelevant, as the controversial *Patriot Act* episode remained accessible on multiple legal and illegal platforms. The policy's success was Pyrrhic, to say the least. The attempt to undo an act of mediatized "political jamming"[100] ended up heightening viewers' interest in watching the blocked content as the banned episode went viral on the social web, reaping more than 4 million YouTube views.

The *Patriot Act* case highlights the difficulty states may face in controlling the circulation of digital content. Historically, the sovereignty imperative governed state investments in media technologies. Since the 1960s, Saudi Arabia has invested heavily in broadcast technologies to counter foreign propaganda, fend off political ideologies, and uphold its values.[101] The advent of satellite technology complicated attempts to stem the tide of border-crossing content, leading the kingdom to accommodate satellite technologies and tolerate measured deregulation and economic liberalization.[102]

The digital turn created even greater challenges. Digital platforms concentrate production, distribution, and storage in the hands of a few supranational companies, undermining the ability of nation-states to retain their political, cultural, and economic sovereignty. Although technology platforms and digital entertainment companies recognize restrictions, adopt geo-blocking, and support content localization in individual nation-states, it is hard for states to control the flow of undesired material, especially as digital platforms become integrated into people's everyday lives. If anything, improvised state responses to these challenges reflect the complexity of exerting influence while being embedded in a supranational market for digital content.

Part IV

IMITATION AND INNOVATION

Inside the Political Economy of the Digital

The Middle East's economies are visibly changing. From the emergence of an eclectic generation of multinational entrepreneurs and the unprecedented number of transnational startups to the state's recalibrations of development planning and its varied commitment to digital transformation, the knowledge economy has been at the center of attention of policymakers and business leaders in the region. Yet these changes overlap with entrenched practices and tendencies that nurture stasis. Technical limitations aside, bureaucratic rigidity, political restrictions, and a host of market-specific obstacles underscore resistance to change. By and large, the region remains characterized by relatively stable, nationally bounded spheres of economic activities. Despite the vitality of certain sectors, economic activity is largely circumscribed by state regulation, channeled into markets that feed oligopolies, and reproduced as a business culture derived from the region's historical legacies.

To make sense of these conflicting pulls, this part of the book delves into the political economy of the digital and maps out trends and practices that have emerged in conjunction with the digital turn. In doing so, it shifts the focus away from traditional economic rankings, indicators, and projections (and the digital economies' respective performance or output) toward an understanding of how different policies, processes, and practices affect the political economy of the digital in the region. It pays particular attention to initiatives and activities that lay out original pathways while also reaffirming the state's ability to remain a locus of power. It also covers industries and sectors in which the digital economy is emerging and describes sociopolitical organizational forms that have developed around the digital. Besides illuminating how the region's economies are changing, this part also reveals historical trends, trajectories, and patterns that complicate our understanding of how the political economy of the digital manifests itself in the Middle East.

Chapter 9

In Pursuit of the Knowledge Economy

The extent to which the digital turn is reshaping the Middle East's economic future is evident in many countries' aspirations to become knowledge economies. These orientations also reflect broader dynamics brought about by the twin forces of globalization and informatization. In many ways, they are part of a long and arduous path toward modernization that brought hopes and promises to the region but also incurred apprehension and misgivings. Throughout the twentieth century, the emergence of the modern state intertwined with discourses of economic modernization. Conceived as a set of policies and plans for achieving a high level of socioeconomic development, ambitious modernization efforts were projected as hegemonic visions that eschewed public scrutiny and repudiated critical opposition. In the 1960s, for example, Tunisia's Habib Bourguiba and Egypt's Gamal Abdel Nasser developed their modernization projects over the objections of critical voices, who included both Western-educated intellectuals who advocated precipitous change and traditionalist social factions who challenged these visions. Today, as this chapter reveals, economic strategists and policymakers emphasize the need for states to focus on a knowledge-based economy even when they have persistent structural issues or sociodemographic challenges. With the digital turn, the state remains beholden to the unfulfilled promises of economic modernization, which it cannot control and toward which it continues to be ambivalent. At the same time, the state is responding to the ever more pressing demands and expectations of an aspiring young population with varying levels of digital access.

Promises and Aspirations

Over the past few decades, digital transformations have had a profound effect on the nature and structure of the global economy, impelling a move to a postindustrial economy based on technologically advanced, knowledge-intensive industries.

The Digital Double Bind. Mohamed Zayani and Joe F. Khalil, Oxford University Press. © Oxford University Press 2024.
DOI: 10.1093/oso/9780197508626.003.0009

State and market interest in traditional manufacturing and low-tech industries has receded, giving way to value-added goods and services aimed at increasingly sophisticated and fickle consumers. Initially projected in the writings of postindustrial sociologists and later codified by international organizations such as the OECD, World Bank, and UN,[1] the global reorientation toward a knowledge economy shifted the focus from physical to intangible assets; it also entailed structural changes in the labor force and market.[2] To be sure, the old builds on the new; even knowledge economies depend on natural resources and material factors as much as they rely on talent, incentive, and innovation.[3] Whereas in developed nations the knowledge economy is a central feature of growth, this transformation remains largely an aspiration in less developed countries.

The inability of countries in the Middle East to adequately address growing socioeconomic challenges highlights the limits of traditional development approaches and creates widespread frustration. Generally, the region's economies have not kept pace with population growth and changing societal needs. The events of the Arab uprisings further accentuated the need for change.[4] Demographic trends put more pressure on states to achieve economic development, stimulate growth, and create adequate employment opportunities.[5] Youth unemployment in the region exceeds the global average (29% in North Africa and 25% in the rest of the region in 2019)[6] and is consistently the primary challenge facing Arab nations. With a higher-education gross enrollment ratio (GER) of 42% in 2018, there is a need for national (and regional) job markets to absorb growing numbers of graduates.[7] Projections of rapid population increase in the region over the next three decades point to a significant increase in the working-age population.[8] Faced with these challenges, more Middle Eastern states are realizing that GDP growth rests on their response to global changes and their adaptability to the demands of the knowledge economy in the hopes that this strategy can help them overcome economic stagnation and enhance development.

Regionally, these transitions matter for resource-rich countries facing pressures to reconsider their economic model, as well as for resource-limited countries confronting acute economic challenges. Although the physical depletion of oil reserves is far from imminent, fluctuating oil prices and emerging alternative energy sources and technologies that herald a post-carbon era have put into question the sustainability of the Gulf region's economic well-being and accentuated the importance of developing its adaptive capacity. These countries recognize the inevitability of a shift from dependency on natural resources and seek to pivot toward being knowledge-producing and knowledge-employing societies—a move that will also likely entail changing the region's employment focus on the public sector. Beyond the Gulf states, whose digital transformation is relatively on course, transitioning from growth dependent on natural resources to growth based on knowledge would help diversify the region's economies, promote new sectors, create jobs, and boost long-term growth.

Ambitious National Strategies

The road to a knowledge economy is complicated by factors linked to the structure of the region's political economy, whether rentier, traditional, state capitalist, or neoliberal. Several countries in the region have declared policy goals, formulated ICT-centered national visions, announced strategies for transitioning to knowledge economies, and endeavored to create an environment that facilitates such an economic shift. For the UAE, the transition to a knowledge economy has been a central economic pillar, and the scale of its investment in such an economy is considerable. Abu Dhabi and Dubai, in particular, have emerged as global economic hubs. They combine state-of-the-art technical infrastructure with a business-friendly environment, adequate legal and institutional frameworks, and effective e-government. The Saudis are also eyeing economic sectors that could enable the kingdom to leapfrog in the region's knowledge economy. The Saudi Vision 2030 plan and its National Transformation Program aspire to transition toward upskilling its expanding youth population, upgrading the kingdom's communications networks, and instituting programs that incentivize innovation—and doing all of these in a sustainable and socially delicate way.[9] Similarly, Bahrain's Economic Vision 2030 commits the government and the private sector to "establishing a platform for advancing innovations to market readiness, which will help Bahrain tap into the global knowledge economy."[10] All these countries have taken steps toward developing knowledge economies, from reforming education to improving the business environment and from increasing e-business readiness to setting up e-government platforms. Other countries, such as Jordan, Morocco, Tunisia, and Egypt, have acknowledged the role of the knowledge economy in facilitating socioeconomic development, formulated sectoral or national plans, and undertaken government initiatives.

Despite these pronouncements and policy aspirations, the knowledge economy has not taken hold. One of the widely recognized indices for assessing readiness for the knowledge economy is the joint UNDP-MBRF Global Knowledge Index (GKI), which surveys 154 countries. Based on the World Bank's Knowledge Assessment Methodology, the GKI ranking relies on performance indicators in education, research and innovation, ICT, economy, and the "general enabling environment."[11] In spite of the shortcomings of these measurements in terms of data and methodologies, the results highlight noteworthy trends.[12] In 2021, the top regional performer was the UAE, which is ranked eleventh globally, while Qatar ranks second regionally and thirty-eighth globally. The other five Gulf countries are in the second quartile, with notable variations in performance: Saudi Arabia ranks third in the region (globally at 40), followed by Kuwait (48), Oman (52), Egypt (53), and Bahrain (55). In the third quartile, we find Tunisia (83), Lebanon (92), Morocco (101), Jordan (103), and Algeria (111). Trailing are Iraq (137), Sudan (145), and Yemen (150 of 154).

While differences in performance generally correlate closely with country income type (e.g., oil vs. other sources of income), there are notable differences even among countries with similar economic profiles. Compared with other Gulf states, which have made significant progress in their endeavor to transition to a knowledge economy, Kuwait continues to rely heavily on hydrocarbons, and its economy is one of the least diversified and most volatile in the region.[13] Even high-ranking countries such as the UAE and Qatar (both of which rank above the world average in all indicators) are not uniformly prepared when it comes to sectoral indices. For example, the UAE is the second-best performer globally in the economy category but ranks twenty-eighth in the R&D category and twenty-seventh in the broader enabling environment category. Those deficits impede the UAE's ability to absorb, adapt, and create knowledge.[14] Conversely, Lebanon ranks at 138 in enabling environment but 31 in the higher-education category. Algeria—where the dominance of the hydrocarbon sector de-incentivizes the development of a knowledge economy—trails the chart in all sectoral indices except pre-university education, where its performance is on par with the world average.

Overall, the GKI data reveal that resource-rich countries such as the Gulf states have invested in developing a knowledge-economy infrastructure and taken concrete measures to propel their economies toward that goal.[15] Countries in the Levant and North Africa are either in the initial stages of digital transformation or have devised knowledge-economy plans and strategies, the implementation of which is contingent on the availability of human and financial resources, the condition of the infrastructure, or the willingness to undertake necessary reforms. Others still lag. For example, in Iraq and Syria, knowledge economy development has been slow, readiness low, and efforts to transition economically hampered by underinvestment in the enablers of the knowledge economy.[16] Yemen and Libya, on the fringes of the global economy and disrupted by war, operate virtually outside the global knowledge economy.

Persistent Anachronisms

Building a knowledge economy requires more than improvements in the ICT infrastructure. It entails establishing an entire ecosystem, which involves multiple stakeholders and encompasses diverse sectors. Key to such enabling environment are an adequate educational system, policies, and frameworks that produce more adaptive institutional bodies, and a strong culture of research, innovation, and entrepreneurship.[17] Yet the region faces many problems in developing its capacity to innovate, for reasons including the nature and quality of education and the dearth of research.

Establishing quality education and training systems is a prerequisite for building a knowledge economy, but investment in people and knowledge assets has not kept up with ICT investments. States with solid educational traditions, such as North African countries, have not been able to maintain the rigor of their educational systems or keep pace technologically. Resource-rich countries with adequate ICT infrastructure but lackluster educational systems are still navigating education reform. These deficiencies affect higher education, as growth in the number of universities and colleges has been inadequately supported by elementary and secondary educational systems.[18] There is also a problematic gap between educational programs and employment opportunities that needs to be addressed.[19] Specifically, the educational system is not conducive to training a creative labor force, nor is it linked to labor market requirements, which results in a mismatch between the skills required to operate within the workforce and those acquired in school by job seekers.[20] Significantly, the path to the promises and riches of a knowledge economy requires adjustments in education and beyond, which then result in a fundamentally changed population—often creating people within each country who are willing either to radically challenge the status quo or to vehemently defend it. Despite curriculum reform and ICT implementation across schools, knowledge economy skills and competencies remain underdeveloped, and "much deeper institutional reform is necessary to fulfill the policy aspirations rather than speculating over progress through technology-enriched futures."[21] Overall, these efforts cannot be said to have transformed education and learning in ways that adequately respond to development demands and job-market exigencies.[22]

Another lacuna mitigating against the development of the knowledge economy is the region's relative lack of research intensity and innovation performance. Building a knowledge economy requires unleashing creativity and innovation—not an area of strength for much of the region. Investment in R&D as a percentage of the GDP is distinctly low in the Arab world. In 2020, the average public spending in the region on R&D did not exceed 0.72% of the GDP (compared with the world average of 2.63% and a high of 5.44% in Israel, a global outlier). National expenditures ranged from 1.45% in the UAE, to 0.96% in Egypt, to a dismal 0.04% in Iraq.[23] Research output, patent applications, and scientific journals are also weak relative to other global regions. Research is not a priority in most Middle Eastern universities, and research efforts are generally not oriented toward innovation and entrepreneurship. The relation between innovation (measured by gross expenditure on R&D) and economic performance (measured by GDP) in general is not strong.[24] Nor have science, technology, and innovation policies in the region sufficiently or effectively catalyzed knowledge production.

Historically, research in the region was developed mainly under the purview of the state, through national research agencies, and often in partnership with developed nations. With the adoption of economic liberalization policies, the receding role of the public sector, and the advent of globalization, investment in R&D dwindled. With global economic downturns (from the 2008–2009 global economic crisis to the 2020s global pandemic) devastating the region's economies, the Middle East is moving from the intense globalization of the 1980s and 1990s to state-initiated "de-liberalization," a shift justified on security grounds.[25] Such measures risk increasing digital inequalities as they limit foreign direct investment (FDI) and technology transfers to build capacity. Adding to these external factors is waning state support for research and innovation and either an inability or unwillingness to pursue a decentralized institutional research environment. Attention to institutional entities that support knowledge-based enterprises and innovation activities (such as research and innovation parks) is insufficient, and the number of centers in the region is limited. A few countries have commendably invested in higher education and other national initiatives conducive to knowledge creation, such as government-sponsored science and research parks. Yet in many cases, these investments do not succeed as innovation centers and have neither resulted in strong research networks nor translated into a dynamic research culture.[26] A flourishing knowledge economy relies on investments in science, technology, and innovation (STI) and is often contingent on specific technology transfers that are typically limited to North-North trade. Several security and economic barriers limit such technology transfers to developing countries.[27]

Additionally, technological innovation and promotion in the region are hindered by weak protection and enforcement of intellectual property rights. The Gulf countries have demonstrated efforts to support the filing of patents, secure legal protection of rights, draft laws, abide by international agreements, and enforce copyright protections. Still, these actions did not eradicate copyright violations or guarantee a complete transition to emerging economies. Other countries in the region have made concrete attempts to educate and nurture entrepreneurship focused on producing and protecting digital assets.[28] An absence of both political commitment and cultural receptiveness to enforcing payment for intangible assets, software, and content (all of which are often freely accessible) remains a perpetual challenge.

There are occasional bright spots. In the Gulf subregion, there have been concerted efforts to build capacity in research and knowledge sectors as some states bankrolled state-of-the-art education cities, sponsored branch campuses of reputable American institutions of higher education, and built research parks that draw on world knowledge and thrive on international talent—from Saudi Arabia's King Abdullah University of Science and Technology to Qatar Foundation's Education City (home to a cluster of leading American research universities), and from Dubai's Knowledge Village to Oman's Knowledge Oasis Muscat.[29] However, such ambitious higher-education initiatives are the exception rather than the rule across the region and, so far, have had limited diffusion into the broader economy.[30] These lacunae accentuate the need for resource-rich states to move away from subcontracting knowledge creation, utilization, and dissemination[31] and for the other states in the region to develop and incentivize local research capacity while tapping into global knowledge. The same goes for human development. Countries that have made headway in developing a knowledge economy rely heavily on foreign labor. In contrast, many countries with indigenous talent and local capacity lack the ICT infrastructure, financial resources, and political will to transition toward a knowledge economy. Despite the region's complementary assets, a limited number of private-sector actors are driving regional synergies in lieu of intergovernmental Arab agencies.

The nature of the region's economies further hampers efforts to move toward a knowledge economy. Except for the Levant and the Gulf, the economies of the region have a penchant for dirigisme. In Lebanon, Jordan, and Palestine, the business sector is largely vibrant and independent of the state, while in the oil-rich rentier states, the economy is linked to a system of patronage that blurs the line between economic clout and political power.[32] Elsewhere in the Middle East, though, members of the business elite lack the motivation or the resources for digital entrepreneurship, as their success generally is not dependent on their ingenuity but on their proximity to the political elite.[33] Additionally, the preponderance of the public sector over more competitive economic sectors skews the labor market toward low productivity and de-incentivizes competition and high performance.[34] As a consequence, the overall business environment is not conducive to building a knowledge economy.[35] Even where these capacities are starting to develop, they tend to be in specific or narrow sectors.[36]

These considerations aside, a supportive environment is also premised on technological and managerial modernization that is generally inadequate or ineffective in the Middle East. For example, despite the proliferation of business incubators, their effect has been uneven. Incubation and innovation have not been structurally integrated, and they tend to "lack appropriate management and professionalism, connections to adequate technical or commercial networks, and sufficient quantities of venture capital."[37] Supporting growth and entrepreneurship requires a broad range of financial services not readily or uniformly available across the region. For instance, a knowledge economy is contingent on instituting financing mechanisms that make available and mobilize seed, angel, and venture capital. Because knowledge creation and diffusion depend on financial sectors that result from financial policies, the inadequacy of economic and institutional frameworks compounds the problem.[38] For a knowledge economy to take hold, it is imperative to adopt supportive legal frameworks, improve the governance environment, and institute transparent regulations.

The Challenges of E-Governance

Perhaps more than any other economic system, the knowledge economy requires a healthy climate for business premised on good governance and transparent regulations, the rule of law, the elimination of corruption, and the improvement of government efficiency. The digital turn has induced several states in the region to adopt e-governance to varying degrees in order to develop "the use of the technologies that can help govern and be governed."[39] The application of ICTs requires an overhaul of existing laws, regulations, and policies, with broad business and community involvement, to ensure that service expectations are met. This includes, for example, developing e-commerce regulations such that all transactions are conducted following standard privacy and security provisions. A foundational step toward e-governance is rolling out e-government initiatives that allow increased access to government information and services, improved quality of public-service delivery, and effective transactions on government portals.

The adoption of e-government also contributes to the creation of a culture premised on openness and transparency while promoting a pro-business environment. Some countries at the forefront of e-government trends—namely, the UAE, Saudi Arabia, Bahrain, Kuwait, and Qatar—rank high globally on the UN E-Government Development Index. For these tech-ready states, e-government and m-government (mobile-based government) services are key components in an integrated national vision that seeks to increase operational effectiveness, reduce public-sector costs, and foster an enabling investment environment. In the case of the UAE, among the motivations to publicly commit and fully support e-government is the desire "to seed the field for private investment in the country's growing technology sector."[40] Similarly, effective e-governance cuts the red tape around the transnational operations of companies, people, ideas, and capital. In the instance of Dubai Internet City, the implementation of e-governance provided a seamless gateway to setting up businesses, handling licenses and permits, and facilitating access to government services.

The leading performers in e-government stand out as the exception rather than the rule. Across much of the Middle East, e-government remains largely underdeveloped despite considerable foreign aid, technical support, and funding. The absence of a strong political will and inadequate ICT infrastructure thwart efforts to improve e-governance. Equally problematic are issues of access and skill, as low internet penetration and varying levels of users' digital literacy skills prevent the growth of e-government and limit its reach across the various segments of society. For instance, Egypt, Morocco, and Algeria have moderate e-government readiness, which places them below the global average in the UN E-Government Development Index, while Sudan and Yemen score noticeably lower.[41] In many cases, government portals amount to little more than repositories of information. Where interactive data-exchange services are available, government portals allow users to request select services online—though administrative processes are typically done manually on-site rather than using end-to-end processing because the front- and back-office operations are not fully integrated.

The extent to which the digital turn has enabled the Middle East to transition from cumbersome bureaucracies to seamless online technocracies should not be overstated. The push for e- and m-government faces challenges even in countries with high performance levels in this region. Although the digitization of government processes has led to qualitative improvements in services and more effective capabilities, e-government practices have not attained "an integrated e-government."[42] Institutional hindrances add to the challenges emanating from an incomplete ecosystem for the advancement of e- and m-government (third-party suppliers, cybersecurity, regulatory framework, etc.).[43] Additionally, e-government initiatives are often undermined by the preponderance of bureaucratic practices, dwindling civil-service values, inadequate training, and the absence of a genuine desire for government agencies to change. The general public's weak predisposition toward government services online and virtual transactions in general, as well as concerns over information privacy and security, further undermine the adoption of such initiatives.

In spite of modest progress, the digitization of government services has not been transformative, nor have digital technologies bridged the gap between the state and citizens or redefined the way governance is conceived. While offering better services and user experiences, e-government has not strengthened citizen empowerment, and the prospects for ICTs to facilitate the adoption of open government and achieve good governance in the region remain dim. Typically, digital initiatives such as e-government are valued for their reinvention of how government works as well as for what the government stands for, as these initiatives can help provide better communication with the public, enhance relations with the private sector, improve the effectiveness of civil service, remove red tape, and increase productivity and efficiency.

Developing and implementing e-government projects and applications is one thing; fostering e-governance is quite another. As Kumar Cherupelly notes, "ICTs do not have any intrinsic ability to undermine existing traditional institutions of power, economic or social, unless agents direct them towards such ends. Digital space . . . . is partly embedded in actual societal structures and power dynamics."[44] When it comes to instituting open government, reducing corruption, promoting transparency, supporting inclusion, and enhancing good governance, the promise of e-government in the Middle East remains unfulfilled. The successful implementation of e-government would necessitate several adjustments considering how social relations in parts of the region tend to be rooted in practices that favor social hierarchies, nepotism, and face-to-face interactions. Yet even when challenged by evolving communication practices and changing user dispositions, those markers of traditional forms of sociality persist.

While e-government offers citizens the opportunity to participate in certain forms of public consultation and allows them to lodge complaints against the inefficiencies of government departments, overall, the proclivity of e-government to genuinely promote e-citizen engagement and foster better governance in the region remains intangible. Echoing how the adoption of ICTs in the region has not yielded more developed e-societies, the advancement of e-government is far from promoting a digital agora. Nor has the adoption of e-government had a perceptible impact on much of the region. Leveraging ICTs to modernize public administration, increase efficiency, and improve services is not equivalent to reorienting toward a knowledge economy that energizes various sectors and yields high-value-added jobs. Yet another challenge to e-governance in the region stems from the disparate implementation of good governance principles considering the resilience of the political structures and economic systems.[45] E-government makes the economy nimble and more efficient, which helps attract investments, but when states move toward e-government, people who operate within the existing system often lose privileges they enjoy and expect. For example, e-government's cashless transactions reduce the ability of some civil servants to make extra income through bribes and thus challenge the foundations of a system that trades government jobs for political favors and compensates low wages with unsanctioned bribes.

Furthermore, the efficiency gains of digitization may entail other trade-offs. Digitization can help upskill the workforce and trigger job creation.[46] In the Gulf region, though, ICT-intensive jobs tend to be filled by expatriate labor, whereas for the locals, shrinking government jobs are coveted for their security as well as their enviable benefits. For rentier states aspiring to be knowledge economies, increased digitization reduces their ability to provide their citizens with lifetime jobs that constitute a key dimension of a ruling bargain premised on citizens trading political rights for prosperity. These dynamics need to be understood within the peculiarity of the region's political economy.

The Development Conundrum

The Middle East has struggled to integrate the global drive toward the knowledge economy. Such a transition requires changes in the region's economic structure and functioning, as well as broader, more profound reforms. Both have been slow to materialize. Several barriers continue to hinder such efforts, including uneven development, remnants of post-Arab socialism, deficient economic models, rampant corruption, and weak institutionalization of reform. In Lebanon, where the transition toward a knowledge-based economy is driven by a robust education system and a vibrant entrepreneurship culture, progress is held back by endemic political instability and a weak ICT infrastructure.[47] Conversely, in Kuwait, where the knowledge economy still has shallow roots, there exist a relatively strong ICT infrastructure and ample financial resources but limited human resources and political support. In countries that lack adequate infrastructure, such as Sudan, the knowledge economy has yet to significantly materialize.[48]

Although the Gulf countries have been the regional leaders in the knowledge economy, their progress is bound by an anachronistic political economy. Hydrocarbon wealth helped modernize these states and create ambitious infrastructure developments but also reinforced structures of power by instilling a rentier culture that determines the nature and extent of change.[49] Distributive policies (including generous handouts, an elaborate welfare system, and near-guaranteed employment in the public sector) and the selective redistribution of wealth helped create prosperity, breed acquiescence, and shore up support while also feeding networks of kinship and patronage in a process that extends the exercise of political power within bureaucratic administrations.[50] As these benefits become entitlements deeply ingrained in society, they play an essential role in molding citizenship and defining the state-society relationship.[51] Elsewhere in the region, the culture of entitlement to free services, which persists in spite of the retrenchment of the welfare state, constrains competitiveness and undermines change, while the prevalence of *wasta* (nepotism) contributes to the decline of societal productivity.[52]

The distributive nature of hydrocarbon economies and the networks of dependency fostered by clientelism[53] stand at odds with the ethos of the knowledge economy. At least in theory, citizen entitlement depresses the motivation to attain education and develop entrepreneurship, as the public sector is held to absorb those citizens who do not have the necessary skills, qualifications, or disposition to work in a competitive, private-sector environment. These trends are problematic in two ways. First, the system engenders inefficient economies premised on a ruling bargain whereby the state "guarantees" jobs through a massive public sector and maintains living standards by subsidizing citizens' needs. Second, the system is content with a bloated and largely uncompetitive public sector, in which the driver of the knowledge economy is a private sector served mainly by expatriate workers, overdependent on migrant labor, and often subsidized by the state. Effectively, even in Gulf states that have immersed themselves in the knowledge economy, much of the local population is digitally invested as users and consumers but has yet to fully engage the possibilities of that transformation. A transition from rent-seeking practices to a value-added economy would require reconsideration of the social contract that has perpetuated the system even before the establishment of the modern Gulf states.[54]

Beyond these limitations, factors favoring the reinvention of crony capitalism stunt the development of a knowledge economy. The dominant business approach throughout the Gulf region is anchored in a rentier model characterized by the lack of a truly competitive market environment. The abundance of state resources energizes the economy and facilitates certain investments but also helps "create complacency and underpin traditional approaches that hinder adjustment to the new era."[55] Although private-public initiatives have helped stimulate change at the margins, business regulations limit shares of foreign ownership, and international companies typically operate through local, well-connected partners adept at navigating the local bureaucracy, which effectively perpetuates the rentier system.[56]

These dynamics are particularly evident in the telecommunications sector in the Gulf. Although governments introduced competition and economic stakeholders became more diversified, the state remains a key player. The financial dependency of the telecommunications sector is such that the incumbent, semi-privatized, state-dominated system spawns entities that operate at the intersection of the corporate and the nepotic, the private and the public. With many countries embracing the privatization of state-owned companies, a hybrid neoliberal system emerged whereby semiprivate companies are carved out of government operations. Although these companies have managed to overcome entrenched bureaucratic cultures and provide efficient services, they are only operationally dissociated from the government, and a degree of state influence persists.[57] What prevails is a murkily eccentric "creative protectionism"[58] that ironically stymies real competition in the name of liberalization.[59] Oddly, while resources bolster investment in the next-generation ICT environment, protecting the telecoms' revenues to the detriment of the economy prevents the exploitation of the potential of digital technologies. This results in an odd situation in which the early adopters of 5G technologies expand capacity but end up blocking VoIP services such as WhatsApp.

Whence comes the double bind: many states eye the opportunities that come with adopting knowledge-based economies as an integral part of a sustainable development framework, while at the same time, they remain wary of the disruptive effect of such orientation and its uses, which could unsettle the premise upon which the existing system of power and privileges rests. At the very least, the pursuit of the knowledge economy calls for implementing robust e-governance, which invites public scrutiny of diverse issues ranging from financial transparency to freedom of speech. It also requires overhauling the very meaning of knowledge (as organically developed, not imported) and how knowledge is produced (partnerships, critical thinking, etc.) and packaged for local and regional use. In the next chapters, we dissect a sociotechnical landscape that is taking shape despite the aforementioned structural challenges and limitations. In doing so, we shed light on imitation and innovation in emerging globally connected and integrated knowledge-based economies that remain responsive to regional histories, logics, and mechanisms of modernization.

Chapter 10

Cultural and Creative Industries

Digital cultural and creative industries have become integral to the way the knowledge-based economy operates. These sectors bring together culture, leisure, and entertainment in formats that have never been experienced before, from online games to streaming services and from digital publishing to virtual museums. With today's technology, consumers can access media on a variety of platforms for different uses. This chapter examines the region's digital cultural industries, which are associated with the production, storage, distribution, and exhibition of cultural goods and services.

Particularly noteworthy is how the cultural industries' strategies have evolved. Digitization once merely referred to a conversion from analog format. Now, digitization means an elaborate and integrated process for the development, distribution, and exhibition of content in digital form. This realm is marked by the coexistence of traditional media institutions, which engage in digital transformation to ensure their continued relevance to consumers and advertisers and digital-only platforms, which produce content to expand into global digital markets. While economic, political, and cultural clout of traditional media industries may be waning, the reconfiguration and underlying political economy of digital media are still taking shape. Examining the interlocking histories, strategies, and transformations of digital cultural industries advances our understanding of key stakeholders in the knowledge economy.

Toward an Arabized Internet

The story of "Arabizing the internet"[1] has yet to be told. It includes the ambitions and triumphs, as well as the deceptions and failures, of generations of technology actors who shaped the development of a subset of digital cultural industries in the region. To understand the nonlinear trajectory of the regional industries and the characteristics of the emerging ecosystem, it is useful to dwell on the expansion from software development to search engines.

The Digital Double Bind. Mohamed Zayani and Joe F. Khalil, Oxford University Press. © Oxford University Press 2024.
DOI: 10.1093/oso/9780197508626.003.0010

In the 1970s, the software sector in the Middle East began to take shape in the form of consultancy services offering limited proprietary solutions for companies (finance, banking, accounting, and logistics). In the 1980s and through the 1990s, the widespread adoption of personal computers, the introduction of the internet, and the development of robust mobile communication networks accentuated the need for regional companies to develop their capabilities and expand services for their consumers—specifically, small and medium-sized companies. Against the backdrop of deep globalization, the better-prepared regional players enjoyed a first-mover advantage. Today the region boasts one of the world's largest user bases and teems with companies that offer mobile applications, over-the-top services, and web solutions.

For many countries, software development has emerged as a strategic sector, part of their pursuit of a digital economy. In Lebanon, ICT is a key sector, with more than 550 companies, 10,000 employees, and a sectoral GDP estimated to reach USD 7 billion by 2025.[2] Similarly, Jordan's ICT sector is estimated to contribute around 12% of GDP, with plans to increase revenue by 25% to 30%, create 130,000 to 150,000 jobs, and establish 5,000 to 7,000 new businesses by 2025.[3] Egypt boasts the largest IT sector in the region, with a particular focus on electronics design and products and systems development. The country's software ecosystem includes both developers with added value and vendors of international software. In spite of this headway, Egypt's software industry is unevenly developed. With few exceptions, the proprietary software sector remains invested in consultancy operations and is primarily engaged in customizing, implementing, and servicing international versions from global software companies.

Not all ICT activity is directly featured in GDP measures, partly because many ICT products and services are intentionally low-priced, free, or part of the informal economy. There is a growing interest in the adoption of open-source software (OSS), which uses freely accessible source codes that are relatively easy to modify, customize, and redistribute. Considered a revolutionary departure from intellectual property models in software products, OSS offers valuable tools to increase access to knowledge (A2K) given economic and educational limitations in the region.[4] At other times, the cause of ICT activities' low contribution to GDP is less salutary. The average rate of software piracy in the Middle East region and the African continent remains high, at 56% in 2017 (compared with the global rate of 37%), for both individual and institutional violations.[5]

By focusing on how users interact with digital tools, these companies use their limited human and other resources to respond to the growing demand for localized products and develop synergies with global companies. They are invested in traditional business models that represent ownership, management, and control of conventional intellectual property rights. The software companies are subject to two competing forces that challenge their growth potential: limited state or corporate resources allocated to R&D (compared with global players) and the related competitive disadvantage of potentially costly, regional, "one-size-fits-all" products against globally customizable products or free-access software. Nevertheless, many local companies have succeeded in carving a space in the regional landscape.

As in many places around the world, the IT sector in the Middle East is genuinely multinational, benefiting from inward foreign investments, the free movement of labor, and globally integrated businesses. The development of Arabizing publishing software was instrumental in the digital transformation of various industries, from accounting departments and banking sectors to the printing and publishing industries themselves. As early as 1986, Diwan, a UK-based IT company that pioneered desktop publishing (DTP) in the Arabic language, developed the DTP application al-Nashir al-Sahafy for the Macintosh operating system.[6] In Egypt, affordable talent, particularly the low cost of highly skilled IT professionals, has lured large international companies. For example, IBM established a research center dedicated to offering Arabic-related solutions, and Microsoft's Innovation Center engages in concept-level problem-solving with local academic and business partners. Similarly, since its founding in 2000, Dubai Internet City has become the regional home for leading global ICT firms from Cisco to Facebook.

Though limited, there is even a trend of outward foreign investment by Middle Eastern companies acting across the region and beyond. This is the case of Sakhr Software Company, which stands out as a global leader in developing, producing, and implementing technology solutions for computers and the internet with a focus on Arabic content. The company was initially established as Al Alamiah Electronics company in 1982, a division of a family-owned electronics distributor in Kuwait. Over the next four decades, it benefited from its position as a gateway to an emerging market, growing from a small regional operation servicing Gulf countries into a global solutions provider. The company offered Arabic-language support for computer software during its early years[7] and briefly ventured into computer hardware production. Because it understood the construction and complexity of the Arabic language, the company was able to position itself uniquely in the market. Following the Iraqi invasion of Kuwait in 1990, Sakhr relocated to Egypt, where it boosted its R&D capabilities and reoriented its operations to focus on commercial products and solutions. It continued to create innovative computer software, such as tools for Arabic optical character recognition (OCR), while leveraging its development capabilities for the internet with an Arabic online handwriting recognizer and other solutions. In the early 2000s, Sakhr reorganized and expanded its operations by purchasing a silicon-based software company, obtaining US and Canadian patents, and becoming an official Microsoft partner (in 2008). The value of Sakhr lies as much in its adaptability as in its innovation, namely in enabling its Arabic-language corporate clients and computer programmers to participate in digital transformation in their native language. Sakhr capitalized on trans-regional capabilities, Arab talent, and Kuwaiti business capabilities to develop and market IT solutions for the region.

Sakhr's success illustrates how indigenous software companies can excel in developing products as varied as software packages for personal computers, sophisticated programs for banks and corporations, and e-government solutions, all with Arabic-language capabilities. One way to bridge the digital literacy divide in the Middle East is to provide local-language tools for participation. Arabic is the fifth most-spoken language globally, an official language in twenty-two countries, one of the six official languages of the UN, and the native language of more than 400 million people, as well as a foreign language of interest for more than 1.5 billion Muslims worldwide. Despite the scale of the language's reach and potential markets, however, Arabic has faced challenges. In particular, it is not easily customized into Western software. It is a morphological language whose script uses diacritical marks, and there are numerous variations in its construction and composition, not to mention the plethora of spoken Arabic dialects used in everyday online communication. These represent limitations for companies seeking to repurpose their products for the multiple Arabic markets. To address these issues requires indigenous programmers to devise solutions.

In addition to conventional companies such as Sakhr, startup ventures have responded to the language need by developing internet search engines to enhance Arabic content searchability. Before the international interest in Arabic search engines, the regional IT sector developed search capacities. While ventures such as Araby.com, Eb7ath, and Marweb failed, Yamli (Transcribe) offered unique user experiences, including a virtual Arabic keyboard that made web searches easier. Launched in 2007 from the US city of Boston, Yamli was a modest operation with limited features and capabilities before it licensed its technology to the California-based Yahoo! in 2012. The software firm Eiktub (Write) took a different approach, building on the widespread use of Latin script to write Arabic text, known as Arabizi. With Eiktub, users can search the Arabic web using an English keyboard.

These innovations, along with growing international interest in the Arab regional market, reflect the expansion of Arabic-language internet usage, which grew 2,064% between 2000 and 2008,[8] making Arabic the fourth most-common language used on the internet in 2020 (with 5.2% of internet users worldwide).[9] With growth in Arabic internet content, regional tech entrepreneurs have responded with specialized search tools that allow users access to specific content, including searches for Arabic adages (e.g., Yorwa), the Koran (e.g., Alwafa), banking services (e.g., Bnooki), Arabic academic online databases (e.g., e-Marefa), and Arabic websites (e.g., Arabo). Although many of these local search engines did not survive, the ones that did struggled against competition or co-optation from global companies and their localized services.

The development of search engines is also a by-product of the digital turn's political, economic, and socio-technological embeddedness. In the aftermath of 9/11, governments and firms sought to use technologies to identify security threats. The advent of Web 2.0 heightened Arab states' interest in the surveillance and monitoring of the blogosphere and social media. To meet these needs, enhanced search capabilities were developed and introduced into the commercial market afterward. Similarly, the development of Arabic-only search engines reflected the drive of tech programmers and the ambitions of tech entrepreneurs more than market research insights. Yamli, for example, was developed to satisfy the need for news searches during the Lebanon War of 2006.

Eventually, such projects struggled due to limited access to global tech markets. Global competition featured a combination of strategic planning and financial depth the region was hard-pressed to match. Transliteration-based search engines (typing words using the English keyboard, which the tool then converts into the native script) became obsolete in 2009, when Google's Ta3reeb (Arabization) and Microsoft's Marin were launched. Initially, international search engines such as Google, Yahoo!, Bing, and others did not fully recognize or accommodate the characteristics of the Arabic language or the needs of Arabic users. While some (such as Google) invested in developing their in-house capabilities with offices and developers operating across the region, others (such as Yahoo!) tapped into existing ventures for solutions. Google customized search engines by country and offered a generic Arabic version as part of its global strategy, while Yahoo! acquired the Boston-based Yamli to offer smart Arabic keyboard capabilities. In the process of focusing on the Arabic language, the software and search engine industries may have momentarily serviced the most pressing needs of the local market but failed to engage in a global market.

Web Portals, E-Publishing, and Digital Journalism

Although the software industry has largely succeeded in addressing obstacles related to integrating the Arabic language in the digital era, the transition from print to digital journalism presents different challenges and introduces new players.[10] E-publishing (the creation of content for the web or mobile phone) started with technologies used to digitize print material, primarily documents of historical value. From the Egyptian Centre for Documentation of Cultural and Natural Heritage to the Omani Ministry of Culture and Heritage, various regional entities have actively engaged in digitizing, preserving, and improving access to historical manuscripts. Consolidating these efforts are initiatives to promote the licensing and development of new Arabic content (text and otherwise) for online distribution, such as Qatar's Creative Commons, which allows the legal licensing of material, and Abu Dhabi's Taghreedat (Tweets), which aims to increase Arabic content on platforms from Twitter to Wikipedia. These initiatives aside, the digital transformation of traditional print media and book publishing remains hampered by logistical, structural, and market factors.[11]

The underdeveloped digital book publishing industry in the region reflects a general hesitancy toward digital conversion. Initially, digital publishing software lacked the technical sophistication required to handle the complexities of the Arabic language. E-publishing thus emerged as an informal market that co-opted the legal copyright holders by producing digitally scanned copies of print originals and circulating them online for free. Arab publishers' reluctance to embrace e-books, with only approximately 10% of the one million books published in Arabic annually being digitized, has led to a piracy rate of around 60% in the print market and a staggering 98% in the e-book market.[12] Within this environment, e-publishing developed slowly, partly because of regulations designed for the predigital world and a lack of copyright protection for authors and publishers. The digitization of the book industry also entailed a gradual decentralization such that the production and distribution of books are no longer limited to specific countries. A dispersed network of centers such as Sharjah Publishing City in the UAE and online self-publishing platforms such as Egypt's Kotobna (Our Books) arose to challenge Beirut as the region's publishing capital. Today the e-book market is largely dispersed between sites such as Al Manhal, Maktabat Al Jalis, Arabic e-library, Neelwafurat, Arabic Book Library, Alwaraq, and Maktabati. Interest in the e-book market has been favored by the wide adoption of smartphones, changing user habits, accessibility, and, since 2020, the effects of COVID-19. With the renewal of the Arabic novel, authors have capitalized on the potential of the e-book market. Young, digitally savvy authors draw on digital tools for inspiration (blogs turned into novels), while publishers are eager to use media tools to reinvent their businesses. These adaptations have given rise to nontraditional publishers such as Dar Dawen (House of Blog) in Egypt, which compiles blogs into print books while reformatting and promoting them online. Notwithstanding these initiatives, digital book publishing in the region remains a fledgling industry.

The migration of traditional newspapers to digital platforms has been similarly slow and uneven. As early as the 1990s, digital technologies facilitated the wide distribution of London-based pan-Arab newspapers such as *Asharq Al Awsat* and *Al Hayat*. Using satellite technology, the copy and layout of these papers were fed to printing presses across the region (and beyond) for local printing and distribution. Some Arab publishers were considered among the early beneficiaries of the internet, using it to enhance their tools and expand their circulation.[13] Between 1995 and 2000, more than sixty Arabic newspapers began offering online versions, starting with the UAE-based *Al Khaleej* newspaper in 1995.[14] Generally, the digitization race was less motivated by innovative business strategies than by the pressure to have a web presence and the fear of being left behind. Gradually, with changing demographics, ownership patterns, and readership habits, newspapers adopted an audience "pull" strategy; instead of merely pushing their print content online, they attracted readers with the web version.

The digital transformation that aimed to expand readership has compounded the problems of an already struggling newspaper industry. The internet perplexed an industry built around a combination of government or political support, business patronage, and advertising revenue. With the readership of print newspapers dropping from 42% in 2013 to 16% in 2019[15] and declining even further with COVID-19,[16] it was only a matter of time before the incumbent model was challenged, especially with a global journalism crisis characterized by steadily shrinking print readership, growing online competition, and the migration of advertisement revenue.[17] The crisis hit even the region's most established newspaper markets. Nowhere was this more acutely felt than in Lebanon, a regional publishing hub.[18] In 2016, the prestigious newspaper *Assafir*, a voice for Arab causes and home to many prominent leftist intellectuals and celebrated Arab writers since 1974, ceased its print and web presence, citing financial hardship.[19] Faced with mounting debts, its competitor *Al Anwar* (established in 1959) also ceased its print and online operations in 2018. Of the main newspapers with relative independence, *Annahar* (established in 1933) sought to diversify its offerings by including video content and a subscription model. Other publications did not fare any better. Despite its regional reach, the expatriate-focused *Daily Star* (established in 1952) suspended its print publication in 2020 and limited its operation to its online edition before closing entirely in 2021. Elsewhere in the region, newspapers' digital transformation has resulted in various funding models that favor more direct political patronage over traditional commercial media practices.

As incumbents struggle to adapt or exit, new players have entered the fray. With Web 2.0, an alternative form of journalism emerged—a form independent of state control and centered around a plethora of sites dedicated to the aggregation and production of news. These new forms of digital journalism are anchored in practices of citizen journalism that initially developed with blogging and are also rich in investigative content and multimedia storytelling. By favoring short-form content, relevant hyperlinks, user commentary, and social-media integration, digital journalism aims to attract the region's largest demographic groups (readers younger than thirty). Benefiting from a gray regulatory area, independent actors and political activists established news sites to report and comment on political, economic, and social conditions locally and regionally. For example, the Nawaat site started in 2004 as a collaborative blogging platform before transforming into a news-and-views site after the Tunisian revolution in 2011. In turn, Nawaat inspired Mamfakinch, a popular Moroccan blog site associated with the country's February 20 protests, and then transformed into an alternative-news site. Similarly, Mada Masr brought together former journalists with activists to launch a platform for independent journalism within Egypt's politically charged environment in 2013.

In recent years, alternative journalism has flourished across the region, benefiting from changes in laws on freedom of information (in countries such as Jordan, Morocco, and Lebanon), professional development and networking organizations (such as the Arab Reporters for Investigative Journalism), and foreign media assistance funding from European and American organizations (such as Internews and International Media Support). For such journalism, a digital presence offers production and distribution possibilities that speak to an audience of digital natives while being less hindered by editorial control and physical censorship than print journalism. While the digital turn ushered in a form of journalism characterized by real-time reporting of news produced and distributed online, the current iterations of citizen journalism are challenging legacy news media.

Not all digital journalism is alternative or anti-hegemonic. Many digital news ventures have kept to the region's traditional journalistic practices, including patronage and partisanship. On the one hand, their sources of funding (national or foreign) open them to criticism regarding their professional integrity. On the other hand, their search engine optimization (SEO) strategies have failed to create a true alternative to the mainstream. Instead, the plethora of news media sources invited competition from mainstream traditional media with established news credibility. For example, in Lebanon and Iraq, political parties operating radio, television, and print media have actively developed news aggregators that support self-serving political ideologies.

Unlike news sites that produce original content, web portals collect and distribute news stories, videos, and pictures from various sources, often in real time. Initially tied to websites, portals have migrated to the app environment over time while also diversifying their content (press releases, websites, etc.) and expanding their service offerings (email, web hosting, etc.). Some portals aggregate news stories from mainstream sources, while others favor partisan or biased original content. When it comes to specialized news portals, consider Zawya (part of Refinitiv Middle East) and AMEinfo.com (owned by Mediaquest Corporation, a publisher of specialized magazines). Established in 2000, Zawya is a source of business news and analysis about regional and global markets, while AMEinfo.com (2003) started hosting press releases in English and Arabic before developing its own news stories and analyses. Whereas Zawya operates as a freemium service, AMEinfo.com is supported by advertising. With these portals, information became a commodity whose function is to enable access to a range of economic data about the Middle East's emerging markets. In a region where reliable information is often scarce, controlled, or inaccessible, such web portals have become valuable sources of information about various economic sectors.

Initiatives such as these build on a history of experimentation with the development of digital services. Among these is Maktoob, which serves as an early example of the entrepreneurial possibilities the digital turn opened for the region.

Founded in 1998, Maktoob (Letter) was a trailblazer in the internet sector. Incubated in Jordan and then operating in Dubai, Maktoob was the brainchild of Samih Toukan and Hussam Khoury, who were part of an early generation of Jordanian tech enthusiasts who benefited from the country's political, economic, educational, and cultural climate to offer digital solutions and innovations. Unlike existing webmail services, Maktoob initially targeted the region by uniquely providing its users with Arabic support and by introducing a virtual keyboard and then a range of content channels and services (such as chatting) for which there was no Arabic interface. Building on its growing user base, Maktoob transformed into a portal and adopted a dual strategy of internal development and acquisition, which yielded Tahadi (MMO/MMORPG games), Araby (search engine), Sukar (private online shopping), and Maktoob Research (online research service). As a portal, it secured content in the form of Maktoob blogs, launched in 2005, to serve its then 4 million users.[20] To generate revenue, Maktoob also developed content-sharing agreements with various regional and international media companies and partnered with Beirut-based ARABvertising.net, a banner advertising network.[21] By 2005, it acquired Strategy.com to manage media and advertising content and services.[22] It also developed Onwani (My Address) as a web-hosting and domain-registration service, and CASHU to ensure electronic payments to its paid services. Maktoob's pioneering activities in a nascent sector allowed for much experimentation, adaptation, and innovation.

Maktoob's success led it to be a part of regional and then global capital markets. At first, it lured Abraaj Capital, a UAE-based private equity firm, to purchase 40% of its shares in a USD 5.2 million buyout deal in 2005. The portal was then redesigned, offering a free and unlimited mailbox capacity, a news section including analysis, a dedicated women's section, and an upgraded blog section. With Abraaj Capital, Maktoob also developed management and corporate competencies that positioned it well to navigate an uncharted territory for regional startups. Between 2005 and 2007, Maktoob took up majority stakes in the popular sports news portal Sport4ever.com and acquired the online shopping site Adabwafan.com in partnership with ARAMEX International.[23] It also strategically acquired the UAE-based stock market and business portal Uaesm.com and the Saudi-based women's site AlFrasha.com. Such a diverse and attractive portfolio made Maktoob the most-visited website in the Arab world and the 102nd most-visited website globally.[24] By 2007, Abraaj Capital sold its profitable shares to Tiger Global Management, a US-based firm investing in global tech industries. Over the next two years, Maktoob consolidated its assets and continued to grow, achieving 16.5 million unique users (one in three online people in the region).[25] Maktoob became a wholly owned subsidiary of Yahoo! in 2009. The estimated USD 164 million deal excluded the remaining Maktoob Group companies—including Souq.com, CASHU.com, Araby.com, and Tahadi.com—which continued to operate under a new entity known as Jabbar Internet Group.

As one of the most significant acquisitions in the region, Maktoob opened the door for local internet companies to play on the world stage. Perhaps its most enduring legacy lay in its early realization that digital-only content and services can be profitable in a region still holding on to traditional media. Despite this burgeoning and active sector, Maktoob's success as a portal has not been replicated, and the users it commanded have since been fragmented and incorporated into global platforms.

A Booming Gaming Sector

Despite rampant piracy, the Middle East (or at least its wealthier states) is considered a lucrative market for video games, due in part to its young demographics and spending power. The MENA's average revenue per user (ARPU) is among the highest globally at USD 181, compared with China's USD 48.[26] In 2021, the video games market in the Middle East and North Africa reached a value of USD 3.12 billion and is projected to reach USD 5.4 billion by 2027.[27] The largest video game market in the region is Saudi Arabia, estimated at USD 680 million, followed by Iran at USD 431 million and UAE at USD 280 million. Estimates place the region's cumulative annual growth rate (CAGR) revenue between 2019 and 2024 at 8.1%, compared with a global rate of 6.4%.[28] The region's potential has garnered international interest with promotional campaigns and activities, including the localization of games (e.g., Ubisoft), assigned servers for the region (e.g., EA Games, Blizzard Entertainment), and dedicated social-media channels addressing regional audiences in their language (e.g., Ayoub6669 and KhaleDQ84EveR). The popularity of e-sports—a growing subsector focused on organized sporting competitions for multiplayer video games—has further energized the regional games market and raised the stakes. As a result, the gaming industry and e-sports overlap and compete over investments, state support, industry recognition, and target consumers. Yet the region's gaming strength remains constrained by economic and political factors.

At its core, the gaming industry includes hardware and software producers and game developers, publishers, and distributors. As early as the 1980s, the software development company Sakhr assisted the localization of gaming hardware and software. It introduced an Arabic version of Microsoft's MSX computers, which acted as video game consoles complete with TV connection, cartridge slots, controllers, and an Arabic keyboard. Sakhr also developed educational games and partnered with Japanese developers such as Konami to release Arabic versions of their games. Among Sakhr's software engineering feats is its localization of *Captain Tsubasa Vol. II* (1990), which was very popular across the Arab world. The restructuring Sakhr underwent after its move to Egypt in the mid-1990s, though, led it to abandon its hardware operations and refocus its software development on Arabic-language products and business solutions. That decision, in turn, was a reaction to growing competition from global hardware developers such as Nintendo and Sega, the rampant piracy of video games, and concerns over censorship of violent titles.

The waning interest in hardware and software development in the 2000s corresponded to growing activities in developing, publishing, and distributing PC and mobile games. Sony's release of *This Is Football 2004*, which featured regional clubs, inaugurated a new era of video games in the region. Other producers, such as EA, Konami, Ubisoft, and Tencent Games, also localized products, and the latter two even established regional offices. What started as a basic translation of menus and instructions became transliteration of plots, commentary, and local features. Still, the localization of international games posed a challenge because of difficulties stemming from the complexity and structure of the Arabic language and the need to capture cultural nuances and respect local sensitivities.[29] This was evident in the gaming community's reaction to issues of prejudice against and misrepresentations of Arabic and Islamic cultures in big-budget games, as was the case with mistaking Arabic for Urdu in *Call of Duty: Modern Warfare 2* (2009) or treating the region as an apocalyptic wasteland in *Spec Ops: The Line* (2012).[30] Problematic depictions such as these prompted independent and state-supported developers in the region to develop identity-centered or ideologically laden video games. Early attempts to develop indigenous games include the Syrian Dar Al Fikr, which released *Tahta el Ramad* (*Under Ash*, 2002), while the Central Internet Bureau of Lebanon's Hezbollah launched *Al Quwwat al Khassa* (*Special Forces*, 2003). Both of these releases are fighting games revolving around missions in which the player is an Arab Muslim hero, instead of assuming the stereotypical role of terrorist or villain. This type of political (counter-)propaganda game was a response to games such as *Delta Force* (1998) and *America's Army* (2002), which negatively portrayed Arabs and Muslims.[31]

Beyond their cultural significance, games constituted a promising business sector. Eyeing the economic potential of the gaming industry, several governments developed programs and launched initiatives to promote education and innovation. For example, Bahrain supported the launch of Bahrain Polytechnic (2008), an institution offering courses in game development, and Unreal Bahrain (2017), a community for developers. But success on this front has been uneven. Game development and publishing have been concentrated in Jordan, Egypt, and Saudi Arabia, with only a few studios operating elsewhere in the region. The evolution of these scattered centers of production parallels that of the gaming industry itself. The introduction of the internet gradually shifted young people's interest from PC and console games to online gaming, which often involved playing in groups at local area network (LAN) centers operating as internet cafés. In the 2000s, with the introduction of connected consoles and massively multiplayer online (MMO) games such as *World of Warcraft*, transnational online gaming became popular in the region.[32] By 2007, PC and console games started to shift toward mobile gaming applications, reaching a peak with Pokémon in 2016. The introduction of 5G has allowed virtual reality (VR) and cloud gaming to gain ground, particularly in the Gulf. Changes in the development and publishing of games went hand in hand with distribution channels across the region shifting from brick-and-mortar stores such as GameStop to online stores of tech giants such as Apple and Google. Today the region represents the fastest-growing online gaming population globally, at 25% year-over-year growth, and includes one of the youngest demographics of gamers anywhere.[33]

The introduction of e-sports (and its associated gaming arenas) reveals the industry's popularity, depth, and scope and accentuates the potential for profitability.[34] As one of the fastest-growing sectors of the gaming industry, e-sports refers to the professionalization of games such as *Fortnite*, *League of Legends*, and *Call of Duty* and also to gaming competitions, including the League of Legends World Championship, Dubai's Esports Festival, and Saudi's Gamers8, in which participants compete in teams, either in their homes or in large arenas. Although concentrated in the Gulf region, the increase in e-sports teams has given rise to dedicated leagues with a broad international following. Similarly, Saudi Mosaad "Msdossary" Al Dossary, who joined Shawn "Jay-Z" Carter's Roc Nation Sports, is the second player from Saudi Arabia to win the FIFA eWorld Cup and was named the e-sports Console Player of the Year in 2018.[35] With their knowledge of multiple languages, Arab game players and teams (such as Nasr Esports and Yalla Esports) can navigate both regional and global markets, making them attractive to foreign teams and international brands. Competitions are also profitable for top-ranked players, including Team Liquid players such as Lebanese "GH" Merhej and the Jordanian-Polish star Amer "Miracle" Al-Barkawi, the latter of whom earned nearly USD 3.2 million in thirty-six tournaments to rank eighth in earnings worldwide.[36]

In addition to events, leagues, competitions, and content, e-sports owe their growth to media exposure and livestreaming platforms (e.g., Twitch). Events designed for gaming arenas are streamed to virtual audiences, and leagues and players are represented by PR and communications companies dedicated to digital platforms (e.g., Swipeleft). Millennium Arabia, part of Webedia Arabia, which has a fan base of more than 50 million Arabic speakers, produces Hala Gamers (Welcome Gamers), which features interviews, gameplay moments, reports, tips, and tricks for the e-sports community.[37] Supporting these developments is an interlocked gaming environment. Participation in the Arabic-language community on the Twitch platform, which enables users to broadcast their gameplay live, has increased dramatically, as has YouTube viewership of such events. Saudi Telecom introduced dedicated servers for specific games, while Kuwaiti Zain launched a platform, Zain Esports, to develop tournaments and events. In 2019, Dubai-based W Ventures partnered with RedPeg to invest USD 50 million in the regional gaming ecosystem.[38] This increased professionalization has also attracted local and global partnerships to invest in the regional expansion of the e-sports ecosystem.

Though its global integration has increased, the gaming industry in the region remains culturally and linguistically fragmented and reflects both geopolitical dispersions and infrastructural impediments. Many would-be users cannot access the games, and those who can have a limited choice when it comes to games in local dialects. Even so, culturally attuned gaming practices are typically not reflected in games developed outside the region. The lack of both availability and reliability of regional servers poses a critical infrastructural challenge. With few exceptions, such as Bahrain's and the UAE's Amazon Web Services, players in the Gulf region are easily connected to Asian servers, while those in the Levant and North Africa connect to European servers. The latter are prone to latency, which interferes with winning decisions and negatively affects the game experience. Equally significant is the economic divide in the adoption of games and the development of the industry. In the Levant and North Africa, freemium PC players tend to be more dominant than the costlier consoles widely adopted in the Gulf. Such divides affect the popularity of games (e.g., *League of Legends* vs. *Fortnite*) and the level of government support, with the Gulf leading the way in organizing and promoting game development and e-sports championships. Compounding these difficulties are concerns over the absence of a regulatory framework to handle issues related to game exploitations for money laundering, the practice of bribery, and—perhaps more important—concerns over gambling, which is religiously forbidden and legally banned.[39] Interestingly, even conservative countries in the region have capitalized on the popularity of these games, as in the instance of the charity tournament organized by the Saudi Arabian Federation for Electronic and Intellectual Sports (SAFEIS) in 2020, the proceeds of which funded campaigns and efforts to help slow the spread of COVID-19.[40] Just as with team sports, more states are extending their reach to support e-sports and organize the gaming sector in an attempt to reap political, economic, and cultural rewards.

The emphasis on the exhibition side of the ecosystem—characterized by the building of venues, ownership of teams, recruitment of players, and organization of leagues and tournaments—may come at the expense of investments in game development itself and, more broadly, the local knowledge economy. Effectively, longer-term state and market investments in innovation are being sidetracked by short-term rewards of championships.

Into the Streaming Era

The digital turn did not have a uniform effect. Whereas many economic incumbents continued to do what they had always done (capitalize on market share and the established ecosystem of legacy media), a handful of disruptive ventures pursued a digital-first strategy that helped them carve out a space in a reconfigured media environment.

Within this emerging video-streaming environment, the Saudi-owned Shahid (Watch) has been a trailblazer owing to its synergies with the region's most prominent television network, MBC Group, and its experience with the market since 2008. Prompted by the growing appeal of pirated content on DVDs and YouTube, MBC decided to offer its *musalsalat* (TV drama series) and comedy series on a dedicated "catch-up" platform, Shahid, originally free of charge. It became a hit in the region and across the diaspora, encouraging a redesign of the platform and the addition of more than two hundred unique titles in 2011.[41] Over the next ten years, Shahid increased its viewership through distribution partnerships with international networks (e.g., US Sling and DISH) and regional telecom operators (e.g., Etisalat and Zain). MBC invested USD 1.3 billion in acquiring and producing 46,000 hours of Arabic entertainment during this growth phase.[42] The network upgraded Shahid into the subscription video-on-demand (SVOD) model with digital-first local offerings and exclusive content from Disney, Fox, and ABC Studios.[43] By 2020, the rebranded and relaunched Shahid became central to MBC's long-term strategy—a recognized brand with an extensive archive, rights, content productions, and long-established corporate relationships. With the Saudi government now owning 60% of MBC Group, Shahid stands to offer a state-sanctioned platform that could regionally compete against streaming platforms such as Netflix.[44]

This success comes with trade-offs. The survival of MBC Group's other media assets could be in jeopardy. For one, the revenue model of SVOD remains uncertain, considering the limited commitment to Shahid VIP (the service's subscription arm) and the insufficient revenues of digital advertising. Another trade-off is that the increased competition between streaming platforms diverted production budgets to scripted programs and away from nonfiction shows, mainly live TV, which still enjoys popularity with audiences and advertisers. The coexistence of traditional broadcast with streaming services, as in the case of the broadcast channels and Shahid, suggests that a complete digital transformation of MBC may signal the demise of the satellite broadcasts upon which it has thrived all along.

MBC Group's initial experimentation with Shahid may prove to be a harbinger of the future for the region's television industries. The aftershocks of the Arab uprisings and the popularity of social media have dealt a blow to satellite television's popularity. Streaming poses a serious challenge to the future of satellite television beyond news and sports. At the same time, the pay-TV satellite model is being challenged by competition from local and global streaming platforms. Although Shahid is partially supported by the Saudi kingdom, its ability to develop independent revenue models reveals the potential viability of commercially oriented digital media. While COVID-19 expanded digital media adoption and increased demand for original content, it remains to be seen whether such growth is sustainable or likely to succumb to the forces of churn, namely customers canceling their services when they exhaust new offerings.

Ongoing disruptions in the music industry offer another instance of imitation and innovation in the knowledge economy. The digital turn in music consumption in the region presents both continuities of music piracy and changes with the advent of streaming. While piracy has plagued the regional music industry ever since the arrival of cassette tapes, the ability to digitally copy or download music has reinforced an informal economy centered around the sale of CDs and flash drives of pirated music; targeting both regional and international music and video content, piracy benefits from peer-to-peer (P2P) file-sharing sites as well as lax copyright laws. The advent of streaming forced radio stations to transform their production, make their broadcasts available online, and actively engage their listeners on social media. Such responses broadened their geographic reach and demographic sway. Although technically this change entailed little more than livestreaming their broadcast signals, it gradually energized the development of apps and exclusive digital content. It was particularly popular among the diaspora, with several apps, such as Radio Arabic, offering streaming access to hundreds of regional stations.

Nowhere is the effect of such disruptive technology more patent than in the case of Anghami (My Tunes).[45] Initially based in Beirut, Anghami was designed to offer music compression compatible with the region's limited fixed and mobile internet infrastructure. It provided a freemium model that leveraged its connections with mobile networks to offer subscription options with multiple pricing tiers. With its ad-supported version reaching more than 13 million people, Anghami has developed into a media company focused on production (including music, podcasts, and events).[46] Streaming platforms such as Deezer and Spotify also sought to expand in the region and to localize their playlists and Arabic interface with local teams. Deezer, in particular, emerged as a critical player in the region's growing digital music industry when it attracted the direct investment of Saudi mogul Alwaleed Bin Talal and his record label (the region's largest), Rotana, in 2018. Between 2018 and 2022, Deezer boasted exclusive access to Rotana, before the latter was signed back to Anghami.[47] From a consumer's perspective, the difference between these streaming platforms is less about price than user experience and exclusive content, including a reliable and rich service.

Within audio streaming, the podcasting scene is characterized by disorganization, limited commercial or consumer awareness, and self- or government censorship. Although podcasting started in 2006, Arabic podcasts appeared late, but they grew quickly and massively, from three hundred in 2018 to more than one thousand in 2021.[48] Despite attempts at self-organization such as the Middle East Podcast Forum (established in 2008), the podcast scene is controlled by both commercially oriented and nonprofit networks such as Kerning Cultures,

Mstdfr podcasts, House Zofi podcast entertainment network, Finyal Media, Sowt, and Amaeya Media. Interestingly, these networks produce shows in English and Arabic with local and regional guests, though localized content is more prevalent, as in the case of the Jeddah-based podcast network Mstdfr. With 20% of women in Saudi Arabia listening to podcasts at least once a week, there is a growing demand for podcasts featuring strong, inspiring women.[49] Although technology-driven podcasts are the most popular, music, comedy, news, sports, and education are increasingly strong niches. Branching out from traditional offerings, Kitab Sawti offers both podcasts and Arabic audiobooks. Established by Swedish entrepreneurs in 2016, Kitab Sawti was acquired by the Stockholm-based Storytel before it relocated to Dubai,[50] yet such demand for local content did not translate into significant advertising interest or commercial exploitation. To broaden podcast appeal, collectives and networks such as Jawla and Zamakan have been formed to curate Arabic podcasts and make them available on multiple platforms, including Apple, Google, Anghami, Deezer, and Spotify. Despite its growing popularity, podcasting continues to operate within the parameters of a regional media culture that tends to adopt self-censorship to preempt heavier-handed state censorship. At the same time, podcasts are considered more private, personal media and therefore escape the scrutiny of public mass media.

Together, these developments suggest that the advent of streaming has accentuated the tension between an aging traditional broadcasting system whose constitutive elements operate in silos and a digital media system in which the promises of streaming remain unfulfilled. Many traditional media production and distribution companies have not capitalized on the potential of the digital or remain largely unprepared to harness its advantages. The production, distribution, and exhibition cycle is beholden to interests that often treat the digital as more of a threat than an opportunity. In contrast, an expanding range of local and international audio- and video-streaming platforms are targeting broad demographic groups and, in the process, forming new media-consumption habits and accommodating a borderless audience. While the primary focus is on developing exhibition platforms within existing infrastructural, economic, and legal limitations, audio and video streamers are keen on developing and producing content with local and global appeal.

Whether the speed and velocity of change in the advertising industry will encourage or hinder streaming platforms will depend on a host of factors. In the meantime, streaming will still have to contend with other digital platforms vying for consumers' leisure time, including social-media apps. Streaming may have broken the monopoly of broadcast over audio and video content, but it has yet to satisfy a demanding audience. After all, streaming media industries are superimposed over pre-streaming industries, thus challenging the old order without necessarily effacing it.

Evolving Digital Media Industries

Underpinning the region's burgeoning tech industry is a developing media eco-system characterized by new processes, practices, and products. This ecosystem is global by design but local by practice. It is integrated into global technological and financial structures while catering to local or regional needs and tastes. It revolves around enterprising individuals animated more by "grand ideas" than by politi-cal and economic motivations. It involves traditional media players and digital natives who coexist within a market in constant flux, with evolving processes and practices that manifest themselves around the three areas of production, distribu-tion, and exhibition of digital content. In some ways, then, this nascent ecosys-tem reinforces cultural, political, and economic factors associated with traditional media industries while simultaneously unsettling an established ecosystem built around economic and political networks whose stakeholders include the state and its proxies.[51]

Digital content—audio, visual, and textual—is increasingly ubiquitous and challenges traditional media's popularity, genres, aesthetics, and programming. Creators rely on grants, advertising revenues, subscriptions, and other arrange-ments to survive (and sometimes thrive). Both conventional and digital-native content developers are involved in repackaging or repurposing content. While MBC Group made its content available on its Shahid streaming service, its com-petitors acquired content from established suppliers. New digital players intrinsi-cally adopt corporate convergence and synergistic practices and, in the process, create relationships that are at once symbiotic and interdependent. Consider Webedia Arabia, one of the largest Arabic networks, which commands a cross-platform audience of more than 50 million people. As the regional affiliate of the French-based Webedia since 2018, this network was born out of the merger of Diwanee, UTURN Entertainment, Fullstop Creatives, and Made in Saudi Films.

Despite such successes, the region's development of original digital content continues to suffer from inequitable monetization, deficient regulation, and uneven digital access and literacies. Over the past decade, Arabic digital content has consistently made up 3% of the total global internet content.[52] There is also a sharp revenue gap between legacy content producers and digital-native content creators. For the former, digital offerings constitute an added value and an addi-tional revenue stream. For the latter, the digital is a precarious lifeline that depends on attracting followers, advertising revenue, or financial support that is particu-larly threatened by piracy (which also afflicts legacy providers). Some countries have taken measures to counter piracy in response. Egypt forced a shutdown of websites that were illegally streaming local movies and in 2019 set up the more affordable (and presumably government-run) site Watch iT.[53] Nevertheless, anti-piracy laws continue to be disregarded, as evidenced by mirror websites such as

Egynow, Koora Live, and Yalla Goal, which offer pirated streaming to local and international soccer games, including the FIFA World Cup 2022.

Traditionally considered the infrastructure of digital media economies, telecoms ensure the digital distribution of content through mobile and fixed internet despite varying levels of e-readiness. Telecoms have also taken on new roles as content acquisition or development players. For example, Saudi Telecommunication Company (STC) acquired partial ownership of Intigral—a digital sports and media company, which supplies Jawwy as STC's on-demand service. To boost demand for traffic, telecoms created initiatives such as tie-in promotional campaigns offering free access to digital content providers. For instance, the streaming service StarzPlay Arabia partnered with Ooredoo to bundle free subscriptions with specific data packages. Telecoms also offered spaces for apps to interact with consumers. In a market with limited credit-card penetration but high mobile ownership, telecoms deploy their billing system to collect dues on behalf of app subscriptions. In the case of the music platform Anghami, recourse to the telecoms as payment gateways was a key strategy in increasing its subscription base. Add-on services like these turned telecoms into integrated digital service providers (IDSPs) operating as platforms for their services and those of other stakeholders within an emerging ecosystem. The centrality of their operations to the region's evolving digital media industries raises questions about net neutrality and their role in content censorship and surveillance. The debate over net neutrality is gaining momentum as consumers, internet activists, and market forces become increasingly aware of its repercussions. In some countries, regulatory bodies are using the principle of net neutrality to protect consumers and safeguard competition. Tunisia's licensing of telecom operators, for example, guarantees consumers access to all types of connections including VoIP. In other countries, a series of net-neutrality consultations have begun in an effort to ensure that adequate policy frameworks are adopted (as in the case of Saudi Arabia's Communications and Information Technology Commission).

Other stakeholders in the ecosystem focus on content exhibition through app development, design, and marketing. Following Apple's successful marketing campaign "There's an app for that" (2009), the region's ICT community heeded the call. With apps becoming widely used even in aspiring digital economies, online businesses and service providers alike have invested in cross-platform capabilities, with many maintaining responsive and mobile websites while developing specific apps. From business and government e-services to social-media and chat applications, everyday uses of apps are expanding. The value of the MENA mobile apps market is estimated to have grown from USD 762 million in 2014 to USD 1.233 billion in 2019.[54] Bandwidth-hungry apps and services are expected to drive a regional surge of 430% in data consumption between 2021 and 2027.[55] Beyond their role in productivity and communication, apps play a significant role as exhibitors of digital content. Offering information as a service, several apps combine the marketing of goods and services with entertainment and news content. The UAE-based health platform Altibbi (The Medical), an app that operates on the freemium model, offers 24/7 telehealth service and access to medical videos and articles in Arabic.

Apps provide opportunities for producers to reach users beyond the physical and geographic limitations of other distribution channels. As expected, apps have become the prime gateway to digital content not only on mobile phones but on set-top boxes, smart TVs, and game consoles. Regional media companies such as OSN's streaming platform, OSN+, combined access to select HBO and Paramount+ content, and beIN's TOD platform blended the network's multiple linear sports channels with a large catalog of entertainment content, while MBC partnered with Samsung to add a Shahid button on TV remote controls designed for the region. To support the promotional efforts of regionally developed apps, a range of design and marketing companies have emerged across the region. The development, design, and marketing of apps have become a constant tech exhibition feature, most prominently at regional venues such as GITEX, and a central component of the region's startup culture.

In keeping with the view that such transformations are evolutionary, not revolutionary, tensions between the upstream (development/production) and the downstream (distribution/exhibition) are two factors that delimit this emerging ecosystem.[56] Although the downstream is increasingly dominant, its domination remains incomplete. Traditional media has retained control over content and can still muster the clout and financing to withstand or co-opt cash-strapped new entrants. Further complicating this regional ecosystem is the proliferation of nontraditional content (e.g., YouTube video channels and other social-media content), often produced by digital natives who are better positioned to profit from the "attention economy,"[57] which increasingly grabs audiences' engagement. In addition, the time spent consuming digital content is shortened as apps have also transformed the way we purchase products and services. These trends elucidate the impact of the digital turn on consumption patterns and on how services (including media content) and goods are exhibited and traded. Significantly, telecoms and apps are more than points of access to digital content; they are essential to a burgeoning tech economy, which is the focus of the next chapter.

Chapter 11

Emerging Digital Economies

No less important than the uneven changes in the digital cultural industries are the peculiar trajectories of digital economies. Of particular interest is how, with their tangible and intangible assets, digital economies emerge as the harbingers of wider changes to business practices and ecosystems and as enticing sources for new wealth creation in the region. Three cases of trailblazing ventures, each representing a sector and creating a "template" for other startups in the region, are particularly interesting examples in this regard: the shopping platform Souq, the ride-hailing app Careem, and the music-streaming platform Anghami. Despite these ventures' success, the digital economy in the region remains nascent. As some of the inherent contradictions associated with the introduction of the Internet of Things (IoT), artificial intelligence (AI), and cloud computing suggest, the nature of this emerging economy is intricate, its supporting ecosystem developing, and its trajectory defined by both excitement and apprehension. While the digital represents the next frontier in the region's economy, its development is neither uniform nor analogous to more established digital economies associated with the network society. The resulting regional digital economies are partly shaped by temporal and spatial disjunctures, partly by the pace and velocity of the region's digital turn. Against that backdrop, discourses that elevate the region to be "the next Silicon Valley" call for a critical analysis that reveals how such depictions of the Middle East's digital turn have become so common as to be virtually meaningless.

Fledgling E-Commerce Platforms

The adoption of ICTs has fueled the development of e-commerce, especially within affluent states such as Saudi Arabia and the UAE. Since 2014, e-commerce in the MENA region has been growing by 25% yearly, and its value is expected to exceed USD 50 billion in 2025.[1] In 2021, Saudi Arabia had more than 36,000

The Digital Double Bind. Mohamed Zayani and Joe F. Khalil, Oxford University Press. © Oxford University Press 2024.
DOI: 10.1093/oso/9780197508626.003.0011

registered online stores and platforms, up from 25,105 in 2019, with a combined market value of approximately USD 10 billion.[2] In countries such as Jordan, where no tariffs are levied on e-transactions related to imported goods by individual consumers, e-commerce has flourished.[3] Out of roughly 2.6 million internet users in Kuwait, 2.4 million shop online in an e-commerce market whose scale is estimated at USD 1 billion.[4] Fast-growing business structures such as m-commerce (mobile commerce) and s-commerce (social commerce) reveal new practices and dispositions, with more users being drawn to e-commerce platforms and availing themselves of wider choices from the convenience of home.

To be sure, the total volume of e-commerce remains relatively small. Even in the region's most active market, the UAE, e-commerce accounted for a mere 4% of all retail sales in 2019.[5] In 2020, it jumped 53% to a share of 10% of all retail sales, owing partly to COVID-19 restrictions and the various e-shopping platforms developed in response to lockdowns.[6] Fears over the security of online payments and internet fraud remain prevalent, spurring alternative payment methods such as cash on delivery (COD) and bill presentment. In some instances, home-grown click-and-mortar companies and e-businesses have adopted online payment methods that rely on bank-sponsored, internet-only credit cards or prepaid options such as CASHU.[7] Although there is steady overall growth in online transactions, cash remains the preferred means of payment in the region, even in Gulf countries that hold the highest per capita average of devices and connections.[8] In other countries, supporting services, such as payment systems, credit-card penetration rates, and postal services, have not kept up with e-commerce development. Although many Arab countries have introduced electronic-commerce legislation, in most cases, the existing applicable laws that regulate this sector, including electronic signature, are not fully developed, and most governments do not actively promote electronic trade.

Although online shopping activities may not lead to actual online purchases, they nevertheless have an impact on other—and broader—related developments. Sharing shopping experiences with other users, chatting about purchasing decisions, soliciting consumer input, and comparing prices form an e-commerce lifestyle even when customers eventually buy offline. Thus, offline shopping is itself getting a boost from online shopping activities. It is common for consumers who are hesitant to buy products online, or those who cherish haggling in the souk or bazaar, to engage in hybrid shopping activities that start online and end offline, in brick-and-mortar stores or other face-to-face shopping experiences. In contrast, when it comes to travel services, more consumers in the Gulf region are predisposed to book their trips online than through a travel agency.[9]

The appeal of online shopping is reshaping the relationship between businesses and consumers. Increasingly, retailers are cultivating an online presence and relying on social-media advertising to reach consumers and data analytics to optimize advertising campaigns. More brands are also resorting to content creators and social influencers with marketing prowess and large numbers of followers on social media to promote their products.[10] Companies such as the Dubai-based, Saudi-owned ITCAN help address the growing need for digital marketing services. The flourishing of business-to-customer (B2C) e-commerce is also driving the growth of other related services, including expansion in express-logistics operations. The potential of e-commerce in the region is most evinced by new ventures such as CommerCity—a Dubai-initiated, USD 733 million free zone designed to attract FDI and meet projected e-commerce needs in areas such as logistical support, electronic payment, and IT solutions.[11]

Despite these initiatives, e-commerce development is hampered by multiple deficiencies and inhibitors. To start with, the e-commerce sector is fragmented. It would be misleading to consider the growth of e-commerce in affluent states with relatively high levels of IT readiness as representative of the entire Middle East. According to the B2C E-Commerce Index 2020, the MENA region is marked by significant gaps in IT readiness, with Gulf countries consistently (and, in some cases, significantly) outranking non-Gulf countries: UAE (37), Saudi Arabia (49), Qatar (50), Oman (54), Kuwait (58), Lebanon (64), Bahrain (66), Jordan (76), Tunisia (77), Libya (85), Morocco (95), and Syria (133).[12] These disparate rankings reflect infrastructural limitations, logistical challenges, limited consumer acceptance, and inadequate legal frameworks.

Consumers are also reluctant to embrace e-commerce because of ecosystem considerations. Their concerns range from the privacy of their personal information to the security of online transactions and the level of comfort with electronic payment. Generally, Middle Eastern societies value social and business ties rooted in face-to-face communication, verbal interaction, price negotiation, personal relationships, and the building of trust between parties.[13] These societies tend to be cash-oriented,[14] slowing the adoption of e-commerce. The sector's development also faces logistical hurdles, from the unreliability of delivery services to the lack of a favorable online environment. In some Middle Eastern countries, central banks restrict sending funds abroad, which limits online trade across borders.[15] In other cases, add-on fees, including shipping, logistics, and customs tolls, which affect competition with traditional retailers, disincentivize potential online customers.[16] E-commerce also competes with the social environment in which visiting sprawling shopping centers and luxurious malls (an established business sector with high financial stakes for local investors) is a favorite pastime.[17]

From Tech Tinkerers to Digital Sectors

In the Middle East, as elsewhere, digital innovation is associated with tech tinkerers who build new tools, reconfigure existing practices, and offer solutions to problems. In their relentless tinkering, whether by chance or by design, these individuals frequently become disruptors.[18] In interview after interview, these tech enthusiasts express a sense of shared motivation to address the region's endemic problems and be part of its techno-futures.[19] Equipped with computer skills, some of these tinkerers became digital entrepreneurs, creating opportunities through the initiation, financing, and implementation of ICT-driven solutions. Together they represent a strong network of individuals willing to explore new pathways for innovation—not stigmatized by the failures of modernization the region previously experienced.

The call of entrepreneurship does not appeal only to those with digital skills and expertise. Over the past two decades or so, ICTs have attracted a broad spectrum of players, including startup entrepreneurs focused on transforming ideas into viable digital solutions; not-for-profit entrepreneurs who take on social, cultural, or environmental issues; and others. The pathways for startup entrepreneurs vary, from ICT developers who build products and offer services to digital content producers. The case of Maktoob illustrates how technical ingenuity and business initiatives combine to produce a successful startup. Some entrepreneurs tend to align their platforms with state, philanthropy, or corporate initiatives for social responsibility. For example, mobile applications are transforming traditional charity activities with popular applications such as Megakheir (Egypt), Arzaq (Saudi Arabia), and Sada9a (Morocco). Startups such as the Cairo-based platform MoneyFellows have even digitized the traditional money-based social circles (known as *gam'eya*) common in Egypt.

Geographically, digital entrepreneurship can be mapped along the three distinct geopolitical regions: North Africa, the Levant and Egypt, and the Gulf. While making significant strides in the digital economy, North Africa supplies more digital labor than digital entrepreneurship. The mismatch between the subregion's relatively high educational status and its less developed digital industries causes a brain drain primarily flowing toward Europe and the Gulf. While Morocco has actively promoted digital social entrepreneurship, Tunisia passed the Startup Act to encourage the emergence of the local ecosystem. In the Levant, a cottage industry has developed with limited support from governments, nonprofit organizations, and private investors. For instance, in Palestine and Syria, a gaming industry has emerged in which small studios take the lead on development and marketing. In Lebanon, the Central Bank introduced a USD 600 million fund to support startups, and the private sector has developed initiatives such as Beirut Angels to increase information sharing among investors—though these initiatives have been stalled since 2018, when the financial crisis hit the country. Similarly, Egypt and Jordan have created enterprise-incubation schemes in software development, though admittedly these successful initiatives remain isolated cases.[20] In all these instances, governments have invested in selected segments of the economy while other key economic sectors are largely unaffected by the knowledge economy. It remains to be seen whether these tech sectors can support further development to stimulate job creation for the region's sizable younger generation.

The Gulf region has gone a long way toward institutionalizing digital entrepreneurship by providing infrastructural, logistical, regulatory, and financial support. While the UAE leads the charge with the pace and level of digital entrepreneurship, other Gulf countries, particularly Saudi Arabia and Qatar, have stepped up their entrepreneurial efforts, including supporting a range of high-tech industries. Since the 1980s, Kuwait played a pioneering role with investments in computer and software products before the UAE emerged as a major regional investor, extending its support to semiconductor and space technology.[21] By instituting regulatory frameworks for e-commerce, the Gulf has begun to address data piracy and privacy issues. E-government services have made establishing a business more cost-effective and streamlined, while institutional assistance in navigating regulatory compliance requirements and financing opportunities have made transitioning to the digital economy seamless. The Gulf region has also made digitalization a cornerstone of development plans. With the announcement of its first Information and Communications Technology Strategy in 1999, Dubai began its journey toward digital transformation with the successive launches of Dubai Internet City (DIC, 2000), Dubai e-government (2005), and Smart Dubai (2014), among other projects. The national digital economy of the UAE is projected to experience a significant increase, rising from its value of USD 38 billion in 2023 to USD 140 billion by the year 2031.[22]

The role of DIC cannot be overstated. It was the region's first technology innovation zone with an integrated ecosystem for ICT industries, which proved to be an economic driver for startups. Capitalizing on Dubai's model of economic free zones, the launch of DIC attracted many regional and international companies to establish or relocate their operations there. As a special economic free zone, DIC offers licenses to foreign-owned ICT businesses and freelance contractors, along with an array of financial and regulatory incentives.[23] With companies such as Oracle and Microsoft setting up shop, DIC gradually became a hub for local, regional, and global ICT companies wanting to operate in the region. As ICT technologies got more integrated into converging telecommunications, media, and computer technologies, DIC became the anchor zone for other clusters, such as Dubai Media City (dedicated to content development and production) and Dubai Knowledge Village (focused on education and training).[24] Together these clusters helped build an integrated ecosystem for DIC's estimated 1,200 businesses, 24,000 professionals, and 100,000 freelancers.[25] Beyond these figures, DIC's ecosystem fosters collaboration across different sectors, including mobile companies, satellite providers, and content producers, as well as hardware, software, and applications industries. Among noteworthy initiatives is the launch of the Innovation Hub, which aims to bring together fintech and innovation communities and is part of efforts to broaden DIC's resident businesses to include global enterprises, such as the China-based video game publisher Tencent Games and the American multinational IT company Hewlett Packard Enterprise, alongside several small and medium-sized enterprises.[26] With this mix of local support, regional interest, and global connections, DIC emerged as an economic driver for startups eager to benefit from these partnerships and collaborations. Start-ups in Dubai witnessed a notable increase in collective funding, surpassing USD 2 billion in 2022, doubling the amount secured in 2021, and representing over 30 percent of funding rounds in the Middle East and North Africa region.[27]

Although DIC offers a blueprint for developing an ecosystem for innovation, differences in political systems and market structures may limit the ability of many Middle Eastern states to develop similar free-zone frameworks. The region's business environment has traditionally focused on natural resources and raw materials (e.g., oil and phosphate), human capital (e.g., skilled labor or professionals), and traditional industries (e.g., tourism or agriculture). The nature of the ecosystem required to foster a digital economy has forced governments to contemplate changing their familiar models, reckon with the risk of losing some control over the economy, and succumb to the lure of foreign investments. By establishing tailored investment schemes, governments—most notably in the Gulf—are accommodating a startup culture bound to disrupt existing modes of financing practiced in traditional economic sectors while simultaneously creating new synergies. The UAE's sovereign wealth fund, Mubadala, has added to its American and European startup investments a commitment to support Middle Eastern ones, setting up one fund with USD 250 million for startups located in the region and another USD 100 million for startups associated with Abu Dhabi's "global ecosystem."[28] Joining these funding venues are two talent-honing initiatives that are part of Twofour54, Abu Dhabi's media free economic zone: Creative Lab, for developing promising ideas and supporting creativity, and Apps Arabia, for transforming ideas into mobile applications. Such initiatives aim to develop local talent, attract foreign human capital, and spearhead the startup ecosystem.

Other countries in the Middle East have sought to employ similar strategies. Egypt has invested in initiatives that support an enabling ecosystem and foster tech innovation, making it the region's fastest-growing startup ecosystem and its second largest.[29] With the private sector taking a leadership role, workspaces (such as the GrEEK Campus) dedicated to technology and innovation offer startups room to connect and grow.[30] Similarly, Lebanon's private sector has stepped up to create coworking spaces, such as Beirut Digital District (BDD), that could foster an ecosystem in the absence of state support.[31] Elsewhere in the region, some countries are pushing for a regulatory overhaul to address entry and exit barriers for venture capital, company creation (or closure), bankruptcy, data privacy, and security regulation. The business community has yet to fully embrace the financing of digital entrepreneurship. This is particularly challenging for emerging economies where risk-averse local investors are reluctant to support startups and states are hindered by limited resources.

Despite these challenges, the startup ecosystem is gradually if unevenly institutionalizing, driven by the region's interest in diversifying its economies and leveraging traditional funding resources toward knowledge economies. The burgeoning startup culture is no longer dependent on local replications of emerging market trends, much less the result of individual tinkerers and isolated experimentations. The emergence of trailblazing companies has ushered in a new phase in which multiple stakeholders are driven by various, often divergent, interests. Since 2016, investments in MENA startups have consistently reached a yearly value of around USD 1 billion, compared with USD 15 million in 2009.[32] While this figure includes Turkey and Pakistan, the leading investment destinations are the UAE (by funding amounts), Egypt (by number of deals), and Saudi Arabia (by greatest percentage increase in funding).[33] In a pre-pandemic report, the leading countries in terms of investment deals were the UAE, Lebanon, Egypt, Saudi Arabia, and Jordan. Interestingly, the UAE also led in the value of investments, thanks to high-value deals such as Careem (2016–2018), Souq (2016), and StarzPlay Arabia (2017 and 2022).

The availability of regional corporate venture capital and the emergence of various incubators and accelerators have strengthened the startup ecosystem with possibilities for synergies, scaling, and attracting other investors, operational support, and a customer base. With forty-eight investors in MENA-based startups in 2019, Saudi Arabia is the most active regional investor.[34] Take, for instance, the Singapore-based Wego travel search engine, which attracted an investment of USD 12 million from Saudi-owned MBC Group. This synergy allowed Wego to tap into MBC Group's various digital platforms, capitalize on its local customer database, and benefit from its corporate alliances.[35] As part of its increased regional engagement, Google for Startups Accelerator Middle East and North Africa was launched in 2021. The first cohort of ten technology startups came from six Arab countries and is part of a more extensive Google program dedicated to the Middle East.[36]

Still, the region remains limited in public listings and initial public offerings (IPOs). Many startups either are dormant or end up prematurely exiting in direct equity sales to large, local, family-owned, regional, or (in some instances) multinational companies.[37] Cases include Thompson Reuters's acquisition of the business information portal Zawya (2012); Japan's Cookpad's purchase of the Lebanese culinary website Shahiya (2014); and the European food-delivery service Delivery Hero's acquisition of Kuwait's Talabat (2016). Regional and global capital tends to be apprehensive about operating in emerging markets, often for reasons associated with varying levels of transparency compounded by high levels of corruption. The unfolding dynamics of this ecosystem are connected to the region's overall (family) business environment, the type and level of investors, and the regulatory structure.[38]

Fortunately, there are promising developments nationally, regionally, and globally. Nationally, many countries in the region have embraced ICT policies and supplemented them with state financing. An investment community is developing within the banking industry with the help of established digital entrepreneurs. While primarily offering seed investment and acting as mentors, incubators, or accelerators, this community provides essential expertise and experience for startups. The region already has several "serial entrepreneurs" who have gone on to launch new startups in the hope of replicating their initial success. Finally, digital entrepreneurs are intrinsically "global" and can grow and scale across borders. An unprecedented global movement of labor and capital animates the digital Middle East, with many regional cities becoming international hubs for business. At the same time, the decentralization of jobs and the proliferation of tech poles (from India to Malaysia and from Russia to Dubai) in the digital sector have increased IT outsourcing and thereby limited the transfer of expertise. Unlocking the digital Middle East's potential on the global stage will require balancing state support, private capital, and business endeavors, including entrepreneurial ingenuity, scale, and management.

Playing on a Nebulous World Stage

Over the past two decades, pioneering tech-centered activities have produced a ripple effect. More startups have emerged across the region as former employees of aspiring unicorn companies (those with a valuation of more than USD 1 billion) went on to (co)found their own ventures and become successful entrepreneurs themselves. The reorientation toward the knowledge economy and the promise of these startups have helped attract state and corporate investments. In 2022, venture deals in the region totaled more than USD 3 billion for 627 different startups, compared with USD 15 million for a mere five startups in 2009.[39] The sources of investment in regional startups are also more diverse than ever. Whereas regional startups traditionally sought to attract Western investors, there is a growing interest in inter-MENA funding, South-to-South collaborations, and investments from Asian countries. For example, China has increased its trade relations and company presence in the region. In 2016, a Chinese consortium acquired the Dubai-based ad tech company Media.net for a reported USD 900 million, making it the third-largest acquisition deal in the history of the ad tech industry globally.[40] Meanwhile, some Arab entrepreneurs resort to Chinese expertise in video game development, design, and publishing, as is the case, for example, with the Hangzhou-based Falafel Games, which is behind *Knights of Glory*, *Fathal*, and *Full House Party*.

Unlike Middle Eastern media moguls who thrive on political clientelism, digital entrepreneurs are motivated by grand ideas and energized by stories of tech-inspired success. These entrepreneurs are equipped with the technological know-how to develop innovative solutions and are experienced in navigating the region's complex legal, regulatory, financial, political, and sociocultural landscape. Pioneering ventures such as Souq (e-commerce), Careem (mobility), and Anghami (entertainment) exemplify the vibrancy and diversity of the startup community in the region. Each of these startups marked a milestone in the region's digital turn and became a player on the global stage.

SOUQ: FROM AN AUCTION WEBSITE TO A SHOPPING PLATFORM

The growth of e-commerce is closely related to the emergence of multiple platforms vying to connect suppliers with the region's sizable consumer base. The idea of an online souq (market) emerged from the success of Jordanian entrepreneurs Samih Toukan and Hussam Khoury. With less than USD 50,000 in initial investment and under Ronaldo Mouchawar as cofounder and CEO, Toukan and Khoury first developed Mazad-Maktoob as an initiative of the web-based portal offering online classified ads and an auction platform.[41] Capitalizing on Maktoob's infrastructure, they relocated to Dubai to develop an independent brand, Souq. com. When Souq officially launched in 2006, Dubai had already established itself as a destination for digital entrepreneurs, investors, and e-commerce companies and as a logistics hub with Dubai's airport and Jebel Ali port. By 2009, Souq was operating under Toukan's Jabbar Internet Group, a company formed after Yahoo! acquired Maktoob to include payment gateway CASHU, advertisement network ikoo, gaming publisher Tahadi, and others.[42]

Souq's development is intertwined with the digital turn and reflects how business models adapt to changing technologies. Souq began as an auction website, similar to eBay, and soon included real estate and other classified advertisements. Before its fifth anniversary, Souq reached around 39 million visitors and roughly USD 1 million in auction transactions per month. By then, it had expanded its warehouses and sorting operations to the UAE, Saudi Arabia, Kuwait, and Egypt and devised shipping arrangements to other countries.[43]

With the infusion of USD 10 million from Jabbar Internet Group in 2009, Souq benefited from dynamics that coincided with a move from web to mobile platforms. The region was ready for Souq to make a double transition: from auction to B2C platform (in 2010) and from a website to an app (in 2012). During these two years, user experience changed noticeably, as suppliers started categorizing their goods by stock-keeping unit (SKU)[44] and consumers became linked to local and global retail merchants on widely adopted smartphones. Because retailers were reluctant to trust shopping platforms as an intermediary, and with credit-card penetration limited, Souq embraced alternatives. While it accommodated COD transactions, it also enhanced the CASHU payment gateway—the independent online payment provider that was relaunched under the name PayFort to serve regional online businesses.[45] No less challenging were the inadequate systems for logistics and the unreliability of delivery systems. Even in modern Gulf cities, residential postal codes are largely deficient, leading to potential product delay or loss. The geolocation features of smartphones became an essential part of solving this "last mile" logistical challenge, with both customer and delivery personnel using connected devices. Gradually, Souq became a virtual marketplace that ensures end-to-end service, including payment and delivery.

Souq's multiple expansions put it on a growth path but also highlighted the need for additional capital, which existing investors could not offer. Having collaborated with Tiger Global Management on Maktoob, the founding investors believed that such partnership offered international exposure, networking, and advice from expert investors. Attracting the likes of the South African global media group Naspers as investors, Souq raised a total of USD 425 million in funding.[46] With 45 million visits per month, Souq did more than acquire a sizable market share: it helped transform the region's shopping culture.

In 2016, Souq reached a valuation of USD 1 billion, drawing increased global attention to its activities.[47] After a long negotiation, in 2017, Amazon acquired Souq for an undisclosed amount (estimated at USD 650 million in cash).[48] Amazon's initial decision to keep the Souq brand guaranteed the trust of its customer base, vendors, merchants, and sellers and a culturally competent local talent pool. Without this trust, customer acquisition and local market access would have been both time-consuming and resource-intensive. In addition, Souq's payment and logistics solutions became the backbone of Amazon's expansion in the region. To localize its brand, in 2019, Souq's UAE-based website changed to Amazon.ae, offering its customers access to 30 million products compared with Souq's 9.4 million.[49] Evidently, Amazon is not without competition both regionally (Noon.com, MarkaVIP, and Namshi.com) and globally (Alibaba.com).

CAREEM: DIGITAL EXPERIMENTATION AND BUSINESS ADAPTATIONS

Two years after Amazon acquired Souq, in 2019, another US-based, multinational, technology-enabled company expanded into the Middle East. Just like Maktoob and Souq, the ride-hailing startup Careem attracted the attention of global tech players eager to claim a footing in the region, and in acquiring Careem, the global giant Uber Technologies joined Yahoo! and Amazon in staking a claim in the Middle East's digital economy. After web portals and e-commerce, the region's logistics and transportation industries became subject to digital transformation. The region is a significant hub for global airline and maritime travel and shipping industries, with some of the world's busiest airports (Doha and Dubai), canals (the Suez), and ports (Alexandria and Jebel Ali). By contrast, public transportation, including taxis, is a highly regulated industry with limited competition, even with varying degrees of labor segmentation (Egyptian drivers drive Cairo's 120,000 locally assembled taxis, while Dubai's 12,000 imported taxis are driven by expatriate drivers).[50]

The digital transformation has favored the emergence of new business models, the increased integration of transportation (of people as well as goods), and various financialization schemes. Based in Dubai, Careem (Generous) was established in 2012 by Mudassir Sheikha and Magnus Olsson, two veteran management consultants. The fact that this was "a high-risk investment," as its founders ascertained in their initial pitch deck, did not dissuade their first investors from backing the startup with USD 1.7 million.[51] Seven years later, Uber acquired Careem for USD 3.1 billion—the largest technology-related transaction in the region at the time.[52] By January 2020, Careem had become a wholly owned subsidiary of Uber while maintaining independent brand control and management.

Initially, Uber was reluctant to pursue the acquisition of Careem in light of the different local markets, distinctive regulatory structures, and local resistance to the business model of these ride-hailing companies. An added challenge was that Careem was already operating in nearly one hundred cities in fifteen different countries in the MENA region and South Asia, resulting in diverse business practices, from the prevalence of cash payments to the power (or lack thereof) of driver unions. Eventually, Careem's adaptability and experimentation with solutions to many of these issues during its expansion made the acquisition particularly attractive. Careem's capitalization on WhatsApp in countries such as Iraq, which has low bandwidth and suboptimal internet connectivity, allows customers with limited access and literacies to book their rides using the Careem bot.[53] In the lead-up to becoming an Uber subsidiary, Careem developed a portfolio of acquired companies and assets, including Saudi-based home delivery service Enwani (2015), Pakistan-based cab service Savaree (2016), India-based shuttle-service app Commut (2018), and UAE-based bike-sharing service Cyacle (2019). Each of these companies injected Careem with talent, consolidated resources, and attracted additional investments.

These acquisitions also allowed Careem to branch into other fields. Careem targeted niche groups such as the millions of pilgrims visiting Saudi Arabia, offering them a bus-transport service.[54] In addition to the quality of its fleet and professionalization of its "captains" (the company's term for drivers), Careem invested more than USD 150 million in building a delivery platform, Careem Now, covering everything from food to pharmaceuticals.[55] This strategy leveraged the company's infrastructure and network to compete with delivery platforms in the food industry, such as Talabat and Deliveroo. To support these expansions, Careem introduced Careem Pay, which expands payment options through the app to include credit and debit cards, mobile wallet, and COD. In Egypt, for example, Careem and Uber compete against each other and against regional ride-hailing apps such as the Egypt-based Halan, the Dubai-based Swvl, and the Saudi-based

UVA. Despite some similarities between Careem and Uber in terms of strategies (e.g., rewards programs and community services), their relatively distinct operations and investment approaches allowed for the development of synergies while maintaining distinctively competing brands.

Although the COVID-19 pandemic limited the mobility of people, the mobility of goods of all types has ballooned. With traditional business down by 80% in 2020, Careem had to adapt by consolidating its offerings into one app, dubbed the SuperApp, with an initial investment of USD 50 million.[56] With Careem Pay at the center of this consolidation, the SuperApp is designed for daily uses beyond hailing a ride. In practice, Careem has been able to leverage its strengths in three complementary mobility sectors: people (car, bike, rickshaw), products (food, e-grocery, delivery), and money (bill payment, mobile recharge, P2P transfer).

For many years, the main objective of the nascent startup community was to lead companies either to an acquisition and eventually an exit (Souq/Amazon) or to a merger (Careem/Uber). Facilitating these pursuits is an emerging ecosystem with multiple stakeholders, including tech-oriented investment groups, a maturing startup community, and resourceful regional telecom operators.

ANGHAMI: THE SOUND OF LEGAL STREAMING

Anghami's journey from a local startup into regional and global markets is indicative of the aspirations of an entire generation of tech companies—regardless of whether those aspirations ever fully materialized. Focusing on digital distribution through streaming, Anghami has been a regional pioneer in offering "music as a service." From their original base in Beirut, Eddy Maroun and Elie Habib launched Anghami in 2012 as a Cayman Islands limited liability company with a network of offices and affiliates in Dubai, Cairo, Riyadh, and beyond. In 2021, Anghami established its global headquarters and an R&D center in Abu Dhabi.

Anghami demonstrates the potential of digital startups in the region and how digital transformations affect media distribution and consumption.[57] In its first year of operation, Anghami reached 1 million users, most of whom were millennials.[58] It soon doubled that reach after partnering with MBC Group in a funding arrangement that included free advertising and added exposure on one of the channel's most successful shows, *Arab Idol* (2011–2017). By 2022, Anghami claimed to have 1 million paying subscribers out of 75 million registered users streaming more than 1 billion plays per month.[59] Anghami's multi-application platform[60] is home to 39,000 Arab artists (600,000 songs) and 4 million international artists (56 million songs). Although only 1% of Anghami's content is in Arabic, the consumption of Arabic songs accounts for half of its monthly streamed content,[61] giving the company an edge over global streaming competitors.

Anghami's success rests on its ability to develop its product to match regional tastes, industry conditions, and funding opportunities while also meeting technological challenges. The platform's founders boast that they "understand the artists and the Middle East music better than the competition"[62] and that Anghami's playlists carefully engage with the habits and lifestyles of the various subregions of the Arab world. During the holy month of Ramadan, nearly half of Anghami's consumption is Anasheed (a cappella Koranic recitals). Mindful of the consumer market composition, Anghami also enriched its catalog with more than 1 million Hindi songs to cater to a large South Asian expatriate community in the Gulf and preempt potential competition from streaming platforms such as Gaana and JioSaavn. In addition to music, its content includes more than 250 podcasts from regional creators and global podcasters—ITP Media Group's publications and Eurosports Arabia, Gulf News, Communicate ME, and others.[63]

Anghami's adaptability to the region's music-consumption environment is also evident in its ability to overcome challenges to monetization, including rampant piracy and a culture that favors cash payments. The regional music-production industry and international music distributors have long struggled with content piracy. It is common to have large music catalogs illegally saved on cassettes, CDs, or flash drives and readily bought at curbside kiosks and street stands at very affordable prices.[64] Since its inception, Anghami positioned its music service as an anti-piracy tool, earning it the label of "the Spotify of the Middle East."[65] Considering the prevalence of inexpensive, pirated content, Anghami worked on changing users' dispositions from owning a limited music library to having access to millions of songs. This, in turn, necessitated developing accessible payment systems in a predominantly cash culture and a region with the world's highest unbanked rates. Accordingly, Anghami customized its financing solutions in partnership with telecom operators and advertisers to enable customers to access a premium model with prepaid and postpaid mobile subscription. Other technical adjustments were necessary as well. In a region with a deep digital divide, it was important for Anghami to offer streaming services over both weak and robust infrastructures. The application, the supporting music catalog, and the content delivery network (CDN) service are needed to cope with the recording quality, data transfer speed, traffic fluctuations, and latency. Developed initially between Lebanon and Poland, Anghami's codes were not sacrificed for audio quality and offered premium service access to Dolby Atmos recording. These localization strategies allowed Anghami to stand out in a music-streaming environment increasingly crowded with local and international players.

Anghami's emergence paved the way for various music publishers and telecom operators to develop their music services, such as Anazik and MobSound (Algeria), Etisalat Music (Egypt), and Tapsong (Dubai/Iraq). At the same time, Anghami faced international competition from YouTube Music, Apple, Amazon Music, Digster, and TuneIN. Competition intensified in 2018, when the Swedish streaming service Spotify and the French counterpart Deezer both expanded into the region with offices, curators, and unique offerings.[66] This crowded and competitive environment fed Anghami's ambition to become a global tech company. What began as a startup company with USD 200,000 in founders' seed funding is now a company publicly traded on the NASDAQ stock market.[67] Initially, a series of fundraising rounds led by Middle East Venture Partners (MEVP) attracted regional investors. Similarly, telecom operators such as Saudi Arabia's Mobily and Dubai's du became investors in Anghami (USD 1.5 million and 5 million, respectively).[68] Valued at USD 200 million,[69] Anghami established global headquarters in Abu Dhabi and announced a special-purpose acquisition company (SPAC), Vistas Media Acquisition Company (VMAC), in 2021. Listed on NASDAQ, this company serves as an alternative to an IPO and a faster path to public markets that guarantees relative autonomy. The development of public and private investments in startups reflects the gradual expansion from local to regional and global markets.

These three cases—Souq, Careem, and Anghami—reveal the promise of digital entrepreneurship anchored in local markets and vying for a nebulous world stage. Herein lies the challenge of converting the clarity of local vision, strategies, and outcomes to develop the necessary expertise, attract investments, and gain a strategic positioning in a dynamic global market. Amazon's acquisition and rebranding of Souq, Uber's retention of Careem as a subsidiary, and Anghami's decision to go public on NASDAQ indicate a maturing indigenous entrepreneurial culture. Instead of looking for quick exits, investors and entrepreneurs are increasingly focused on retaining equity, or even scaling up for the world stage. However, these few cases should not be mistaken for the trees that might obscure our view of the forest of a competitive global digital economy.

Digital Frontiers

As a metaphor that shapes how we think about technology, "frontiers" designates both temporal and spatial dimensions. Temporally, the invocation of frontiers is a reminder of how technologies are introduced and sustained at different tempos across the Middle East. For instance, the transition to 5G mobile connectivity is not simply an upgrade of the technology but rather a complex and layered undertaking. In addition to the different regulatory, technological, and infrastructural adjustments that 5G deployment required, geopolitical considerations also proved challenging, even for leading regional countries. To take just one example, the Chinese-Saudi agreements to adopt Huawei's 5G technologies, cloud computing, and data centers have raised US concerns over the security infrastructure of a key Gulf ally.[70] Spatially, the reference to frontiers is a reminder of the macro and micro forces that shape and organize the digital landscape. Expanding digital frontiers is more about negotiating political, economic, and sociocultural change than introducing new information technologies. Embracing cloud computing could be interpreted as an opportunity for states, communities, and businesses to extend their operations toward de-territorialized infrastructures. In effect, new digital frontiers demarcate ruptures and continuities between technologies, both transitioning and transforming. Examining the MENA region's emerging digital frontiers involves reflecting more broadly, both spatially and temporally, about technologies and the political, economic, and sociocultural dynamics associated with them. Understanding these emerging frontiers entails thinking of technologies less as "shiny gadgets" that can be acquired and more as embedded elements of the region's futures.

Among the various sectors that epitomize these emerging digital frontiers in the region, three merit particular attention: the Internet of Things (IoT), artificial intelligence (AI), and cloud computing. IoT refers to how digital or mechanical machines connected to the internet can send and receive data, from kitchen devices to car features. With AI, these machines can simulate intelligent behavior by learning from their data and experiences. IoT and AI are increasingly connected with the extensive information inputs that big data gleans and the network of remote servers that cloud computing affords for data storage, management, and processing. The potential of these interrelated developments represents the region's next frontier, making state support for and commercial interest in these technologies critical to the region's digital transformation.

According to the 2019 Middle East Barometer Report, one-third (34%) of regional companies have adopted IoT as part of their digital transformation plans.[71] Trends in IoT spending are concentrated in industrial sectors such as intelligent grid (8.4%) and manufacturing operations (8.1%), as well as consumer sectors such as smart homes (5.7%).[72] In 2019, the two leading regional countries in IoT spending were Saudi Arabia (USD 1.49 billion) and UAE (USD 650 million). IoT spending in the Middle East region and the Africa continent (MEA) was estimated at approximately USD 17.63 billion by 2023, up from USD 8.47 billion in 2019.[73] Notably, the UAE, Egypt, Qatar, and Saudi Arabia are making significant investments in IoT infrastructure, as has Tunisia by launching a satellite, Challenge One, that specializes in IoT.

Realizing the full potential of IoT will require developing AI technologies that collect, process, and analyze the multitude of data coming from countless points. A PwC report estimates that AI's impact on regional economies could reach USD 320 billion by 2030.[74] Across the region, there is a race to acquire the infrastructure and skills required to develop machine-learning algorithms. AI projects encompass various sectors and industries and include diverse activities such as data mining historical records, developing solutions for early disease detection, managing urban environments, and reconfiguring cyber-surveillance techniques. Robots form a particularly spectacular showcase for AI. Ibn Sina—named after Avicenna, developed in the UAE, and introduced at the Gulf Information Technology Exhibition (GITEX) 2009—is the first Arabic-speaking android robot that recognizes faces, retrieves information, and connects to the internet.[75] Since Ibn Sina's debut, there have been growing efforts to introduce AI across a range of consumer, enterprise, banking, and government activities. AI has also been at the center of efforts to develop initiatives that rely on cloud computing and big data. In 2017, the UAE launched a national strategy for AI that seeks to expand services, sectors, and infrastructure projects for a post-mobile phase.[76] To support its endeavors and develop capacity in AI, the UAE established the Mohamed bin Zayed University of Artificial Intelligence (MBZUAI).[77] In neighboring Saudi Arabia, the Saudi Data and Artificial Intelligence Authority (SDAIA) provides operational solutions (e.g., government cloud services), innovations (e.g., smart cities), and regulations for harnessing the potentials of AI. Similarly, the Qatar Center for Artificial Intelligence (QCAI) has emerged as an innovation and solutions hub for society and businesses with various applications. By 2030, AI's contribution to Kuwait, Oman, Bahrain, and Qatar could amount to USD 45.9 billion (8.2% of GDP), on par with Egypt's USD 42.7 billion (7.7% of GDP).[78] While these endeavors have not yet produced AI language models such as OpenAI's ChatGPT, Google's BERT, or Facebook's RoBERTa, the establishment of and investment in research centers in some of the region's countries point to a commitment to make AI an important component of their digital economies.

IoT and AI depend on cloud computing, which offers a lower-cost infrastructure that responds to an increasingly volatile and rapidly changing technological environment. The growing interest in and demand for reliable and secure cloud computing services are indicators of the region's digital transformation. In turn, providers of cloud computing recognize the opportunity to extend their presence to the MEA cloud computing market, which is expected to grow to USD 31.4 billion by 2026.[79] The landscape includes hardware and telecommunications companies as well other tech vendors from the United States (Microsoft, IBM, Google), China (Alibaba Cloud), the UAE (Etisalat, BIOS Middle East Group, eHosting DataFort), and Qatar (Ooredoo, Malomatia). The growing interest in cloud services is also an indicator of the increase in startups that require the cloud's flexibility to scale their operational needs up or down as they grow or shrink. Amazon Web Services (AWS) was among the early players to establish operations in the region, with its first cloud computing center in Bahrain (2017) and in the UAE (2022). Qatar also boosted its digital infrastructure, with Microsoft launching a cloud datacenter (2022) and Google establishing a new Google Cloud region (2023). These services have been valuable for the development of a digital media industry in the region (including leading streaming services such as Anghami and Shahid), particularly regarding data storage, as well as processing and overcoming latency issues. Just as the migration from legacy systems to cloud services is an essential part of digital transformation, the growing investment in the region's future by companies providing cloud services is a reassuring factor for skeptical businesses.

One pointed manifestation of how IoT, AI, and cloud computing have gained ground in the region is the growing adoption of fintech. International fintech solutions, such as e-payments and e-banking, support e-commerce by integrating technology into financial services offerings. After regional banks' initial reluctance to embrace these technologies, fintech deployment is now on the rise with investment, regulatory, and public adoption. Deloitte identifies three defining stages of fintech's presence: the first wave (2019–2020) focused on enhancing existing key processes (security, crowdfunding), the second wave (2020–2021) enhanced value proposition (crypto-solutions, e-wallets), and the third wave (2022–2025) offers innovative value propositions (data analytics, Islamic fintech).[80] Innovative solutions for remittances, such as NOW Money and North Ladder, reflect the public's needs in highly integrated economies (such as the UAE's) where growth in fintech is regionally unmatched. Even before Qatari banks adopted Apple Pay, the state's financial authorities licensed the locally developed mobile payment app SkipCash. In less fintech-ready countries, such as Egypt, many underserved consumers tap into platforms such as Dayra, which provides financial services to consumers in informal economies, or Cassbana, which offers financial identities to unbanked consumers. In Jordan, the central bank introduced regulatory frameworks for fintech operations that include crowdfunding and cryptocurrency, among other financial instruments. The Arab Monetary Fund's 2021 Index of Modern Financial Technologies in the Arab Countries places the UAE, Saudi Arabia, Bahrain, Tunisia, and Egypt at the top of the region's list for fintech adoption.[81]

Much like fintech, smart cities evince how new, digitally based industries are taking hold and opening promising new frontiers—though these industries do not necessarily solve the challenges the region faces. When considering the impact of digital technologies on urban development, the case of Dubai offers a glimpse into the possibilities digital transformation affords for sustainable urban living. In 2014, Dubai launched the Smart Dubai initiative aimed at improving the everyday urban experience, reducing the cost of basic services, and softening negative environmental impacts. The program entails actions from providing access to hundreds of e-government services to the use of integrated, network-connected drones to improve mobility and delivery services. A digital landscape now overlies the city's urban plans. Other cities around the region have followed suit or are advocating smart cities. The most ambitious of those may be Neom, a mega-tech city designed to attract new, technologically adept communities and serve as a tourist destination in the northwestern part of Saudi Arabia.

While some countries sought to adapt infrastructures to transform existing cities into smart cities, others built smart cities from the ground up. This is the case with Abu Dhabi's Masdar City and Doha's Lusail City, which represent the next generation of major, purposefully built smart cities.[82] These energy-efficient smart cities are high-tech environments that provide city dwellers with advanced services and feature fully integrated infrastructures with state-of-the-art computational technologies. They are also designed to manage urban processes and resources efficiently, including optimizing mobility and minimizing carbon emissions. Premised on sustainability, such live/work community initiatives reveal an emerging digital frontier for urban planning and economic growth.

Resource disparity and differing levels of ICT infrastructure across the Middle East make such smart-city projects more the exception than the rule. Many traditional cities in the Middle East are dense, in terms of both population and built environments, and in such places adopting a smart-city model in which urban settings are better planned and managed is a daunting challenge. Old cities such as Baghdad, Beirut, and Cairo—with their degraded infrastructures and now-antiquated planning—pose notable challenges to deploying smart-city solutions.

Effective integration of the various dimensions and sectors that enable smart-city projects remains a key issue. More than simply a collection of initiatives adopting new technologies linked to critical networked infrastructure, these are complex urban projects sustained by an entire ecosystem that involves multiple stakeholders and relies on the efficiency of various sectors. Even within areas that have pursued smart-city projects, the benefits and spillovers have been limited. Smart-city projects build on international best practices but lack local talent resources, adaptive know-how, and innovative capacities to implement these projects and manage their operations. Nor have the laws, policies, and standards adapted to the requirements and expectations of the smart-city model. For example, data regulations and policies have failed to keep pace with a range of integrated data-driven operations, from digital identity to digital payment.[83] Even in Gulf countries that have undertaken large-scale development projects, these cities constitute a complex "socio-technical system of systems"[84] with several challenges. Considering the region's large carbon footprint, it is fitting to ask whether the sustainable designs of these technology-driven urban projects can make a significant impact environmentally.

The foregoing analysis suggests that the push toward techno-futures is premised on acquiring IoT, AI, and cloud computing capabilities and deploying them across different sectors, including fintech and smart cities. Three observations can be made regarding this race into the next frontier. First, new information technologies, much like previous forms of infrastructure, require negotiating political, economic, and sociocultural change. While it is easier for richer countries to acquire the infrastructure and develop the talent to operate them, there is always a need for these technologies to be politically sanctioned, economically viable, and culturally accepted. Second, analyzing the impact of these emerging technologies requires thinking less about their technical capabilities and more about their uses in politics, the economy, and culture at large. As demonstrated throughout this book, the digital turn is marked by contradictions, tensions, and ambiguities that affect the adoption of technologies at all levels. Third, reading the new digital frontiers as encompassing the entire region is misguided and risks homogenizing the MENA digital experience. If anything, existing gaps are widening as we move toward new frontiers. While IoT, AI, cloud computing, smart cities, and fintechs are gaining ground in certain parts of the region, beyond the Gulf states these digital frontiers are still out of reach.

The Middle East Is No Silicon Valley

"Silicon Valley" has become synonymous with high-tech innovation and wealth generation. After all, California is the birthplace of big-tech companies such as Apple, Alphabet, and Meta. Along with hundreds of startups, these tech giants came to represent the unbounded possibilities of the internet and the extent to which it transformed our everyday lives. What is often forgotten, though, is that the history and name of Silicon Valley stretch back decades before even Steve Jobs's (and Steve Wozniak's) Apple computer was first assembled. The term is linked to the semiconductor industry and its factories, which replaced the Santa Clara Valley's fruit orchards during the 1950s and 1960s. The story of Silicon Valley, then, is one of transition from an agrarian to an industrial to a knowledge economy—one where transformation and innovation in the tech industry are entangled with the drives and motivations of multiple stakeholders, including the state (military spending on defense-related R&D), research institutions (Stanford University), adventurers, experimenters, and "risk capital" investors.[85] With every technological breakthrough, the Silicon Valley ecosystem has built on previous tech experiences (and a long culture of exploration dating back to westward expansion, which lends California its "vibe" to this day) to model the future of innovation and business.

The Silicon Valley model and the economic growth it spurred have taken hold beyond California, spreading across the United States and beyond. As the epitome of digital capitalism, it became a global descriptor for technology hubs energizing urban regeneration projects, including Silicon Hills in Austin, Silicon Prairie in the US Midwest, and London's Silicon Roundabout, all the way to Bengaluru, which emerged as "India's answer to Silicon Valley."[86] In the Middle East, Israel features Tel Aviv as "the next Silicon Valley," while neighboring Jordan was proclaimed "Silicon Wadi" (Arabic for "Valley"). Then, of course, there is Dubai's Silicon Oasis, a free economic zone designed to attract technology companies.[87] Such designations are premised on the ability of these hubs to develop an ecosystem that encompasses educational institutions, leading tech companies, digital infrastructure, investment funds, state and private incentives, regulatory environment, and geographical access to talent and markets. Yet none of these has recaptured what stands out in the case of Silicon Valley: its culture of openness and acceptance, learning and mentoring, and tolerance for failure.

In the elusive quest to replicate Silicon Valley, some countries invest in digital technology, infrastructure, and training, while others leverage their human resources capabilities, foster a culture of innovation, and access markets. Combining these elements is essential for an ecosystem to emerge, but the accumulated historical experiences are also necessary. As early as the 1980s, educational institutions in Tunisia and Jordan started focusing on computer science programs. In more recent years, several universities dedicated to science and technology were established throughout the region. With technologically savvy, globally oriented youth, innovation is emerging as an expectation and a currency for success. Significantly, governments are themselves diversifying their economies away from single-sector dependencies toward a knowledge economy. Judging by previously discussed indicators, several states in the Middle East are taking measures to develop a Silicon Valley–like ecosystem, including the introduction of regulations, frameworks, and initiatives, along with incentives and opportunities, to support regional innovators and attract global investors. Unlike California's Silicon Valley, which came about through successive business-led economic development, the regional cloned versions are a by-product of state planning, often with little input from the private sector.

Both market and state have supported the emergence of this ecosystem. Across the region, but more so in the emerging Gulf states, governments developed funding agencies and regulatory structures, including the Small and Medium Enterprises General Authority (Monsha'at) in Saudi Arabia, the Oman Technology Fund, MENA's 500 Startups, Egypt's Technology Innovation and Entrepreneurship Centre (TIEC), and the Dubai Future Foundation. Between 2000 and 2010, venture capital firms in Dubai alone grew from six to thirty-one. Global venture capital firms such as Wafra, Lumia, Global Founders Capital, 500 Startups, Softbank, and AppHarvest have also invested in regional companies such as Kitopi, Mamopay, and Eat. Similarly, accelerator Wamda established its venture capital fund Wamda Capital (2014), while seed investment companies and early-stage venture capital firms such as Flat6Labs expanded their operations beyond Cairo. In addition to the cases discussed in this part of the book, there are other success stories, such as Fawry's USD 100 million IPO, and Delivery Hero's acquisition of Instashop in a USD 360 million deal. In the first quarter of 2023, despite global negative macroeconomic factors and geopolitical tensions, the MENA region recorded USD 818 million in funding across 94 deals, with Saudi Arabia achieving a record high of USD 359 million.[88] These developments nurtured a shared view among Middle East tech enthusiasts, investors, and some official circles that wherever technology becomes accessible, people will connect, collaborate, innovate—and create wealth in the process. Sheikh Mohammed bin Rashid Al Maktoum's reprise of the famous proclamation "Innovate or face extinction" encapsulates this drive.[89] To help establish a digital economy, the ruler of Dubai signed a deal in 2021 with a number of tech giants to implement a coder training program for one hundred thousand young people in hopes of creating one thousand tech companies that would go global.[90]

Despite such sustained and costly efforts, the Middle East is no Silicon Valley. Amid the region's politicians' aspirations, investors' ambitions, and innovators' dreams, it is easy to lose sight of the fact that Silicon Valley is deeply intertwined with American political, economic, and cultural dynamics—as well as the fact that it has been in development for more than half a century. Politically, the discourses, plans, and promises of state leaders in the Middle East are often disconnected from the material realities of the region. Lessons from the modernization projects of the 1960s and 1970s loom large over these states' abilities to thrust themselves, as latecomers, into a globally competitive field. An additional challenge is an imbalance between the resource-rich and talent-rich countries—not being mutually exclusive categories. This gap in capabilities is particularly noteworthy considering the lack of regional cooperation and the state's pivotal role in the economy, both of which are detrimental to the growth of the knowledge economy. On one hand, rentier and semi-rentier economies are often anathemas to competition; on the other, in the few liberal economies in the region, large family-owned conglomerates or state proxies control capital and direct their investments toward traditional sectors believed to offer more secure returns.

Despite the backing and support of regional and global investment funds, both innovators and investors lack financial skills. Understandably, most innovators are not trained as entrepreneurs, nor can they access the mentoring required to enter the business world. In contrast, investors with proper financial training have yet to embrace digital startups as viable investments. According to Wamda Research, funding, talent, and communication gaps hinder initial investments beyond the USD 500,000 threshold.[91] Innovators are constrained by a lack of access to capital and financial support from the banking sector. Even where capital is available, it tends to favor traditional sectors such as real estate, banking, telecommunications, and tourism; together these represent a significant share of domestic and foreign investment, but they are also sectors in which returns are implicitly guaranteed by the government. For example, considering the nature of the region's omnifarious economy, investors prefer the reliability (and profitability) of real estate investments over the unpredictability (and riskiness) of technology startups. Because the region's transparency and freedom-of-information regulation are deficient, investors also lack the data they need to calculate risk. When available, data are fragmented, covering only a handful of countries whose political agendas and economic interests lie in making such information available. The (rare) public market research tends to focus on traditionally active markets, particularly the Gulf and Egypt, which contributes to the emergence and development of solutions that cater almost exclusively to national settings and local communities rather than the broader region.

Not only is innovation intertwined with political incentives and economic opportunities, but it also rests on a culture nurtured at schools, developed in universities, and flourishing in small and medium enterprises (SMEs). In the Middle East, where schools generally operate with traditional curricula and outdated pedagogical practices, students learn to use tools but not to experiment with technologies. At the university level, the scarcity of research and innovation centers limits the opportunities to build and expand experiences. The few places where these centers exist are often limited in scope, focused on national priorities, and in some cases populated by foreign rather than Arab talent. The achievements of SMEs do not seem to be on par with their traditional economic weight and their long history and tradition of creative ingenuity.

Every bit as limiting as these structural factors is the region's intolerance for failure. To put it plainly, "failed entrepreneurs" are legally challenged, culturally stigmatized, and economically dissuaded from reentering the marketplace. The tech world is full of stories of innovators unable to overcome bankruptcy, restricted from raising seed funds, and judged on the outcome rather than the process. Those who endure failure often face a double marginalization from the business and tech communities. Instead of harnessing the benefits of personal experiences—even negative ones—to promote collective success, the stigma of failure prevents innovators from engaging in disruptive, bold, and creative ideas.

Despite these limitations, there are lessons learned, experiences translated, and collaborations nurtured between the region and global tech hubs. Two examples of regional startups that leveraged the ecosystem of Silicon Valley are worth considering: AJ+, a digital journalism venture, and Instabeat, a wearable technology venture.

In the early 2010s, Al Jazeera Network sought to develop an innovative digital journalism startup, AJ+, which could position it to succeed in the face of massive changes to journalism. To translate a project idea into a competitive digital news venture that could compete with the likes of Vox News and Buzzfeed, the project's incubating team relocated from Doha to the San Francisco Bay Area. For such an ICT-centered operation to succeed, it needed the technological expertise of diverse professionals, from data journalists to development software engineers, with skill sets not readily available in the Middle East. As an established and well-funded media organization, Al Jazeera had the power and means to push its new venture globally. Operating out of Current TV's former training center in the Bay Area allowed the AJ+ team to immerse itself in an exceptional high-tech environment that values experimentation and to develop ties with leading tech companies and social-media platforms.[92] Notwithstanding the digital aspirations of regional firms, Silicon Valley's much-hyped environment of trust, inclusivity, collaboration, commitment, security, and diversity has yet to emerge in the MENA region.

Other startups were able to develop and execute business concepts only to be faced with different challenges. Inadequate access to capital, mentoring, and data has limited startups' ability to scale up and thus move to a growth stage that would enable them to contribute new technology, offer better services, or create job opportunities. Instabeat, a startup designed to provide high-tech tools to track and improve swimmers' performance, was the brainchild of entrepreneur Hind Hobeika. A swimmer herself, Hobeika introduced her concept on the 2010 season of the regional reality-TV show *Stars of Science*. As the contest's winner, Hobeika was granted seed funding. With the assistance of a multinational team, her startup Instabeat industrialized a wearable technology product for the global market of competitive swimmers, particularly in the US, Australia, and Europe.[93] Having failed to scale up Instabeat, she relocated to California. Partnering with Alex Asseily, a young Lebanese technology entrepreneur and cofounder of Jawbone, Hobeika raised USD 6 million from Middle East investors, including Berytech Fund, Wamda Capital, and Jabbar Capital, as well as angel investors.[94] Conceived in Lebanon, operating out of San Francisco, and manufactured in China, Instabeat illustrates how startups in the MENA region have overcome the limitations of their business environment by tapping into the culture of Silicon Valley and creating global connections.

Today, states' embrace of the knowledge economy and the market's enthusiasm for startups have resulted in an emerging, albeit deficient, ecosystem. At its heart, the digital economy marks a continuation of unevenly distributed resources and opportunities that benefit the privileged few at the expense of the many. At the same time, it is important to go beyond narratives that portray the digital economy as merely being "more of the same." Such narratives reinforce preconceptions about the region as being resistant to change. In many ways, the digital economy also marks a reconstitution of social practices and cultural traditions. As the digital economy gradually integrates into everyday life, it becomes imperative to examine its sociocultural dimension.

Building on the previous parts of this book, which explored the digital turn's technological, political, and economic dimensions, the next part considers how digital transformations are intertwined with cultural politics and what they mean for the self and the other. Significantly, while the digital turn has profoundly impacted the social and cultural realms, the intricate and diffuse nature of such changes makes them particularly elusive. After all, the digital increasingly occupies sociocultural spaces that were once considered sacred and personal.

Part V

CONNECTIVITY AND COLLECTIVITY

Cultural Transfigurations of the Digital

The more information technologies become affordable, accessible, and user-friendly, the more digital media permeates people's everyday lives. The near ubiquity of information technologies has recentered lived experiences around the digital. Today, everyday interactions, social ties, friendship networks, and practices of socialization are all touched by the digital. The speed, mobility, and multifaceted nature of the digital are altering many facets of sociality. The exponential growth in the usage of popular and emerging social-media platforms in the Middle East is unsettling traditional conceptions of the self, redefining lived experiences, and reformulating the nature of social relationships. Those changes are particularly evident for the youth of the region.

To explore these changes, one must examine how the self is mediated and recreated on social networks and the extent to which the digital has reconfigured different sociocultural practices. Specifically, we must ask: What are people doing online, and how are their lives being carried out with the digital? How is the adoption of digital tools changing the dynamics of social ties and transforming socialization practices? What new forms of social connectedness are developing? And what happens when life becomes increasingly centered around digital apps and services? More than promoting new modes of usage and communication habits, the widespread use of digital technologies and the degree of hyperconnectivity have engendered an ontological shift—though arguably with less intensity in the Middle East than in "network societies." Some of the manifestations of this shift can be witnessed in emerging cultural practices and forms of social engagement. In this respect, the question of how individuals experience the digital turn is as important as the question of what individuals do (or don't do) with particular technologies, precisely because this experience has both the power and the tendency to reshape these individuals' understanding of their identities and their conception of the self.[1]

While many of the practices and habits associated with digital technologies reflect global trends, sociocultural experiences in the Middle East produce specific variants of these behaviors. Because internet use is "a socially defined activity," as Jon Anderson reminds us, "it reflects before it inflects the society using it."[2] The technology may be the same across contexts, but the patterns of usage, adaptation, and appropriation of the digital are situated within particular local realities and therefore must be considered within those contexts. Tensions, discordances, and disjunctures develop at the intersection of antinomies: the individual and the collective, the self and the other, the public and the private, the modern and the traditional. As sociocultural change associated with the digital turn is often subtle and incremental, assessing emerging trends requires an appreciation of the complex and hybrid nature of these trends' constitutive dynamics. Those dynamics, in turn, are indicative of the double bind that characterizes the Middle East's encounter with the digital.

The analysis unfolds along three complementary lines of analysis that underscore the history, intensity, and complexity of the digital turn and its emergence as a contested arena in which competing sociocultural forces intersect. The first line of analysis explores how the advent of particular technologies helped project digital lives and create online spaces that continue to challenge prevailing sociocultural norms. The second looks at what being in a connected culture means for significant demographic groups, in particular youth (who are socially stigmatized yet increasingly assertive) and women (who are traditionally constrained but defiant). The third line teases out what the integration of ever-changing technologies into everyday life means for the construction of the self and its relation to the social other. While the cumulative effect of these unfolding trends is hard to measure, the dynamics that underlie various sociocultural changes provide rich insights into the region's digital double bind.

Chapter 12

Virtual Lives and Digital Spaces

Communicative practices unleashed by the digital turn have expanded and reconfigured sociocultural dynamics. Particularly germane to our examination is how individuals and collectives are introducing dynamics of empowerment at the grassroots level. We focus on three articulations of these cultural engagements with the aim of exploring how digitality is pushing boundaries and reformulating practices defined by dominant social, political, and economic systems: how women renegotiate gender roles while navigating cultural expectations of conformity, how believers reinterpret religion beyond state and state-sanctioned religious discourses, and how publics rearticulate the notion of citizenship.

The cultural adoption of the digital turn is particularly evident in the ways groups and individuals contest power, assert positions, and advance alternative discourses. It can also be seen in how states, regimes, and institutions have capitalized on the digital to co-opt change, maintain their authority, and advance their agendas. In conservative settings, for instance, women activists appropriated digital technologies to continue their efforts to challenge established sociocultural norms.[1] Their activities have created an additional sphere of participation that promises to empower them but also makes them vulnerable to state co-optation. Similarly, the digital has expanded the sphere of religion by enmeshing it with everyday communicative practices. This development has reconfigured how people relate to religion and how religious authority is defined but has also altered the very nature of religious expression. Yet these same digital tools have been appropriated by groups that espouse religious radicalism and hide on the dark web.[2] Finally, whereas digitality has helped citizens develop and articulate alternative forms of citizenship, the state also capitalizes on the digital to project the national sociocultural identity it has constructed and to advance its favored narratives of citizenship. In all these cases, the kind of mediation the digital affords to contest established sociocultural practices and bypass institutional forms of power and authority is both multidirectional and mutating.

The Digital Double Bind. Mohamed Zayani and Joe F. Khalil, Oxford University Press. © Oxford University Press 2024.
DOI: 10.1093/oso/9780197508626.003.0012

Cultural Dispositions and Transgressive Spaces

Online forms of engagement are shaped by the sociocultural milieu in which they occur. Focusing on the heterogeneity of sociocultural contexts reveals how these forms of ICT-centered socialization have reacted to and were often subject to specific norms and traditions, manifesting practices and uses that are not easily encapsulated by the binaries of conservative and conformist. Those sociocultural contexts do not preclude the nonconformist use of information and communication. Some online forms of communication, after all, offer possibilities for pushing boundaries and expanding transgressive spaces for both men and women. Importantly, those transgressions do not necessarily amount to digitally bound empowerment. Some engagements with social media tend to produce variations of conformity, perpetuate existing power relations, and reinforce users' traditional gender roles.

Such dynamics are not necessarily new, but the Middle East's digital turn made them more visible and arguably more complex. Take, for example, Saudi Arabia, whose sizable young population is among the region's most active on social media. Considering that Riyad was named the Arab world's digital capital in 2020, it is all too easy to forget that the advent of the internet two decades earlier was met with misgivings about the flow of undesired information and images, leading some Saudi clerics to issue fatwas (religious decrees and legal pronouncements passed by qualified religious scholars) that disapproved or only conditionally approved of the internet's usage.[3] This resistance calls to mind how the introduction of television in the kingdom in the mid-1960s was deemed an un-Islamic innovation (or *bidaa*)[4] and the advent of satellite television in later years was condemned in numerous fatwas as encouraging deviance.[5]

How women have been associated with some of the ills of information technologies is instructive. The adoption of various ICTs brought deep concerns about their potentially unsettling effect on what are otherwise firmly codified gender relations. In a setting where women's modesty and respectability are typically associated with their seclusion from male-dominated spaces, the prospect that such technologies could facilitate mingling (*ikhtilat*) between the sexes, even if virtual, provoked a stern reaction from state institutions and conservative forces who attempted to maintain physical boundaries and moral rectitude by controlling access and usage. Such reactions—which reflect discourses that project women as the embodiment of *fitnah* (enchantment and therefore sexual temptation and potentially sin and affliction to the *umma*) and portray their desirability as undermining morality and disrupting the social order[6]—reinscribe prevalent sociocultural conceptions of femininity and of the female body within everyday techno-cultural practices. Even as the state promoted the adoption of communication technologies, it had to reckon with their potential to tarnish the image of a pious nation and undermine the authority of the religious establishment that manages public life. Ironically, the proliferation of (often controversial) fatwas that reassert such authority was facilitated by the rise of social media—though the instrumentalization of fatwas in the kingdom goes back decades earlier.[7] Many of these fatwas were directed at women, aiming to gain control over various aspects of their lives (and bodies).[8] The urgency of many of these fatwas emanated from a proclaimed need to save women from the trappings of modernity.

The introduction of camera-equipped cell phones in the early 2000s brought deep concerns. A slew of incidents in 2004 revolving around leaked, illicit photos showing unveiled women at female-only wedding ceremonies in the kingdom led to a state ban on the use of cell phones during all-female social events and on the sale of camera phones altogether.[9] Such reactions are as much about the position of women in society as they are about the characteristics of the technology. Yet restrictions on camera phones proved hard to enforce with wider adoption of cell phones and the emergence of a gray market for the sale of camera-equipped phones. The restrictions eventually fizzled—as was the case with the ban on satellite dishes in reaction to the onslaught of transnational channels to the kingdom.[10] During this same period, other technological innovations, such as Bluetooth technology, helped unleash new ways of transgressing state-sanctioned mores, causing another moral panic. Bluetooth enables anonymous messaging to other phones nearby without knowing the receiver's phone number or going through the telecom company. Many young men and women seized the opportunity to flirt in public spaces or "make digital advances."[11] The sociocultural context remained relevant as technology changed and users adapted, shifting to messaging on Snapchat, Instagram, and TikTok. These digital forms of mingling, which circumvented the watchful eye of the conservative community, stretched the boundaries of what is socially permitted. In some cases, such recurring transgressions impelled the state to loosely apply the law and, when opportune, display a responsiveness to the aspiration for change by making a token overture toward the youth.

With digital tools promoting social networking, the appeal of an app such as Snapchat acquires an added significance when considering some of its features which promise both publicity and privacy. Saudi Arabia is one of the biggest national markets for Snapchat. Of the kingdom's internet user base in 2022 (around 20 million out of a population of nearly 35 million), 68.8% of users actively employed the app, which was also nearly uniformly adopted across genders (50.5% male users and 49.4% female users).[12] In part, Snapchat's privacy protection drives its popularity, particularly because other end-to-end encryption messaging apps, such as WhatsApp, offer only a limited ability of users to control the dissemination of videos. Local modes of usage reflect global trends and are partly motivated by widely shared concerns about the impingement on privacy and the fate of user data that find their way to social-networking sites. For women, the choice of particular platforms and modes of usage cannot be disengaged from cultural politics of visibility[13] that predate the digital. Significantly, privacy as a

concept is as much cultural and political as it is technical and legal.[14] Within conservative settings, it is largely constructed in relation to a clearly delineated "private sphere," which serves to maintain gender relations, thus relegating women to
a familial sphere that is also linked to such concepts as honor, femininity, tribal
identity, religiosity, and modesty.

Snapchat's core technology enshrines the mortality of videos, as media content is deleted immediately after it is seen. That ephemerality particularly appeals
to female users eager to partake in the contemporary urge for self-representation
but apprehensive that images and videos of them may be reshared beyond trusted
circles of friends—or, worse, become permanently public. Instead of smashing
norms, their use of technology complicates how conceptions of public and private
are appropriated. Social-media platforms are helping women overcome barriers to
broader social communication and facilitating women's access to and sharing of
information on matters related to their lives, while also enhancing their voices[15]—
though they often do so within the constraints of traditional norms and societal
expectations.[16] These practices need to be understood in relation to agency but
also in the context of digital cultures, namely the trend of social-media entertain-
ers, celebrities, and influencers who have reshaped the notion of privacy and of
women's visibility in public.

Similar dynamics have developed around women's online activism, even if the
scope and scale of such activism are limited. Digital social activism provides evidence of growing dispositions and subtle changes unfolding at the intersection of
the online and offline worlds. In this regard, the appeal of Twitter among Saudis
is informative. The kingdom boasts one of the highest Twitter user bases in the
region (after Turkey).[17] More than merely a new form of connecting, communicating, and networking, Twitter helps create and nurture alternative communities.
At least prior to the state's proclaimed modernization efforts and its gesture of
more tolerance toward women, being active on the microblogging site afforded
many women social recognition in a patriarchal society where social norms and
expectations perpetuate gender roles.

These maneuvers are not specific to Twitter. Young urban Saudi women have
long devised ways to work around barriers and shift existing boundaries. Among
the strategies they employ are selective adherence to dress codes and the culti-
vation of unsanctioned forms of self-representation.[18] In some instances, cultural
restrictions have fueled women's artistic sensibility and unleashed their ability to
imagine and revel in transgressive online spaces. One pioneering example of this is
Girls of Riyadh, a 2005 epistolary novel in the form of emails that vividly describe
Saudi women's attempts to expand their freedoms and negotiate their existence
in the face of limitations imposed on them by society.[19] It is not that women were
silent prior to the digital era; rather, their "voices," as one Saudi critic notes, "were
not heard through the layers of social censorship."[20] The significance of the book
lies in both its content, illustrating how girls navigate social restrictions with

digital tools, and its style, featuring compiled email exchanges. It represents a generation of female writers who honed their skills through online discussion groups and blogs. Even so, women's movements are not a monolithic category, as each embodies different perfectives on social change.[21]

These cases exemplify how various forms of contention are making it harder for the political and religious establishment in conservative Middle Eastern states to continue to exert strict control over public life, dictate norms for social conformity, and maintain expectations of acquiescence. Many young women have taken to the internet to advocate social change. One example is Saudi women's online activism against the kingdom's long-standing ban on women driving vehicles, which ranged from women activists defiantly posting videos of themselves behind the wheel to taking to Twitter to challenge the ban.[22] But the publicity of such activism on social media invokes other forms of sociocultural control such as tribal pride, honor, and shame.

To be sure, the struggle for Saudi women's right to drive predates the digital era. As early as 1990, some forty-seven women drove a dozen cars through the streets of Riyadh before they were arrested.[23] These rare forms of female civil disobedience fizzled amid the events of the 1991 Gulf War. In the mid-2000s, the sporadic use of digital media gave such activism an added element of "publicness."[24] Over time, different forms of online engagement enabled women to challenge their situations by imagining modes of self-expression that contested prevailing role construction while advocating change.

The decision to end the driving ban in 2017, though, was not the direct result of social-media campaigns by women's rights advocates but was rather part of a new modernization agenda.[25] Edging toward a "state feminism" was as much motivated by "the state's quest for new local allies"[26]—namely women—as it was impelled by socioeconomic imperatives, particularly the pressure "to reduce dependence on expatriate labor and to diversify its economy."[27] In this sense, the same form of economic development that leads to prosperity and stability is also socially unsettling. As much as the increased participation of women in the workforce may challenge "traditional notions of masculinity among young men,"[28] independent women's voices tend to be perceived as an encroachment on the authority of a "masculine state."[29] Interestingly, what was trending on the day the driving ban was effectively lifted was not the stories of female activists who had been reined in but instead a YouTube clip of a young Saudi woman (Leesa A) driving, dancing, and rapping in Arabic, expressing joy and gratitude for being granted the right to drive.[30]

The speed and velocity of change in the kingdom make the Saudi case all the more noteworthy. Yet such a case is more illustrative than it is broadly representative, as women's lives differ markedly across the Middle East. More than simply inviting skepticism about cyber-utopian narratives celebrating ICT-driven change, the dynamics that transpire point to a double bind that accompanies the introduction and adoption of new information technologies. As society changes, so does the technology, and as these technologies take hold, citizens use them to challenge those in power, who in turn deploy these same technologies to mold practices of citizenship.

Competing Voices of the Sacred

The internet has given rise to a diverse cyber-Islamic environment in which users go beyond a narrow spiritual focus to address issues of everyday life.[31] The way Muslims, as the majority religious group in the region, acclimated to digital tools has contributed to the rise of new socioreligious and political identities and enhanced both community interaction and networking. It has also reconfigured religious authority further, yielding a contested space with competing voices that oscillate between the modern and the traditional, the state-sanctioned and the rebellious, the orthodox and the radical. The digital has both expanded the sphere of religion by newly enmeshing it with everyday communicative practices and reconfigured the very nature of religious expression.

These developments are part of a long line of changes in the production, dissemination, and consumption of religious knowledge and the way people relate to religion and religious authority. Traditionally, Koranic recitations, preachings, books, and pamphlets played an important role in spreading religious teaching before broadcasting expanded the reach of state religion.[32] In the latter decades of the twentieth century, new "technological instruments of the modern mass culture" were appropriated. These included early physical media forms such as cassette tapes, which were used to disseminate sanctioned sermons and oppositional views,[33] and later CD-ROMs, which became an important medium for circulating different interpretations of religion outside the mosque.[34] Such innovations challenged what had been a near-total state monopoly over "official" religion, which used radio and television to assert its religious authority. In Egypt, Al Azhar had regular appearances on state television, while in Saudi Arabia, dedicated broadcast channels were devoted to recitation of the Koran. Live broadcasting of hajj rituals, which pilgrims perform in Mecca, on the pan-Arab satellite channel MBC in the late 1990s ushered in a new era of transnational religious broadcasting. The mediatization of Islam came full force in the 2000s with the proliferation of satellite religious channels and their unsanctioned content, which formally broke the monopoly of the religious establishment and state media.[35] During the same period, digital Islam further loosened the state's grip on religious discourse, rendering religious interpretation less restricted, religious authority more dispersed, and religious discourses more fragmented.

A precursor to the digitization of religious outreach (da'wa) was the mediatization and popularization of Islam at the hands of media-savvy preachers who sought to reinvigorate religious discourse. Among these, three figures who achieved transnational celebrity stand out as religious personalities: Egyptian preacher Amr Khaled, Kuwaiti preacher Tareq Al-Suwaidan, and Palestinian-Saudi preacher Ahmad Al Shugairi. All three came from outside the religious establishment and became religious revival celebrities, with millions of fans and social-media followers attracted to their progressive religious discourses. They exploited various media platforms to advance a new form of social religiosity, using an approach that mixes religion and entrepreneurship with infotainment.

Khaled drew a large following by using language that is both colloquial and accessible, passionate delivery, and a relatable preaching style but also by promoting a message in sync with contemporary life. He advocates an Islam that is personable and relevant to people's daily lives and therefore easy to identify with. Al-Suwaidan makes religion more relevant to people's professional lives. An entrepreneur, preacher, writer, and producer of religious shows, Al-Suwaidan offers guidance and mentorship promoting self-development by sharing stories of successful historical figures, from the revered companions of the Prophet to the glorious era of the Al Andalus (referring to parts of the Iberian Peninsula that Muslims ruled centuries ago). Combining preaching, leadership, and management, his approach features a conversational tone and is geared toward self-development and designed to motivate and reenergize youth and the broader target audience to be more proactive and oriented toward change. Al-Suwaidan's various media offerings blend religious knowledge from traditional sources and historical events with more contemporary issues in a way that refocuses religion on people's pursuits and their preoccupations of daily life, thus shifting the attention from the doctrinaire to the practical. Other preachers have oriented their efforts toward social activism. Al Shugairi's television programs explore social and economic development in search of inspiration in successful stories. Al Shugairi started as a host on *Yalla Shabab*, a religious TV program for youth, before launching his own show discussing social issues from smoking to illegal parking. Its title, *Khawatir* (*Reflections*), refers to the reflections he offers aimed at self-improvement and community development and motivated by the vision of an improved society that is simultaneously Islamic and modern.

Khaled, Al-Suwaidan, and Al Shugairi all hold relatively liberal religious views and adopt a modern form of religious expression that is relevant to people's daily lives. Integrating religion and infotainment, they offer a practical and adaptable religiosity that reconciles public life and religious belief, self-reflection and piety, materiality and spirituality. This individualized form of religious expression appeals particularly to audiences motivated by morality and civic responsibility rather than doctrine and ideology.[36] It also prioritizes the sphere of cultural and religious identity over issues of nationality and citizenship, and social action and self-change over political action and regime change.

These religious celebrities' relevance hinges on their ability to repackage their content and reconfigure their approaches for a changing variety of platforms.

Members of this older generation of religious celebrities owe much of their fame and success to satellite television, which allowed them to position themselves as alternative religious authorities and as "Islam's new interpreters."[37] As religious entrepreneurs, Khaled, Al-Suwaidan, and Al Shugairi are tied to business interests originally founded with legacy media but which quickly transitioned to digital platforms.[38] Although their major draw was television, they also used cassettes and CD-ROMs, and with the advent of Web 2.0, they capitalized on online tools such as video blogs and YouTube channels to share their messages and expand their reach. For example, Khaled has millions of followers on Facebook and Twitter, and his elaborate web page receives substantial traffic.[39] Similarly, Al Shugairi uses his YouTube channel and other social media to expand his reach. His projects are supported by a strong web presence, and some of his television shows, such as *Qumra*, offer multimodal content.

More recent forms of religious engagement developed exclusively online. Among the well-established and highly trafficked Islamic websites aimed at *da'wa* is Islamonline.net, which was designed to spread awareness of the Islamic faith, addressing both Muslims and non-Muslims. The brainchild of then–Qatar University student Maryam Al-Hajri, IslamOnline was launched in 1997 (in collaboration with Al-Hajri's mentor, Hamid Al-Ansari) by Al Balagh Cultural Society. A key influence on the site was Yusuf Al-Qaradawi (1926–2022), a prominent, controversial Qatar-based Egyptian theologian and religious authority who is considered as representing a moderate form of Sunni Islam, the *wasatiyya* (centrist). Al-Qaradawi had been a popular figure on Al Jazeera's widely watched religious discussion program, *Al Sharia wal Hayat* (*Islamic Law and Life*). With its administrative and technical operations based in Doha and its editorial office in Cairo, IslamOnline gradually established a strong presence, gaining international popularity after the September 11 attacks, with many users taking part in its interactive forum.

IslamOnline is indicative of reconfigurations in an increasingly fragmented Islamic public sphere that gave rise to "new Islamists," who project an *umma* (a global Muslim community) that is anchored in "religious communalism and collectivism."[40] This is evident in its attention to advice (nasiha), counseling, interactivity, and education, as well as in its keenness on being open to a wide spectrum of religious sensibilities and its desire to enlist various religious and nonreligious actors in its work. Because the *umma* for IslamOnline takes precedence over the state, the website is more concerned with sociality than with politics. Published in both Arabic and English, the website serves the dual purpose of affirming religious life and building a communal identity. It offers editorials, news articles, and reflections on religious practice and provides a forum for discussing a broad range of issues related to Islam and daily life. Additionally, the site offers interactive counseling, issues online fatwas or edicts, and serves as a repository for Islamic knowledge on a variety of issues.

Significantly, the platform is not monopolized by clerical perspectives. Instead, it draws on various international collaborators and contributors, from sharia experts to academics, and promotes vibrant discussions about topical subjects. Such interactions, many of which come from Indonesia and diasporic communities in the West, give the platform a transnational dimension. The sense of community it fosters helped it expand the traditional borders of the *umma* and promote community faith as a potent element in the experience of users attracted to the platform. The digital nature of IslamOnline adds to its appeal to educated, middle-class youth whose social lives are increasingly intertwined with new ICTs. Operationally, IslamOnline is run by some 350 staff members, predominantly Egyptian men and women.[41] Naturally, the site's association with an eminent theologian was mutually beneficial: Al-Qaradawi lent IslamOnline legitimacy and shaped its religious identity, while the vibrant, multilingual nature of the website drew in Muslims (and often non-Muslims) from around the world, enhancing the Egyptian cleric's reputation as a "global mufti."[42] The wide appeal of IslamOnline that led to its expansion into different foci and media arms also mired it in multi-layered tensions.[43] This culminated in a widely publicized crisis in 2011, following the restructuring of IslamOnline and its funder's decision to close the Cairo operation (and eclipse Al-Qaradawi himself) amid disagreements about the organization's identity, editorial direction, and management, all of which reflect deeper ideological battles and geopolitical rivalries in the region.[44]

The political context of digital Islam in the region is important. Varying forces have shaped how it manifests in different countries. The crackdown on political Islam (Egypt), widening sectarian divisions (Iraq, Syria, Lebanon, Bahrain), the consolidation of ethno-religious identities (Kurds, Yazidi), and doctrinal or religious contestation (Iran, Saudi Arabia) have all produced a religious multivocality and decentralization (with often conflicting interpretations and practices of religion). In shaping religious identity, the perceived assault on Islam as such is no less significant than those contexts. In a post-9/11 environment marked by growing Islamophobia, the advent of digital Islam contributed to a heightened sense of *umma* and helped online spaces acquire users spanning regions and countries. This is the case with the controversy surrounding the Danish cartoons, the French ban on hijab, the anti-Islam film *Innocence of Muslims* in the United States, and the burning of the Koran in Sweden. Many people were drawn to these new forms of religiosity because they offered a sociocultural space in which people could find strength and solidarity, as well as access to resources and spiritual support. Significantly, while digital Islam has proven to be a uniting element by virtue of transcending borders and reaching different demographics, it has also been highly divided along ideologies, ethnicities, and orientations—so much so that traditional religious institutions were alarmed.

Online experiences have reshaped how people conceive of themselves and their religiosity and what it means to be simultaneously religious and modern.[45]

These developments need to be understood within the twin contexts of the "commodification of religion" and the "Islamization of modernity."[46] The hyper-mediatization of Islam, initially on satellite television and then more intensely with digital tools, has given religion an entertainment dimension, which contributes to "the depoliticization of Islam."[47] Even more, the fact that the digital turn has manifested itself remarkably in the sphere of religion—of all places—defies the perception of Islam as retrograde. This is evident in the wide range of Islamic services that have become available, from e-fatwas to online services that support *zakat* (obligatory almsgiving) and from Muslim dating apps to *athan* (call for prayer) apps, but also in the ways Muslims are "using the latest information and communication technologies to question and challenge the religious order."[48] The digital also underscores specific interpretations that are subsequently promulgated as unchallengeable.

The same dynamics have prompted conservative preachers and religious institutions, as well as violent groups and extremist organizations, to assert a stronger presence online, which is indicative of "the spurious relation between *da'wa* and radicalization."[49] In the 2000s, Al Qaeda and its many branches used satellite television to advocate the reestablishment of an Islamic state, reach targeted believers, and dominate news coverage.[50] Later the internet became an important means of communication outreach "for its pronounced, digitalized multiplier effects on jihadist consciousness-raising and operational activities."[51] Subsequently, Al Qaeda's affiliates used YouTube to rally newcomers to jihadism. The arrival of a younger generation of radicalized and digital-native recruits has significantly enhanced Al Qaeda's ability to reach global communities and maintain a digital connection with group members and supporters.[52] Militant groups such as Al Shabab in Somalia were among the first to capitalize on Twitter to spread their propaganda and coordinate their operations. ISIS even developed a dedicated digital media operation to raise funds, recruit operatives for its cause, disseminate its ideology, and foment radicalization.[53] Its use of the internet to spread spectacles of terror with gory videos containing incendiary violence and gruesome beheadings is shockingly brutal, inciting revulsion and stoking fear.[54]

Social-media platforms (such as Telegram), which are famously used by dissidents in organizing anti-regime rallies and activities, emerged also as powerful tools in the hands of terrorist organizations such as ISIS. Unfettered access to global audiences means terrorists can create "hypermedia events"[55] and disseminate images and messages far and wide, often bypassing traditional media. Despite efforts to combat these tendencies, the appropriation of the internet by extremist groups remains largely unchecked, particularly as the root causes of extremism itself persist in a region that is in convulsion and in a broader context where Islamophobia is on the rise. Although these extremist groups have garnered considerable attention, they operate on the fringe of society and as such are unrepresentative of the broader forms of religious dynamics developing on the internet.

Digital media increased the accessibility of religious discourses but also accentuated their heterogeneity. The popularity of alternative religious discourses and the proliferation of religious interpretations online contributed to the informalization, contestation, and reconfiguration of religious knowledge.[56] In turn, this manifested itself in the fragmentation of religious authority, long monopolized by learned religious scholars (*ulama*) and sanctioned by the state. It further resulted in the delocalization of Islam beyond its traditional center (Mecca) and beyond established institutions for Islamic learning (Al Azhar).[57] Religious institutions could not keep up with a sprawling conversation over an increasingly popular medium that crosses national, demographic, and sectarian boundaries. The advent of digital Islam means that no single party or player controls doctrine, making it hard for nation-states and religious establishments to have a monopoly on how religiosity is managed and religious identity molded.

Digital Narratives of Citizenship

Throughout the Middle East, the relationship between the state and its citizens continues to be in flux. As noted earlier, attempts to reclaim sociopolitical rights or gain legal status as citizens continue to drive various forms of activism. Part of this drive, although not readily evident, involves citizenship less in terms of political rights and legal status (*jinsiyya*) than as a form of affect (*mouwatana*). What distinguishes such "affective citizenship" is how it "mobilizes feelings of civil belonging, loyalty, and solidarity."[58] While feelings denote embodied emotions associated with an individual actor, affect designates relational (and therefore collective) practices premised on engagement.[59] The digital has accentuated the polysemous nature of affective citizenship in terms of the tools and platforms used and the narratives and interpretations they animate. With the digital turn, affective citizenship serves to advance both states' and citizens' particular narratives and conceptions of identity. Just as the state has instrumentalized the digital to mold national identity and nurture affective citizenship (for ideological or political ends), traditionally marginalized groups have found in the digital a more leveled, if still contested, arena in which they can develop emotional resonance, assert identity, and redefine citizenship.

DIGITAL MUSEUMS AND NATIONAL IDENTITY

Traditionally, culture has been at the center of state efforts to ingrain rallying narratives of citizenship. The state has long engaged artists and assumed cultural production to promote nation building, affirm national identity, and promote a sense of nationhood. Increasingly, rapid changes in information technologies and communication practices are reorienting state efforts to mold citizenship through the instrumentalization of the digital. Besides social-media campaigns, some states have formulated digital cultural strategies to reinvigorate nationalism and advance particular forms of state-centered national identity.

Museums have played a significant role in nurturing nationalism. For decades, states have used museums as shrines for fostering affective citizenship. Throughout much of the region, though, museums have been slow to change and adapt to the digital era. This may be unsurprising, because museums are inherently conservative and inward-looking institutions whose traditional focus is the preservation and presentation of heritage.[60] Yet where states availed themselves of the opportunities offered by digital technologies, they reinvigorated the role museums play in their societies and beyond. The motivations for developing digital museums vary, and so do the forms and defining features of these cultural and artistic projects. Meriting particular attention are digital initiatives in Gulf states that have strategically invested in art and culture, with an unprecedented scale and pace of development, including art acquisitions, cultural project adoption, and heritage events. These countries have spent lavishly on extravagant, high-prestige museum projects, including Abu Dhabi's Louvre and Guggenheim and Qatar's Museum of Islamic Art and National Museum, and ambitious cultural developments, such as Sharjah's Art Foundation, Bahrain's Arts Center, and Saudi Arabia's King Abdulaziz Center for World Culture and the MiSK Art Institute. Increasingly, these cultural projects are acquiring digital dimensions that range from curating virtual exhibitions to offering digital displays of art. They have also become central to educational efforts, through in-person or virtual tours, interactive activities, and teaching material. Whereas most of these initiatives have some form of online presence, the more ambitious ones have partnered with online platforms such as Google Arts and Culture to bring their collections to a broader audience.[61] Imposed service innovation[62] during the COVID-19 pandemic expedited digital transformation (with digitization and platform development). It induced some museums in the region (such as Qatar's Museum of Islamic Art) to reorient themselves toward virtual exhibits and others (such as Dubai's Museum of the Future)[63] to position themselves as sites of imagined futures, thus expanding the reach of these institutions—though often at the expense of the communal experience museums typically foster.

Community building and citizenship molding aside, one motivation energizing the digital expansion of regional museums is nation branding, accomplished by developing cultural capital to improve the Gulf states' international reputations, raise their profiles, and advance their prestige. Acquiring exclusive artworks and artifacts and collaborating with reputable global art institutions and museums could help these states project a progressive image of themselves and garner soft power. Several of the region's ambitious artistic projects convey an image of religious openness and cultural tolerance reflective of these states' diverse and multicultural (expatriate) populations but also indicative of their desire to project a particular image about themselves to an international audience.[64] Financial potency and technological readiness enable these museums to extend their reach and influence in the service of this strategy: "By buying and conserving Islamic art and mixing it with global artifacts, they produce a kind of pan-Arab or pan-Islamic sphere that differs from previous iterations in catering to global tastes."[65] In doing so, they extend and diversify the nation-branding footprint. These cultural projects are not uniform across the region. Whereas the UAE adopted a cosmopolitan approach premised on partnership with Western museums and connections with international institutions, Qatar sought to develop homegrown museum projects by building its collection and training curators.

State-led efforts to develop a culture industry invested in the revival of Arab and Islamic heritage are an affirmation of the region's predominantly Arab and Muslim identity. This is all the more significant considering the tensions between the conservative cultural traditions in these Gulf monarchies and the effects of rapid development and fast-paced globalization.[66] To bridge these gaps, Gulf states have adopted forms of "culture creation"[67] that promote cosmopolitanism and global consumption among the citizenry while preserving cultural heritage and protecting national identities.[68] The reliance on digital imaging tools solved another problem. Whereas institutions such as the Egyptian Museum in Cairo could draw on archaeological treasures, Gulf states lacked endowments of national relics that could populate their museums. Digital imaging tools could recreate artifacts and render the past without such physical mementos.

The combination of financial resources and digital capabilities enables Gulf states to have at their disposal previously inaccessible archives from colonial powers, which are then appropriated to bestow historical credibility on state-sanctioned narratives. Digitizing museum collections, enabling virtual tours, developing interactive exhibitions of digital resources, and promoting online art initiatives have helped these museums (and others) increase their reach, enhance their engagement, and better target specific users. Chief among these targeted audiences are networked citizens and youthful audiences who are heavy users of social media and operate at the intersection of the physical and the virtual. In particular, the adoption of digital museums helps attract and cultivate youthful audiences, whose members constitute the largest demographic category in the region and are less likely to visit traditional exhibits or cultural spaces. By engaging them, museums can also align the youth with state agendas and expectations. Investing in digital library archives, building digital museums, and extending cultural events to online spaces are among the many ICT-centered initiatives undertaken with the goal of reviving the national memory, celebrating the local culture, and preserving the region's heritage.

Engaging in art projects and setting up state-of-the-art museums with local reach and global appeal underscore the Gulf's efforts to reconcile tradition and modernity.[69] Yet there are more direct interests at work. With the exigencies of an inevitable transition to a post-petroleum economy eroding the social bargain that binds rentier Gulf states and their citizens and with a once firmly held social contract under strain,[70] the need to nurture the national identity has never been more pressing.[71] State-sponsored art and cultural initiatives serve the Gulf region's strategic vision of promoting more sustainable economic avenues away from hydrocarbon economies.[72] Such museums are also part of an endeavor to position Gulf capitals as creative cities where art and culture play a significant role in attracting people, businesses, and investments.[73] The cultural politics of these endeavors is such that citizenship and nationhood are invested in an affective relationship with the past.[74] By evoking the past and reconstructing these countries' histories, museums help forge contemporary national(ist) narratives that strengthen the bond between citizens and communicate a rallying vision of who these nations are and where they are heading.[75]

DIGITAL AFFECTS AND COUNTERNARRATIVES

States are not the only ones to capitalize on the digital to nurture affective citizenship. Whereas museums in the Gulf have been bankrolled and appropriated by the state to reclaim national identity, in the case of Palestine, several cultural initiatives (including digital museums) have been developed by NGOs to help bolster national identity in "the absence of the state."[76] The mid-2010s saw the inauguration of three museums in the West Bank: one to commemorate Palestinian leader Yasser Arafat, another to pay tribute to the Palestinian national poet Mahmoud Darwish, and, more prominently, the Palestinian Museum—a multimillion-dollar project devoted to the history and aspirations of the Palestinian people. Situated in Ramallah, the political and cultural center of the West Bank, the museum stands out as much for its imposing physical presence and architectural ingenuity as for its inherent impermanence, being vulnerable to the possibility of destruction or closure. Interestingly, the original conception of the museum emphasizes both its materiality and its immateriality. Considering the simultaneous concentration and dispersion of the Palestinian population, the digital dimension of the museum is central both to the project and to efforts to bring together Palestinians and foster affective citizenship.

The Palestinian Museum is designed to bypass geographical boundaries and geopolitical restrictions in an imagined future state. Surrounded by checkpoints, Palestinians live in a land divided into a patchwork of areas ghettoized by separation walls that effectively prevent the formation of a contiguous state.[77] Those obstacles stifle the encounters, engagements, and exchanges around which museum cultures thrive. Accordingly, the museum was envisaged as "post-territorial" (in its need to encompass Palestinians who are scattered transterritorially) and as "a mobilizing and interactive cultural project that can stitch together the fragmented Palestinian body politic by presenting a wide variety of narratives about the relationships of Palestinians to the land, to each other, and to the wider world."[78] No less important than the national centeredness of the museum is its "transnational"[79] dimension, which helps reconnect Palestinians. A key component of the Palestinian Museum is its Digital Archive Project, which contains a rich collection of historical documents, photographs, and artwork that records the history and culture of Palestine as well as oral narratives of displaced Palestinians.[80] Initiatives such as the Museum from Home and the Palestine Perseveres campaign encourage ordinary Palestinians to post personal photographs that document stories with the aim of preserving and reviving the national memory. The digital dimension makes the museum a more equitable and encompassing venue, such that stories told by Darwish's parents or Arafat's widow are as worthy of being displayed at the museum as anybody else's. What entices people to participate, besides the ability to share pictures that capture particular moments in their lives, is the ultimate affective belonging to, and participation in, the construction of a national narrative, made all the more insistent by Palestine's perpetual statelessness.

More than simply facilitating access to cultural artifacts and displays, though, digital archiving helps bring Palestinians together around a past in order to keep their story alive and reasserts their aspiration for an independent state. On one level, digital archiving is a critique of the complacency of the Palestinian National Authority. Undertaking such an ambitious national project independent of the state's cultural patronage articulates a growing disconnect between the Palestinian people and an increasingly unpopular Palestinian National Authority.[81] On another level, such an unbounded cultural project nurtures affective citizenship, which in itself is a form of "resistance" against displacement and dispossession and an affirmation of a Palestinian identity, land, and continued survival.[82] On yet another level, the transnational dimension of the project strengthens international solidarity with and support for the Palestinian cause abroad by conveying a relatable side of the conflict's story.

Other independent digital projects have been launched seeking to draw on history and culture to nurture this affective dimension and reassert a Palestinian identity. For example, Gaza launched a digital cultural project through the platform Kanaan (named after the Canaanites, the original inhabitants of Palestine) to safeguard its rich past and document its historic buildings.[83] These digital archives provide a window into historical and archeological sites that are otherwise inaccessible to non-Gaza residents.[84] Rediscovering Palestine's rich history often serves as a conduit for emotional identification, which in turn nurtures a sense of belonging. Similarly, the Majazz Project is an online platform dedicated to restoring Palestinian musical heritage, including lost Palestinian songs and rare traditional recordings.[85] More than preserving and displaying tangible and intangible heritage, projects such as these offer interpretations of the past that communicate a particular conception of the present. They also keep the Palestinian story alive despite systematic and multiple approaches to limit Palestinian content online and silence Palestinian voices.[86]

Elsewhere in the region, more modest social-media initiatives emerged as reflections on local, indigenous cultures, times, and places. One is the Digital Khaleeji Art Museum, which was launched by two young Emirati sisters, Manar and Sharifah Alhinai, to support and promote Gulf talent. Focusing especially on art either by or about women, the project challenges Orientalist tropes about the region and promotes a better understanding of Middle Eastern women, who are generally misrepresented in international media.[87] The Middle East Archive Project is another online initiative centered around virtual storytelling using personal photos and crowdsourced material from the MENA region. In the words of its founder, Darah Ghanem, this social-media archive seeks "to challenge mainstream and orientalist narratives about the region" and to redefine what the Middle East means by foregrounding identities, profiles, and races that have been marginalized throughout the region's contemporary history.[88]

Digital initiatives such as these articulate an alternative conception of citizenship that acts as a collective foundation, symbolic though it may be, for emotions. Aspects of these dynamics and the agencies that developed around them are evident in the counternarratives marking the second wave of the Arab uprisings. A case in point is mobilization in Lebanon and Iraq—two tension-ridden countries where the state's ability to define citizenship has been weakened by nonparticipatory forms of governance, a self-serving political class, networks of patronage and clientelism, rampant corruption, and endemic mismanagement. In 2019, scores of Lebanese and Iraqis took to the streets to express mounting discontent with systems of governance they saw as repeatedly failing them.[89] In Lebanon, citizens protested against both a government-proposed tax on WhatsApp calls and the mishandling of an economic crisis, while in Iraq, protesters denounced the deterioration of basic services and the government's failure to eliminate corruption. Equipped with mobile phones, protesters in both countries called for the resignation of the government and the dismantling of what they perceived as a corrupt political system that feeds on institutionalized divisions and engenders deeper schisms between the countries' ethnic and religious constituents. In Iraq, as in Lebanon, protesters from different segments of the population were united in protesting their government and contesting a system they adamantly wanted to see overhauled. For them, sectarianism has come to serve as a form of sociopolitical demarcation that symbolizes (and promotes) corruption.

These public displays of contestation are simultaneously a rejection of sectarianism and a projection of a new vision: a more encompassing conception of collective identity that affirms one's claim to equal rights (*al musawat fi al huquq*), citizenry (*muwatana*), and coexistence (*taayush*). Widely shared scenes of protesters chanting slogans that call for unity and oneness became powerful statements about the nature of citizenry to which they aspire. In an era in which subjectivities are constructed at the intersection of online and offline worlds, in a context where place and platform are intertwined, the use of digital tools to live, relay, and connect with these moments allows people to identify closely with these impromptu, unrehearsed, unstructured moments that showcase affective belonging. By using mobile devices to record, share, and amplify these spontaneous "acts of citizenship,"[90] protesters imbue the notion of citizenry with an affective dimension. Throughout these events, it is not so much the expediency of digital communication that has brought people together but the call for unity and the display of affective citizenship.

Chapter 13

The Demographics of a Connected Culture

By some measures, the Arab Middle East, and particularly its youth, is highly connected to the Internet. According to 2022, ITU data, 70% of individuals in the Arab world use the internet, which places the region's average above those for the world (66%).[1] Of the region's roughly 400 million internet users, access rates are 75% among men, 68% among women, and 68% among youth (ages fifteen to twenty-four)[2] Yet these numbers do not tell the full story. In addition to considering what the scale of internet penetration suggests about the region's digital access, it is also useful to explore what the current affordances of the digital in the Middle East, which operate on the techno-social level, reveal about opportunities and challenges for the region's communities and cultures.

While children, youth, and women constitute distinctly significant segments of the population, their interests are poorly served and their voices inadequately represented in the development, organization, and management of Arab societies. Decisions about the acquisition, adoption, and use of technologies primarily remain the purview of a predominantly older, male demographic whose interests and priorities determine policy. Accordingly, states have consistently attempted to censor and regulate information technologies under the pretext of maintaining societal norms. When media content and digital communication threaten to unsettle the status quo, states intervene, invoking the need to safeguard the social order.[3] This approach is motivated by cultural preservation but also stems from long-standing views about the role and status of children, youth, and women in society. While such logics continue to shape how these demographic categories are perceived and treated in Middle Eastern societies, the digital turn has also given rise to media uses and communication practices that challenge established sociocultural norms—as evidenced by the reaction against them.

How the digital turn unfolds in relation to significant cultural and demographic shifts deserves greater attention. In this chapter, we first explore unique aspects of

The Digital Double Bind. Mohamed Zayani and Joe F. Khalil, Oxford University Press. © Oxford University Press 2024.
DOI: 10.1093/oso/9780197508626.003.0013

how the digital turn impacts connected children (from birth to age fifteen), then focus on how digital spaces offer openings as well as enclosures among the region's largest age group (youth ages fifteen to twenty-four), and conclude by addressing the lingering issue of the digital gender divide.

Growing Up with the Digital

The global interest in twenty-first-century skills has brought digital literacy and its relationship to children's education and entertainment to the center of public attention. Although children around the world increasingly benefit from the opportunities digital media affords, the implications of such digital encounters depend on the specific contexts within which they unfold.[4]

The Middle East's economic, political, and sociocultural conditions are reflected in how the digital turn has impacted children. Whereas the region's digitally advanced countries have adopted digital technologies as skill-enhancing pedagogical tools, less developed countries bemoan how limitations of infrastructure and literacies reinforce structural inequalities (such as internet speed), exacerbate long-standing divides, and introduce new barriers.[5] These conditions are further complicated by growing anxieties about digital content, fueled by the moral panic that traditionally accompanies the introduction of new media and the adoption of new technologies.[6] As children's lives on- and offline coalesce and alter existing forms of communication and modes of sociality, questions about missed opportunities and potential harms acquire renewed relevance.

The demographic category of "children" is socially constructed and therefore differs across time and cultures.[7] Whereas Western constructions of childhood emphasize the status of the child as an individual with agency, across the Middle East, the term exists within the cultural framework of collectivism (family, neighborhood, tribe, village, etc.).[8] In this context, adults' roles and responsibilities are central to the upbringing of children, from passing on tradition and fostering identity to instilling values and nurturing faith. In traditional Middle Eastern societies, parents and caregivers acted as role models, ushering children into the various developmental stages leading to adulthood. Various societal changes—from family structures to rising standards of living and from mass education to new forms of communication—have had a notable impact on the family structure and the social formation of the individual, effectively challenging conventional role models.[9] Replacing the traditional extended clan are nuclear families and variably single-parent households that experience different challenges compounded by the exigencies of particular sociocultural environments. Inevitably, as Arab societies become increasingly subject to processes of acculturation, traditional family role models shift and are redefined. Children find themselves more intensely exposed to different role models, interacting in multiple languages, and operating in heterogeneous communities.[10] These changes all influence who the children are, how they behave around others, and what decisions they make.

Changes in communication brought new complexities that coincided with an era of high globalization characterized by the intense and unprecedented flow of images, ideas, and lifestyles. The introduction of satellite channels in the 1990s challenged parental control over children's television access, viewing habits, and content preferences. From educational programs to music videos and from cartoon shows to interactive live programs, Arab children were exposed to different messages and practices through programming on specialized children's channels. Nevertheless, adults continued to shape children's social world, including their education and leisure activities and, more relevant, their access to technology. Fear that such content would threaten the social values and well-being of children prompted states and market to invest in regional television content (e.g., Al Jazeera Children's Channel, now part of the beIN Media Group) or create alternative content (e.g., the religious Al Majd Kids channel). The debate regarding whether moral panics over children's television programming were justified remained inconclusive and eventually waned, only to reemerge when the internet started to compete with familiar programming on satellite television for children's time and attention.

The introduction of the internet bred public anxiety over unhindered access to potentially uncontrolled, unrestricted foreign content. The television screen was an inherently bounded sphere in which programming executives, state regulators, and adults largely oversaw the flow, quantity, and quality of content. The internet was structurally different. Unlike older technologies, digital media is available on mobile tools, transforming everyday practices and making them more accessible and pervasive. With the abundance of personal devices from cell phones to consoles, many parents became wary of the extent to which familial relations and delineated media environments were receding in the face of children's proclivity to develop para-social relationships with digital characters online. In some ways, video-sharing platforms (e.g., YouTube and later TikTok) and video games (e.g., *Minecraft*) are for today's children what television channels such as Spacetoon and Nickelodeon were for children who grew up during the transition from broadcast to satellite television. Both video-sharing platforms and video games depart from the incumbent media's stale, monotonous content to offer a tapestry of colorful, interactive, and fast-paced content for children eager to immerse themselves in avenues for leisure and discovery. And just as many of today's parents wanted to have their own television sets as children, their own children now pressure them for their own mobile devices. While television reigned in twentieth-century media, it now competes with an ever-expanding array of communication tools and digital media devices, including cell phones, portable media players (iPads), interactive multiplayer video games, and online social networks.[11]

The speed with which children are gaining access to digital tools is unprecedented. It is estimated that 26% of children and youth from birth to age twenty-five in the region have access to the internet at home, compared with the global percentage of 33%.[12] Considering the higher rate of mobile connectivity among the region's adult population and that many children access the internet through their parents' mobile phones, this is a conservative estimate, which means the immersion of the region's children in the digital world is likely on par with global trends. The unprecedented level of immersion means multiple facets of children's everyday lives are associated with internet practices and played out on digital devices. The digital turn is uncharted territory not only for parents but for the state and its institutions, considering their authority over public life. Increasingly, regulatory authorities in the region are playing catch-up. The exceedingly open environment of contemporary digital media enables behaviors that defy the state's ability to intervene even while it challenges family control over children's viewing.[13]

Children's attraction to the digital often renews old anxieties in the previous generation. For some, children's largely unhindered access to screens is making more real than ever the predicament Kahlil Gibran wrote of in his poem "On Children"—namely that "your children are not your children."[14] In many cases, these apprehensions emanate from a nostalgia for a predigital world defined less by technologies of communication and information flows than by personal communication and conventional social ties. For skeptical parents, many of whom are themselves heavy mobile users, the promises of the internet are tinged with its undesired effects. According to this group, the compulsive use of digital devices has proved disruptive to existing forms of sociality and to traditional ways of living. The internet can broaden opportunities for children, but constantly evolving forms of digital engagement also pose new risks.

The dearth of region-specific research leaves a void that is often filled by normative interpretations derived from Western contexts. Comparative research reinforces existing inequalities between the region and the rest of the world by focusing on access and affordances or underscoring Western research interests by highlighting regional standards of privacy or commercialization of its digital industries, for example. Local research on children and the internet warns against the consequences of children's growing internet addiction[15] for traditional gender definitions, cultural values, social norms, and linguistic practices.[16] These apprehensions partly account for growing dispositions among parents to support internet censorship that could reinforce cultural protectionism while also advocating efforts to develop more culturally relevant digital entertainment.[17] In contrast, various NGOs offer digital literacies to both parents and children to mitigate the risks and limitations of the internet. For example, Jordan's Queen Rania Foundation spearheaded initiatives for Arabic digital literacy and early childhood development that recognize the centrality of digital tools to children's social world,[18] while Google launched Abtal Al Internet (Internet Heroes), an initiative in Arabic designed to educate children about digital citizenship and safe internet practices.[19]

The unprecedented exposure to languages, representations, traditions, and social behavior is sometimes celebrated as integration into a global (understood as Western digital) culture that proclaims rich diversity and inclusive identities. Coexisting with this celebration is concern about foreign cultural influence and a generational divide, as children, being "digital natives," develop skills and literacies little understood by parents, teachers, and policymakers. Even so, adults' widespread access to and use of digital tools and increasing institutional, educational, and religious endorsement of the digital turn have led to several initiatives to maximize opportunities and minimize risks, especially in digitally advanced Arab states. With support from international organizations, government bodies, and commercial ventures, digital educational technologies have been at the forefront of bridging the generational gap and offering children alternatives to Western digital platforms and applications. Considerable efforts have been made to transition print publishing to the digital age[20] and develop interactive tools and digital resources for learning Arabic.[21] In the e-books sector, the Saudi early-education app Lamsa and the Egyptian app for interactive stories Rawy Kids stand out for their rich catalogs and ability to incorporate animation, games, and videos for preschoolers. Other initiatives have focused on specific children's demographics, such as Keefak (How Are You) for the Lebanese diaspora and BabaNoor for children with learning disabilities.

The COVID-19 pandemic has starkly revealed the vast disparities between nations regarding online teaching. In some countries, such as the Gulf states, a robust infrastructure already allowed them to make a smoother transition. Elsewhere, though, many students and teachers lacked access to suitable technology or reliable internet connections. Additionally, outdated curricula, traditional subjects, and insufficient funding for faculty created further obstacles. These difficulties are particularly acute in public schools, where critical thinking is often stifled and budgets unevenly allocated. While private schools tend to tackle these problems, they do so at prohibitive cost. This sharp contrast between the public and private systems has been worsened by limited access to ICTs.

Clearly, the ubiquity of digital devices and the abundance of nonlocal content have created opportunity while accentuating discordance. Children and youth rarely see themselves adequately represented in the digital content they consume. In globalized games such as Call of Duty and Battlefield, Middle East landscapes are featured as backdrops; Arab traditions, dialects, and costumes are mixed up; and Arab characters are rarely portrayed in positive ways. Similarly, parents do not recognize their culture in the largely Westernized digital content their children often prefer. While regional parental and political agendas seem to focus on bridging digital divides and addressing sociocultural issues related to Arabic language and the region's culture, international organizations such as UNICEF[22] and ESCWA[23] are increasingly interested in developing and legally enforcing measures for protecting children from internet-based abuse, from online bullying to sex trafficking. In practice, the region's children and youth are subject to competing and often conflicting messages from their parents, educational and religious institutions, and the interlocking commercial interests, technological tools, and cultural forces of globalization.

These considerations aside, the digital turn has undoubtedly transformed children from "audiences" whose access to media content is relatively limited and fairly controllable into "users" who are often in control of the type and amount of digital content they consume through a constantly changing set of devices. The implications of these developments are particularly manifest with youth, whose appropriation of the digital is the focus of the next section.

The Youth Bulge and Digital Natives

Youth in the Middle East often find themselves navigating competing and contradictory forces. In some states, the youth population must be controlled and utilized to muster support for the regime, while in others, youth must be appeased to preempt rebellious inclinations. The region's governments dedicate ministries for youth affairs and manage young people's access to sports, cultural, and social activities. Similarly, educational institutions play an important role in shaping young people's identities and promoting specific career paths, while religious authorities guide their spirituality. Beyond these influences, young people's lives are also subject to the forces of globalization in its socioeconomic articulations and its disruptive manifestations. Over the past few decades, extremist religious groups have been vigorously recruiting youth from across the region and its diaspora to serve as literal or figurative soldiers in their ideological battles. In contrast, foreign (mostly European and American) aid and international organizations nurture a Western-friendly youth population, often through public diplomacy efforts ranging from media workshops to educational fellowships.[24] Alongside these conflicting ideological forces is a glamorized and hedonistic culture of consumption fostered by the region's increased integration into global economies. The outcome is communities of style, practice, and interest that transcend linguistic and geographic barriers and are embedded in global—mostly Western—trends. Such youth cultures have developed around various types of fashion, movie, and musical genres, among other forms of cultural production and modes of consumption.[25] Although Arab youth cultures have historically manifested themselves in the arts (e.g., modern poetry), lifestyle (e.g., the mall culture), and music (e.g., Arab pop), they have become particularly pronounced with the proliferation of satellite television and, more intensely, with the onset of the digital turn. Together these sociocultural forces construct and shape the experience and meaning of youth in the Middle East.

Young people are generally viewed as being in a transitional stage between childhood and adulthood, making the definition of "youth" fluid. Various age brackets have been applied for statistical purposes, but these remain somewhat arbitrary and subjective. For example, the UN and the World Bank define youth as being from fifteen to twenty-four years of age,[26] while the Islamic Development Bank and the Arab League use a more expanded definition of youth as ages fifteen to thirty-five).[27] These age brackets are hard to delineate when considering how youthfulness is valued socioculturally (e.g., employment, marriage) and enmeshed with political economy (e.g., marriage loans, emigration). Age markers such as these are further complicated when accounting for generations that are often viewed as part of the youth category, such as Generation Alpha (born in the early 2010s and throughout the 2020s), Generation Z (born in the late 1990s and early 2000s), and millennials (born between 1981 and 1996.

Demographically, the Middle East's children and young people (from birth to age twenty-four) constitute nearly half of the population[28] in a region witnessing the most rapid population growth in its modern history, with people ten to twenty-four years of age representing around 26% of the population.[29] The sheer size of this demographic group, known as the "youth bulge," helps to illuminate its increasing socioeconomic and political importance.[30] More relevantly, this sizable group represents an entire generation—"an Arab digital generation"[31]—that identifies (and is identified) with the introduction and development of digital technologies. Young people were among the first groups to seek and integrate digital tools into their everyday activities, and today's youth continue to be the leading users of the internet. Young people make up the core of the 88% of the population that is online daily and of the 94% who own a smartphone.[32] The scale of internet adoption by youth should not obscure structural or infrastructural limitations.

From its beginning, the internet posed challenges to policymakers and parents who found themselves conflicted over the potential of this new development. On one hand, the internet (and having strong digital skills) was believed to be the gateway to better employment. With unabated unemployment rates that are double the world average,[33] the state and business communities are developing programs and initiatives to remedy the skills mismatch between education and the job market. Countries such as Oman and Qatar have made great strides in integrating digital skills into their curricula.[34] Jordan has pioneered private-public partnerships in boot camps, training, and funding to support digital initiatives such as Edraak.[35] Where youth were able to overcome digital disparity and skill deficits, they have contributed to the growth of the digital sector and, in many cases, have helped energize digital innovation and entrepreneurship.[36]

On the other hand, sociocultural concerns about young people's exposure to unregulated content persist. In reaction, the state has interfered, to varying degrees, to ensure that access to internet content is controlled, particularly when it comes to culturally sensitive material (e.g., content deemed to be pornographic). This is not entirely experienced as oppression, as observers steeped in Western free-speech discourses might assume. Even today, there is an expectation among many people in the region that the government should exert some form of control over internet content, particularly objectionable material.[37]

Such sociocultural and structural contexts have a strong bearing on how we approach the question of Arab youth and the digital, not least the need for such analysis to recognize young people's individual and collective agency. The acquisition of digital tools and skills has offered pathways for young people to express themselves and develop more open and egalitarian forms of engagement within their societies. Intersecting with this sense of individualism is a competing sense of collectivism that transcends the traditional markers of family or geography— one that centers on the use of digital media, including apps, gaming, e-learning, e-commerce, and social media.

The rise of individualism and the renewed sense of collectivism make it difficult for young people to relate to the kind of expected passivity, complacency, and dependency characteristic of the predigital era. As an example, consider young people's patterns of news consumption. Data suggest that social media is a key sources of news stories for the majority of Arab youth (79%).[38] As individuals and communities, young people are attracted to content that speaks to their lives, experiences, and perspectives; when such content is not available, they create it themselves. While they may show little interest in formal or party politics, the youth are inevitably enmeshed in everyday politics. These trends are evident across the social-media spectrum, from the way young people identify with the startup culture to the multiple ways they recognize their ethnic, class, or gendered identities.

Women and the Digital Gender Divide

The status of women in the Middle East has long been at the center of political, cultural, economic, and religious debates both within and outside the region. The digital has intensified these debates. On one hand, the digital has brought renewed faith in women's empowerment.[39] Many women have found the internet to be a platform to voice their views and defy male control of public discourses. Some have gone further, engaging in grassroots activism, economic advancement, and entrepreneurship. On the other hand, there is deep skepticism about the ability of the digital turn to significantly alter women's status. If anything, the digital turn has increased concern that existing limitations for women in the region will be transposed into the online sphere and perhaps even compounded by new challenges that exacerbate gender inequalities.

Even with increased access and diverse use, a substantial digital gender gap persists. Overall, this gap impacts women's ability to benefit fully from the affordances of ICTs. Notably, low internet penetration is not the only barrier to disseminating ICTs among women. The divide is also influenced by other gender barriers, including education levels, illiteracy rates, and ICT skills. Cultural attitudes, internalized norms, and preconceptions about women are also important factors. Gender differentiation is generally an outcome of socialization, and the role of family and society cannot be overstated in terms of control or protection regarding internet access. These issues are exacerbated by limited independence, financial and otherwise. Where internet access and mobile ownership are relatively high, women often operate in a hostile environment that includes misogyny, bullying, and harassment. Like other marginalized groups, women are as vulnerable online as they are offline. Because the Middle East has the lowest rate of female participation in the workforce of any global region,[40] it would be misguided to think the advent of a knowledge economy and increased use of technology in the workplace would be sufficient to level the playing field for women. They are simply not yet reaping the benefits.

Although the paucity of gender-disaggregated data relating to internet use makes it difficult to assess the extent of the digital gender gap in the region, available statistics provide revealing trends. ITU data from 2021 show that only 56% of the Arab female population uses the internet, compared with 68% of Arab males.[41] Within the region, there are notable differences between countries. In Kuwait and Lebanon, internet usage is roughly even by gender, and in Jordan, women's internet access (83%) only minimally lags men's internet access (86%). By contrast, in Morocco, nearly 23% fewer women than men have internet access, and the gender gap increases to 29% in Tunisia.[42] These disparities do not always correlate with income level. In Iraq, an upper-middle-income country, 67% of women use the internet compared with 84% of men. In Egypt, a lower-middle-income country, 47% of women use the internet compared with 69% of men. According to the 2020 GSMA Mobile Gender Gap Report, women in low- and middle-income countries are 8% less likely to own a mobile phone than men, whereas the gender gap in mobile internet use is 21%.[43] Other factors affect digital gender gaps, such as issues of income level, education, social class, age, and divisions between urban and rural populations.

Digital gender equity bears on issues of human rights, social justice, and social change. Low rates of internet access deprive women of economic opportunities and affect their ability to take part in internet-based economic activities and emerging knowledge-based economies.[44] Despite the global push toward "gender mainstreaming"[45] aimed at making the experiences and concerns of women and men part of the process of policymaking and program implementation, the rate of women in the STEM fields (science, technology, engineering, and mathematics) remains relatively low, and the number of women in ICT careers is markedly lower than that of men.[46] Similarly, and despite advances in gender parity, women continue to be an underrepresented group in decision-making, policy, and regulation in the IT sector.[47]

While ICTs are helping women pursue economic opportunities, the adoption of ICTs is not necessarily altering issues of gender inequity. In fact, the digital gender divide reflects broader socioeconomic and cultural dimensions of gender inequalities. Statistically, most Arab countries figure in the third and fourth quartile of the 2022 Global Gender Gap Index, which is based on four indicators: economic participation, educational attainment, health and survival, and political empowerment. In a survey of 149 countries, the top three performers in the region are the UAE (ranked 68), Lebanon (119), and Tunisia (120).[48] In the long run, the pressing question is whether the digital can help address these inequalities and bridge the gender divide or is more likely to transpose it, reinvent it, and deepen it with digitization.

These dynamics come into play more fully with the expanded presence of female entrepreneurs. According to one survey, Tunisia, Algeria, Egypt, the UAE, and Saudi Arabia are the top-ranked Arab countries when it comes to the presence of female business owners (as a percentage of total business owners) in 2018.[49] Although more women are capitalizing on communication technologies and digital tools to enhance their participation in the workplace, their advancement is undermined by existing conditions, structural limitations, and power dynamics. As a result, the digital is creating opportunities for women to be financially independent, which in turn can secure other forms of independence, but it is also reproducing existing disparities and engendering another set of challenges. A case in point is the Facebook trade (or *tijarat al face*) in Khartoum, where women sell products acquired from regional commercial centers such as Dubai through all-female Facebook groups. Ethnographic work on such small-scale forms of entrepreneurship suggests that the internet enables networked Sudanese women to operate on the margins of a male-dominated trade sector in a society where constructions of womanhood are traditionally premised on women's exclusive dedication to their homes and families.[50] Being active on digital platforms enables women to overcome social limits on physical mobility, create economic value, and pursue online commercial activities from their homes. Navigating family responsibilities and work opportunities enables these female entrepreneurs to redraw the boundaries between private and public life. ICT-centered activities on social-media platforms create opportunities for economic empowerment and social maneuvering by widening these women's social circles and adding meaning to their social lives.[51] Significantly, while such small-scale forms of entrepreneurship give women a degree of autonomy, they are tolerated only as long as they do not conflict with women's adherence to cultural expectations about gender roles or lead to assertions of independence or questioning of patriarchal ideologies.

Beyond the case of Sudanese women entrepreneurs, the digital turn has favored the rise of a new type of female economic actor whose pursuit of autonomy and attainment inspires other women.[52] Among these are successful digital entrepreneurs who have created multimillion-dollar digital brands, predominantly in the fashion and lifestyle niche.[53] These range from Palestinian entrepreneur Mona Ataya, who cofounded and headed Mumzworld, a leading e-commerce company (later acquired by Saudi Tamer Group) in the region specializing in mother, baby, and child products, to Iraqi-American Huda Kattan, a makeup artist and top-ranked influencer who is among the world's richest self-made women and whose brand, Huda Beauty, has more than 50 million Instagram followers. The women's startup scene also includes incubators for women's digital startups and supportive ventures, such as Womena, a Dubai-based media platform dedicated to gender tech inclusion, and the Gaza Sky Geeks, a Gaza-based tech hub and startup accelerator with a focus on women.

While these success stories have inspired an increasing number of female entrepreneurs, women continue to face constraints. Startup and online ventures may advance women's entrepreneurship, but they nonetheless leave women in the region with the intractable challenge of reconciling societal norms regarding the demands of career pursuits and professional fulfillment with those of personal and traditional family obligations.[54] Professionally, although the digital is fostering a more equitable environment and a meritocratic system that challenges traditional barriers, the demands of successful entrepreneurship and multistake business processes that depend on a complex ecosystem subject women to other forms of exploitation inherent in the very nature of digital capitalism (e.g., commodification of data, paid work and "leisure time," and value derived from digital activity). Even so, successful female entrepreneurs are not representative of the majority of women in the Middle East. Access to technology does not necessarily reduce the gender gap. Digital leapfrogging opportunities do not constitute a clear path to eradicating gender inequalities.[55] For the average woman, such opportunities do not remedy socioeconomic marginality as is often believed. Structural barriers and disadvantages—from class determinants to sociocultural censure and from capital access to resource accrual—hamper women's agentive use of digital technologies and engender further marginalization.[56]

Chapter 14

Collectivity, Identity, and Multivocality

Mediated youth culture has changed over time. With the digital turn, contemporary Arab youth cultures continue to coalesce locally and integrate globally. These youth cultures allow for the emergence of a pronounced digital self within predominantly collectivist societies. For youth, traditional and socially mediated networks are concurrently liberating and constraining. Young people often experience a tension between the desire to display their individuality and the expectation to heed social norms. From this milieu, forms of cohabitations between competing voices within society emerge. In the process, the sociocultural dynamics of the digital turn manifest as complex, multilayered dynamics that shape subjectivities. Young people thus emerge as simultaneously independent individuals and dependent community members.

Living on Social Networks

Increasingly, the lived experience of young people is shaped by what they experience online and what they do offline. Being nearly always connected, the interpersonal relationships that characterize traditional social networks (primarily friends and family) are increasingly mediated through digital platforms and social-media applications.

On average, people in the MENA region spend 3.5 hours daily on social media, with the average person being active on roughly eight different social-media platforms[1] and with nine out of ten youth using at least one social-media platform daily.[2] Patterns of use and accessibility differ across socioculturally, economically, and politically diverse subregions and countries. On the whole, however, the region's high rates of social-media adoption are in line with global trends and with patterns of usage in the OECD countries.[3] Saudi Arabia and Egypt dominate the social-media networks. Data from 2022 show that Egypt—the most populous

The Digital Double Bind. Mohamed Zayani and Joe F. Khalil, Oxford University Press. © Oxford University Press 2024.
DOI: 10.1093/oso/9780197508626.003.0014

country in the region—is a key national market for Facebook, with more than 44.70 million monthly mobile users (42.50% of the population), compared with more than 11.40 million (32% of the population) in Saudi Arabia, the region's largest ICT market. On Instagram, though, usage data is comparable in the two countries, with 15.45 million users in Saudi Arabia and 16.00 million users in Egypt. The kingdom also has more than 29.30 million active YouTube users and dominates both Snapchat (with 20.30 million users) and Twitter (with 14.10 million users prior to the launch of Meta's Twitter-like Threads) regionally. Globally, Saudi Arabia reigns as the sixth-largest market for Snapchat and the eighth-largest market for Twitter. Undoubtedly, young people continue to drive the growth on these social media, with millennials leading the development on Twitter and Facebook, Generation Z fueling growth on Snapchat and Instagram, and Generation Alpha dominating livestreaming apps such as TikTok, Likee, and Twitch.

A close examination of social-media adoption in the MENA region points to sustained and diverse online interactions, personal and professional usage, and increased engagement. While it is difficult to account for the diversity of young people's online interactions, it is possible to highlight common trends and identify defining characteristics based on widely adopted online activities and user habits, which tend to correlate with access to better infrastructure. In line with global trends, many young people in the Middle East engage in consuming and sharing videos (47%) and music (34%).[4] However, when it comes to sharing personal content online, youth across the region differ in ways that reflect their sociocultural contexts, with 65% in Lebanon sharing personal photos or videos compared with 26% in Qatar.[5] Similarly, young people in the region tend to acquire news primarily from online sources (61%)[6] and to consume entertainment on digital venues, including those animated by social-media influencers (50%).[7] Importantly, young users are not merely passive consumers of content. They also use social networks to discover, negotiate, and perform their identities, from female cyber activists using social media to demand gender parity[8] to Amazigh youth launching a health campaign in their indigenous language. Still other youth capitalize on social networks for self-advancement and professional pursuits. While many young people use social media to network, promote themselves, or identify job opportunities, the most venturesome use social media as marketing platforms. In particular, young innovators have been entrepreneurial in using social networks to advertise services, conduct business transactions, and organize product deliveries. Whether to produce and consume content, show solidarity, or develop business, young people have adopted social media as both modus vivendi and modus operandi.

An analysis of the growing prominence of digitality in young people's lives needs to situate that development within the context of political dynamics and economic structures. From the onset of the digital turn, both state policies and market exigencies incentivized young people to develop digital skills. Where mandated by the state and integrated into educational programs, digital skills became a gateway for future-oriented employment, entrepreneurship, and investment opportunities. Once acquired, these skills helped youth navigate their way into an encompassing, unbounded, and consuming sphere where information, communication, and creation overlap and intersect. For savvy users adept at using communication technologies, operating online became second nature. These young people now communicate information, defend their ideological stances, voice their opinion on issues, and articulate their own understandings of everyday affairs by creating and posting content and by sharing, liking, and commenting on posts. Together, information, communication, and creation amount to the development of individual voices, with more users adopting social networks as a platform for identification and for distinguishing themselves as individuals with independent voices. Yet, while imposing and pervasive, these voices tend to be fragmented and dispersed. These engagements also encompass disinformation, inauthentic behavior, and fraudulent transactions that replicate aberrations common in face-to-face interactions offline, accentuating the need for all users to develop digital literacies.

Living on social networks is reshaping social values and even challenging the kind of collectivist culture that has long characterized the Middle East. In practice, there is a form of cohabitation, delicate and tenuous as it may be, between a traditional sense of belonging to a community whose interests are prioritized over those of its members and a growing expression of individualism characterized by the pursuit of personal goals and interests that supersede those of the group. On one level, social networks encompass interactions and personal relationships as the foundation of collectivist societies. Such social formations are prominently based on shared identity markers, including kinship, nationality, language, interests, and religion. On another level, social networks constructed around social media often underscore the personal rather than the collective. Individuals are distinguished by their technical savvy, content creativity, and ability to attract followers.

Young people's tensions between expressing individual voices and their collective belonging did not originate with the digital. The history of such tensions shows that they can follow surprising paths that differ from the revolutionary, individualistic futures some have projected. The introduction of satellite television in the 1990s initially brought apprehensions that access to borderless media content could disintegrate the sense of communal belonging, that the proliferation of channels and de facto fragmentation of audiences could erode a sense of national and inter-Arab social cohesion. Instead, the proliferation of media fed a renewed sense of Arabness—of belonging to a broader linguistic, geographical, and cultural community—that transcended state borders. Similarly, in the digital era, individual subjectivities are defined less in contradistinction to the communal self than in relation to it.

Tensions between forms of sociality centered around collectivism and individualism, both alternative and mainstream, are expressed against changing notions of the private and the public. Digital social networks have contributed to new forms of socialization, including those related to internet privacy and public postings. These digital forms of socialization include dating applications such as Tinder or Grindr, which are used by an estimated 14% of the region's population.[9] With a younger generation of Arabs migrating their leisure time to social media and streaming platforms, these ongoing tensions manifest themselves even more intensely in the digital sphere. Whether socially enforced or religiously dictated, the separation between private and public spheres has been challenged by introducing relatively open digital spaces. In the process, young people have redefined the parameters of privacy by selectively including or excluding particular communities and individuals online. Across the Middle East, new forms of socialization benefit from platform affordances where young people, particularly women, would share avatars instead of pictures of themselves, limit the visibility of their accounts, exclude certain friends and family members from "official" accounts, or create mirror accounts and develop aliases. Young people are conscious of their level of privacy, particularly as social-media accounts become accepted and normalized and their profiles and images become more readily consumable.

The use of personal devices has enhanced young people's ability to foreground their identities and assert their individuality. Spending so many hours engaging through social networks amounts to being connected to and spending time with others. Yet the substance of these activities points to the rise of new collectivities transcending existing barriers. While young people tend to be removed from (and often distrustful of) the sphere of formal politics, they develop communities around issues of "everyday politics," which center on the topics that affect them on a personal level and the challenges they encounter in their daily lives, including subjects as diverse as unemployment, the environment, migration, and dance parties. Being at the receiving end of state policies and government choices that affect their lives, young people are constantly negotiating their evolving identities and roles within their societies.[10] The tensions that animate the multiple levels of sociality between collectivism and individualism are particularly evident in how youth negotiate their voice and presence on social networks.

A case in point is *Ayza Aggawez* (*I Want to Get Married*), a television series based on a book that was inspired by a blog. Both the content, including the storyline and the characters, and its multimodal narrative production reveal much about the tension between collectivism and individualism. In 2006, when many Egyptian blogs were focused on political issues surrounding Mubarak's succession, Ghada Abdel Aal, a young woman from Al Mahalla, a large industrial city in Egypt, started a blog recounting her personal experiences and the challenges many of her female friends encounter as they navigate the community's sociocultural norms for finding a suitor. She chronicled her encounters and reflected on her experience using witty, critical, and poignant journal-style blog entries that became instantly popular among a generation of young Egyptians dealing with the same issues. Whereas in many societies the choice of a spouse is a personal decision, in Egypt's largely conservative communities courting happens in public under the scrutiny of the family and the neighborhood community. In the blog, Abdel Aal questioned the immediate and extended community's probing involvement in a personal matter. The blog resonated with young women precisely because it exposed deep-rooted tensions between individual choices and collective values in a changing society in which females are increasingly educated and independent. While Abdel Aal's blog may be read as an articulation of incongruencies between the values of traditional and westernized societies, or between middle- and upper-class communities, at its core, it is also about young people developing competencies and affordances to turn information and communication into critical reflection and artful creation whereby imaginatively crafted messages acquire a broad circulation and a strong resonance.[11]

Becoming a "blogthrough"[12] that attracted wide attention helped *Ayza Aggawez* cross over from digital media spaces to traditional media. Dar al Shuruq, one of the region's prominent publishers, printed a book version of the blog, which was subsequently translated to other languages.[13] In 2010, MBC, the region's most popular entertainment channel, turned the book into a sitcom, which broadened its appeal further. Capitalizing on the success of *Ayza Aggawez* while giving it a new spin, Netflix produced a sequel to the series, *Finding Ola*, which featured the lead character as a forty-year-old newly divorced mother navigating even more difficult social pressures in a world where dating apps coexist with arranged marriages and where social influencers compete with community elders as role models. The various iterations of *Ayza Aggawez* and Abdel Aal's own journey highlight a creative tension between markers of collectivism and individualism that reflect societal changes and how individuals navigate them in the digital era. They also demonstrate young women's ability to harness digital platforms to communicate their subjectivities and advocate for alternative cultural politics.

Living on social networks imbues life with a sense of urgency, epitomized in the virality and instantaneous nature of messages, which amounts to a practical antidote to feelings of powerlessness as individuals build solidarities within and across boundaries. There is an unprecedented immediacy with which individuals and groups can reach local, regional, and global users. Young people's ability to forge a life outside traditionally established cultural norms and social structures is often considered a threat to the fabric of these collectivist societies. Gender roles and sexual identities have become arenas in which old, patriarchal norms and the very "habitus and practices that limit not only women's but also men's sexuality"[14] are challenged. Similarly, other collectivities have found strength in digital platforms where women's voices are consolidated in religiously defined digital spaces.[15] Such largely gender-based collectivities are built around everyday politics and transcend traditional boundaries that often limit women's participation in public life. In the Middle East, these practices reconnect with a long history in which the young served as the vanguard of sociopolitical change and in which poets, journalists, and artists illuminated plights of social injustice across the region and beyond.

Socially Mediated Publicness

More than ever before, young people's ways of living are performed and consumed in public. Publicness has become a defining element of emerging digital-culture practices, an ever-changing process through which young people, in particular, appropriate various digital platforms, shape the context of their usage, and engage with certain content. In the process, they transgress established social boundaries, claim a space, and communicate specific conceptions of the self. An examination of young people's agency reveals how the socially mediated publicness of culture is imagined and produced. Tightly connected with these dynamics are the development and articulation of identity politics that revolve around digital practices and everyday forms of sociality.

The use of communication technologies to negotiate and assert identity politics is hardly new. What is notable is the unprecedented degree of young people's appropriation of social-media affordances and the extent to which social-media usage and communication habits permeate everyday life. In addition to online forums, this publicness developed around and found an outlet in blogs. Blogging allowed the proliferation of autobiographical writing and other creative forms of expression through diverse content (audiovisual, photos, sketches, etc.) and types of engagement (collective blogging, anonymity, commentary, etc.). From personal narratives to poems and film reviews to food critiques, blogs fused the fictional and the real, the private and the public, and the personal and the social. With the widespread adoption of smartphones, social media gradually replaced blogs as tools for projecting the self and constructing social identity. Facebook status updates, Instagram stories, and Twitter statements offered a magnified sense of publicness predicated on the ability to engage with and compete over "followers" whose interactions take various forms of engagement (likes, shares, comments, replies, etc.). Notably, this socially mediated publicness has encompassed private moments and intimate occasions. In many instances, it has replaced community events. More conspicuously, during the COVID-19 pandemic, these online community interactions became even more common, as obituaries, condolences, and testimonials were shared online to conform with guidelines for physical distancing.

The changes in the mediation landscape have altered user habits while simultaneously positioning users and platforms at the center of the communication process. The advent of the digital both generates and orients specific practices. What was traditionally the purview of a dominant social class—the sociocultural, political, and economic elites who are adept at using mass media to mold the public—is gradually slipping into the hands of young smartphone users. Their engagement in everyday life, whether as producers or (more often) consumers, allows them to contest the elites' preferred content and reclaim a sociocultural sphere.

Consider the controversy surrounding Mahraganat, a popular Egyptian street music associated with a DJ dance movement, the January 25 revolution, and oppositional culture more broadly.[16] At the core, such music challenged an imagined role for Egyptian art. The movement drew the ire of the Egyptian Musicians' Syndicate, a pro-establishment professional union that grants artists permission to perform. The union banned Mahraganat music from public performance and revoked the membership of its singers. Yet the genre thrived. Emerging from the *sha'bi* (popular) neighborhoods, Mahraganat music became enormously popular, transcending social classes. Its performances were avidly consumed on mobile phones through YouTube. Beyond its controversial cultural standing, Mahraganat is noteworthy because it promotes, among other trends and activities, collective dancing and vocal acts that challenge inherited visions of the self and its publicness. The famous song line "I drink alcohol and smoke weed," from the super-hit "Bent el Geran" ("The Neighbor's Daughter"), is a proclamation of agency in the form of a Mahraganat YouTube song against state-sponsored, religiously sanctioned, class-based hegemonic culture. As such, Mahraganat's digital distribution and exhibition represent shifting notions of publicness and reconfigurations of identity politics insofar as they compete with established gatekeepers of Arab pop, the dominant commercial musical genre.

Other artists have used digital platforms to make their voices heard. Bands such as Egypt's Cairokee and Masar Egbari (Mandatory Direction) or Lebanon's Soap Kills and the disbanded Mashrou Leila (Leila's Project) have occupied digital spaces from P2P sharing to streaming and from Soundcloud to YouTube. These various artists and collectives have been labeled as underground or avant-garde. They offer an alternative to commercial music by tackling themes of unemployment, corruption, education, and sexual orientation, among others. As a result, these artists have come to represent different aspirations of young people and resonating expressions of identity politics in a space that favors conformity, univocality, and mass consumption. Such underground music, with its Western rhythms and sensitivities, contrasts sharply with Mahraganat's street sounds and politics. While each genre represents a polar extreme of class and gender-identity politics masquerading as cultural production and consumption practices, their prevalent use of mediated publicness is a manifestation of the digital turn.

Unlike traditionally mediated publicness, which takes place in print and broadcast fields that are not interactive, digital publicness is dialogical, allowing for multilevel, multimodal communication. These new pathways for participatory communication are extensive and often come at the expense of other values, such as anonymity. A case in point is how digital social connectivity, such as meeting someone or finding a suitable partner, takes over traditional, socially organized matchmaking practices. Digital publicness turns a communal approach into an individual act. The dating app Tinder and the social proximity networking app WhosHere compete with the customary introductions offered by friends and family or the professional assistance of an *alkhattaba*, a traditional matrimonial matchmaker (now also the name of a matchmaking app). Where affordable and accessible, these apps offer young women, in particular, a choice of how and whom they want to date while giving them control over when and how much information to reveal about themselves. All these elements are essential considerations in societies in which gender relations are codified and social conservatism precludes unabashed forms of socialization. The appeal of such networking services has given rise to a range of homegrown digital services and apps that are culturally adapted, from the Beirut-based Matchmallows and Wango, which highlight emotional intimacy and value women's perspectives, to the Palestine-based Wesal or the Dubai-based Veil, which are more attuned to Islamic values. For most users who seek free services, Facebook acts as a surrogate dating tool through its friend request service and its messenger app (although the app also facilitates online harassment and generates social spam). Such networking practices are redefining publicness and reconfiguring privacy.

Digital platforms not only offer avenues for individuals to perform socially mediated publicness, but they also provide marginalized groups traditionally excluded from the public with possibilities to build solidarity and gain recognition within and across societies. This is particularly evident for displaced communities. Across the region, refugees have been subject to rules and restrictions imposed by their host states and the benevolence of aid organizations. Aside from political mobilization, digital tools have been used to foster and extend traditional community and familial links between community members, both in refugee camps and in the diaspora. In such digital spaces, political discourses and mobilization give way to nostalgia for the hometown, news about families, and solidarities between members of the same village, town, clan, or extended family. These digital feeds are venues where the dead are remembered and newborns are celebrated but also where public requests can be made for collaborative problem-solving or crowdfunding for needs such as assistance with medical intervention, housing relocation, or employment. While particularly developed and well documented within Palestinian communities,[17] these digital practices are also widespread among Yemeni, Syrian, and other refugees in the region. Although not exclusive to young people, many Facebook pages and WhatsApp groups that foster refugee or diaspora communities are managed by youth. By forging networks and developing alliances in these seemingly apolitical sites, these groups enact a socially mediated publicness that often eludes the eyes of the state. Such alliances are not perfect, and conflicts exist online just as they do offline, making the platform a less-than-peaceful rendering of communal life. Here moderation becomes the key to coexistence.

Young people use digital technologies to negotiate, test, and transgress established sociocultural boundaries. Young women, in particular, have harnessed the affordances of digital technologies to develop messages that speak to their conditions, reflect their politics, and expand their sphere of influence. Even before the global online viral #MeToo campaign of 2017, the Middle East had its digital collective movements to advance women's rights. In 2011, Saudi Arabia's #Women2Drive was a continuation of the 1990s movement and a precursor to lifting the ban on female drivers. In Egypt, the #NudePhotoRevolutionary campaign followed Egyptian activist Aalia Elmahdy's nude self-portrait on her blog. Morocco's #RIPAmina, Lebanon's #Abolish522 and #Undress522, and Jordan's #Sarkhet_Ahlam were social-media campaigns all targeting penal-code laws that sanctioned "honor killing" or allowed rapists to escape prosecution if they married their victims. Later the global #MeToo movement was appropriated as a way for young people to globally connect these campaigns. Several movements emerged across the region, drawing attention to harassment against women, calling out specific harassers, and demanding tougher legal sanctions. Although limited in its spread, the Saudi #MosqueMeToo draws attention to violence perpetrated against women of particular classes and ethnicities in religious spaces. In Morocco, the campaign Masaktach (As a Woman, I Will Not Be Silenced) operated Facebook and Twitter accounts that denounced harassers while maintaining the anonymity of the victims. In Kuwait, the Instagram account Lan Asket (I Shall Not Keep Quiet) released videos exposing and addressing harassment issues. In Egypt, a group of activists developed HarassMap, an interactive map for reporting harassment incidents and a platform for campaigns, with the help of NGOs and the open-source, Kenya-based software application Ushahidi. Although these campaigns may be inspired by global movements, they do not merely replicate them, nor does the young people's world narrowly reflect what is globally trending, politically expedient, or locally compliant.

As young people engage and appropriate digital media, they develop new forms of publicness that echo or emulate interpersonal settings or broadcast media. Seen from a macro sociological perspective, the various manifestations of cultural imperatives and individual agency accentuated by the digital turn are potentially indicative of incremental social change centered on young people's ability to espouse identity politics in a socially mediated publicness. The cohabitation between traditional celebrities and those dubbed "social-media influencers" provides one example of such change, which is the focus of the next section.

Digital Cohabitation

Examining the cohabitation of influencers and traditional celebrities who migrated to social media reveals seemingly irreconcilable and paradoxical everyday practices enabled by the digital. This digital cohabitation hinges on the question of authenticity. Influencers are people who built audiences using digital media; by

contrast, celebrities transferred their fame, which was gained on traditional channels (media, sports, the arts, etc.), to the digital sphere. These micro and macro
celebrities[18] have acquired the power to affect followers with whom they have built
social relationships based on authority, knowledge, position, or connection. Both
influencers and celebrities occupy various social-media platforms, yet they differ
in their goals, followers, content type, and influence level. Many of the region's
influencers operate as textbook cases of digital marketing premised on cultivating an image, manipulating algorithms, and developing content; however, a few
have been able to monetize their success. What seem like contradictory impulses
at the level of authenticity are dialectical tensions: both influencers and celebrities
occupy the same virtual space and, at times, are even constitutive of each other's
substance or form. So far, celebrities seem content to comply with digital cohabitation and extend their fame to these areas, while organic influencers are relegated
to being brand ambassadors. Celebrities and influencers alike capitalize on followers who value unique and genuine voices and a perceived sense of authenticity.

The emergence of noncelebrity influencers is associated with the popularity
of reality television in the 2000s.[19] Many among the current generation of star
singers (such as Diana Karazon, Amal Bouchoucha, Mohamed Assaf, and others) were groomed on reality TV shows such as *Super Star*, *Star Academy*, or *Arab
Idol*, which capitalized on the affordances of an evolving "hypermedia space" of
multimodal communication that enabled them to sustain the commercial and
dramatic logics of reality TV.[20] Suddenly famous for their athleticism, beauty, or
singing talents, these mostly young figures challenged established stars even as the
format seemed to offer the public the opportunity to select their favorite newcomers. While these shows' audiences voted for their favorite singers using SMS
and websites, their choices were facilitated and arbitrated by a set of gatekeepers, from judges to television executives.[21] Beyond voting, ordinary young people
demonstrated their support for their favorite contenders with YouTube clips and
comments, Facebook fan pages, and other social media content. These young and
talented contestants pioneered digital cohabitation. By combining traditional and
digital channels, they showcased their talent and strategically revealed facets of
their lives to build their followings.

The rise of influencers accentuated the reconfiguration of stardom. If mainstream media promoted the "ordinariness" of reality television stars who embodied self-commodification and self-branding, digital media valorized those
characteristics. Ambition and boldness became a structuring principle for acquiring online influencer status. By the end of the 2010s, fame became less dependent
on mainstream media's promotion and designation and more pointedly centered
around online personality, message, and platform. Owing in part to its features
(e.g., audiovisual, filters, photos, texts, captions) that facilitate the production of
edited and live content, Instagram has become a favorite platform for independent and alternative Arabic music (e.g., Arab Sounds, Scene Noise), rappers (e.g.,

Rap Scene), and local musicians (e.g., Moroccan Rap Memes, Saudi Musicians). Popular platforms such as TikTok, which engage a younger user demographic, feature more experimental talent (e.g., MENA Heat). The cumulative effect of these digital spaces tends to unsettle narrow or fixed definitions of talent, offer parallel venues for "discoverability," and expand the nature and scope of artistic expression.

Such cohabitation is not simply about choices of platform and modes of self-presentation. It is also about constructing a message that appears authentic despite, in reality, being the strategic result of many considerations, including politics. For many influencers, the politics of everyday life takes over politics in the traditional, narrow sense to become a defining characteristic of authenticity. This is particularly evident in the rise of the media phenomenon Bassem Youssef, an Egyptian cardiac surgeon turned YouTube comedian, television talk-show host, and eventually a social-media influencer. Youssef's unprecedented fame needs to be understood in relation to the broader social milieu, which values both his professional pedigree as a physician and his practice as a comedian. Operating from this privileged status, Youssef served as an aspirational, authentic figure when traditional media personalities were tainted by their association with the regime. Because Youssef (as discussed earlier) resisted the pressure to engage in self-censorship during a post-revolution period of political turmoil, his show was canceled on several satellite channels, and he was forced to leave Egypt. Youssef found himself caught between digital media's perceived freedom and traditional media's controlled speech, in a predicament indicative of the challenges digital cohabitation poses. Although his episodes continue to live on YouTube, his career took a new turn, as he shifted attention to Egypt's political scene after the uprisings and a focus on social change in the region. He reinvented himself as a social-media influencer, using his fame to promote lifestyle changes and environmentally friendly products. Although in Youssef's case such cohabitation came at a high professional and personal cost, many others still aspire to cohabitate between audience-limited digital spaces and speech-limiting satellite television—though these are not mutually exclusive spaces. Such is the case with Egyptian Youssef Hussain, whose JoeTube satirical comedy on YouTube was renamed *Joe Show* and broadcast on Al Araby TV.

To be successful, both traditional and digital influencers must be genuine in their content. In doing so, they must consider how states and markets control influence. The state has proactively passed cyber laws that effectively reorient these influencers from political and economic topics to sociocultural ones. Authenticity must thus be produced within the confines of what is tolerated. Fears of state intervention mean that influencers commonly self-censor to avoid breaking unwritten laws in undefined areas such as "public order and morals" and "religious values." Regulation is not the only tool governments wield. The state may organize initiatives that bring together social-media influencers, members of the business community, religious leaders, and law enforcement agencies to mirror the best practices around the ethics of digital marketing, the social impacts of digital technologies, and online radicalization. One such case is Saudi Arabia's MiSK Foundation, which convened several Shoof (Look) and Mugharedoon (tweeps) forums with the purpose of fostering education, innovation, and entrepreneurship. Similarly, in Jordan, the private and state sectors, with foreign support, partnered to develop initiatives that serve rural or remote communities, such as Al Aqaba's Digital Village, which includes an Innovation Center. Practically speaking, however, it is difficult to control the variety of digital content genres in circulation, including music remix and parody, political satire and comedy, animated cartoons, makeup and lifestyle, technology reviews, and DIYs.

As an alternative to direct control or enticement, some states opt to regulate influencers as service providers and thereby control how content is monetized. In the UAE, where many influencers reside, a trade license is required to receive paid sponsorships. Such attempts to formalize influencers include inviting the Arab-Israeli vlogger Nuseir Yassin from the Nas Daily Facebook page to establish a training center in Dubai. Known for his more than one thousand one-minute travel videos, Yassin is essentially an entrepreneur financed by Dubai's New Media Academy to train Arab content creators. By transforming popular influencers who typically thrive on self-sustaining digital activities into licensed content producers, the state is reaping the benefits of the influencer economy while projecting a rallying "national brand in cyberspace."[22]

These dynamics produce parallel discourses featuring the tame and the contentious. Seemingly banal, mundane, and unremarkable everyday content coexists on platforms that also feature often explosive public contention over social norms and cultural orthodoxies, particularly around class, gender, ethnicity, and religion. The Arab uprisings drew attention to how identity had become relevant as a tool of political mobilization and resistance and was situated within a context of relationships and networks with other people, politics, products, and places. For post-Arab-uprisings youth, online content creation is different from the political activism that characterized the prerevolutionary blogging, vlogging, and other social-media activities. While earlier forms of digital activism were valued for breaking state control over information, today's content finds inspiration and motivation in coping with the struggles of everyday life. Such content encompasses information and mobilization about issues ranging from individual identity and community values to visions of a postwar Syria and a united Libya.

As young people communicate through social media, they become aware of the immediately visible public (family, friends, and beyond) and the potentially obscured audience (those who share similar interests and are masked by algorithmic structures). They develop groups on messaging platforms such as WhatsApp, or they limit the visibility of social-media accounts and use them to share private messages, personal opinions, or other content. At the same time, they join or develop larger online communities to draw attention to various forms of social injustices, human rights abuses, and local and regional issues. For example, solidarity with the Black Lives Matter movement found traction in the region, prompting reflections on racism and stereotyping in the Middle East. In the absence of official and broad public acknowledgment of systemic racial discrimination in the Middle East, social media amplified the voices of many black Arabs demanding to have their stories heard and their injustices redressed. Seizing on the global moment of reckoning, some traditional celebrities such as singer Tania Saleh and actress Mariam Hussein posted blackface images, only to be criticized for their appropriation of racist entertainment practices that originated in—and have long been condemned by—American and British culture.[23] Such controversy extended an American national issue (systemic racism in the United States) into a new awareness and Middle Eastern regional debate about the ways in which minorities, including ethnic groups, are treated across the Middle East.

Within ad-supported ecosystems, social media seems to favor the development of counter-hegemonic discourses that manifest themselves as controversial topics and in turn boost their revenue. Despite legal criminalization and social stigma, lesbian, gay, bisexual, transgender, and queer (LGBTQ+) populations in the Middle East are developing collective and individual ways to organize and express themselves, grow communities, and influence public discourse. Digital initiatives operate alongside traditional advocacy groups that combine civil society's organization strategies with digital outreach, campaigns, and information. Often working with international organizations, groups such as IraQueer, Algeria's Association Alouen, and Lebanon's Helem have developed their social-media presence to advance solidarity campaigns and challenge a legal system that penalizes nonconformity.

Campaigns and advocacy efforts are not the only ways collectivities operate in the digital. Everyday functions matter as well, such as online venues that foster a safe environment for LGBTQ+ communities, affirming their presence and giving them a voice. A case in point is My.Kali. Published since 2007 and named after its founder, the Jordanian model and activist Khalid "Kali" Abdel-Hadi, My.Kali is the region's first publication that addresses homophobia and transphobia while seeking to empower young people to challenge gender-binary institutional traditions. Managed by university students and circulating online, this relatively underground magazine acquired popularity in artistic circles while fostering a link among Jordan's LGTBQ+ communities and beyond. It allegedly even inspired Khalaf Yousef, a Jordanian Muslim cleric, to announce his homosexuality publicly on his YouTube channel, a move that ultimately compelled him to seek refuge in Canada.[24] Because of the exposure associated with the act of coming out, only a few social-media influencers in the LGTBQ+ community—such as Lebanese comedian Shadden Fakih (@shadyonshka) and Egyptian Dalia Al-Faghal (@dalia.alfaghal)—still live in the region, while the most famous and digitally active members of the region's LGBTQ+ community live in the diaspora.

Elsewhere, platforms with more privacy such as Instagram have offered groups such as Drag Queens of Lebanon a site to record and share their performances and even organize an Arab Drag Queen Championship. Shunned by society's social conservatism and excluded from traditional media, drag queens such as Queen Sultana (@SultanatheQueen), La Kahena (@la_kahena), and Latiza Bombé (@latizabombe) took to social media to engage the community in a relatively safe space, amplify their voices through humanizing their existence, and generate income from their performances. For these individuals, as for many others who are active on social media, the digital offers extended venues and multiple ways for the self-expression of identities. However, these amplified spaces for self-assertion are precarious at best, as prejudice and prosecution of LBGTQ+ communities are institutionalized, and individuals and communities who claim their right to digital cohabitation remain largely unsafe and unprotected. In Morocco, for instance, more than one hundred gay men were exposed as such after being identified on location-based apps during the COVID-19 lockdown. The controversy was sparked by a transgender Instagram influencer, Naoufal Moussa, known as Sofia Taloni, who intended to "humanize" sexuality and who has since apologized for "outing" the men.[25] In this case, digital cohabitation induces self-assertion and promotes acceptance but also feeds intolerance and invites reprisal.

Paradoxically, the authenticity of social-media influencers, both organic and migrant, points to real voices that are entangled in the politics of everyday life while also being subject to forces of standardization and commodification. Similarly, the cohabitations between banality and contentious discourses are increasingly crowding digital spaces and resulting in ever more controversies. Cohabitations are not a priori related, let alone opposed. They also involve different areas of sociality. At best, such cohabitation reveals a diverse, fluid, and elusive digitality.

Beyond Digital Subjectivity

In a region as socioculturally diverse, economically eclectic, and politically charged as the Middle East, issues of subjectivities are controversial and often mired in considerations of gender, ethnicity, and class, among others. These issues are interwoven with the region's political economies and its multiple modernities but also with enduring, culturally essentialist interpretations of Middle Eastern societies. Celebratory accounts of the digital empowerment of youth, women, and minorities in the Middle East should be pitted against the myriad ways the digital has reinforced hegemonies over these same subjects it is assumed to be "liberating." Digital experiences do not simply play out a Western, consumerist, democratizing script but reflect local contexts that can accelerate, undermine, and transform the digital.

As a pervasive part of social life, digital technologies affect people's subjectivities and impact users' perspectives on, expectations regarding, and understandings of the world around them. Although personal and private, subjectivities also have substantial intersubjective social dimensions, as members of the same community tend to react similarly in similar situations. With the digital becoming part of everyday life, these subjectivities extend beyond circumscribed cultural spaces to occupy techno-cultural geographies[26] that define the self and shape understandings of and attitudes toward others. The celebrity cases of Huda Beauty and the TikTok girls bring to light different experiences of young women whose increased online visibility represents multiple vectors of competing subjectivities about gender, politics, economy, and the conditions of sociality and digitality.

Huda Kattan is an Iraqi-American celebrity makeup artist, beauty blogger, entrepreneur, and philanthropist. After formal training in Los Angeles, she worked as a makeup artist for cosmetics giant Revlon in Dubai. Concomitantly, she developed a beauty-related WordPress blog, Huda Beauty. What started with an occasional post about makeup tips in 2010 became an influencer-marketed cosmetics line just two years later. Kattan's breakthrough came when her original collection of false eyelashes was taken up by American media personality Kim Kardashian. The Huda Beauty brand thereafter expanded internationally to more than 140 beauty products generating an estimated annual revenue of USD 200 million.[27] Catering to specific tastes and aesthetics while also showing business ingenuity and harnessing digital capabilities, Kattan built a billion-dollar empire with Huda Beauty Brand (skin-care label), Wishful (skin-care line), and Kayali (fragrance line), amassing a personal wealth of more than USD 500 million.[28] Despite its global success, Huda Beauty remains a family business, just like many companies based in the Middle East. As a third-culture millennial influencer turned entrepreneur, Kattan takes pride in her ability to bypass traditional marketing strategies and instead capitalize on her 52 million Instagram followers to promote her products.

Embraced as the Kim Kardashian of the beauty-products influencer economy,[29] Kattan attracted global attention. She is frequently portrayed by various sources as an example of sanctioned subjectivities centered around gender, ethnicity, and class; these portrayals reflect the contexts from which they arise. Thus, within the US business community, Kattan is celebrated as successful immigrant woman of color; in Dubai, she is seen as the epitome of cosmopolitanism and entrepreneurship; in the mainstream media, she serves as a symbol of women's leadership and empowerment. These dominant frames constitute internalized subjectivities, thus serving as an intersubjective referent for what women could—or should—be. For intersectional individuals such as Kattan, these subjectivities are not easily separated from the sociocultural fabric. Kattan has capitalized on her fame, her fortune, and, most effectively, her Instagram platform to support social causes and lobby the beauty industry against "toxic" beauty standards promoted by social media.

As an entrepreneur with a strong social-media presence, Kattan has not shied away from politics, either. Most notably, in 2021, she spoke about the "unjust situation in Palestine" and criticized Instagram's practice of deleting posts about Palestine.[30] Cognizant of how multiple and colliding subjectivities define her positionality, Kattan notes: "I know I have a beauty brand, and I am not supposed to talk about politics or whatever, but . . . I want to stand for what is right whether or not it makes me unpopular."[31] Taking a political stance, it was believed, would poten-tially threaten her digital popularity, which is largely based on her apolitical posts about beauty and fashion. In the background is her cognitive-affective framework, anchored in American exceptionalism, Dubai's cosmopolitanism, and global con-sumer capitalism. At times, she steps outside this framework to assert convic-tions of particular values that stem from competing positionalities. Her Instagram posts are examples of intersubjective communication in which she recognizes the potentially harmful implications of her political stances for her brand. In brief, the kind of entrepreneurship that is celebrated is both threatened and threatening.

In the popular imagination, digital media empowers users to share their unique voices. Digital researchers who criticize such narratives emphasize the economic basis of the online economy, namely that digital media usage takes place in a con-text where content is commodified, attention is a source of advertising revenue, personal information is data to be mined, and increased engagement leads to bet-ter monetization opportunities.[32] Such characterization of digital technologies, however, seems simplistic insofar as it portrays digital use as transforming passive and disengaged subjects into individuals whose subjectivities are inevitably co-opted by forces of commodification. After all, digital media are producing venues and spaces for intersubjective communication—enabled through such functions as "friend" and "follow"—that are often drawn from the unmediated world. In practice, spaces of solidarity or contention are created, and users benefit from an assumed freedom for self-expression. Beyond the deterministic models of com-modified subjectivities, intersubjectivities could be constructed through engage-ments with technological infrastructures, sociocultural contexts, and political and economic institutions. These alternatives do not seamlessly commodify subjec-tivities; instead they create fissures, frictions, and spaces for resistance.

Despite digital inequalities in access and literacies, the growing number of young people using social media allows for more culturally and economically diverse digital subjectivities to emerge. Just as Kattan's case highlights the dynam-ics between personal politics and brand image in the instance of an influencer, the case of Egypt's "TikTok girls," as they came to be known, points to different manifestations of digital subjectivities in gender and class. In Egypt, the COVID-19 pandemic increased the popularity of social media, particularly among young women, allowing some to earn a living wage from their online activities. While some young women flourished, other social-media influencers were rebuked for creating content that was perceived as violating family principles and societal values. This is the case with Mawada El-Adham and Haneen Hossam, two female influencers then in their early twenties who came under public scrutiny in 2020. El-Adham danced and lip-synced videos on TikTok. Calling herself Egypt's Fourth Pyramid, Hossam, who comes from a family of modest means, often appeared wearing a hijab with tight jeans, which made her videos a media sensation across the social spectrum. While Hossam and El-Adham moved in different social circles in Egypt, their digital subjectivities, manifested in their social-media popularity, collided. Being a social-media influencer proved profitable for Hossam, while El-Adham's 3.1 million followers on TikTok made her a magnet for influencer marketing agencies.

The TikTok girls were performing to millions of followers, as well as potential advertisers and sponsors, displaying an image of what it means to be young and online. Yet the same social media that avowedly empowered these women also brought them under scrutiny. El-Adham's flashing of her newfound wealth and the content of her videos alarmed "Al Mouwatineen Al Shurafaa" (self-proclaimed "Honorable Citizens"), unidentified people who reported her to the authorities for immoral acts. Hossam posted a promotional video on Instagram describing how women could earn up to USD 3,000 for creating marketing clips on the video-chatting platform Likee. The posts were met with rebukes from a fringe of social-media users and drew the attention of the authorities, who were quick to accuse the TikTok girls of "promoting women selling sex online."[33] El-Adham and Hossam were sentenced on retrial to three years in prison and a fine of USD 10,000 each.

Known as the prosecution of the TikTok girls, the cases of El-Adham and Hossam became a source of controversy. On social media, many commentators lamented the moral shortcomings of the young female generation. More than merely another case of moral panics triggered by new media content and practices, the arrest of the TikTok girls can be read as an attempt by the guardians of the dominant system and religious orthodoxy to reaffirm their authority. The targeting of these young women amounts to reasserting religious and political control over women's bodies and lives by sanctioning those whose digitally enabled intersubjective communication is perceived as disturbing public order, unsettling patriarchy, and threatening men's privilege. Some commentators spoke out strongly against the backlash, citing it as an unacceptable pretext for limiting freedom of speech. Most ingenious, perhaps, was a sarcastic Arabic hashtag (translated as #If_Egyptian_families_permit)[34] questioning the cultural norms and legal rationale that legitimized the TikTok girls' arrests. Using poignant Egyptian wit, the campaign highlighted how systematic crackdowns targeted women, particularly those from lower socioeconomic backgrounds.

Such cases underscore challenges for empowerment discourses and invite critical reflection on how subjectivities are sanctioned and chastised. Whereas Kattan's model of subjectivity defies the best practices of communication capitalism (protecting the brand), the TikTok girls' case reveals frictions between young people's subjectivities and the persistent social reality represented by the sociopolitical axis. These complex tensions point to significant conundrums ranging from women's experiences of gender and class politics to the structure of the social environments that instrumentalize religious interpretations to constrain women further legally and politically. In both cases, the digital offers pathways and mechanisms to move beyond inherent subjectivities to develop attitudes and predispositions that affect behaviors and generate concrete interactions with followers beyond those in women's more limited offline social circle. More broadly, the foregoing discussion offers some pathways for rethinking and privileging sociality in discussions of the digital turn. With the expansion of digital communicative and organizational resources, everyday people have renewed various forms of sociocultural interactions such as commenting on news stories and pursuing activities to help pass the time during lockdowns. The celebration of the digital turn as a globally integrative force by which children, youth, and women in the Global South could have the "good life" (understood as "a Western lifestyle") fails to acknowledge the double bind that such pursuits entail.

Social change and mutable yet durable aspects of gender-, race-, and class-based power structures are integral to the digital turn. Focusing on children, youth, and women concretely locates the double bind in what culture does and how people experience it. The discourses regarding digital empowerment project imaginaries of a Middle East in which children's rights are respected, young people's privacy is protected, and women's equality is achieved. However, these very same tools testify to encroachments on children's rights, increased surveillance of young people's activities, and reconfigured yet undiminished patriarchy. People in the Middle East are engaging more intensely with sociality through different means, digital or unmediated, than have historically been acknowledged and, in the process, are transforming their relationship to traditional sources of power (whether family, tribe, community, or state). Such pursuits often fall short of participating in a more overt political movement and therefore are not taken seriously in discussions about the Middle East's digital turn, representing a missed opportunity to inform our understanding of its impacts as well as its potential.

Afterword

Unraveling the digital Middle East has taken us to a territory that lies beyond conventional approaches to the region's relationships with technology. Our inquiry broadens such understandings, taking the discussion into sociality from media-focused communication practices to ICT-related developments that mark this historical juncture. Today's techno-centric cultures are redefining economic structures, challenging political systems, and reconfiguring everyday practices. When considering these transformations, one confronts a steady stream of stories about the digital Middle East. In this current of commentary, the digital heralds a new era that is rendering the region's seemingly inescapable predicament of resistance to change to be itself a thing of the past. Underlying these narratives are particular conceptions about both technology and the Middle East itself. To equate the digital with change, promised or actualized, is to subscribe to a set of techno-imaginaries that often are disconnected from the material—and immaterial—conditions of everyday life, particularly those outside the celebrated network societies.

We situate the digital Middle East within transformations ushered in by the exigencies of the information era but also in relation to entrenched systems and enduring practices that have marked the region for decades. The confluence of these two disparate realities warrants critical engagement with the underlying question of change and stasis. Such an undertaking does more than question the assumptions of development theorists who posit technology as the driver for change and the essentialist accounts of cultural critics who argue that stasis withstands even the most advanced technologies. It shifts the analysis from focusing on the manifestations and effects of change to exploring the conditions and logics of the digital turn. Accordingly, this book invites a theoretical recalibration that maps out particular structures and their underlying logics but also illuminates contradictions and disjunctures that complicate our understanding of the digital Middle East.

The digital turn that we capture provides a spatiotemporal anchorage for examining complex and interrelated dynamics associated with how information and communication technologies are introduced, deployed, and used. This turn is indissociable from ongoing political, economic, and sociocultural dynamics that overlap with, but are not necessarily the result of, technological transformations. Thus conceived, the digital turn refers to the scope and scale of the region's technological transition and the coexistence of multiple, often competing temporalities of change. The analysis we offer delves into how the same digital strategies, policies, tools, and practices that foster change also perpetuate stasis. The ensuing disjunctures, which punctuate the digital turn, often manifest themselves as irreconcilable tendencies. Therein lies the digital double bind—dynamics that maintain stasis even as they avowedly challenge it.

Insofar as it articulates contradictory pulls that complicate our understanding of the relationship between change and stasis, the digital double bind that we depict is far from an essentializing formulation. The complex dynamics that underlie the digital double bind that we unravel are neither specific to the Middle East nor unknown to many parts of the Global South. Though persistent issues of unequal connectivity, digital divide, and digital literacy continue to inflect the digital turn, a critical engagement with the digital in the Global South needs to go beyond the question of access to address the perpetuation of existing cultural, political, social, and economic inequalities and opportunities as consequences of historical legacies, demographic compositions, and structural predispositions. Capturing these logics requires a nuanced undertaking beyond West-centric treatments of the Global South, which either essentialize it or homogenize what are otherwise richly complex dynamics that have garnered the attention of an emerging body of critical scholarship on Latin America, Asia, and Africa. Notably, examining the digital double bind calls for locally grounded, socially attentive, and culturally embedded research and also necessitates adopting a *longue-durée* approach that helps eschew the pitfalls of presentism. Conceiving of conflictual pulls as constitutive of the digital double bind provides a useful framework for dissecting overlapping logics of change and stasis beyond facile analyses mired in technological determinism.

The digital double bind acquires an added relevance when considered in relation to the dynamics adumbrated by the advent of global digital capitalism. Together they complicate such conventional categories of economic analysis as market structure, relations of production, exchange value, and wage labor but also introduce new challenges related to changing forms of market territoriality, practices of surveillance, and strategies of data colonialism. These considerations challenge assumed distinctions between nations based on ICT indicators and technological prognostications. Such distinctions rest on the presumption of an "ideological divide" between a Global North regarded as having evolved into a network society and a Global South preoccupied with issues of modernization. These considerations also unsettle conventional categories and labels of development and problematize globalized discourses that promulgate the digital as the path for social change.

Though more pronounced in the Global South, the constitutive logics (and illogics) of the digital double bind that we illustrate are not extraneous to the network society or antithetical to experiences of the digital in the Global North. How those logics are perceived and rationalized is another matter. Typically, issues related to digital surveillance, data monetization, and excess (dis)information in the Global North are treated as anomalies—as exogenous dynamics—rather than as structuring logics inherent in the system. Thus obscured, such manifestations of the digital double bind are projected as aberrations, disruptions, and excesses—in short, as conjunctural rather than constitutive.

Critical geography and postcolonial studies posit that the interests of the Global North have largely defined the geographical boundaries of the Global South. In the same spirit, we claim that the digital double bind could serve as an analytical modality for questioning key aspects of the network society's technological paradigm and organizational structure. Such an undertaking requires that we consider the Global North less as a model that works than as one working model among others. In-depth studies about technology and change within the Middle East and across the Global South, and potentially extending to manifestations of techno-cultural geographies of the Global North, will help uncover even more complex facets of the digital double bind.

These formulations leave us with the question of whether the region can escape the digital double bind. Considering that the essence of any double bind is entrapment, this question may at first seem rhetorical. The disposition to conceive of change and stasis as mutually exclusive positions, however, derives from binary thinking that fails to recognize how the digital turn is associated with spatiotemporal dynamics and how it engenders nuanced choices. If one is to make sense of the double bind, the analysis needs to address not how it is confirmed or challenged but what continues to make it a defining feature of the digital turn. Ultimately, what stands about the digital turn is less its promise or its teleological ending than the process of struggle, creation, and adaptation it engenders.

Notes

Chapter 1

1. Castells, *The Rise of the Network Society*; Castells, *The Network Society*.
2. Castells, "The Network Society Revisited," 2.
3. Bateson et al., "Toward a Theory of Schizophrenia."
4. Stevens, "The Political Ways of Paradox," 214.
5. Romm, *Double Bind*; Jamieson, *Beyond the Double Bind*; Irby et al., *Women of Color in STEM*; Duffy and Pruchniewska, "Gender and Self-Enterprise."
6. Cooper, *Double Bind*.
7. Collett, Giappone, and MacKenzie, *The Double Binds*; Nagle, *Multiculturalism's Double Bind*; Hall, "Media Power."
8. Spivak, *An Aesthetic Education*, 10–11.
9. Hall, "Media Power," 21.
10. In popular culture, Joseph Heller's satirical war novel *Catch-22* (1961) and its subsequent film and television adaptations offer a common understanding of the double bind as a no-win situation.
11. For a treatment of the digital and the double bind in relation to media and the internet, see Thompson, *The Media and Modernity*, and Mansell, *Imagining the Internet*, respectively.
12. Cusolito et al., *The Upside of Digital*; Elmasry et al., "Digital Middle East"; Deloitte, "National Transformation"; Arab Advisors Group, "Digital Index"; Arab Commission for Digital Economy, "The Arab Digital Economy Strategy"; GSMA, "The Mobile Economy 2020," 13.
13. On the relevance of history to understanding technology and social change, see Silverstone, "What's New about New Media?"; Briggs and Burke, *A Social History of the Media*.
14. This is a much theorized and debated term in the interdisciplinary fields of science and technology studies (STS), digital humanities, and digital cultures.
15. Mumford, *Technics and Civilization*.
16. Practically, each environment reveals a particular *techne*, which amounts to the coexistence of multiple *technes*. For our purposes, though, the attention to *techne* offers a critical lens for examining sociocultural experiences, which goes beyond a descriptive account of systems, services, and applications.
17. Sabry and Khalil, *Culture, Time and Publics*, 8.
18. Hoy, *The Time of Our Lives*.
19. For a critical discussion of how conceptions of the temporal reveal colonial dimensions, see Fabian, *Time and the Other*.
20. Barak, *On Time*.

21. Zayani, *Digital Middle East*.
22. Stetter, *The Middle East*.
23. On digital capitalism, see Fuchs, *Digital Capitalism*; Betancourt, *The Critique of Digital Capitalism*; Pace, "The Concept of Digital Capitalism."
24. Ajami, *The Arab Predicament*.
25. Kraidy and Krikorian, "Mediating Islamic State"; Abdulmajid, *Extremism*; Winkler and Damanhoury, *Proto-State Media System*.
26. Canclini, *Hybrid Cultures*, 1. It is worth noting that there is a long-standing debate about the Middle East experience with modernity and the "postmodern condition." See, for instance, Ahmed, *Postmodernism and Islam*. During the last decade, and partly as a result of the socio-cultural, political, and economic conditions that emerged since the Arab uprisings, such debate gained a new relevance. See, for instance, Sabry, "On Historicism"; El-Ariss, *Trials of Arab Modernity*.
27. On sociotechnical imaginaries, see Jasanoff and Kim, *Dreamscapes of Modernity*; Rottenburg, "Digital Imaginaries."
28. Mansell, *Imagining the Internet*, 81–82.
29. Hepp, *Deep Mediatization*; van Dijck, Poell, and de Waal, *The Platform Society*.
30. Downing et al., *The Sage Handbook*, 145.

Chapter 2

1. Alterman, "The Middle East's Information Revolution"; Ghareeb, "New Media"; Mawlana, "The Arab World."
2. Alterman, "IT Comes of Age," 41.
3. Murphy and Zweiri, *The New Arab Media*, xiii.
4. Zayani, *Networked Publics*.
5. Howard and Hussain, *Democracy's Fourth Wave?*; Gerbaudo, *Tweets and the Streets*; El Nawawy and Khamis, *Egyptian Revolution 2.0*.
6. Gonzalez-Quijano, *Arabités numériques*, 25.
7. Smith, "The Middle East's Other Revolution."
8. This section is not intended to offer a detailed history of the Middle East as a term or to advance a specific definition of the region. Rather, it aims to offer the reader a basic overview of the complexities associated with delineating the Middle East.
9. Worrall, *International Institutions*.
10. Oruc, *Sites of Pluralism*.
11. Khalil et al., *Handbook*.
12. Maxim, *The Colonial and Postcolonial Middle East*; Mohamedou, *State-Building*.
13. Gason and Yachin, "How the Abraham Accords Are Shaping."
14. Amanat, "Is There a Middle East?," 5.
15. Said, *Orientalism*.
16. Culcasi, "Constructing and Naturalizing"; Kurzman, "Cross-Regional Approaches."
17. Anderson, *Imagined Communities*.
18. Iskandar, "Media as Method."
19. Amanat, "Is There a Middle East?," 7.
20. Gonzalez-Quijano, *Arabités numériques*, 25.
21. See, for instance, Ball and Mattar, *Edinburgh Companion*.
22. Al-Awdat, *Renaissance and Modernity*, 59–90.
23. Gorman and Irving, *Cultural Entanglement*.
24. Boyd-Barrett and Mirrlees, *Media Imperialism*, 16.
25. Lerner, *The Passing of Traditional Society*. For a critical discussion of Lerner, see Shah, *The Production of Modernization*; Wilkins, "Considering 'Traditional Society.'"
26. Deuchar, "Nahda."

27. The first half of the twentieth century was marked by an Arab literary renaissance and an intellectual resurgence, as exemplified in the works of literary giants, in Egypt and elsewhere in the Mashriq, from Taha Hussein to Abbas Mahmoud El-Aqqad and from Ahmed Shawqi to Mikhail Naimy. See Hussein, "The Modern Renaissance"; El-Ariss, *The Arab Renaissance*.
28. Wilkins, *Prisms of Prejudice*, 27–28; Hazbun, "The Uses of Modernization Theory."
29. Elmusa, "Dependency and Industrialization," 253.
30. Wilkins, "Considering 'Traditional Society.'"
31. Khader, "The Social Impact."
32. Zahlan, *Technology Transfer and Change*; El-Obeidy, "Scientific System."
33. Wilkins and Mody, "Reshaping Development Communication," 386.
34. Katz, *Dependency Theory*.
35. Thomas, "Development Communication," 8–9.
36. Galtung, "A Structural Theory."
37. Amin, "Keynote Address."
38. The NAM presented a political agenda, while the Group of 77 proposed an economic agenda, driven primarily by the newly created UN Conference on Trade and Development (UNCTAD). They then united their efforts and endorsed the call for a New World Economic Order at the NAM meeting in Algiers in 1973.
39. In 1974, Tunisian prime minister Hedi Nouira coined the term "new world information order." Another Tunisian, Mustafa Masmoudi, along with Egyptian Gamal El-Oteifi, also served on the MacBride Commission (1977–1980), a UNESCO panel charged with addressing issues of communication imbalances. See Oledzki, "Polish Perspectives"; Masmoudi, "Le nouvel ordre mondial."
40. Thomas, "Development Communication," 8–9.
41. Shareef, *Arab Satellites*.
42. El Louadi, "The Arab World"; Sardar, *Science and Technology*; Segal, "The Middle East."
43. In addition to the international development industry, the main donors are Arab and Muslim countries, especially between the oil boom of the 1970s and the 2000s. Much of that aid was provided on the basis of ideological, political, and other conditions. See Momani and Ennis, "Between Caution and Controversy"; Watanabe, "Gulf States' Engagement."
44. Wilkins, "Development and Modernization."
45. Kerr, "Arab Socialist Thought."
46. Owen, "The Arab Economies."
47. Even Gulf states that benefited from the energy crisis that sent Western economies into turmoil in the 1970s were not immune from economic tribulations, and following the oil price collapse in the mid-1980s, they experienced chronic revenue deficits. See Miller, *Desert Kingdoms*, 93; Zanoyan, "After the Oil Boom."
48. Singer, "The 1980s"; Leopardi and Trentin, "The International 'Debt Crisis.'"
49. McAnany, *Saving the World*, 30. For a critical engagement with the question of development in relation to media in the region, see Kazan, *Mass Media, Modernity, and Development*; Guaaybess, *Media in Arab Countries*.
50. Ward and Rustow, *Political Modernization*.
51. Diamond, "Promoting Democracy."
52. Hazbun, "The Uses of Modernization Theory"; Pressman, "Power without Influence."
53. Seib, *Toward a New Public Diplomacy*; Seib, "US Public Diplomacy."
54. Wilkins, "Considering 'Traditional Society'"; Rist and Camiller, *The History of Development*.
55. Sosale, "Toward a Critical Genealogy," 35–37; McAnany, *Saving the World*, 8.
56. Ajami, *The Arab Predicament*.
57. Al Azm, "Self-Criticism."
58. Hanafi, *On Political Culture*, 22–23.
59. Laroui, *Arabs and Historical Thought*.

60. Pormann, "The Arab 'Cultural Awakening'"; Reynolds, *The Cambridge Companion*; Dickinson, *Arab Film and Video Manifestos*; Burkhalter, Dickinson, and Harbert, *The Arab Avant-Garde*.
61. Ajami, *The Arab Predicament*.
62. Kassir, *Being Arab*; Kassab, *Contemporary Arab Thought*.
63. Mosco, *The Digital Sublime*.
64. Hess and Zimmermann, "Transnational Digital Imaginaries," 158; Stalder, *The Digital Condition*, 8–9.
65. Taylor, *Modern Social Imaginaries*.
66. Bouchard, *Social Myths*.
67. Treré, *Hybrid Media Activism*, 110.
68. Couldry, *Media, Society, World*.
69. Wheeler, *Digital Resistance*.
70. Giglio, "Tunisia Protests"; Zhuo, Wellman, and Yu, "Egypt."
71. Ghonim, *Revolution 2.0*.
72. Vallor, *The Oxford Handbook*; Aouragh, "Framing the Internet."
73. Haughølle, "Rethinking the Role"; Wilson and Corey, "The Role of ICT"; Guesmi, "The Social Media Myth"; Smidi and Shahin, "Social Media"; Khatib, "Social Media and Mobilization."
74. Diamond and Plattner, *Liberation Technology*.
75. Jones, *Digital Authoritarianism*.
76. Biltgen and Ryan, *Activity-Based Intelligence*.
77. Youngs, "Digital Globalization and Democracy," 148.
78. Mosco, *The Digital Sublime*.
79. Menabytes, "Careem."
80. See, for instance, Pepe, *Blogging from Egypt*; Lenze, *Politics and Digital Literature*; El Khachab, *Making Film in Egypt*; Günther and Pfeifer, *Jihadi Audiovisuality*.

Part II

1. Hesmondhalgh, "The Infrastructural Turn."
2. Bowker et al., "Toward Information Infrastructure"; Karasti, Baker, and Millerand, "Infrastructure Time."
3. Plantin and Punathambekar, "Digital Media Infrastructures," 164.
4. Shafiee, "Science and Technology Studies," 3.
5. Star and Bowker, "How to Infrastructure."
6. McCormack, "Elemental Infrastructures."
7. Masmoudi, "The Arab World," 139.
8. Determann, *Space Science*, 15–16, 23.

Chapter 3

1. Youssif, "Development," 96.
2. Sakr, *Satellite Realms*, 16.
3. Boyd, "The Evolution of Electronic Media"; Mellor et al., *Arab Media Globalization*.
4. Between 1964 and 2001, Intelsat was as an intergovernmental consortium that owned and operated a constellation of satellites. It provided a model of the Arab League's establishment of its own intergovernmental satellite organization, ArabSat.
5. Boyd, "Development of Egypt's Radio."
6. Shareef, *Arab Satellites*, 9.
7. Shareef, *Arab Satellites*, 12.
8. Pelton and Howkins, *Satellites International*, 135.
9. Kraidy and Khalil, *Arab Television Industries*, 17–18.

10. Zayani, "Transnational Media." Ironically, neighboring Iran developed its own network of satellites under the shah as part of a state-led drive for modernization. These same technologies would later be appropriated for promoting the Islamic Republic following the Iranian Revolution.
11. Shareef, *Arab Satellites*, 18–19.
12. Guessoum, "The Arab World."
13. Sakr, *Satellite Realms*, 10.
14. Sakr, "Satellite Television and Development."
15. Kavanaugh, *The Social Control of Technology*, 138; Determann, *Space Science*, 63–64; Sakr, *Satellite Realms*, 10.
16. Al Ani, "Iraq's Al Abid Satellite Launch System."
17. Boyd, "The Arab World"; Sakr, *Satellite Realms*, 10–11.
18. Borowitz, *Open Space*, 308.
19. Sakr, *Satellite Realms*, 16.
20. This new generation of satellites employed digital technologies, which enhanced reception and improved image quality (including digital encryption, compression, and transmission) and energized additional digital transformations.
21. Even before the advent of transnational satellite television, such satellite technology enabled satellite-linked printing of transnational Arab newspapers, for instance.
22. Determann, *Space Science*, 155.
23. Gaillard-Sborowsky, "L'espace."
24. Margit, "UAE, Saudi Arabia, Turkey."
25. Amlôt, "Lockheed Martin."
26. Determann, *Space Science*, 159–160.
27. Al Jazeera, "Qatar Launches."
28. Gulf Times, "Es'hailSat."
29. Gulf Times, "Es'hailSat."
30. Es'hailSat, "Qatar Enters Space Age"; Haddad, "The Contribution."
31. Haddad, "The Contribution."
32. Malecki and Wei, "A Wired World," 363.
33. Starosielski, *The Undersea Network*, x.
34. Malecki and Wei, "A Wired World," 363–365.
35. Gelvanovska, Rogy, and Rossotto, *Broadband Networks*.
36. Chattopadhyaya, "How Well."
37. Kemp, *The East Moves West*, 243.
38. Kavanaugh, *The Social Control of Technology*, 68.
39. These include, for example, King Abdul Aziz City for Science and Technology in Saudi Arabia, AUB in Lebanon, AUC in Egypt, and Al Kawarizmi Computing Center in Tunisia.
40. Amin and Gher, "Digital Communications," 135.
41. ITU, "Internet for the Arab World."
42. Wheeler, *The Internet*, 32.
43. Kalathil and Boas, *Open Networks*.
44. Ghareeb, "New Media," 416.
45. Goodman and Green, "Computing," 22; Mihoub-Dramé, *Internet*, 33; Human Rights Watch, "The Internet."
46. Dutta and Coury, "ICT Challenges," 125.
47. Ghareeb, "New Media," 396.
48. Anderson, *Arabizing the Internet*, 22.
49. Wheeler, "Empowerment Zones"; Wheeler, *The Internet*, 34–35.
50. Anderson, *Arabizing the Internet*, 5.
51. Anderson, *Arabizing the Internet*, 19.
52. Kavanaugh, *The Social Control of Technology*, 29.
53. Human Rights Watch, "The Internet."

54. Al-Kinani, "Factors of Culture."
55. Filiu, *The Arab Revolution*, 45.
56. Hamdy, "ICT in Education."
57. Abdulla, *The Internet*, 20–21.
58. ESCWA, "National Profile Saudi Arabia."
59. World Bank, "Individuals Using the Internet: Arab World."
60. Anderson, "Producers," 426.
61. Anderson, *Arabizing the Internet*, 23.
62. Miniaoui, *Economic Development*.
63. Hillman, *The Digital Silk Road*.
64. Chaziza, "Gulf States Go Digital"; Araz, "The UAE Eyes AI Supremacy"; Middle East Eye, "Israeli Defense Companies."
65. Abraham, "5G Implementation."
66. Greene and Triolo, "Will China Control the Global Internet?"
67. Soliman, "How Tech Is Cementing."
68. Middle East Eye, "Google Plans Fibre-Optic Cable"; Jones and FitzGerald, "Google Plans Fiber-Optic Network"; Jones, "Google Plots New Europe-Asia Path"; Internet Society, "Middle East and North Africa Internet Infrastructure," 13; Qui, "Google's Blue-Raman Cable."
69. Dutta and Coury, "ICT Challenges," 119.
70. Human Rights Watch, "The Internet."
71. Anderson, "Producers," 425.
72. Wagner, "Push-Button Autocracy."
73. Tawil-Souri, "Digital Occupation."
74. Internet Society, "Enabling Digital Opportunities."
75. Ayton, "Lebanon's Illegal Internet Boom."
76. Pack, "Asian Successes."
77. Steinmueller, "ICTs and the Possibility for Leapfrogging," 194; Calestous, "Leapfrogging Progress."
78. ITU, "Measuring Digital Development 2021," 8.
79. Bhagavan, "Technological Leapfrogging," 48.
80. Sakr, *Satellite Realms*, 16.
81. ESCWA, "National Profile Yemen," 5.
82. Schanzer, "Yemen's War on Terror," 522; Zanini and Edwards, "The Networking of Terror," 36.
83. Vacca, *Guide*, 468.
84. El-Katiri and Fattouh, "Energy Poverty," 37.
85. ITU, "Measuring the Information Society Report 2018."
86. Holland, "The New Dawn."
87. Steel, "Navigating (Im)Mobility," 245.
88. Soyres et al., "What Kenya's Mobile Money Success Could Mean."
89. A study on perceptions and attitudes toward the use of AI shows a receptiveness toward the use of digital technologies to serve health needs (ranging from 66% in Saudi Arabia to 65% in Qatar to 62% in UAE). See PwC, "What Doctor?"
90. Soliman, "COVID-19."
91. Steinmueller, "ICTs and the Possibility for Leapfrogging," 194; Bhagavan, "Technological Leapfrogging," 48.
92. Fong, "Technology Leapfrogging," 3708.
93. Dutta et al., "Global Innovation Index Ranking 2021," 30–31.
94. Third and Kao, "ICT Leapfrogging Policy," 329.
95. Downs, Kiyasseh, and Quaintance, "Silicon Wafers and Semiconductors."
96. Al Murshidi, "STEM Education."
97. Parcero and Ryan, "Becoming a Knowledge Economy."
98. Ewers and Malecki, "Leapfrogging," 498.

99. Anderson, "Producers," 420.

100. Warf and Vincent, "Multiple Geographies," 95.

101. Arab Commission for Digital Economy, "The Arab Digital Economy Strategy."

102. Dubai Internet City, "About Us."

103. Bin Bishr, "How Digital Technology Is Transforming Dubai."

104. Kalaldeh and Al Homsi, "Jordan's Startup Economy."

105. Kalaldeh and Al Homsi, "Jordan's Startup Economy."

106. Al Bawaba, "Abraaj Capital Sells Stake."

107. Altaba, "Yahoo! to Extend Reach"; Crunchbase, "Jordanian Startups."

108. Askhita, "The Internet in Syria."

109. World Bank, "Individuals Using the Internet: Syrian Arab Republic."

110. Reporters without Borders, "Syria."

111. Yamamoto, "The Current Situation."

112. Tkacheva et al., *Internet Freedom and Political Space*, 73.

Chapter 4

1. Pellicer and Wegner, "Quantitative Research."

2. Cisco, "Cisco Global Digital Readiness Index 2019," 5.

3. Dutta and Lanvin, "The Network Readiness Index 2022."

4. Economist Impact, "Inclusive Internet Index 2022."

5. Economist Impact, "Inclusive Internet Index 2022."

6. Since 2017, ITU expert panels have agreed on a new set of indicators, but no data have been collected.

7. ITU, "Measuring the Information Society Report 2017," 73.

8. Elmasry et al., "Digital Middle East."

9. Arab Advisors Group, "Digital Index."

10. Cisco, "Cisco Global Digital Readiness Index 2019."

11. Dutta and Lanvin, "The Network Readiness Index 2020," 44.

12. Arab Commission for Digital Economy, "The Arab Digital Economy Strategy."

13. Deloitte, "National Transformation."

14. UN, "Sustainable Development Goals."

15. ITU, "Information Society Statistical Profiles," 9.

16. ITU, "ICT Facts and Figures 2010."

17. ITU, "ICT Facts and Figures 2015"; ITU, "ICT Facts and Figures 2016."

18. ITU, "Measuring Digital Development 2019."

19. ITU, "Measuring Digital Development 2021."

20. World Bank, "Individuals Using the Internet: Arab World."

21. World Bank, "Individuals Using the Internet: Arab World."

22. ITU, "Information Society Statistical Profiles," 6; Dean, "Accelerating the Digital Economy," 4.

23. ITU, "ICT Facts and Figures 2010."

24. ITU, "ICT Facts and Figures 2015."

25. ITU, "Measuring Digital Development 2021," 8.

26. ITU, "Measuring Digital Development 2021," 17.

27. ITU, "Measuring Digital Development 2021," 9.

28. GSMA, "The Mobile Economy 2022," 14; GSMA, "The Mobile Economy 2020," 13; GSMA, "The Mobile Economy 2015," 12.

29. GSMA, "The Mobile Economy 2020," 13.

30. GSMA, "The Mobile Economy 2020," 9; GSMA, "The Mobile Economy 2014," 23.

31. ITU, "International Bandwidth Usage." The figures are in trillion bits per second and refer to the number of units of data transmitted or received each second.

32. ITU, "Measuring Digital Development 2021," 14.

33. ITU, "Measuring Digital Development 2020."

34. Calabrese, "The Huawei Wars"; Soliman, "The Gulf."
35. Cabral, "UAE Seeks to Play."
36. Blaubach, "The 5G Divide."
37. ITU, "Measuring Digital Development 2021," 3–4.
38. ITU, "Measuring Digital Development 2019," 3.
39. ITU, "Measuring Digital Development 2021," 12.
40. ITU, "Measuring Digital Development 2022."
41. ITU, "Measuring Digital Development 2020."
42. ITU, "Measuring Digital Development 2021," 15.
43. ITU, "Measuring Digital Development 2021," 16.
44. Alliance for Affordable Internet, "Affordability Report," 22–24; Alliance for Affordable Internet, "Affordability Drivers Index."
45. World Bank, "Literacy Rate."
46. ITU, "Measuring Digital Development 2020."
47. ITU, "Measuring Digital Development 2021," 19.
48. UNCTAD, "ICT Policy Review."
49. Eaves, "An Analysis."
50. World Economic Forum, "Digital Policy Playbook."
51. Office of the Minister of State for Administrative Reform, "Lebanon Digital Transformation Strategy."
52. Atia, "Analyzing ICT Policies."
53. ESCWA, "Arab Digital Development Report."
54. Kemp, "Digital 2020."
55. Oxford Business Group, "Strategies to Transform Jordan."
56. Smith, "Digital Transformation"; Deloitte, "National Transformation."
57. UAE Government Portal, "UAE Centennial 2071."

Chapter 5

1. Although "digitality" has been associated with Nicholas Negroponte's description of the condition of living in a digital culture, the term here refers to the series of immaterial transformations associated with the expansion of digital infrastructure. Rather than describe the living conditions of a digital culture in the context of a networked society, digitality is confined with the everyday-life conditions of the digital turn. For more on digitality, see Negroponte, *Being Digital*; Hassan, *The Condition of Digitality*.
2. Jenkins, *Convergence Culture*. See also Chadwick, *The Hybrid Media System*.
3. Bruns, *Blogs*.
4. Deuze, *Media Life*.
5. Gabbard and Park, *The Information Revolution*; Alterman, *New Media, New Politics?*; Ghareeb, "New Media"; Fandy, "Information Technology."
6. Anderson and Hudson, "Internet Pioneering."
7. Al Mamlaka TV, *Digital Kingdom*.
8. Anderson and Hudson, "Internet Pioneering."
9. See, for example, Gabbard and Park, *The Information Revolution*; Alterman, *New Media, New Politics?*; Armbrust, "A History of New Media."
10. Almowanes, "History of Computing"; Abunadi, "Influence of Culture."
11. Sakr, *Satellite Realms*; Wheeler, "Empowering Publics."
12. Beblawi, "The Rentier State."
13. Foote, "CNE in Egypt."
14. Sakr, *Satellite Realms*, 1.
15. Kraidy and Khalil, *Arab Television Industries*.
16. Eaves, "An Analysis," 1.
17. Al Mamlaka TV, *Digital Kingdom*.
18. Human Rights Watch, "The Internet."

19. Arabian Business, "Saudi to Set Up."
20. Copestake, "Could Ramallah Become."
21. Hub71, "Mubadala Launches."
22. ESCWA, "Arab Horizon 2030," 57.
23. ESCWA, "Arab Horizon 2030," 59.
24. Whereas "backhauling" results from overloading the internet backbone instead of rerouting traffic between connecting points, with "tromboning," traffic is routed to large exchange nodes and back.
25. Yil-Kaitala, "Revolution 2.0."
26. Ben Gharbia, "The Internet Freedom Fallacy"; Hussain, "Digital Infrastructure."
27. Kalathil and Boas, *Open Networks*.
28. Baiazy, "Syria's Cyber Operations."
29. MBZUAI, "About."
30. Consultancy-me.com, "GCC's E-Commerce Sector."
31. Elmasry et al., "Digital Middle East."
32. Eickelman and Piscatori, *Muslim Politics*.
33. The ESCWA report "Arab Horizon 2030," 34, notes that "the track record of existing Arab digital strategies and the continuation of a business-as-usual approach would not lead to meaningful results, even in the more affluent GCC countries."
34. Fandy, "Information Technology," 378.
35. Star and Bowker, "How to Infrastructure."
36. ITU, "Internet Surge Slows."
37. ITU, "Development Sector."
38. Arora, *The Next Billion Users*.

Part III

1. Certeau, *The Practice of Everyday Life*.
2. Mouffe, *Dimensions of Radical Democracy*.
3. McClure, "On the Subject of Rights," 123.

Chapter 6

1. Coleman and Blumler, *The Internet*; Maira, *Missing*.
2. Coleman and Blumler, *The Internet*, 4.
3. France, "Why Should We Care?," 105.
4. Benkler, *The Wealth of Networks*.
5. Bernal, "Diaspora."
6. Castells, *The Internet Galaxy*.
7. Nagel and Staeheli, "ICT and Geographies."
8. Appadurai, *Modernity at Large*.
9. Andersson, "Digital Diasporas."
10. Norris, "Preaching to the Converted?"
11. Therwath, "Cyber-Hindutva."
12. Georgiou, "Gender."
13. Hall, "Cultural Identity and Diaspora."
14. Naimy, *The Lebanese Prophets*.
15. Lloyd, "Transnational Mobilizations," 373.
16. Georgiou, "Diaspora in the Digital Era," 80.
17. Georgiou, "Diasporic Media," 90.
18. One of the earliest networks in the region was established by IBM to connect researchers around the Gulf to databases and shared resources. See Al-Sulaiym, Al-Muammar, and Bakry, "GULFNET."
19. Society.Culture.Lebanon Conference, "Towards a New Lebanon."

20. Siapera, "Minority Activism."
21. Georgiou, "Diasporic Media."
22. Brouwer, "Dutch Moroccan Websites"; Aly, *Becoming Arab*.
23. Electronic Intifada, "About the Electronic Intifada."
24. Brown, "Virtual War."
25. Yin, "The Electronic Intifada"; Ghabra and Hasian, "Tough Love."
26. Elaph, "Publisher's Message."
27. Rinnawi, "Imagined Coherence."
28. Georgiou, "Diaspora," 85.
29. Foucault, "The Subject and Power."
30. Andén-Papadopoulos and Pantti, "The Media Work."
31. Moss, "The Ties That Bind."
32. Rheingold, *The Virtual Community*.
33. Alomosh, "Virtual Communities."
34. Kalathil and Boas, *Open Networks*.
35. Wheeler, *The Internet*.
36. Freedom House, "Freedom on the Net."
37. Al-Saggaf and Williamson, "Online Communities"; Al-Saggaf, "The Digital Divide."
38. Kepel, *Jihad*, 215.
39. Swalif.net later turned into a technology news site.
40. Al Saha, "The Al Saha Forum."
41. Fares et al., "Readers and Members."
42. Kraidy and Khalil, *Arab Television Industries*, 36; Sakr, *Satellite Realms*, 10.
43. O'Reilly, "What Is Web 2.0."
44. Montague, "The Baghdad Blogger."
45. Melzer, "Gay Iraqi."
46. Pax, *Salam Pax*.
47. Khalil, "Youth-Generated Media."
48. Kraidy, *The Naked Blogger*.
49. BBC, "Saudi Arabia's Ban."
50. Wheeler, "Saudi Women Driving Change?"
51. BBC, "The Story behind No Woman, No Drive."
52. Al-Mukhtar, "Fageeh Stands Up."
53. This is the case, for instance, with the film *Al Erhab Wal Kebab*, which offered a satirical image of the Muslim Brotherhood.
54. Marx, "Bassem Youssef."
55. Tartaglione, "Jon Stewart Bids Farewell."
56. Al Hasniya, "Arab YouTubers"; Metafora Productions, "Joe Show."
57. Trans-locality is a concept used in research related to culture and migration. It emphasizes the importance of treating citizenship and identity as concrete rather than universalizing them. See Deirdre, "Translocal Circulation"; Datta and Brickell, *Translocal Geographies*.
58. Shiblak, "Arabia's Bedoon."
59. Blilid and Favier, "Du monde réel."
60. Costa, *Social Media*.
61. Kreyenbroek and Allison, *Kurdish Culture*.
62. Merolla, "De la parole aux vidéos."
63. Palestinian National Internet Naming Authority, "Promote Palestine."
64. Al-Ghathami, *The Culture of Twitter*.

Chapter 7

1. Mihoub-Dramé, *Internet dans le monde Arabe*, 111–116.
2. Howard, *The Digital Origins*, 84–107.

3. Ulrich, "Historicizing Arab Blogs."
4. Perlmutter, *Blogwars*, 66.
5. Etling et al., "Mapping the Arabic Blogosphere."
6. In 2006, there were an estimated 40,000 blogs. See HRinfo, "Implacable Adversaries."
7. Lynch, "Blogging"; El-Nawawy and Khamis, *Egyptian Revolution 2.0*, 34.
8. Ghannam, "Social Media," 5.
9. Aday et al., "Blogs and Bullets," 3.
10. Hofheinz, "Arab Internet Use."
11. Albloshi and Alfahad, "The Orange Movement," 227.
12. To prevent reader confusion, we chose to utilize terms for movements that are widely used in international media, even though these terms may not align with the local designations for these movements.
13. Sun, "Blue Revolution."
14. Schleusener, "From Blog to Street"; Karolak, "Civil Society."
15. Douai, "Online Politics," 142–145.
16. Zayani, *Networked Publics*, 131–167.
17. Haugbolle, "From A-Lists to Webtifadas."
18. Riegert and Ramsay, "Activists, Individualists, and Comics."
19. Riegert, "Understanding Popular Arab Bloggers," 470.
20. Lim, "Clicks."
21. Radsch, "Core to Commonplace."
22. Lim, "Clicks," 239.
23. Isherwood, "A New Direction."
24. Faris, *Dissent and Revolution*, 8–9.
25. Radsch, "Core to Commonplace."
26. Isherwood, "A New Direction."
27. Howard and Hussain, *Democracy's Fourth Wave?*, 38.
28. Zayani, "Social Movements."
29. Radsch, "Core to Commonplace."
30. Faris, "The End."
31. Sreberny and Kiabany, *Blogistan*.
32. Sreberny, *Small Media*.
33. Chalcraft, "Popular Movements"; Zayani, "Courting and Containing"; Bayat, "The 'Street'"; Pollock, "The Arab Street"; Regier, "The Arab Street."
34. Shirky, *Here Comes Everybody*; Shirky, "The Political Power"; Morozov, "Think Again"; Gladwell, "Small Change"; Aouragh, "Framing the Internet."
35. Charrad and Reith, "Local Solidarities."
36. Kenner, "Arabic Facebook Launches."
37. Alaimo, "How the Facebook Arabic Page."
38. Howard and Muzammil, *Democracy's Fourth Wave*.
39. Zayani, *Bullets and Bulletins*.
40. Nanabhay and Farmanfarmaian, "From Spectacle to Spectacular," 576.
41. King, *Arab Winter*.
42. Zayani, *A Fledgling Democracy*.
43. Haugbolle, "Spatial Transformations."
44. Atallah, "How Internet Has Become a Battleground."
45. Abdulraza, "Iraq's Protests."
46. Bailey, *Understanding Alternative Media*.
47. Kushkush, "Sudan's Diaspora."
48. Thieux, "Les réseaux sociaux."
49. Silva, "Algeria Protests"; Bior, "Sudan's Social Media."
50. One need only recall the 1994 Zapatista uprising in Mexico (when activists used web pages, email lists, bulletin boards, and chat rooms to communicate their message, coordinate their

activities, and rally support against NAFTA's enactment) and the 1999 WTO protests in Seattle (when numerous organizations protested the meeting and established a media center supported by the internet to communicate and spread the news).

51. Khanfar, "At Al Jazeera."
52. Diamond and Plattner, *Liberation Technology.*
53. Berridge, "Briefing."
54. Hosea, "Libya Unrest."
55. Kandaka, "Sudan Uprising."
56. Hagenah, "How the Women-Only Facebook Group."
57. Tilly, *The Contentious French*; Tilly, *Regimes and Repertoires.*
58. Rolfe, "Building an Electronic Repertoire."
59. Bartu, "The New Arab Uprisings."
60. Northlet, "Imagining."
61. Ouaras, "Tagging."
62. Northlet, "Imagining."
63. International Crisis Group, "Algeria."

Chapter 8

1. Feldstein, "The Global Expansion."
2. Mellor, *Arab Digital Journalism*, 25–26.
3. Eid and Douai, *New Media Discourses.*
4. Owen, *Disruptive Power,* 17.
5. Yangyue, *Competitive Political Regime.*
6. Deibert, "The Geopolitics of Internet Control."
7. Shishkina and Issaev, "Internet Censorship."
8. Committee to Protect Journalists, "10 Worst Countries."
9. Donaghy, "Falcon Eye"; Radsch, "Treating the Internet."
10. Aboulenein, "Egypt Blocks 21 Websites."
11. Fahmi, "Egypt Tightens Grip on Media."
12. Agence France-Presse, "Saudi Arabia Criminalises Online Satire."
13. Associated Press, "Saudi Arabia and BlackBerry."
14. Woodhams, "Digital Authoritarianism."
15. Middle East Eye, "EU States 'Approved'"; TIMEP, "Export of Surveillance"; TIMEP, "Use of Surveillance Technology."
16. Meaker, "Death by Spyware"; Marczak et al., "The Great iPwn."
17. Chulov, "Syria Shuts off Internet Access."
18. Index on Censorship, "Sudan Blacks Out Internet."
19. Moore-Gilbert, "Mediated Mobilisation," 80.
20. Moore-Gilbert, "Mediated Mobilisation," 85.
21. Iddins, "Mamfakinch," 3582.
22. Abadi, "The February 20th Movement," 124.
23. Al-Ghazzi, "'Citizen Journalism.'"
24. Andén-Papadopoulos, "Media Witnessing."
25. Boex, "YouTube and the Syrian Revolution."
26. Su, "How One Syrian Fought."
27. Human Rights Watch, "If the Dead Could Speak."
28. Shehabat, "The Social Media Cyber-War."
29. Abdelaziz and Yan, "Video."
30. Grohe, "The Cyber Dimensions."
31. Springer, *Cyber Warfare*; Harris, "How Did Syria's Hacker Army"; Fowler, "Who Is the Syrian Electronic Army?"
32. Lee, "The Impact of Cyber Capabilities."

33. Maximillian, "Networked Communication," 101.
34. Donaghy, "Falcon Eye."
35. Right, "Most-Followed Politicians."
36. Jacinto, "Can Hariri's 'Selfie Diplomacy.'"
37. Abouzeid, "Lebanon's Hariri."
38. Gresh, "Dubai's Police Chief."
39. Al Qassemi, "Gulf Governments."
40. Antwi-Boateng and Al Mazrouei, "The Challenges"; Al-Mansouri, Al-Mohannadi, and Feroun, "Digital Diplomacy"; Akdenizli, "Twitter Diplomacy."
41. Westall and McDowall, "Saudi Arabia's Rulers."
42. Alkarni, "Twitter Response"; Westall and McDowall, "Saudi Arabia's Rulers."
43. Gillespie, "The Instagram Influencers."
44. Al-Saggaf and Simmons, "Social Media."
45. Rossel and Finger, "Conceptualizing E-Governance."
46. According to one report, more than two-thirds of organizations in the Gulf cite cybersecurity as one of the biggest challenges of digital transformation. Another survey of IT security practitioners also raises concerns about several IoT security threats given the rapid deployment of digital transformation. See Trade Arabia, "Data Security"; Zawya, "Enterprises in the UAE/KSA."
47. Navarria, "E-Government."
48. Navarria, "E-Government."
49. Weldali, "Awqaf Ministry."
50. Karaki-Shelhoub, "Population ID Card Systems," 140.
51. According to the International Labour Organization, migrant workers in the six GCC states account for more than 10% of all migrants globally, and in the case of Qatar and the UAE, they make up more than 80% of the population. See International Labour Organization, "Labour Migration."
52. Ajana, *Governing through Biometrics*, 5.
53. Kirk, "Why Abu Dhabi Doubled Down"; Odell, "Inside the Dark Web"; BBC, "How BAE Sold Cyber-Surveillance Tools," 8.
54. Bridge, "Abu Dhabi."
55. Qatar News Agency, "Qatar 2022 Hayya Card."
56. Al-Rawi, *Cyberwars in the Middle East*; Sexton and Campbell, *Cyber War*.
57. The cybersecurity market in the Middle East is expected to reach more than USD 28 billion in 2025, growing at an average rate of 12% yearly. See Al-Ayed, "Saudi Arabia Spends $2Bn."
58. In addition to government institutions, several businesses and public figures have been victims of "mercenary" hackers who target mobile phones and applications with increased sophistication. See Satter and Bing, "'Mercenary' Hacker Group."
59. Chawki et al., *Cybercrime*.
60. See, for example, Langton, "Dozens of Cyber Attacks"; Al Mukrashi, "Oman Government Website."
61. Mabon, "Aiding Revolution?"
62. El-Guindy, "Cybercrime in the Middle East," 18.
63. Perlroth, "Hacking Group."
64. Saad, Bazan, and Varin, "Asymmetric Cyber-Warfare."
65. Al Amro, "Cybercrime," 36; Perlroth, "In Cyber Attack."
66. Pagliery, "The Inside Story."
67. Zetter, "Meet 'Flame.'"
68. Knopová and Knopová, "The Third World War?," 28.
69. Nakashima and Warrick, "Stuxnet."
70. Sanger and Mazzetti, "U.S. Had Cyberattack Plan."
71. Zetter, "The NSA Acknowledges"; Bastani, "Structure of Iran's Cyber Warfare."

72. Warner, "Crown Prince."
73. Rudner, "'Electronic Jihad,'" 10.
74. Watts, *Messing with the Enemy*, 47–48.
75. Atwan, *Islamic State*.
76. Khalil, "Turning Murders into Public Executions"; Mirgani, *Target Markets*, 98–102.
77. Jones, *Digital Authoritarianism*; Feldstein, *The Rise of Digital Repression*.
78. Fanon, *The Wretched*.
79. James, *Nasser at War*.
80. Zaharna, *Battles to Bridges*, 29–53; El-Affendi, "The Conquest"; Seib, "Public Diplomacy"; El-Nawawy, "U.S. Public Diplomacy."
81. Prashad, *Arab Spring*.
82. Bradshaw, Bailey, and Howard, "Industrialized Disinformation."
83. Grossman and Ramali, "Outsourcing Disinformation."
84. Silverman, Lytvynenko, and Kung, "Disinformation for Hire"; El Gendy, "Social Media."
85. Hoffman, "'Bots' and Bans."
86. Miller, *The Gulf Crisis*.
87. Mneimneh, "The Gulf Crisis."
88. Al-Rawi, *Cyberwars*.
89. MarkMonitor, "beoutQ Investigation"; LaMay, "Qatar's beIN Sports," 305.
90. Piracy Monitor, "beoutQ."
91. Sardarizadeh, "Facebook."
92. Schiller, *Digital Capitalism*.
93. Graham, "BlackBerry Crippled."
94. Cox, "Signal Claims."
95. Farid, "Egypt Is Blocking Voice Calls."
96. Wam, "Dh500,000 Fine."
97. Mazzetti, Perlroth, and Bergman, "It Seemed Like."
98. Radcliffe, "Skype Banned."
99. Khalil and Zayani, "Deterritorialized Digital Capitalism."
100. Cammaerts, "Jamming the Political."
101. Boyd, *Broadcasting*.
102. Mellor, "Bedouinization or Liberalization."

Chapter 9

1. Bell, *The Coming of Post-Industrial Society*; World Bank, *Building Knowledge Economies*.
2. World Bank, "Transforming Arab Economies," 5.
3. Ojanperä, Graham, and Zook, "The Digital Knowledge Economy Index."
4. Ghanem, *The Arab Spring*, 39–64.
5. Murphy, "Problematizing Arab Youth."
6. UNICEF, "MENA Generation."
7. World Bank, "School Enrollment."
8. UNICEF, "MENA Generation."
9. Khorsheed, "Saudi Arabia"; Saudi Ministry of Economy and Planning, "Saudi Arabia's Ninth Development Plan."
10. Bahraini Ministry of Interior, "From Regional Pioneer."
11. UNDP and MBRF, "Global Knowledge Index."
12. Ojanperä, Graham, and Zook, "The Digital Knowledge Economy Index."
13. Brinkley et al., "Kuwait."
14. Ahmed and Alfaki, "Transforming the UAE."
15. Tadros, "The Arab Gulf States."
16. From the perspective of the World Bank, a knowledge economy framework rests on four pillars: an economic and institutional regime, a well-educated and skilled population,

a dynamic information infrastructure, and an efficient innovation system. See Aubert, Karlsson, and Utz, "Building Knowledge."

17. Chen and Dahlman, "Knowledge Economy."
18. See, for instance, El Kogali and Krafft, *Expectations and Aspirations*; Boutieri, *Learning in Morocco*; Alaoui and Springborg, *The Political Economy of Education*; Kirdar, *Education*; Abi Mershed, *Trajectories of Education*.
19. ESCWA, "Arab Horizon 2030."
20. World Bank, "Transforming Arab Economies," 14.
21. Lightfoot, "Promoting the Knowledge Economy."
22. Arab Social Media Report, "Transforming Education."
23. World Bank, "Research and Development Expenditure."
24. Omar, "Innovation and Economic Performance."
25. Springborg, "Globalization."
26. World Bank, "Transforming Arab Economies," 31.
27. ESCWA, "Intellectual Property."
28. Wyne, "Country Insights."
29. Schiwietz, *American Higher Education*.
30. Brinkley et al., "Kuwait."
31. Bizri, "Research, Innovation, Entrepreneurship," 225.
32. Dana, *Economies*; Lawson, "The Political Economy of Rentierism."
33. See, for example, Haddad, *Business Networks*.
34. Omar, "Innovation and Economic Performance"; World Bank, "Transforming Arab Economies," 14–18.
35. Bizri, "Research, Innovation, Entrepreneurship," 202.
36. In 2021, a total of 256 funding institutions (venture capital firms, accelerators, family offices, and government initiatives) invested $1 billion into regional startups. See MAGNiTT, "2021 MENA Venture Investment Report"; MAGNiTT, "2021 MENA Venture Investor Ranking Report."
37. World Bank, "Transforming Arab Economies," 25.
38. Asongu, "Financial Sector Competition."
39. Rossel and Finger, "Conceptualizing E-Governance," 399.
40. Newcombe, "The United Arab Emirates."
41. UN, "UN E-Government Survey 2020."
42. Radcliffe, "E-Government," 247.
43. Younes, "A Generic Five-Stage Model," 46.
44. Cherupelly, "E-Governance," 88.
45. Denner, "Open Government," 20.
46. O'Donovan, *Pursuing the Knowledge Economy*.
47. Ben Hassen, "The State of the Knowledge-Based Economy."
48. Alfaki, "Sudan Regional Stand."
49. Anderson and Djeflat, *The Real Issues*, 6.
50. Anderson, "The State," 14.
51. Hvidt, "Transformation," 14–18; Jones and Sahraoui, *The Future*.
52. Eibl, *Social Dictatorships*; Ramady, *The Political Economy*, xiii; Sidani and Thornberry, "Nepotism."
53. Ghaffar, "Clientelism"; Elvira, Schwarz, and Weipert-Fenner, *Clientelism and Patronage*.
54. Brinkley et al., "Kuwait," 28.
55. Anderson, "Special Considerations," 396–397.
56. Bizri, "Research, Innovation, Entrepreneurship," 199; ITU, "Measuring the Information Society 2010."
57. Howard, *The Digital Origins*, 122.
58. Neate, "Rupert Murdoch."
59. Barrett, *Dubai Dreams*, 43–44.

Chapter 10

1. Anderson, *Arabizing the Internet*; Gonzalez-Quijano, *Arabités numériques*, 56.
2. Investment Development Authority of Lebanon, "Sectors in Focus."
3. Oxford Business Group, "Strategies."
4. Shaver and Rizk, *Access to Knowledge*.
5. Business Software Alliance, "Global Software Survey."
6. Diwan, "About Us."
7. Anderson, *Arabizing the Internet*, 21–22.
8. Dirar et al., "Development Arabic Search Engine."
9. Internet World Stats, "Internet World Users."
10. Mellor, *Arab Digital Journalism*; El-Issawi, *Arab National Media*.
11. Al Qasimi, "Digital Publishing."
12. Khaleej Times, "UAE"; Al Tarras, "Arabic E-Books."
13. Alterman, *New Media, New Politics?*
14. Alshehri, "Electronic Newspapers."
15. Middle East Media, "Media Use by Platform."
16. Adgate, "Newspapers Have Been Struggling."
17. Phillips, *Journalism in Context*.
18. El-Richani, "Whither the Lebanese Press."
19. Khalifeh, "Pressing Issue."
20. Al Bawaba, "Maktoob.com Picks Up Majority Stake."
21. Arabvertising.net, "Arabvertising.net Engineers"; Arab News, "Maktoob Chief."
22. Al Bawaba, "Maktoob.com Acquires Premier."
23. Al Bawaba, "Maktoob.com Picks Up Majority Stake."
24. Al Bawaba, "Abraaj Capital Sells Stake."
25. Altaba, "Yahoo! to Extend Reach."
26. Allison, "The 'World's First Virtual Gaming Festival.'"
27. Saleh, "MENA."
28. PwC, "MENA Entertainment and Media Outlook."
29. Al Otaibi, "The History, Pitfalls, and Opportunities."
30. Wilkins, *Prisms of Prejudice*.
31. Šisler, "Digital Arabs."
32. Schleiner, *Transnational Play*.
33. Allison, "The 'World's First Virtual Gaming Festival.'"
34. Since January 2020, "e-sports" has been a keyword that consistently gets more than 100,000 mentions on social media in the Middle East. See Ntloko, "A Data-Driven Analysis."
35. FIFA, "FIFA eWorld Cup Champion."
36. Atalah, "Game On."
37. Godinho, "Saudi's Millennium Arabia."
38. Nabil, "W Ventures to Invest."
39. Pahuja, "The Global Rise."
40. Al Bawaba, "Saudi Arabia Launches."
41. MBC, "MBC Group Re-Launches Shahid.net."
42. Cherian, "MBC's Shahid."
43. Zawya, "MBC Launches New Version."
44. Paul, "Chairman of Saudi Media Group MBC."
45. Khalil and Zayani, "Digitality and Music Streaming."
46. Paracha, "Anghami Commits $3 Million."
47. Stassen, "After Previously Being Exclusively Available."
48. Arabic Podcast, "Podcast in Numbers."
49. Allison, "Major New Study."
50. Paracha, "Arabic Audiobook Startup."
51. Khalil, "Modalities of Media Governance."

52. Qatar News Agency, "4th Arab Digital Content Forum."
53. Such platforms have not proved yet to be successful, which points to the relevance of both economic and cultural factors. See Allam and Chan-Olmsted, "The Development of Video Streaming Industry."
54. Bhargava and Al Kaabi, "How Young Arabs Are Fuelling," 15.
55. GSMA, "The Mobile Economy: Middle East and North Africa 2022."
56. Winston, *Media Technology and Society*; Dwyer, *Media Convergence*.
57. Ling, "Our Well-Being."

Chapter 11

1. Arabian Business, "Inside the Gulf's Digital Retail Revolution."
2. Statista, "Number of Online Stores"; Muhammad, "Saudi Arabia's E-Tail Laws."
3. Fadhelat, "E-Commerce Takes Over."
4. Zawya, "Landmark Group Launches E-Commerce Site."
5. Zawya, "Strong GCC Consumer Optimism."
6. International Trade Administration, "UAE."
7. Vaast, "What Are the Opportunities."
8. Alameddin, "Why Is E-Commerce a Key Economic Driver?"
9. Zawya, "Strong GCC Consumer Optimism."
10. Alsharekh, "Social Media."
11. Wendel, "Dubai Launches."
12. UNCTAD, "The UNCTAD B2C E-Commerce Index."
13. Zakaria, "From the Souk."
14. Ghandour, "An Exploratory Study."
15. Feuilherade, "Foreign Investments," 43.
16. Shuqum, "E-Commerce."
17. Platt, "GCC Mall Culture," 86.
18. Foege, *The Tinkerers*.
19. Hegazi, *Startup Arabia*.
20. Bizri, "Research, Innovation, Entrepreneurship," 202.
21. Vein, "Why Increasing Digital Arabic Content Is Key."
22. Arab News, "UAE."
23. Dubai Internet City and A. T. Kearney, "The IT Market"; Menon, "DIC."
24. Zawya, "Dubai Internet City Welcomes."
25. Zawya, "Dubai Internet City Launches."
26. Zawya, "Gaming Giant."
27. Kamel, "Dubai Start-Ups."
28. Paracha, "Mubadala Launches."
29. Aravanis, "How Social Media Is a Double-Edged Sword"; Industry Development Agency, "The Egyptian Startup Ecosystem"; Karombo, "Egyptian Startups."
30. Refai, "Tahrir Tech"; GrEEK Campus, "The GrEEK Campus Response."
31. Beirut Digital District, "A Unique Cluster."
32. Radcliffe, "COVID Hit Startups Badly."
33. MAGNiTT, "Emerging Venture Markets Report."
34. Nabil, "Investment."
35. Google Developers, "Smart Lock for Wego."
36. Serrano, "10 Startups."
37. MAGNiTT, "Startup Fever."
38. MENA Private Equity Association, "MENA Private Equity & Venture Capital."
39. MAGNiTT, "FY2022 MENA"; Radcliffe, "COVID Hit Startups Badly."
40. Zawya, "Dubai Internet City Partners."
41. Mouchawar, "Souq.com."

42. Ali, "Yahoo Acquiring Arab Portal Maktoob."
43. Arabian Business, "Dubai's Souq.com Secures $75M Funding Boost."
44. An SKU is a unique identifier used to track inventory and differentiate products. SKUs are often used in conjunction with a barcode system to ensure accurate tracking and inventory control.
45. Dalakian, "How CashU Spinoff PayFort Is Trying to Improve."
46. Lunden, "Souq."
47. Nair and Martin, "Amazon in Talks."
48. Lunden and Russell, "Amazon to Acquire Souq."
49. El Sawy, "How Souq's Shift to Amazon.ae Affects UAE Consumers."
50. UN Habitat, "Egypt's Clean Fuels Initiative"; Arabian Business, "Dubai to Add 3,268 New Taxis."
51. Careem, "About Us."
52. Alrawi, "Uber Completes $3.1 Billion Deal."
53. Zawya, "Careem Bot."
54. Odeh and Martin, "Uber's Mideast Addition Careem."
55. Cornwell, "Careem Launches Delivery Service."
56. Hamid, "Careem Invests $50 Million."
57. Khalil and Zayani, "Digitality and Music Streaming."
58. Mid East Information, "Anghami Gears Up"; Stassen, "After Previously Being Exclusively Available."
59. El Fay, "Anghami's Journey"; Tech Plugged, "Anghami."
60. Anghami, "Anghami Raises Funds."
61. Hamid, "Anghami."
62. Valladeres, "How We Started."
63. Communicate Online, "Anghami's Rami Zeidan."
64. Simon, *Media of the Masses.*
65. BBC, "Anghami, a Legal Musical Library."
66. Stassen, "Why Anghami."
67. Digital Bedu, "V1.1.0: Anghami's Elie Habib."
68. Crunchbase, "Anghami Financials."
69. MAGNiTT, "A Rundown of MENA's 3 IPOs in the Last 2 Years."
70. GSMA, "MENA 5G Spectrum"; Al-Atrush and White, "Xi Jinping Hails 'New Era'"; Radwan, "Why China Is a Natural Partner"; Chaziza, "Gulf States Go Digital."
71. Vodafone, "Middle East Barometer Report."
72. Statista, "Expected Share."
73. International Data Corporation, "IoT Spending."
74. PwC, "US$320 Billion by 2030?"
75. Mavridis et al., "Opinions and Attitudes."
76. UAE Government Portal, "UAE Strategy."
77. MBZUAI, "About."
78. Radcliffe, "AI."
79. Global Newswire, "The MEA Cloud Computing Market."
80. Rushdi and Yazizis, "Middle East Fintech Study."
81. Youssef, "'FinxAr.'"
82. Gharib, Tok, and Zebian, "Neoliberal Urbanization"; Tok et al., "Crafting Smart Cities."
83. Khalifi, "The Challenges of Data."
84. Ojo et al., "Designing Next-Generation Smart City Initiatives," 44.
85. O'Mara, *The Code.*
86. Ingham, "Top Cities."
87. Robinson, "Here's Why Israel Could Be the Next Silicon Valley"; Baker, "The Arab World's Silicon Valley."
88. MAGNiTT, "Q1 2023 MENA Venture Investment"; MAGNiTT, "MENA H1 2022 Venture Investment"; MAGNiTT, "Two Decades till Sunrise."

89. Nasrallah, "Sheikh Mohammed bin Rashid."
90. National, "UAE Unveils Coder Training Campaign."
91. Wamda, "Enhancing Access."
92. Zayani, "Digital Journalism"; Youmans, *An Unlikely Audience*, 139–164.
93. Schroeder, "How Hind Hobeika Created"; Ghosh, Keller, and Thapar, "Instabeat: One More Lap"; Ghosh, Keller, and Thapar, "Instabeat: Crossing the Finish Line."
94. Pupic, "In the Pursuit of Greatness."

Part V

1. Levin and Mamlok, "Culture and Society."
2. Anderson, *Arabizing the Internet*, 23.

Chapter 12

1. One of the striking, though not unique, examples of the use of street and digital activism to advance women's rights in conservative settings is the widespread public anger over the death of twenty-two-year-old Masha Amini after Iran's morality police detained her in September 2022 for allegedly failing to wear the hijab in accordance with government regulations.
2. Weimann, "Terrorist Migration."
3. Al-Kandari and Dashti, "Fatwa and the Internet."
4. Boyd, "Saudi Arabian Television."
5. Jafaar, "TV Execs Face New Threats."
6. Mernissi, *Beyond the Veil*, 41–42.
7. Al-Rasheed, *A Most Masculine State*, 108–114.
8. Chraibi, "The King"; Al-Rasheed, *A Most Masculine State*, 108–133; Schanzer and Miller, *Facebook Fatwa*, 37–42.
9. Ghouth, "End Camera-Phone Ban."
10. Mishkhas, "Saudi Arabia"; Sakr, *Satellite Realms*, 20.
11. Sullivan, "Saudi Youth"; Associated Press, "In Saudi Arabia"; Bayazid, "The Evolution of Mobile Phones."
12. Kemp, "Digital 2022."
13. Renard, "The Politics of Unveiling."
14. Benjamin, "Privacy."
15. Elareshi and Ziani, "Digital and Interactive Social Media."
16. Buskens and Webb, *Women and ICT*.
17. Kemp, "Digital 2022"; Statista, "Leading Countries"; Statista, "Most Used."
18. Renard, "Young Urban Saudi Women's Transgressions."
19. Alsanea, *Girls of Riyadh*.
20. Al-Fassi, "Saudi Women," 188.
21. Al-Dabbagh, "Saudi Arabia Women."
22. Al-Sharif, *Daring to Drive*; Altoaimy, "Driving Change."
23. Heintzen, "AP Was There."
24. Otterbeck, "Wahhabi Ideology," 344; Women to Drive Movement.
25. Lim, "Unveiling Saudi Feminism(s)," 463.
26. Al-Rasheed, *A Most Masculine State*, 22.
27. Tucker and Lowi, "Saudi Arabia's Reforms."
28. Thompson, *Being Young*, 4.
29. Al-Rasheed, *A Most Masculine State*, 22.
30. Rannard, "Saudi Wastes No Time."
31. Bunt, *iMuslims*.
32. Eickelman and Salvatore, "Muslim Publics," 15.
33. Sreberny, *Small Media*.
34. Eickelman and Piscatori, *Muslim Politics*, 121; Hirschkind, *The Ethical Soundscape*.

35. Hroub, *Religious Broadcasting*.
36. El Naggar, "The Impact of Digitization."
37. Anderson, "Islam's New Interpreters."
38. Tantawi, "'Modern' Preachers."
39. El Naggar, "The Impact of Digitization."
40. Khamis, "Cyber *Ummah*"; El-Nawawy and Khamis, "Divergent Identities," 33.
41. Abdel Fadil, "The Islam-Online Crisis," 20.
42. Lamloum, "Islamonline"; Graf and Skovgaard-Petersen, *Global Mufti*.
43. Abdel Fadil, "The Islam-Online Crisis."
44. Lamloum, "Islamonline."
45. Azad, "Thinking about Islam," 123.
46. Echchaibi, "From Audio Tapes to Video Blogs," 31.
47. Echchaibi, "From Audio Tapes to Video Blogs," 28.
48. Larsson, *Muslims and the New Media*, 3.
49. Echchaibi, "From Audio Tapes to Video Blogs," 29.
50. Khalil, "Turning Murders into Public Executions."
51. Rudner, "'Electronic Jihad,'" 10.
52. Watts, *Messing with the Enemy*, 47–48.
53. Atwan, *Islamic State*, 15–31.
54. Kraidy, "The Project Image."
55. Kraidy, "Terror."
56. Azad, "Thinking about Islam," 129.
57. El Naggar, "The Impact of Digitization," 202.
58. Coleman and Blumler, *The Internet*, 4.
59. Doveling, Harju, and Sommer, "From Mediatized Emotion."
60. Black, *Museums*, 14.
61. Greenwald, "The New Race."
62. Heinonen and Strandvik, "Reframing Service Innovation."
63. Museum of the Future.
64. Buchholz, *The Global Rules of Art*.
65. Al-Ani and Siebert, "A Digital Transformation," 9.
66. Cooke, *Tribal Modern*.
67. Greenwald, "The New Race."
68. Exell, "Art Is Power"; Exell, "Desiring the Past."
69. Exell, *Modernity and the Museum*.
70. Thompson, *Being Young*.
71. Jones, "The Rhetoric of Self-Definition," 6–7; Greenwald, "The New Race."
72. Mirgani, "Introduction."
73. Florida, *The Rise of the Creative Class*.
74. Ahmed, *The Cultural Politics of Emotions*.
75. Erskine-Loftus, Al-Mulla, and Hightower, *Representing the Nation*.
76. Kraft, "For Still-Stateless Palestinians."
77. Backmann, *A Wall in Palestine*.
78. Toukan, "The Palestinian Museum," 17.
79. Kraft, "For Still-Stateless Palestinians."
80. Palestinian Museum.
81. Toukan, "The Palestinian Museum," 17.
82. Detaille, "Inside the Palestinian Museum."
83. Kanaan.
84. Adli, "Gaza's First Digital Archive."
85. McKernan, "A Journey through the Past."
86. Al Tahhan, "New Platform."
87. Gibson, "These Emirati Sisters."
88. Ghali, "The Middle East Archive Project."

89. Mohsen, "Lebanon and Iraq."

90. Isin and Nielsen, *Acts of Citizenship.*

Chapter 13

1. ITU, "Measuring Digital Development 2022," 2.
2. ITU, "Measuring Digital Development 2022," 3–5.
3. For example, the Arab version of the reality television show *Big Brother* was deemed culturally disruptive and eventually banned. See Kraidy, *Reality Television.*
4. Livingstone et al., "Global Perspectives."
5. Wiseman and Anderson, "ICT Integrated Education."
6. For a cleric's response to parents on this issue, see, for example, Al-Hakeem, "Ruling on
   Watching Cartoons."
7. Sabry and Mansour, *Children and Screen Media.*
8. Awan and Steemers, "Arab and Western Perspectives."
9. El-Haddad, "Major Trends"; Anser, "Divorce."
10. Holes, "Language and Identity."
11. Tayie, "Children and Mass Media."
12. UNICEF, "How Many Children."
13. ESCWA, "Review."
14. Gibran, *The Prophet*, 15.
15. Rahmani, "Children Internet Addiction."
16. Boutieri, *Learning in Morocco.*
17. Martin, Martins, and Wood, "Desire for Cultural Preservation."
18. Queen Rania Foundation, "Resources for Early Childhood Development."
19. Saeed and Badr, "Google Launches."
20. Ali, "The Role of Electronic Publishers."
21. Zaatar and Bodada, "Digital Media."
22. UNICEF, "Children in a Digital World."
23. ESCWA, "Review."
24. Paragi, *Foreign Aid.*
25. Kraidy, *Hybridity.*
26. UNDP, "Arab Human Development Report."
27. Islamic Development Bank, "Youth Development Strategy." It is important to note
    that individual states also adopt different age brackets. For example, Tunisia, Lebanon,
    Morocco, and the Palestinian Authority all use fifteen to twenty-nine for their brackets,
    whereas Qatar sets the upper limit at age twenty-five, and Mauritania sets it at thirty-five.
28. UNDP, "Arab Human Development Report."
29. UNICEF, "MENA Generation."
30. Dhillon, *Middle East Youth Bulge.*
31. Sabbagh et al., "Understanding the Arab Digital Generation."
32. GSMA, "The Mobile Economy: Middle East and North Africa 2016."
33. YouGov and Bayt, "The Skills Gap."
34. UNESCO, "Information and Communication Technology."
35. Edraak, "About Us."
36. ITU, "Generation Connect."
37. Dennis, Martin, and Hassan, "Media Use."
38. ASDA'A BCW, "Arab Youth Survey."
39. Manea, *The Arab State.*
40. World Bank, "Labor Force."
41. ITU, "Measuring Digital Development 2021," 3.
42. Raz, "The Arab World's Digital Divide."
43. GSMA, "Mobile Gender Gap Report."
44. Elnaggar, "Towards Gender Equal Access."

45. UN, "Gender Mainstreaming."
46. Elkhalek, "Impact of Knowledge Economy."
47. Newsom, Cassara, and Lengel, "Discourses," 81.
48. World Economic Forum, "Global Gender Gap Report."
49. Dimitropoulou, "Countries."
50. Steel, "Navigating (Im)Mobility," 245.
51. Steel, "Navigating (Im)Mobility," 235.
52. Zahidi, *Fifty Million Rising*.
53. Forbes Middle East, "10 Women."
54. Kristeva, "In Quest of the Feminine," 84.
55. OECD, "Empowering Women."
56. Martinez, Martin, and Marlow, "Emancipation."

Chapter 14

1. Gupta, "Social Media Trends."
2. Arab Weekly, "Social Media Use."
3. Ortiz-Ospina, "The Rise of Social Media."
4. Middle East Media, "Social Media."
5. Middle East Media, "Social Media."
6. ASDA'A BCW, "Arab Youth Survey."
7. Middle East Media, "Social Media."
8. Landorf, "Female Reverberations Online," 5.
9. Costa and Menin, "Introduction"; Statista, "Share of Internet Users."
10. Philo and Swanson, "Afterword."
11. Kraidy, *The Naked Blogger*, 17–18.
12. Perlmutter, *Blogwars*, 66.
13. Abdel Aal, *I Want to Get Married*.
14. Sreberny, "Women's Digital Activism."
15. Mernissi, "The Satellite."
16. Diefallah, "I Come from El Salam."
17. Hajj, *Networked Refugees*.
18. Senft, "Microcelebrity."
19. Kraidy, *Reality Television*.
20. Kraidy, "Saudi Arabia."
21. During the 2017 season of *Arab Idol* (Episode 9, February 24, 2017), a Swedish-based fan group established a PayPal account that bought SMS votes from a Palestinian mobile phone company in support of Yacoub Shaheen, who ultimately was the winner.
22. Uniacke, "Authoritarianism."
23. Osman, "'Blackface' Arab Stars."
24. Al-Shadeedi, "No Ordinary Story."
25. Greenhalgh and Al-Khal, "Morocco Instagram Influencer."
26. Khalil and Zayani, "Digitality and Debordered Spaces."
27. Across the affluent Gulf region, makeup is a lucrative market. Saudi Arabia's sales alone were estimated at USD 5.5 billion in 2022. See Zawya, "Kingdom Accounts."
28. Forbes Middle East, "30 Women."
29. Shapiro, "Is Huda Kattan."
30. Arab News, "Beauty Mogul Huda Kattan."
31. Arab News, "Beauty Mogul Huda Kattan."
32. Goldhaber, "The Value of Openness"; Andrejevic, "Estranged Free Labour"; Lovink, *Networks*; Couldry and Mejias, *The Costs of Connection*.
33. Al Jazeera, "Egypt Cuts TikTok Influencer Sentence."
34. Egyptian Streets, "Digital Campaign."

References

Abadi, Houda. "The February 20th Movement Communication Strategies: Toward Participatory Politics." PhD diss., Georgia State University, 2015. http://scholarworks.gsu.edu/communication_diss/63.

Abdel Aal, Ghada. *I Want to Get Married*. Translated by Nora Eltahawy. Austin: Center for Middle Eastern Studies at the University of Texas at Austin, 2010.

Abdelaziz, Salma, and Holly Yan. "Video: Syrian Rebel Cuts Out Soldier's Heart." CNN, May 14, 2013. https://www.cnn.com/2013/05/14/world/meast/syria-eaten-heart.

Abdel Fadil, Mona. "The Islam-Online Crisis: A Battle of Wasatiyya vs. Salafi Ideologies?" *Cyber Orient* 5, no. 1 (2011): 4–36.

Abdulla, Rasha. *The Internet in the Arab World*. Bern: Peter Lang, 2007.

Abdulmajid, Adib. *Extremism in the Digital Era: The Media Discourse of Terrorist Groups in the Middle East*. London: Palgrave Macmillan, 2021.

Abdulrazaq, Tallha. "Iraq's Protests and the Technology of Resistance." Al Jazeera, March 12, 2021. https://www.aljazeera.com/news/2021/3/12/iraqs-protests-and-the-technology-of-resistance.

Abi Mershed, Osama. *Trajectories of Education in the Arab World: Legacies and Challenges*. New York: Routledge, 2009.

Aboulenein, Ahmed. "Egypt Blocks 21 Websites for 'Terrorism' and 'Fake News.'" Reuters, May 24, 2017. https://www.reuters.com/article/egypt-censorship-idINKBN18K33J.

Abouzeid, Rania. "Lebanon's Hariri Takes His Political Fight to Twitter." *Time*, November 10, 2011. http://content.time.com/time/world/article/0,8599,2099014,00.html.

Abraham, Samuel. "5G Implementation: How the GCC Leapfrogged the World." *International Finance*, November 13, 2019. https://internationalfinance.com/5g-implementation-how-the-gcc-nations-leapfrogged-the-world/.

Abunadi, Ibrahim. "Influence of Culture on E-Government Acceptance in Saudi Arabia." PhD diss., School of Information and Communication Technology Science, Griffith University, 2013. https://research-repository.griffith.edu.au/bitstream/handle/10072/365226/Abu%20Nadi_2012_02Thesis.pdf?sequence=1.

Aday, Sean, Henry Farrell, Marc Lynch, John Sides, and Ethan Zuckerman. "Blogs and Bullets: New Media in Contentious Politics." Washington, DC: US Institute of Peace, 2010. https://www.usip.org/sites/default/files/resources/pw65.pdf.

Adgate, Brad. "Newspapers Have Been Struggling and Then Came the Pandemic." *Forbes*, August 20, 2021. https://www.forbes.com/sites/bradadgate/2021/08/20/newspapers-have-been-struggling-and-then-came-the-pandemic/?sh=1b6809d112e6.

Adli, Hana. "Gaza's First Digital Archive Documents Rich Cultural History." Al Jazeera, February 28, 2021. https://www.aljazeera.com/features/2021/2/28/gazas-first-digital-archive-documents-rich-cultural-history.

Agence France-Presse. "Saudi Arabia Criminalises Online Satire That 'Disrupts Public Order.'" *Telegraph*, September 5, 2018. https://www.telegraph.co.uk/news/2018/09/05/saudi-arabia-criminalises-online-satire/.

Ahmed, Akbar. *Postmodernism and Islam: Predicament and Promise*. London: Routledge, 2013.

Ahmed, Allam, and Ibrahim Alfaki. "Transforming the UAE into a Knowledge-Based Economy." *World Journal of Science, Technology and Sustainable Development* 10, no. 2 (2013): 84–102.

Ahmed, Sara. *The Cultural Politics of Emotions*. London: Routledge, 2014.

Ajami, Fouad. *The Arab Predicament: Arab Political Thought and Practice since 1967*. Cambridge: Cambridge University Press, 1992.

Ajana, Btihaj. *Governing through Biometrics: The Biopolitics of Identity*. Basingstoke, UK: Palgrave Macmillan, 2013.

Akdenizli, Banu. "Twitter Diplomacy in the GCC: How Foreign Ministers of the Region Are Using Social Media." In *Global Discourse in Fractured Times: Perspectives on Journalism, Media, Education, and Politics*, edited by Yahya Kamalipour, 129–144. Newcastle, UK: Cambridge Scholars, 2018.

Alaimo, Kara. "How the Facebook Arabic Page 'We Are All Khaled Said' Helped Promote the Egyptian Revolution." *Social Media + Society* 1, no. 2 (2015). https://journals.sagepub.com/doi/10.1177/2056305115604854.

Alameddin, Azzam. "Why Is E-Commerce a Key Economic Driver for UAE?" *Khaleej Times*, January, 5, 2020. https://www.khaleejtimes.com/business/local/why-is-e-commerce-a-key-economic-driver-for-uae.

Al Amro, Sulaiman. "Cybercrime in Saudi Arabia: Fact or Fiction?" *International Journal of Computer Science* 14, no. 2 (2017): 36–42.

Al-Ani, Ayad, and Carsten Siebert. "A Digital Transformation of Arab Museums: Challenges and Unconventional Strategies." Digital Arabia Network, 2021. https://digitalarabia.network/media/pages/articles/grab-a-coffee-read/8719c7aa2f-1637052954/museums_in_the_digital_age_20210531_dp.pdf.

Al Ani, Taha. "Iraq's Al Abid Satellite Launch System: A Pioneering Arab Experiment" [in Arabic]. Al Jazeera, December 5, 2021. https://tinyurl.com/muf67mhw.

Alaoui, Hicham, and Robert Springborg. *The Political Economy of Education in the Arab World*. Boulder, CO: Lynne Rienner, 2021.

Al-Atrush, Samer, and Edward White. "Xi Jinping Hails 'New Era' in China-Saudi Arabia Relations." *Financial Times*, December 8, 2022. https://www.ft.com/content/a3ad8e0c-d8e5-4fb3-b3af-39320ecf6b0d.

Al-Awdat, Hussein. *Renaissance and Modernity: Between Confusion and Failure* [in Arabic]. Beirut: Saqi, 2011.

Al-Ayed, Mohammed. "Saudi Arabia Spends $2Bn on Cybersecurity." *Asharq Al-Awsat*, October 7, 2020. https://english.aawsat.com/home/article/2551326/saudi-arabia-spends-2bn-cybersecurity.

Al Azm, Sadiq Jalal. *Self-Criticism after the Defeat*. London: Saqi, 2012.

Al Bawaba. "Abraaj Capital Sells Stake in Maktoob.com Inc.," December 30, 2007. https://www.albawaba.com/news/abraaj-capital-sells-stake-maktoobcom-inc.

Al Bawaba. "Maktoob.com Acquires Premier Media & Marketing Portal," July 13, 2005. https://www.albawaba.com/taxonomy/term/462176.

Al Bawaba. "Maktoob.com Picks Up Majority Stake in Popular Arab Sports Website," April 24, 2006. https://www.albawaba.com/news/maktoobcom-picks-majority-stake-popular-arab-sports-website.

Al Bawaba. "Saudi Arabia Launches $10 Million eSports Charity Tournament to Combat COVID-19," April 23, 2020. https://www.albawaba.com/business/saudi-arabia-launches-10-million-esports-charity-tournament-combat-covid-19-1352721.

Albloshi, Hamad, and Faisal Alfahad. "The Orange Movement of Kuwait: Civic Pressure Transforms a Political System." In *Civilian Jihad: Nonviolent Struggle, Democratization and Governance in the Middle East*, edited by Maria Stepan, 219–232. New York: Palgrave Macmillan, 2009.

Al-Dabbagh, May. "Saudi Arabian Women and Group Activism." *Journal of Middle East Women's Studies* 11, no. 2 (2015): 235–237.

Alfaki, Ibrahim. "Sudan Regional Stand in Knowledge Economy Development." *International Journal of Sudan Research* 6, no. 2 (2016): 67–75.

Al-Fassi, Hatoon. "Saudi Women and Islamic Discourse." *Journal of Women in the Middle East and the Islamic World* 14 (2016): 187–206.

Al-Ghathami, Abdullah. *The Culture of Twitter: Freedom of Expression or the Responsibility of Expression* [in Arabic]. Casablanca: Al Markaz Al Thaqafi Al Arabi, 2016.

Al-Ghazzi, Omar. "'Citizen Journalism' in the Syrian Uprising: Problematizing Western Narratives in a Local Context." *Communication Theory* 24, no. 4 (2014): 435–454.

Al-Hakeem, Assim. "Ruling on Watching Cartoons: Aladdin, Tooth Fairy, Disney, Etc." YouTube, 2020. https://www.youtube.com/watch?v=DPARlBlX5HI.

Al Hasnia, Lama. "Arab YouTubers" [in Arabic]. Raseef22, July 20, 2020. https://tinyurl.com/3zpmrtkz.

Ali, Rafat. "Yahoo Acquiring Arab Portal Maktoob After All." *Guardian*, August, 25, 2009. https://www.theguardian.com/media/pda/2009/aug/25/yahoo-internet.

Ali, Samar. "The Role of Electronic Publishers in Enriching Children's Digital Literature in the Knowledge Society" [in Arabic]. *Arab Literature* 11 (2015). https://platform.almanhal.com/Reader/Article/78278.

Al Jazeera. "Egypt Cuts TikTok Influencer Sentence to Three Years," April 18, 2022. https://www.aljazeera.com/news/2022/4/18/egypt-cuts-tiktok-influencer-sentence-to-3-years.

Al Jazeera. "Qatar Launches Its Second Satellite in Orbit" [in Arabic], November 16, 2018. https://tinyurl.com/574d4p9r.

Al-Kandari, Ali, and Ali Dashti. "Fatwa and the Internet: A Study of the Influence of Muslim Religious Scholars on Internet Diffusion in Saudi Arabia." *Prometheus* 32, no. 2 (2015): 127–144.

Alkarni, Saad. "Twitter Response to Vision 2030: A Case Study on Current Perceptions of Normative Disorder within Saudi Social Media." PhD diss., University of Ottawa, 2018. https://ruor.uottawa.ca/bitstream/10393/38041/1/Alkarni_Saad_2018_Thesis%20.pdf.

Al-Kinani, Ali Nasser. "Factors of Culture Affecting ICT Adoption in an Arab Society." In *ICT Acceptance, Investment and Organization: Cultural Practices and Values in the Arab World*, edited by Salam Abdallah and Fayez AlBadri, 168–175. Hershey, PA: IGI Global, 2011.

Allam, Rasha, and Sylvia Chan-Olmsted. "The Development of Video Streaming Industry in Egypt: Examining Its Market Environment and Business Model." *Journal of Media Business Studies* 18, no. 4 (2021): 285–303.

Alliance for Affordable Internet. "Affordability Drivers Index." https://adi.a4ai.org/affordability-report/data/?_year=2020&indicator=INDEX.

Alliance for Affordable Internet. "Affordability Report 2021." https://a4ai.org/wp-content/uploads/2021/12/A4AI_2021_AR_AW.pdf.

Allison, Austyn. "Major New Study into Podcast Landscape in Saudi Arabia Reveals 86 Per Cent of Listeners Tune in to Brand-Funded Podcasts." Campaign Middle East, August 11, 2020. https://campaignme.com/major-new-study-into-podcast-landscape-in-saudi-arabia-reveals-86-per-cent-of-listeners-tune-in-to-brand-funded-podcasts/.

Allison, Austyn. "The World's 'First Virtual Gaming Festival' GameOn Will Target 2.7 Billion Gamers Globally." Campaign Middle East, July 21, 2020. https://campaignme.com/the-worlds-first-virtual-gaming-festival-gameon-will-target-2-7-billion-gamers-globally/.

Al Mamlaka TV. *Digital Kingdom*. Episodes 1–6, December 2022. https://www.youtube.com/playlist?list=PL8BJpbvti8FtOnzUze0Y3Qi-lK0aY4SpE.

Al-Mansouri, Tarfa, Haya Al-Mohannadi, and Marian Feroun. "Digital Diplomacy during the First 100 Days: How GCC Ministries of Foreign Affairs and Ministers Tweeted the Blockade."

QScience Connect 2 (2021). https://www.qscience.com/content/journals/10.5339/conn ect.2021.spt.1.

Almowanes, Abdullah. "History of Computing in Saudi Arabia: A Cultural Perspective." *International Journal of Social Science and Humanity* 7, no. 7 (2017): 437–441.

Al-Mukhtar, Rima. "Fageeh Stands Up to Tickle Your Funny Bone." *Arab News*, March 20, 2013. https://www.arabnews.com/news/445440.

Al Mukrashi, Fahad. "Oman Government Website Restored after Hack." *Gulf News*, April 20, 2017. https://gulfnews.com/news/gulf/oman/oman-government-website-restored-after-hack-1.2014795.

Al Murshidi, Ghaddah. "STEM Education in the UAE: Challenges and Possibilities." *International Journal of Learning, Teaching and Educational Research* 18, no. 12 (2019): 316–332.

Alomosh, Ahmad. "Virtual Communities in the Arab World." *European Journal of Social Sciences* 8, no. 4 (2009): 569–580.

Al Otaibi, Walid. "The History, Pitfalls, and Opportunities of Arab Video Game Localization." Medium, October 13, 2020. https://medium.com/super-jump/the-history-pitfalls-and-opportunities-of-arab-video-game-localization-5ef523719ac6.

Al Qasimi, Bodour. "Digital Publishing and Its Impact on the Publishing Industry in the Arab World." *Publishing Research Quarterly* 27, no. 4 (2011): 338–344.

Al Qassemi, Sultan. "Gulf Governments Take to Social Media." Huffington Post, May 31, 2011. http://www.huffingtonpost.com/sultan-sooud-alqassemi/gulf-governments-take-to-_b_868815.html.

Al-Rasheed, Madawi. *A Most Masculine State: Gender, Politics and Religion in Saudi Arabia.* Cambridge: Cambridge University Press, 2013.

Al-Rawi, Ahmed. *Cyberwars in the Middle East.* New Brunswick, NJ: Rutgers University Press, 2021.

Alrawi, Mustafa. "Uber Completes $3.1 Billion Deal to Buy Dubai's Careem." *National*, January 4, 2020. https://www.thenational.ae/business/uber-completes-3-1-billion-deal-to-buy-dubai-s-careem-1.959406.

Al-Saggaf, Yeslam. "The Digital Divide within the Digital Community in Saudi Arabia." In *Information, Technology and Social Justice*, edited by Emma Rooksby and John Weckert, 262–282. Hershey, PA: IGI Global, 2007.

Al-Saggaf, Yeslam, and Peter Simmons. "Social Media in Saudi Arabia: Exploring Its Use during Two Natural Disasters." *Technological Forecasting and Social Change* 95 (2015): 3–15.

Al-Saggaf, Yeslem, and Kristie Williamson. "Online Communities in Saudi Arabia: Evaluating the Impact on Culture through Online Semi-Structured Interviews." *Forum: Qualitative Social Research* 5, no. 3 (2004). https://doi.org/10.17169/fqs-5.3.564.

Al Saha. "The Arab Al Saha Forum" [in Arabic]. https://alsahaarb.yoo7.com/.

Alsanea, Rajaa. *Girls of Riyadh.* New York: Penguin, 2007.

Al-Shadeedi, Musa. "No Ordinary Story: The Life of Khalaf Yousef." My.Kali, December 13, 2016. https://medium.com/my-kali-magazine/no-ordinary-story-2a0a58ed35b9.

Alsharekh, Alanoud. "Social Media and the Struggle for Authority in the GCC." *Canadian Journal for Middle East Studies* 1, no. 2 (2016): 8–33.

Al-Sharif, Manal. *Daring to Drive: A Saudi Woman's Awakening.* New York: Simon & Schuster, 2017.

Alshehri, Fayez. "Electronic Newspapers on the Internet: A Study of the Production and Consumption of Arab Dailies on the World Wide Web." PhD diss., University of Sheffield, 2001. https://etheses.whiterose.ac.uk/3503/1/327651.pdf.

Al-Sulaiym, Hamad, Abdulaziz Al-Muammar, and Saad Bakry. "GULFNET: The Academic Network of the Arab Gulf Countries." *International Journal of Network Management* 5, no. 5 (1995): 274–284.

Altaba. "Yahoo! to Extend Reach to Millions of Consumers in the Arab World; Signs Definitive Agreement to Acquire Maktoob.Com," August 25, 2009. https://www.altaba.com/news-releases/news-release-details/yahoo-extend-reach-millions-consumers-arab-world-signs.

Al Tahhan, Zena. "New Platform Documents Digital Censorship of Palestinians." Al Jazeera, November 2, 2021. https://www.aljazeera.com/news/2021/11/2/palestinians-launch-tool-to-document-digital-abuses-against-them.

Al Tarras, Kassem. "Arabic E-Books: A New Solution or Just a Revolution?" *Publishers Perspectives*, May 5, 2014. https://publishingperspectives.com/2014/05/arabic-e-books-a-new-solution-or-just-a-revolution/.

Alterman, Jon. "IT Comes of Age in the Middle East." *Foreign Service Journal* 82, no. 12 (2005): 37–42.

Alterman, Jon. "The Middle East's Information Revolution." *Current History* (January 2000): 21–26.

Alterman, Jon. *New Media, New Politics? From Satellite Television to the Internet in the Arab World.* Washington, DC: Washington Institute for Near East Policy, 1998.

Altoaimy, Lama. "Driving Change on Twitter: A Corpus-Assisted Discourse Analysis of the Twitter Debates on the Saudi Ban on Women Driving." *Social Sciences* 7 (2018): 1–14.

Aly, Ramy M. K. *Becoming Arab in London: Performativity and the Undoing of Identity.* London: Pluto, 2015.

Amanat, Abbas. "Is There a Middle East?" In *Is There a Middle East: The Evolution of a Geopolitical Concept,* edited by Michael Bonine, Abbas Amanat, and Michael Gasper, 1–7. Stanford, CA: Stanford University Press, 2012.

Amin, Hussein, and Leo Gher. "Digital Communications in the Arab World Entering the 21st Century." In *Civil Discourse and Digital Age Communications in the Middle East,* edited by Leo Gher and Hussein Amin. 109–140. Stamford, CT: Ablex, 2000.

Amin, Samir. "Keynote Address at the Second World Congress on Marxism." *Critical Sociology* 45, no. 1 (2019): 7–11.

Amlôt, Matthew. "Lockheed Martin to Build New Satellite Ground System in Saudi Arabia." Al Arabiya, June 8, 2020. https://english.alarabiya.net/en/News/gulf/2020/06/08/Lockheed-Martin-to-build-new-satellite-ground-system-in-Saudi-Arabia.

Andén-Papadopoulos, Kari. "Media Witnessing and the 'Crowd-Sourced Video Revolution.'" *Visual Communication* 12 (2013): 341–357.

Andén-Papadopoulos, Kari, and Mervi Pantti. "The Media Work of Syrian Diaspora Activists: Brokering between the Protest and Mainstream Media." *International Journal of Communication* 7 (2013): 2185–2206. https://ijoc.org/index.php/ijoc/article/view/1841.

Anderson, Benedict. *Imagined Communities: Reflections on the Origin and Spread of Nationalism.* London: Verso: 2006.

Anderson, Jon. *Arabizing the Internet.* Abu Dhabi: ECSSR, 1998.

Anderson, Jon. "Islam's New Interpreters." In *New Media in the Muslim World: The Emerging Public Sphere,* edited by Dale Eickelman and Jon Anderson, 45–60. Bloomington: Indiana University Press, 2003.

Anderson, Jon. "Producers and Middle East Internet Technology: Getting beyond 'Impacts.'" *Middle East Journal* 54, no. 3 (2000): 419–431.

Anderson, Jon, and Michael Hudson. "Internet Pioneering in Four Arab Countries: The Internet as a Force for Democracy in the Middle East." Arab Information Project, 2008. https://aipnew.wordpress.com/.

Anderson, Lisa. "The State in the Middle East and North Africa." *Comparative Politics* 20, no. 1 (1987): 1–18.

Anderson, Thomas. "Special Considerations and Ways Forward." In *The Real Issues of the Middle East and the Arab Spring: Addressing Research, Innovation and Entrepreneurship,* edited by Thomas Anderson and Abdelkader Djeflat, 371–397. New York: Springer, 2013.

Anderson, Thomas, and Abdelkader Djeflat, eds. *The Real Issues of the Middle East and the Arab Spring: Addressing Research, Innovation and Entrepreneurship.* New York: Springer, 2013.

Andersson, Kerstin. "Digital Diasporas: An Overview of the Research Areas of Migration and New Media through a Narrative Literature Review." *Human Technology* 15, no. 2 (2019): 142–180.

Andrejevic, Mark. "Estranged Free Labour." In *Digital Labour: The Internet as Playground and Factory,* edited by Trebor Scholz, 149–164. London: Routledge, 2013.

Anghami. "Anghami Raises Funds to Support Regional Expansion and User Acquisition." PR Newswire, November 2, 2016. https://www.prnewswire.com/news-releases/anghami-raises-funds-to-support-regional-expansion-and-user-acquisition-599643991.html.

Anser, Layachi. "Divorce in the Arab Gulf Countries: A Major Challenge to Family and Society." In *Contemporary Issues in Family Studies: Global Perspectives on Partnerships, Parenting and Support in a Changing World*, edited by Angela Abela and Janet Walker, 59–73. Chichester, UK: Wiley Blackwell, 2014.

Antwi-Boateng, Osman, and Khadija Al Mazrouei. "The Challenges of Digital Diplomacy in the Era of Globalization: The Case of the UAE." *International Journal of Communication* 15 (2021): 4577–4595.

Aouragh, Miriyam. "Framing the Internet in the Arab Revolutions: Myth Meets Modernity." *Cinema Journal* 52, no. 1 (2012): 148–156.

Appadurai, Arjun. *Modernity at Large: Cultural Dimensions of Globalization*. Minneapolis: University of Minnesota Press, 1996.

Arab Advisors Group. "Digital Index in the Arab World 2018," September 2018. https://arabadvis ors.com/product/digital-index-in-the-arab-world-2018.

Arab Commission for Digital Economy. "The Arab Digital Economy Strategy." Center for Economic and Financial Research and Studies and EFSO, 2019. https://arab-digital-econ omy.org/wp-content/uploads/2019/12/Integrated-summary-report-V18-.pdf.

Arabertising.net. "Arabvertising.net Engineers Bridge the Gap between Arab Businesses and Cyberspace." M2 Presswire, October 16, 2000. https://www.proquest.com/wire-feeds/arabvertising-net-engineers-bridge-gap-between/docview/445969835/se-2.

Arabian Business. "Dubai's Souq.com Secures $75M Funding Boost," March 24, 2014. https://www.arabianbusiness.com/dubai-s-souq-com-secures-75m-funding-boost-543653.html.

Arabian Business. "Dubai to Add 3,268 New Taxis to Fleet by 2020," October 19, 2015. https://www.arabianbusiness.com/dubai-add-3-268-new-taxis-fleet-by-2020-609337.html.

Arabian Business. "Inside the Gulf's Digital Retail Revolution," October 19, 2020. https://www.arabianbusiness.com/retail/453366-inside-the-gulfs-digital-retail-revolution.

Arabian Business. "Saudi to Set Up Innovation Five [Five Innovation] Hub Centres with Google," April 18, 2018. https://www.arabianbusiness.com/technology/394430-saudi-to-set-up-inn ovation-five-hub-centres-with-google.

Arabic Podcast. "Podcast in Numbers" [in Arabic]. https://ar-podcast.com/stats/.

Arab News. "Beauty Mogul Huda Kattan Condemns 'Unjust' Situation in Palestine," May 18, 2021. https://www.arabnews.com/node/1860536/offbeat.

Arab News. "Maktoob Chief Says Regional Dotcom Industry Still Strong," November 20, 2001. https://www.arabnews.com/node/216287.

Arab News. "UAE's National Digital Economy to Touch $140bn by 2031: Report," February 1, 2023. https://www.arabnews.com/node/2242741/business-economy.

Arab Social Media Report. "Transforming Education in the Arab World: Breaking Barriers in the Age of Social Learning," June 2013. http://www.arabsocialmediareport.com/UserMan agement/PDF/ASMR_5_Report_Final.pdf.

Arab Weekly. "Social Media Use by Youth Is Rising across the Middle East," January 26, 2001. https://thearabweekly.com/social-media-use-youth-rising-across-middle-east.

Aravanis, Mary. "How Social Media Is a Double-Edged Sword When It Comes to Startups and Small Businesses." Egyptian Streets, February 27, 2020. https://egyptianstreets.com/2020/02/27/how-social-media-is-a-double-edged-sword-when-it-comes-to-start-ups-and-small-businesses/.

Araz, Sevan. "The UAE Eyes AI Supremacy: A Key Strategy for the 21st Century." Middle East Institute, November 19, 2020. https://www.mei.edu/publications/uae-eyes-ai-supremacy-key-strategy-21st-century.

Armbrust, Walter. "A History of New Media in the Arab World." *Journal of Cultural Research* 16, nos. 2–3 (2012): 155–174.

Arora, Payal. *The Next Billion Users: Digital Life beyond the West*. Cambridge, MA: Harvard University Press, 2019.

ASDA'A BCW. "Arab Youth Survey: 12th Annual Edition," October 2020. https://arab.org/blog/arab-youth-survery-2020/.

Askhita, Hasna. "The Internet in Syria." *Online Information Review* 24 (2000): 144–149. https://www.emerald.com/insight/content/doi/10.1108/14684520010330337/full/pdf.

Asongu, Simplice. "Financial Sector Competition and Knowledge Economy: Evidence from SSA and MENA Countries." *Journal of Knowledge Economy* 6 (2015): 717–748.

Associated Press. "In Saudi Arabia, a High-Tech Way to Flirt." NBC News, August 11, 2005. https://www.nbcnews.com/id/wbna8916890.

Associated Press. "Saudi Arabia and Blackberry Agree Deal to Avert a Ban on the Smartphone." *Guardian*, August 7, 2010. https://www.theguardian.com/world/2010/aug/07/saudi-ara bia-deal-avert-blackberry-ban.

Atalah, Nasri. "Game On: The Rise of eSports in the Middle East." *Arab News*, August 7, 2019. https://www.arabnews.com/node/1536316/lifestyle.

Atallah, Nada. "How Internet Has Become a Battleground in the Lebanese Revolution." *Le Commerce du Levant*, December 26, 2019. https://www.lecommercedulevant.com/article/29508-how-internet-has-become-a-battleground-in-the-lebanese-revolution.

Atia, Samir. "Analyzing ICT Policies and Strategies in the ESCWA Region." UN Economic and Social Commission for Western Asia, 2006. https://www.economistes-arabes.org/Cercle_des_economistes_arabes/Samir_Aita_files/arabICTstrategies.pdf.

Atwan, Abdel Bari. *Islamic State: The Digital Caliphate*. London: Saqi, 2015.

Aubert, Jean-Eric, Mats Karlsson, and Anuja Utz. "Building Knowledge and Innovation-Driven Economies in Arab Countries: How to Do It." In *The Real Issues of the Middle East and the Arab Spring: Addressing Research, Innovation and Entrepreneurship*, edited by Thomas Anderson and Abdelkader Djeflat, 359–369. New York: Springer, 2013.

Awan, Feryal, and Jeanette Steemers. "Arab and Western Perspectives on Childhood and Children's Media Provision." In *Children's TV and Digital Media in the Arab World: Childhood, Screen Culture and Education*, edited by Naomi Sakr and Jeanette Steemers, 20–44. London: I.B. Tauris, 2017.

Ayton, Matthew. "Lebanon's Illegal Internet Boom Sparks Crackdown and Calls for Reform." Middle East Eye, May 7, 2017. https://www.middleeasteye.net/news/lebanons-illegal-inter net-boom-sparks-crackdown-and-calls-reform.

Ayubi, Nazih. "Withered Socialism or Whether Socialism? The Radical Arab States as Populist-Corporatist Regimes." *Third World Quarterly* 89, no. 1 (1992): 89–105.

Azad, Hasan. "Thinking about Islam, Politics and Muslim Identity in a Digital Age." *Journal of Islamic and Muslim Studies* 2, no. 2 (2017): 122–134.

Backmann, René. *A Wall in Palestine*. Translated by A. Kaiser. New York: Picador, 2010.

Bahraini Ministry of Interior. "From Regional Pioneer to Global Contender: The Economic Vision 2030 for Bahrain." https://www.evisa.gov.bh/Vision2030Englishlowresolution.pdf.

Baiazy, Amjad. "Syria's Cyber Operations." Jadaliyya, February 15, 2012. https://www.jadaliyya.com/Details/25272/Syria%60s-Cyber-Operations.

Bailey, Olga, Bart Cammaerts, and Nico Carpentier. *Understanding Alternative Media*. Maidenhead: McGraw Hill/Open University Press, 2007.

Baker, Stephanie. "The Arab World's Silicon Valley: Jordan Emerges as an Internet Hub." *Washington Post*, October 12, 2012. https://www.washingtonpost.com/business/the-arab-worlds-silicon-valley-jordan-emerges-as-an-internet-hub/2012/10/18/061a4e9e-0f3c-11e2-bd1a-b868e65d57eb_story.html.

Ball, Anna, and Karim Mattar. *Edinburgh Companion to the Postcolonial Middle East*. Edinburgh: Edinburgh University Press, 2019.

Barak, On. *On Time: Technology and Temporality in Modern Egypt*. Berkeley: University of California Press, 2013.

Barrett, Raymond. *Dubai Dreams: Inside the Kingdom of Bling*. London: Nicholas Brealey, 2010.

Bartu, Peter. "The New Arab Uprisings (Part 2)." Al Jazeera Centre for Studies, January 13, 2020. https://studies.aljazeera.net/en/reports/new-arab-uprisings-how-2019-trajectory-differs-2011-legacy-part-2.

Bastani, Hossein. "Structure of Iran's Cyber Warfare." Institut Français d'Analyse Stratégique, December 13, 2012. http://www.strato-analyse.org/fr/spip.php?article223.

Bateson, Gregory, Don Jackson, Jay Haley, and John Weakland. "Toward a Theory of Schizophrenia." *Behavioral Science* 1 (1956): 251–254.

Bayat, Asef. "The 'Street' and the Politics of Dissent in the Arab World." *Middle East Report* 226 (2003). https://merip.org/2003/03/the-street-and-the-politics-of-dissent-in-the-arab-world/.

Bayazid, Tharaa. "The Evolution of Mobile Phones in Saudi Arabia." Trading Media, 2010. https://bayazidt.wordpress.com/com-546-papers/the-evolution-of-mobile-phones-in-saudi-arabia-the-past/.

BBC. "Anghami, a Legal Musical Library" [in Arabic]. YouTube, April 18, 2018. https://www.youtube.com/watch?v=bs2D68rh394.

BBC. "How BAE Sold Cyber-Surveillance Tools to Arab States." BBC News, June 15, 2017. https://www.bbc.com/news/world-middle-east-40276568.

BBC. "Saudi Arabia's Ban on Women Driving Officially Ends." BBC News, June 24, 2018. https://www.bbc.com/news/world-middle-east-44576795.

BBC. "The Story behind No Woman, No Drive." BBC News, October 28, 2013. https://www.bbc.com/news/magazine-24711649.

Beblawi, Hazem. "The Rentier State in the Arab World." *Arab Studies Quarterly* 9, no. 4 (1987): 383–398.

Beirut Digital District. "A Unique Cluster of Innovation Designed for the Digital & Creative Community." https://beirutdigitaldistrict.com.

Bell, Daniel. *The Coming of Post-Industrial Society*. Middlesex, UK: Penguin, 1973.

Ben Gharbia, Sami. "The Internet Freedom Fallacy and the Arab Digital Activism." *Nawaat*, September 17, 2010. http://nawaat.org/portail/2010/09/17/the-internet-freedom-fallacy-and-the-arab-digital-activism/.

Ben Hassen, Tarek. "The State of the Knowledge-Based Economy in the Arab World: Cases of Qatar and Lebanon." *EuroMed Journal of Business*, July 2020. https://www.emerald.com/insight/content/doi/10.1108/EMJB-03-2020-0026/full/html.

Benjamin, Garfield. "Privacy as a Cultural Phenomenon." *Journal of Media Critiques* 3, no. 10 (2017): 55–74.

Benkler, Yochai. *The Wealth of Networks: How Social Production Transforms Markets and Freedoms*. New Haven, CT: Yale University Press, 2006.

Berger, Mark. "After the Third World? History, Destiny and the Fate of Third Worldism." *Third World Quarterly* 25, no. 1 (2004): 9–39.

Bernal, Victoria. "Diaspora, Cyberspace and Political Imagination: The Eritrean Diaspora Online." *Global Networks* 6, no. 2 (2006): 161–179.

Berridge, Willow. "Briefing: The Uprising in Sudan." *African Affairs* 119, no. 474 (2020): 164–176.

Betancourt, Michael. *The Critique of Digital Capitalism: An Analysis of the Political Economy of Digital Culture and Technology*. New York: Punctum, 2015.

Bhagavan, M. R. "Technological Leapfrogging by Developing Countries." In *Globalization of Technology*, edited by Prasada Reddy, 48–65. Oxford: EOLSS, 2009.

Bhargava, Jayant, and Noura Al Kaabi. "How Young Arabs Are Fuelling the MENA Media Market." Strategy&, November 2014. http://www.admediasummit.ae/en/Images/How-Young-Arabs-are-Fuelling-the-MENA-Media-Market-English_tcm30-22790.pdf.

Biltgen, Patrick, and Stephen Ryan. *Activity-Based Intelligence: Principles and Applications*. Boston: Artecch House, 2016.

Bin Bishr, Aisha. "How Digital Technology Is Transforming Dubai." World Economic Forum, May 16, 2017. https://www.weforum.org/agenda/2017/05/how-digital-technology-is-transforming-dubai/.

Bior, Ayen. "Sudan's Social Media Deemed Major Player in Bashir's Ouster." Voice of America, April 18, 2019. https://www.voaafrica.com/a/sudan-s-social-media-deemed-major-player-in-bashir-s-ouster-/4882059.html.

Bizri, Omar. "Research, Innovation, Entrepreneurship and the Rentier Culture in Arab Countries." In *The Real Issues of the Middle East and the Arab Spring: Addressing Research, Innovation and Entrepreneurship*, edited by Thomas Anderson and Abdelkader Djeflat, 195–227. New York: Springer, 2013.

Black, Graham, ed., *Museums and the Challenge of Change: Old Institutions in a New World*. London: Routledge, 2021.

Blaubach, Thomas. "The 5G Divide in the Middle East." Middle East Institute, May 20, 2021. https://www.mei.edu/publications/5g-divide-middle-east-further-disparity-between-gulf-and-its-neighbors.

Blilid, Abdelaziz, and Laurence Favier. "Du monde réel au monde numérique." *Communication* 35, no. 2 (2018). https://journals.openedition.org/communication/8917.

Boex, Cécile. "YouTube and the Syrian Revolution." *View: Theories and Practices of Visual Culture* 17 (2017). https://doi.org/10.36854/widok/2017.17.681.

Borowitz, Mariel. *Open Space: The Global Effort for Open Access to Environmental Satellite Data*. Cambridge, MA: MIT Press, 2017.

Bouchard, Gérard. *Social Myths and Collective Imaginaries*. Toronto: University of Toronto Press, 2017.

Boutieri, Charis. *Learning in Morocco: Language Politics and the Abandoned Educational Dream*. Bloomington: Indiana University Press, 2016.

Bowker, Geoffrey, Karen Baker, Florence Millerand, and David Ribes. "Toward Information Infrastructure Studies: Ways of Knowing in a Networked Environment." In *International Handbook of Internet Research*, edited by Jeremy Junsinger, Lisbeth Klastrup, and Matthew Allen, 97–117. Heidelberg: Springer, 2010.

Boyd-Barrett, Oliver, and Tanner Mirrlees, eds. *Media Imperialism: Continuity and Change*. Lanham, MD: Rowman & Littlefield, 2019.

Boyd, Douglas. "The Arab World." In *Television: An International History*, edited by Anthony Smith, 182–187. New York: Oxford University Press, 1998.

Boyd, Douglas. *Broadcasting in the Arab World: A Survey of the Electronic Media in the Middle East*. Ames: Iowa State University Press, 1999.

Boyd, Douglas. "Development of Egypt's Radio: Voice of the Arabs under Nasser." *Journalism Quarterly* 52, no. 4 (1975): 645–653.

Boyd, Douglas. "The Evolution of Electronic Media in the Contemporary Middle East." *Revue de l'Occident Musulman et de la Méditerranée* 47 (1988): 23–34.

Boyd, Douglas. "Saudi Arabian Television." *Journal of Broadcasting* 15, no. 1 (1970): 73–78.

Bradshaw, Samantha, Hannah Bailey, and Philip Howard. "Industrialized Disinformation: 2020 Global Inventory of Organized Social Media Manipulation." Programme on Democracy and Technology, January 13, 2021. https://comprop.oii.ox.ac.uk/wp-content/uploads/sites/127/2021/01/CyberTroop-Report20-FINALv.3.pdf.

Bridge, Sam. "Abu Dhabi Launches Coronavirus Quarantine Wristband for International Visitors." *Arabian Business*, September 18, 2020. https://www.arabianbusiness.com/travel-hospitality/452009-abu-dhabi-launches-coronavirus-quarantine-wristband-for-international-visitors.

Briggs, Asa, and Peter Burke. *A Social History of the Media: From Gutenberg to the Internet*. 3rd ed. Cambridge: Polity, 2009.

Brinkley, Ian, Will Hutton, Philippe Schneider, and Kristian Ulrichsen. "Kuwait and the Knowledge Economy." Work Foundation, April 2012. https://core.ac.uk/download/pdf/19578387.pdf.

Brouwer, Lenie. "Dutch Moroccan Websites: A Transnational Imagery?" *Journal of Ethnic and Migration Studies* 32, no. 7 (2006): 1153–1168.

Brown, Hannah. "Virtual." *The Jerusalem Post*, September 27, 2003. https://electronicintifada.net/content/virtual-war/9433.

Bruns, Alex. *Blogs, Wikipedia, Second Life and Beyond: From Production to Produsage*. New York: Peter Lang, 2008.

Buchholz Larissa. *The Global Rules of Art: The Emergence and Divisions of a Cultural World Economy*. Princeton, NJ: Princeton University Press, 2022.

Bunt, Gary. *iMuslims: Rewiring the House of Islam*. London: Hurst, 2009.

Burkhalter, Thomas, Kay Dickinson, and Benjamin Harbert, eds. *The Arab Avant-Garde: Music, Politics, Modernity*. Middletown, CT: Wesleyan University Press, 2013.

Business Software Alliance. "Global Software Survey," 2018. https://gss.bsa.org/wp-content/uploads/2018/05/2018_BSA_GSS_Report_en.pdf.

Buskens, Ineke, and Anne Webb. *Women and ICT in Africa and the Middle East*. London: Zed, 2014.

Cabral, Alvin. "UAE Seeks to Play Pioneering Role in Development of 6G." *National*, November 3, 2022. https://www.thenationalnews.com/business/technology/2022/11/03/uae-seeks-to-play-pioneering-role-in-development-of-6g/.

Calabrese, John. "The Huawei Wars and the 5G Revolution in the Gulf." Middle East Institute, July 30, 2019. https://www.mei.edu/publications/huawei-wars-and-5g-revolution-gulf.

Calestous, Juma. "Leapfrogging Progress: The Misplaced Promise of Africa's Mobile Revolution." Breakthrough 7 (Summer 2017). https://thebreakthrough.org/journal/issue-7/leapfrogging-progress.

Cammaerts, Bart. "Jamming the Political: Beyond Counter-Hegemonic Practices." *Continuum: Journal of Media and Cultural Studies* 21, no. 1 (2007): 71–90.

Canclini, Néstor García. *Hybrid Cultures: Strategies for Entering and Leaving Modernity*. Translated by Christopher Chiappari and Silvia López. Minneapolis: University of Minnesota Press, 1995.

Careem. "About Us." https://www.careem.com/en-AE/about-us/.

Castells, Manuel. *The Internet Galaxy*. Oxford: Oxford University Press, 2001.

Castells, Manuel, ed. *The Network Society: A Cross Cultural Perspective*. Northampton, MA: Edward Elgar, 2004.

Castells, Manuel. "The Network Society Revisited." *American Behavioral Scientist* 67, no. 7 (2023): 940–946.

Castells, Manuel. *The Rise of the Network Society*. Oxford: Blackwell, 1996.

Certeau, Michel de. *The Practice of Everyday Life*. Translated by Steven Rendall. Berkeley: University of California Press, 1984.

Chadwick, Andrew. *The Hybrid Media System: Politics and Power*. Oxford: Oxford University Press, 2017.

Chalcraft, John. "Popular Movements in the Middle East and North Africa." In *The History of Social Movements in Global Perspective*, edited by Stefan Berger and Holger Nehring, 225–263. London: Palgrave Macmillan, 2017.

Charrad, Mounira, and Nicholas Reith. "Local Solidarities: How the Arab Spring Protests Started." *Sociological Forum* 34 (2019): 1174–1196.

Chattopadhyaya, Suvesh. "How Well Is Middle East Ready with Subsea Cables to Be the Hub of Economic Progress." Submarine Cable Networks, April 5, 2018. https://www.submarinenetworks.com/en/insights/how-well-is-middle-east-ready-with-subsea-cables-to-be-the-hub-of-economic-progress.

Chawki, Mohamed, Ashraf Darwish, Mohammad Khan, and Sapna Tyagi. *Cybercrime, Digital Forensics and Jurisdiction*. Cham, Switzerland: Springer International, 2015.

Chaziza, Mordechai. "Gulf States Go Digital with China." East Asia Forum, October 7, 2022. https://www.eastasiaforum.org/2022/10/07/gulf-states-go-digital-with-china/.

Chen, Derek, and Carl Dahlman. "Knowledge Economy, the KAM Methodology, and the World Bank Operations." World Bank, 2006. http://documents1.worldbank.org/curated/en/695211468153873436/pdf/358670WBI0The11dge1Economy01PUBLIC1.pdf.

Cherian, Vijaya. "MBC's Shahid: The Netflix of the Arab World?" *BroadcastPro ME*, February 2, 2020. https://www.broadcastprome.com/opinion/mbcs-shahid-the-netflix-of-the-arab-world/.

Cherupelly, Kumar. "E-Governance in India: Sociological Perspective." *Journal of Politics & Governance* 5, no. 3 (2016): 83–91.

Chraibi, Khalid. "The King, the Mufti and the Facebook Girl." *CyberOrient* 5, no. 2 (2011): 73–90.

Chulov, Martin. "Syria Shuts off Internet Access across the Country." *Guardian*, November 29, 2012. https://www.theguardian.com/world/2012/nov/29/syria-blocks-internet.

Cisco. "Cisco Global Digital Readiness Index 2019." https://www.cisco.com/c/dam/en_us/about/csr/reports/global-digital-readiness-index.pdf.

Coleman, Stephen, and Jay Blumler. *The Internet and Democratic Citizenship: Theory, Practice and Policy, Communication, Society and Politics.* Cambridge: Cambridge University Press, 2009.

Collett, Guillaume, Krista Giappone, and Iain MacKenzie, eds. *The Double Binds of Neoliberalism: Theory and Culture after 1968.* Lanham, MD: Rowman & Littlefield, 2022.

Committee to Protect Journalists. "10 Worst Countries to Be a Blogger," April 30, 2009. https://cpj.org/reports/2009/04/10-worst-countries-to-be-a-blogger.php.

Communicate Online. "Anghami's Rami Zeidan on Podcasts and Audio," March 17, 2019. https://communicateonline.me/category/industry-insights/post-details/exclusive-anghamis-rami-zeidan-on-podcasts-and-audio.

Consultancy-me.com. "GCC's E-Commerce Sector Surging Ahead Thanks to COVID-19," October 9, 2020. https://www.consultancy-me.com/news/3092/gccs-e-commerce-sector-surging-ahead-amid-covid-19.

Cooke, Miriam. *Tribal Modern: Branding New Nations in the Arab Gulf.* Berkeley: University of California Press, 2014.

Cooper, Rodney. *Double Bind: Escaping the Contradictory Demands of Manhood.* Grand Rapids, MI: Zondervan, 1996.

Copestake, Jen. "Could Ramallah Become an Arab World Tech Hub?" BBC News, June 7, 2014. https://www.bbc.com/news/technology-27729793.

Cornwell, Alexander. "Careem Launches Delivery Service, Expects to Close Funding Round Soon." Reuters, December 16, 2018. https://www.reuters.com/article/us-careem-delivery-idUSKBN1OG0CL.

Costa, Elisabetta. *Social Media in Southeast Turkey.* London: UCL Press, 2016.

Costa, Elisabetta, and Laura Menin. "Introduction: Digital Intimacies: Exploring Digital Media and Intimate Lives in the Middle East and North Africa." *Middle East Journal of Culture and Communication* 9, no. 2 (2016): 137–145.

Couldry, Nick. *Media, Society, World: Social Theory and Digital Media Practice.* Cambridge: Polity, 2012.

Couldry, Nick, and Ulises Mejias. *The Costs of Connection: How Data Is Colonizing Human Life and Appropriating It for Capitalism.* Stanford, CA: Stanford University Press, 2019.

Cox, Joseph. "Signal Claims Egypt Is Blocking Access to Encrypted Messaging App." *Vice,* December 19, 2016. https://www.vice.com/en_us/article/nz755w/signal-claims-egypt-is-blocking-access-to-encrypted-messaging-app.

Crunchbase. "Anghami Financials," July 21, 2021. https://www.crunchbase.com/organization/anghami/company_financials.

Crunchbase. "Jordanian Startups." https://www.crunchbase.com/hub/jordan-startups.

Culcasi, Karen. "Constructing and Naturalizing the Middle East." *Geographical Review* 100, no. 4 (2010): 583–597.

Cusolito, Ana, Gévaudan Clément, Daniel Lederman, and Christina Wood. *The Upside of Digital for the Middle East and North Africa: How Digital Technology Adoption Can Accelerate Growth.* Washington, DC: World Bank, 2021.

Dalakian, Glen. "How CashU Spinoff PayFort Is Trying to Improve Cash on Delivery." Wamda, August 14, 2013. https://www.wamda.com/2013/08/cashu-spinoff-payfort-improving-payment-options.

Dana, Leo. *Economies of the Eastern Mediterranean Region: Economic Miracles in the Making.* Singapore: World Scientific, 2000.

Datta, Ayona, and Katherine Brickell. *Translocal Geographies: Spaces Places Connections.* London: Routledge, 2016.

Dean, David. "Accelerating the Digital Economy in the Middle East, North Africa and Turkey." ICANN, 2017. https://www.icann.org/en/system/files/files/accelerating-digital-economy-report-09oct17-en.pdf.

Deibert, Ronald. "The Geopolitics of Internet Control: Censorship, Sovereignty, and Cyberspace." In *The Routledge Handbook of Internet Politics*, edited by Andrew Chadwick and Philip Howard, 323–336. London: Taylor & Francis, 2009.

Deloitte. "National Transformation in the Middle East: A Digital Journey." Deloitte.com, 2017. https://tinyurl.com/mrx47r62.

Denner, Lize. "Open Government and Achieving Good Governance." *Review of Information and Communication Technology for Development in the Arab Region* 21 (2014): 18–22. https://www.unescwa.org/publications/information-communications-technology-development-21st-issue.

Dennis, Everette, Justin Martin, and Fouad Hassan. "Media Use in the Middle East, 2018: A Seven-Nation Survey." Middle East Media, 2018. www.mideastmedia.org/survey/2018.

Detaille, Vittoria. "Inside the Palestinian Museum." *Sekka*, August 8, 2020. https://sekkamag.com/2020/08/08/8260/.

Determann, Jörg. *Space Science and the Arab World: Astronauts, Observatories and Nationalism in the Middle East.* London: I.B. Tauris, 2018.

Deuchar, Hannah Scott. "Nahda: Mapping a Keyword in Cultural Discourse." *Alif: Journal of Comparative Poetics* 37 (2017): 50–84.

Deuze, Mark. *Media Life.* Cambridge: Polity, 2012.

Dhillon, Navtej. *Middle East Youth Bulge: Challenge or Opportunity?* Washington, DC: Brookings Institution Press, 2008.

Diamond, Larry. "Promoting Democracy." *Foreign Policy* 87 (1992): 25–46.

Diamond, Larry, and Marc Plattner. *Liberation Technology: Social Media and the Struggle for Democracy.* Baltimore: Johns Hopkins University Press, 2012.

Dickinson, Kay. *Arab Film and Video Manifestos: Forty-Five Years of the Moving Image amid Revolution.* Cham, Switzerland: Palgrave Pivot. 2018.

Diefallah, Mariam. "I Come from El Salam: Mahraganat Music and the Impossibility of Containment." Jadaliyya, August 25, 2020. https://www.jadaliyya.com/Details/41601.

Digital Bedu. "V1.1.0: Anghami's Elie Habib—An Interview." Clubhouse, March 10, 2021.

Dimitropoulou, Alexandra. "Countries with the Most Female Business Owners in 2018." *CEO World Magazine*, January 21, 2019. https://ceoworld.biz/2019/01/21/countries-with-the-most-women-business-owners-as-a-percentage-of-total-business-owners-2018/.

Dirar, Aamer, Insaaf Salih, Mosab Alrasheed, and Haysam Elamin. "Development Arabic Search Engine." IEEE International Conference on Communication, Control, Computing and Electronics Engineering, 2017. https://ieeexplore.ieee.org/document/7867669.

Diwan. "About Us." https://www.diwan.com/index.php/about.

Donaghy, Rori. "Falcon Eye." Middle East Eye, February 28, 2015. http://www.middleeasteye.net/news/uae-israel-surveillance-2104952769.

Douai, Aziz. "Online Politics in the Arab Blogosphere." In *International Blogging: Identity, Politics and Networked Publics*, edited by Adrienne Russell and Nabil Echchaibi, 133–150. New York: Peter Lang, 2009.

Doveling, Katrin, Anu Harju, and Denise Sommer. "From Mediatized Emotion to Digital Affect Cultures: New Technologies and Global Flows of Emotion." *Social Media + Society* 4, no. 1 (2018): 1–11.

Downing, John, Denis McQuail, Philip Schlesinger, and Ellen Wartella. *The Sage Handbook of Media Studies.* Thousand Oaks, CA: Sage, 2004.

Downs, Nettie, Firas Kiyasseh, and Levi Quaintance. "Silicon Wafers and Semiconductors: A New Black Gold for Abu Dhabi?" *Knowledge at Wharton*, January 2, 2013. https://knowledge.wharton.upenn.edu/article/silicon-wafers-and-semiconductors-a-new-black-gold-for-abu-dhabi/.

Dubai Internet City. "About Us." https://dic.ae/discover/about-us.

Dubai Internet City and A. T. Kearney. "The IT Market—A Middle East Perspective: An Overview of Business Opportunities for Innovative New Companies." TECOM Investments LZ-LLC, 2008. https://tecomgroup.ae/media-center/knowledge-library/.

Duffy, Erin, and Urszula Pruchniewska. "Gender and Self-Enterprise in the Social Media Age: A Digital Double Bind." *Information, Communication, and Society* 20, no. 6 (2017): 843–859.

Dutta, Soumitra, and Mazen Coury. "ICT Challenges for the Arab World." In *The Global Information Technology Report 2002–2003: Readiness for the Networked World*, edited by Soumitra Dutta, Bruno Lanvin, and Fiona Paua, 116–131. New York: Oxford University Press, 2003.

Dutta, Soumitra, and Bruno Lanvin, eds. The Network Readiness Index 2020. Washington, DC: Portulans Institute, 2020. https://networkreadinessindex.org/wp-content/uploads/2020/11/NRI-2020-V8_28-11-2020.pdf.

Dutta, Soumitra, and Bruno Lanvin, eds. "The Network Readiness Index 2022." Washington, DC: Portulans Institute, 2022. https://networkreadinessindex.org.

Dutta, Soumitra, Bruno Lanvin, Lorena Rivera León, and Sacha Wunsch-Vincent, eds. "Global Innovation Index Ranking 2021." World Intellectual Property Organization. https://www.globalinnovationindex.org/gii-2021-report#.

Dwyer, Tim. *Media Convergence*. New York: McGraw-Hill, 2010.

Eaves, David. "An Analysis of the Council of Arab Economic Unity's Arab Digital Economy Strategy." Ash Center for Democratic Governance and Innovation, Harvard Kennedy School, December 2019. https://ash.harvard.edu/files/ash/files/293091_hvd_ash_paper_arab_economic-f.pdf.

Echchaibi, Nabil. "From Audio Tapes to Video Blogs: The Delocalisation of Authority in Islam." *Nations and Nationalism* 17, no. 1 (2011): 25–44.

Economist Impact. "Inclusive Internet Index 2022." https://impact.economist.com/projects/inclusive-internet-index/.

Edraak. "About Us." https://www.edraak.org/en/about-us/.

Egyptian Streets. "Digital Campaign Supports TikTok Women Arrested over 'Egyptian Family Values' Law," July 15, 2020. https://egyptianstreets.com/2020/07/15/digital-campaign-supports-tiktok-women-arrested-over-egyptian-family-values-law/

Eibl, Ferdinand. *Social Dictatorships: The Political Economy of the Welfare State in the Middle East and North Africa*. Oxford: Oxford University Press, 2020.

Eickelman, Dale, and James Piscatori. *Muslim Politics*. Princeton, NJ: Princeton University Press, 2004.

Eickelman, Dale, and Armando Salvatore. "Muslim Publics." In *Public Islam and the Common Good*, edited by Armando Salvatore and Dale Eickelman, 1–27. Leiden: Brill, 2006.

Eid, Mohamed, and Aziz Douai. *New Media Discourses, Culture and Politics after the Arab Spring: Case Studies from Egypt and Beyond*. London: I.B. Tauris, 2021.

El-Affendi, Abdelwahab. "The Conquest of Muslim Hearts and Minds?" Saban Center for Middle East Policy at the Brookings Institution, September 2005. https://www.brookings.edu/wp-content/uploads/2016/06/paper_elaffendi.pdf.

Elaph. "Publisher's Message" [in Arabic], May 1, 2001. https://elaph.com/publishermessage.html.

Elareshi, Mokhtar, and Abdulkarim Ziani. "Digital and Interactive Social Media among Middle East Women." *Media Watch* 10, no. 2 (2019): 235–250.

El-Ariss, Tarek, ed. *The Arab Renaissance: A Bilingual Anthology of the Nahda*. New York: Modern Language Association of America, 2018.

El-Ariss, Tarek. *Trials of Arab Modernity: Literary Affects and the New Political*. New York: Fordham University Press, 2013.

Electronic Intifada. "About the Electronic Intifada." https://electronicintifada.net/content/about-electronic-intifada/10159.

El Fay, Imad. "Anghami's Journey to the Public Markets: Everything You Need to Know." MENAbytes, March 7, 2021. https://www.menabytes.com/anghami-journey-public-markets/?utm_source=dlvr.it&utm_medium=twitter&utm_campaign=anghami-journey-public-markets.

El-Guindy, Mohamed. "Cybercrime in the Middle East." *ISSA Journal* 17 (2008): 16–19. http://www.ask-pc.com/lessons/CYBERCRIME-MIDDLE-EAST.pdf.

El-Haddad, Yahya. "Major Trends Affecting Families in the Gulf Countries." Report for State of the World's Children, UNICEF, May 2003. https://www.un.org/esa/socdev/family/Publi cations/mtelhaddad.pdf.

El Hage, Charles, Karim Sabbagh, Soumitra Dutta, and Paola Tarazi. "Challenges for Information and Communication Technology Development in the Arab World." In *The Arab World Competitiveness Report 2002–2003*, 180–203. Oxford: Oxford University Press, 2003.

El-Issawi, Fatima. *Arab National Media and Political Change: Recording the Transition.* London: Palgrave Macmillan, 2016.

El-Katiri, Laura, and Bassam Fattouh. "Energy Poverty in the Arab World: The Case of Yemen." Oxford Institute for Energy Studies, August 2011. https://www.oxfordenergy.org/wpcms/ wp-content/uploads/2011/08/MEP_1.pdf.

El Khachab, Chihab. *Making Film in Egypt: How Labor Technology and Mediation Shape the Industry.* Cairo: American University in Cairo Press, 2021.

Elkhalek, Abeer. "Impact of Knowledge Economy on the Participation of Women in Labor Market." *International Journal of Business and Economic Development* 5, no. 2 (2017): 15–24.

El Kogali, Safaa, and Caroline Krafft. *Expectations and Aspirations: A New Framework for Education in the Middle East and North Africa.* Washington, DC: World Bank, 2019.

El Louadi, Mohamed. "The Arab World, Culture and Information Technology." In *Encyclopedia of Developing Regional Communities with Information and Communication Technology*, edited by Stewart Marshall, Wal Taylor, and Xinghuo Yu, 21–27. Hershey, PA: IGI Global, 2005.

Elmasry, Tarek, Enrico Benni, Jigar Patel, and Jan Peter aus dem Moore. "Digital Middle East: Transforming the Region into a Leading Digital Economy." Digital McKinsey, October 2016. https://www.mckinsey.com/~/media/mckinsey/featured%20insights/middle%20e ast%20and%20africa/digital%20middle%20east%20transforming%20the%20region%20i nto%20a%20leading%20digital%20economy/digital-middle-east-final-updated.ashx.

Elmusa, Sharif. "Dependency and Industrialization in the Arab World." *Arab Studies Quarterly* 8, no. 3 (1986): 254–267.

Elnaggar, Ayman. "Towards Gender Equal Access to ICT." *Information Technology for Development* 14, no. 4 (2008): 280–293.

El Naggar, Shaimaa. "The Impact of Digitization on the Religious Sphere: Televangelism as an Example." *Indonesian Journal of Islam and Muslim Societies* 4, no. 2 (2014): 189–211.

El-Nawawy, Mohammed. "U.S. Public Diplomacy and the News Credibility of Radio Sawa and Television Al Hurra in Five Countries." *Global Media and Communication* 2, no. 2 (2016): 183–203.

El-Nawawy, Mohammed, and Sahar Khamis. "Divergent Identities in the Virtual Islamic Public Sphere: A Case Study of the English Discussion Forum 'Islamonline.'" *Journal of Arab & Muslim Media Research* 5, no. 1 (2012): 31–48.

El-Nawawy, Mohammed, and Sahar Khamis. *Egyptian Revolution 2.0: Political Blogging, Civic Engagement, and Citizen Journalism.* New York: Palgrave Macmillan, 2016.

El-Obeidy, Ahmed. "Scientific System in the Arab Region: From Prestige Towards Development." *Regional Science Policy and Practice* 5, no. 1 (2013): 97–112.

El-Richani, Sarah. "Whither the Lebanese Press." In *Routledge Handbook on Arab Media*, edited by Noureddine Miladi and Noha Mellor, 167–178. London: Routledge: 2020.

El Sawy, Nada. "How Souq's Shift to Amazon.ae Affects UAE Consumers." *National*, May 1, 2019. https://www.thenational.ae/business/money/how-souq-s-shift-to-amazon-ae-affects-uae-consumers-1.856042.

Elvira, Laura Ruiz de, Christoph Schwarz, and Irene Weipert-Fenner, eds. *Clientelism and Patronage in the Middle East and North Africa: Networks of Dependency.* London: Routledge, 2019.

Erskine-Loftus, Pamela, Mariam Al-Mulla, and Victoria Hightower. *Representing the Nation: Heritage, Museums, National Narratives, and Identity in the Arab Gulf States.* London: Routledge, 2016.

ESCWA. "Arab Digital Development Report 2019: Towards Empowering People and Ensuring Inclusiveness." UN Economic and Social Commission for Western Asia, 2019. https://www. unescwa.org/sites/www.unescwa.org/files/publications/files/arab-digital-development-report-2019-english_0.pdf.

ESCWA. "Arab Horizon 2030: Digital Technologies for Development." UN Economic and Social Commission for Western Asia, 2017. https://www.unescwa.org/sites/www.unescwa.org/files/page_attachments/arab-horizon-2030-digital-technologies-development-en.pdf.

ESCWA. "Intellectual Property for Fostering Innovation in the Arab World." UN Economic and Social Commission for Western Asia, 2019. https://www.unescwa.org/sites/www.unescwa.org/files/publications/files/intellectual-property-innovation-arab-region-english.pdf.

ESCWA. "National Profile of the Information Society in the Kingdom of Saudi Arabia." UN Economic and Social Commission for Western Asia, September 2007. https://www.unescwa.org/sites/default/files/inline-files/SaudiArabia_2005-E.pdf.

ESCWA. "National Profile of the Information Society in Yemen." UN Economic and Social Commission for Western Asia, August 2007. https://www.unescwa.org/sites/default/files/inline-files/Yemen-07-E.pdf.

ESCWA. "Review of Information and Communications Technology for Development in Western Asia" [in Arabic]. UN Economic and Social Commission for Western Asia, 2011. https://archive.unescwa.org/sites/www.unescwa.org/files/publications/files/e_escwa_ictd_11_3_a.pdf.

Es'hailSat. "Qatar Enters Space Age with Launch of Es'hail 1." Es'hailSat, August 1, 2013. https://eshailsat.qa/en/Posts/view/48/12/qatar-enters-space-age-with-launch-of-eshail-1.

Etling, Bruce, John Kelly, Robert Faris, and John Palfrey. "Mapping the Arabic Blogosphere: Politics, Culture and Dissent." Harvard University's Berkman Center for Internet and Society, 2009. http://cyber.law.harvard.edu/sites/cyber.law.harvard.edu/files/Mapping_the_Arabic_Blogosphere_0.pdf.

Ewers, Michael, and Edward Malecki. "Leapfrogging into the Knowledge Economy: Assessing the Economic Development Strategies of the Arab Gulf States." *Tijdschrift voor Economische en Sociale Geografie* 101, no. 5 (2010): 494–508.

Exell, Karen. "Art Is Power: Qatar's Reaction to the Blockade." In *Identity-Seekers: Nationhood and Nationalism in the Gulf Monarchies*, edited by Eleonora Ardemagni, 18–20. Milan: Italian Institute for International Political Studies, 2019. https://www.ispionline.it/it/pubblicazione/identity-seekers-nationhood-and-nationalism-gulf-monarchies-23076.

Exell, Karen. "Desiring the Past and Reimagining the Present: Contemporary Collecting in Qatar." *Museum & Society* 14, no. 2 (2016): 259–274.

Exell, Karen. *Modernity and the Museum in the Arabian Peninsula*. London: Routledge, 2016.

Fabian, Johannes. *Time and the Other: How Anthropology Makes Its Object*. New York: Columbia University Press, 1983.

Fadhelat, Aymen. "E-Commerce Takes Over Traditional Commerce in Jordan" [in Arabic]. Al Jazeera, December 26, 2018. https://tinyurl.com/4rpar5xt.

Fahmi, Kenzy. "Egypt Tightens Grip on Media with New Bill." *Arab News*, July 21, 2018. https://www.arabnews.com/node/1340656/media.

Fandy, Mamoun. "Information Technology, Trust, and Social Change in the Arab World." *Middle East Journal* 54, no. 3 (2000): 378–394.

Fanon, Frantz. *The Wretched of the Earth*. Harmondsworth, UK: Penguin Random House, 1967.

Fares, Tarek, Fares Fares, and Jaber Mohamed. "Readers and Members of the Arab Al Saha Forum" [in Arabic]. https://alsaha.com/.

Farid, Farid. "Egypt Is Blocking Voice Calls Made over Social Media Apps." Quartz Africa, April 25, 2017. https://qz.com/africa/967857/egypt-is-blocking-calls-on-whatsapp-facetime-viber-and-skype/.

Faris, David. *Dissent and Revolution in a Digital Age: Social Media, Blogging and Activism in Egypt*. London: I.B. Tauris, 2012.

Faris, David. "The End of the Beginning: The Failure of April 6th and the Future of Electronic Activism in Egypt." *Arab Media and Society* 9 (2009). https://www.arabmediasociety.com/the-end-of-the-beginning-the-failure-of-april-6th-and-the-future-of-electronic-activism-in-egypt/.

Feldstein, Steven. "The Global Expansion of AI Surveillance." Carnegie Endowment for International Peace, September 17, 2019. https://carnegieendowment.org/2019/09/17/global-expansion-of-ai-surveillance-pub-79847.

Feldstein, Steven. *The Rise of Digital Repression: How Technology Is Reshaping Power, Politics, and Resistance.* New York: Oxford University Press, 2021.

Feuilherade, Peter. "Foreign Investments a Vote of Confidence in Region's E-Commerce." *Middle East* 439 (2013): 42–43.

FIFA. "FIFA eWorld Cup Champion Wins eSports Console Player of the Year Award," November 13, 2018. https://tinyurl.com/mr2ejezz.

Filiu, Jean-Pierre. *The Arab Revolution: Ten Lessons from the Democratic Uprising.* London: Hurst, 2011.

Florida, Richard. *The Rise of the Creative Class.* New York: Basic Books, 2002.

Foege, Alec. *The Tinkerers: The Amateurs, DIYers, and Inventors Who Make America Great.* New York: Basic Books, 2013.

Fong, Michelle. "Technology Leapfrogging for Developing Countries." In *Encyclopedia of Information Science and Technology,* edited by Mehdi Khosrow-Pour, 3707–3713. Hershey, PA: IGI Global, 2009.

Foote, Joe. "CNE in Egypt: Some Light at the End of an Arduous Tunnel." *Transnational Broadcasting Studies* 1 (1998). https://www.arabmediasociety.com/cne-in-egypt-some-light-at-the-end-of-an-arduous-tunnel/.

Forbes Middle East. "10 Women behind Middle Eastern Tech Brands 2021." https://www.forbesmiddleeast.com/lists/10-women-behind-middle-eastern-tech-brands-2021/.

Forbes Middle East. "30 Women behind Middle Eastern Brands 2022." https://tinyurl.com/26w2hwfw.

Foucault, Michel. "The Subject and Power." *Critical Inquiry* 8, no. 4 (1982): 777–795.

Fowler, Sarah. "Who Is the Syrian Electronic Army?" BBC News, April 25, 2013. https://www.bbc.com/news/world-middle-east-22287326.

France, Alan. "Why Should We Care? Young People, Citizenship and Questions of Social Responsibility." *Journal of Youth Studies* 1, no. 1 (1998): 97–111.

Freedom House. "Freedom on the Net Report: Saudi Arabia," 2011. https://freedomhouse.org/sites/default/files/inline_images/Saudi%20Arabia_FOTN2011.pdf.

Fuchs, Christian. *Digital Capitalism: Media, Communication and Society.* New York: Routledge, 2022.

Gabbard, Bryan, and George Park. *The Information Revolution in the Arab World: Commercial, Cultural and Political Dimensions: The Middle East Meets the Internet.* Washington, DC: RAND, 1996. https://www.rand.org/pubs/papers/P7920-1.html.

Gaillard-Sborowsky, Florence. "L'espace dans les pays arabes: Outil de développement et élément de reconnaissance nationale ou régionale." *L'Information géographique* 74, no. 2 (2010): 64–84. https://www.cairn.info/revue-l-information-geographique-2010-2-page-64.htm.

Galtung, Johan. "A Structural Theory of Imperialism." *Journal of Peace Research* 8, no. 2 (1971): 81–117.

Gason, Melanie, and Merav Yachin. "How the Abraham Accords Are Shaping a New Technological Covenant." Tony Blair Institute for Global Change, September 20, 2021. https://institute.global/policy/how-abraham-accords-are-shaping-new-technological-covenant.

Gelvanovska, Natalija, Michel Rogy, and Carlo Rossotto. *Broadband Networks in the Middle East and North Africa: Accelerating High-Speed Internet Access.* Washington, DC: World Bank, 2014. https://openknowledge.worldbank.org/handle/10986/16680.

Georgiou, Myria. "Diaspora in the Digital Era: Minorities and Media Representation." *Journal on Ethnopolitics and Minority Issues in Europe* 12, no. 4 (2013): 80–99. https://www.ecmi.de/fileadmin/downloads/publications/JEMIE/2013/Georgiou.pdf.

Georgiou, Myria. "Diasporic Media across Europe: Multicultural Societies and the Universalism-Particularism Continuum." *Journal of Ethnic and Migration Studies* 31, no. 3 (2005): 481–498.

Georgiou, Myria. "Gender, Migration and the Media." *Ethnic and Racial Studies* 35, no. 5 (2012): 791–799.

Gerbaudo, Paolo. *Tweets and the Streets: Social Media and Contemporary Activism.* London: Pluto, 2012.

Ghabra, Haneen, and Marouf Hasian. "Tough Love: A Diasporic Critique of the Palestinian Boycott, Divestment and Sanctions Movement." *Journal of Communication Inquiry* 42, no. 4 (2018): 340–358.

Ghaffar, Mahmood. "Clientelism within the Arabian Gulf States and Beyond: A Comparative Study." *Central European Journal of International Security Studies* 8, no. 1 (2014): 30–51.

Ghali, Maghie. "The Middle East Archive Project Puts the Arab World in Focus with No Filter." *National*, February 23, 2020. https://www.thenationalnews.com/arts-culture/art/the-mid dle-east-archive-project-puts-the-arab-world-in-focus-with-no-filter-1.983190.

Ghandour, Ahmad. "An Exploratory Study of the Usage Level of E-Commerce among Small and Medium Enterprises in Abu Dhabi." *Global Business and Economic Anthology* 1 (2015): 151–157.

Ghanem, Hafez. *The Arab Spring Five Years Later: Toward Greater Inclusiveness.* Washington, D.C.: Brookings Institution Press, 2016.

Ghannam, Jeffery. "Social Media in the Arab World." Center for International Media Assistance, February 3, 2011. https://www.cima.ned.org/wp-content/uploads/2015/02/CIMA-Arab_ Social_Media-Report-10-25-11.pdf.

Ghareeb, Edmund. "New Media and the Information Revolution in the Arab World: An Assessment." *Middle East Journal* 53, no. 3 (2000): 395–418.

Gharib, Remah, Evren Tok, and Mohammad Zebian. "Neoliberal Urbanization and Smart Cities in the Gulf Region: The Case of Abu Dhabi's Masdar City." In *Gateways to the World: Port Cities in the Persian Gulf*, edited by Mehran Kamrava, 183–202. New York: Oxford University Press, 2016.

Ghonim, Wael. *Revolution 2.0: The Power of the People is Greater than the People in Power.* New York: Houghton Mifflin Harcourt, 2012.

Ghosh, Shikhar, Nicole Keller, and Alpana Thapar. "Instabeat: Crossing the Finish Line." Harvard Business School Case 821–012, July 24, 2020.

Ghosh, Shikhar, Nicole Keller, and Alpana Thapar. "Instabeat: One More Lap." Harvard Business School Case 820–005, July 30, 2019.

Ghouth, Doha. "End Camera-Phone Ban in Weddings, Say Women." *Saudi Gazette*, April 16, 2012. https://saudigazette.com.sa/article/1193.

Gibran, Kahlil. *The Prophet.* New York: Alfred A. Knopf, 1923.

Gibson, Francesca. "These Emirati Sisters Launched an Amazing Digital Museum." Cosmopolitan Middle East, September 17, 2020. https://www.cosmopolitanme.com/life/emirati-sisters-launch-khaleeji-digital-museum.

Giglio, Mike. "Tunisia Protests: The Facebook Revolution." Daily Beast, January 15, 2011. https:// www.thedailybeast.com/tunisia-protests-the-facebook-revolution.

Gillespie, Eden. "The Instagram Influencers Hired to Rehabilitate Saudi Arabia's Image." *Guardian*, October 11, 2019. https://www.theguardian.com/world/2019/oct/12/the-instagram-infl uencers-hired-to-rehabilitate-saudi-arabias-image.

Gladwell, Malcolm. "Small Change: Why the Revolutions Will Not Be Tweeted." *New Yorker*, October 4, 2010. www.newyorker.com/reporting/2010/10/04/101004fa_fact_gladwell.

Global Newswire. "The MEA Cloud Computing Market Size Is Expected to Grow from USD 14.2 Billion in 2021 to USD 31.4 Billion by 2026," June 24, 2021. https://www.globenewswire. com/news-release/2021/06/24/2252730/0/en/The-MEA-cloud-computing-market-size-is-expected-to-grow-from-USD-14-2-billion-in-2021-to-USD-31-4-billion-by-2026-at-a-Compound-Annual-Growth-Rate-CAGR-of-17-2.html.

Godinho, Varun. "Saudi's Millennium Arabia Launch First Arabic Esports Series on Twitter." *Gulf Business*, June 17, 2020. https://gulfbusiness.com/saudis-millenium-arabia-launch-first-ara bic-esports-series-on-twitter/.

Goldhaber, Michael. "The Value of Openness in an Attention Economy." *First Monday* 11, no. 6 (June 2006). https://firstmonday.org/ojs/index.php/fm/article/view/1334.

Gonzalez-Quijano, Yves. *Arabités numériques: Le printemps du web arabe.* Arles: Actes Sud/ Sindbad, 2012.

Goodman, Seymour, and J. D. Green, "Computing in the Middle East." *Computations of the ACM*, 35, no. 8 (1991): 21–25.

Google Developers. "Smart Lock for Wego." https://developers.google.com/identity/casestud ies/wego-smartlock-casestudy.pdf?hl=en.

Gorman, Antony, and Sarah Irving, eds. *Cultural Entanglement in the Pre-Independence Arab World: Arts, Thought and Literature.* London: I.B. Tauris, 2020.

Graf, Bettina, and Jakob Skovgaard-Petersen. *Global Mufti: The Phenomenon of Yusuf Al-Qaradawi.* New York: Oxford University Press, 2006.

Graham, Flora. "Blackberry Crippled in Saudi Arabia and UAE for Being Too Secure." CNET, August 2, 2010. https://www.cnet.com/news/blackberry-crippled-in-saudi-arabia-and-uae-for-being-too-secure/.

GrEEK Campus. The GrEEK Campus Response to COVID-19. https://thegreekcampus.com/corona-response.

Greene, Robert and Paul Triolo. "Will China Control the Global Internet via Its Digital Silk Road?" Carnegie Endowment for International Peace, May 8, 2020. https://carnegieendowment.org/2020/05/08/will-china-control-global-internet-via-its-digital-silk-road-pub-81857.

Greenhalgh, Hug, and Abdulla Al-Khal. "Morocco Instagram Influencer Apologises for Role in Outing of Gay Men." Reuters, May 13, 2020. https://www.reuters.com/article/us-morocco-lgbt-crime-trfn-idUSKBN22P2UI.

Greenwald, Michael. "The New Race for Contemporary Arts Dominance in the Middle East." Belfer Center for Science and International Affairs, Harvard Kennedy School, October 2018. https://www.belfercenter.org/publication/new-race-contemporary-arts-dominance-middle-east.

Gresh, Alain. "Dubai's Police Chief Speaks Out." *Le Monde* Diplomatique, May 19, 2015. https://mondediplo.com/outsidein/dubai-s-police-chief-speaks-out.

Grohe, Edwin. "The Cyber Dimensions of the Syrian Civil War." *Comparative Strategy* 34, no. 2 (2015): 133–148.

Grossman, Shelby, and Khadeja Ramali. "Outsourcing Disinformation." Lawfare, December 13, 2020. https://www.lawfareblog.com/outsourcing-disinformation.

GSMA. "MENA 5G Spectrum: Setting Out the Roadmap," January 27, 2022. https://www.gsma.com/spectrum/resources/mena-5g-spectrum-roadmaps/.

GSMA. "The Mobile Economy Arab States 2014." https://data.gsmaintelligence.com/api-web/v2/research-file-download?id=18809267&file=the-mobile-economy-arab-states-2014-1482139866897.pdf.

GSMA. "The Mobile Economy: Arab States 2015." https://data.gsmaintelligence.com/api-web/v2/research-file-download?id=18809327&file=the-mobile-economy-arab-states-2015-1482139932360.pdf.

GSMA. "The Mobile Economy: Middle East and North Africa 2016." https://data.gsmaintellige nce.com/api-web/v2/research-file-download?id=18809379&file=the-mobile-economy-middle-east-and-north-africa-2016-1482139999344.pdf.

GSMA. "The Mobile Economy: Middle East and North Africa 2020." https://www.gsma.com/mobileeconomy/wp-content/uploads/2020/11/GSMA_MobileEconomy2020_MENA.pdf.

GSMA. "The Mobile Economy: Middle East and North Africa 2022." https://www.gsma.com/mobileeconomy/wp-content/uploads/2022/05/GSMA_MENA_ME2022_R_WebSingles.pdf.

GSMA. "Mobile Gender Gap Report 2020." https://www.gsma.com/mobilefordevelopment/wp-content/uploads/2020/05/GSMA-The-Mobile-Gender-Gap-Report-2020.pdf.

Guaaybess, Tourya. *Media in Arab Countries: From Development Theories to Cooperation Policies.* Hoboken, NJ: Wiley, 2019.

Guessoum, Nidhal. "The Arab World's First Satellite." *Arab News*, April 19, 2020. https://www.arabnews.com/node/1661436.

Gulf Times. "Es'hailSat Chosen by beIN to Telecast UEFA Euro 2016," June 9, 2016. https://www.gulf-times.com/story/497528/Es-hailSat-chosen-by-beIN-to-telecast-UEFA-Euro-20.

Günther, Christoph, and Simone Pfeifer. *Jihadi Audiovisuality and Its Entanglements: Meanings Aesthetics Appropriations*. Edinburgh: Edinburgh University Press, 2020.

Gupta, Neha. "Social Media Trends in MENA in 2020." World Association of News Publishers, June 9, 2021. https://wan-ifra.org/2021/06/tiktok-trumps-snapchat-social-media-trends-in-mena-in-2020/.

Guesmi, Haythem. "The Social Media Myth about the Arab Spring." *Al Jazeera*, January 27, 2021. https://www.aljazeera.com/opinions/2021/1/27/the-social-media-myth-about-the-arab-spring.

Haddad, Bassam. *Business Networks in Syria: The Political Economy of Authoritarian Resilience*. Stanford: Stanford University Press, 2011.

Haddad, Dalia. "The Contribution of Satellite TV Providers in the Telecommunication Sector." Arab Advisors Group Research Report, December 22, 2019.

Hagenah, Iliana. "How the Women-Only Facebook Group Minbar-Shat Helped Overthrow the Sudanese Government." *Elle*, October 4, 2019. https://www.elle.com/culture/career-polit ics/a29355590/minbar-shat-facebook-sudan-revolution/.

Hajj, Nadya. *Networked Refugees: Palestinian Reciprocity and Remittances in the Digital Age*. Berkeley: University of California Press, 2021.

Hall, Stuart. "Cultural Identity and Diaspora." In *Colonial Discourse and Post-Colonial Theory*, edited by Patrick Williams and Laura Chrisman, 392–403. New York: Columbia University Press, 1994.

Hall, Stuart. "Media Power: The Double Bind." *Journal of Communication* 24 (1974): 19–26.

Hamdy, Amr. "ICT in Education in Tunisia." Society of ICT and Education in Africa, June 2007. https://documents1.worldbank.org/curated/en/744461468311467539/pdf/456780BR I0Box31ia010ICTed0Survey111.pdf.

Hamid, Triska. "Anghami: Success Built on Localisation." Wamda, March 7, 2021. https://www.wamda.com/2021/03/anghami-success-built-localisation.

Hamid, Triska. "Careem Invests $50 Million in Super App." Wamda, June 15, 2020. https://www.wamda.com/en/2020/06/careem-invests-50-million-super-app.

Hanafi, Hassan. *On Political Culture* [in Arabic]. Damascus: Dar Alaeddine, 1998.

Harris, Shane. "How Did Syria's Hacker Army Suddenly Get So Good?" *Foreign Policy*, September 4, 2013. https://foreignpolicy.com/2013/09/04/how-did-syrias-hacker-army-suddenly-get-so-good/.

Hassan, Robert. *The Condition of Digitality: A Post-Modern Marxism for the Practice of Digital Life*. London: University of Westminster Press, 2020.

Haugbolle, Sune. "From A-Lists to Webtifadas: Developments in the Lebanese Blogosphere 2005–2006." *Arab Media and Society* 1, no. 1 (2007). https://www.arabmediasociety.com/ from-a-lists-to-webtifadas-developments-in-the-lebanese-blogosphere-2005-2006/.

Haugbolle, Sune. "Spatial Transformation in the Lebanese 'Independence Intifada.'" *Arab Studies Journal* 14, no. 2 (2006): 60–77.

Haugbølle, Rikke. "Rethinking the Role of Media in the Tunisian Uprising." In *The Making of the Tunisian Revolution*, edited by Nouri Gana, 159–180. Edinburgh: Edinburgh University Press, 2013.

Hazbun, Waleed. "The Uses of Modernization Theory: American Foreign Policy and Mythmaking in the Arab World." In *American Studies Encounters in the Middle East*, edited by Alex Lubin and Marwan Kraidy, 175–206. Chapel Hill: University of North Carolina Press, 2016.

Hegazi, Amir. *Startup Arabia: Stories and Advice from Top Tech Entrepreneurs in the Arab World*. Santa Monica, CA: Transformena, 2018.

Heinonen, Kristina, and Tore Strandvik. "Reframing Service Innovation: COVID-19 as a Catalyst for Imposed Service Innovation." *Journal of Service Management* 32, no. 1 (2021): 101–112.

Heintzen, Donna Fenn. "AP Was There: Saudi Women Protest Driving Ban in 1990." Associated Press, September 27, 2017. https://nationalpost.com/pmn/news-pmn/ap-was-there-saudi-women-protest-driving-ban-in-1990.

Hepp, Andreas. *Deep Mediatization*. New York: Routledge, 2020.

Hesmondhalgh, David. "The Infrastructural Turn in Media and Internet Research." In *The Routledge Companion to Media Industries*, edited by Paul McDonald, 132–142. London: Routledge, 2021.

Hess, John, and Patricia Zimmermann. "Transnational Digital Imaginaries." *Wide Angle* 21, no. 1 (1999): 149–167.

Hillman, Jonathan. *The Digital Silk Road: China's Quest to Wire the World and Win the Future.* New York: Harper Business, 2021.

Hirschkind, Charles. *The Ethical Soundscape: Cassette Sermons and Islamic Counter-Publics.* New York: Columbia University Press, 2006.

Hoffman, John. "'Bots' and Bans: Social Media and Regime Propaganda in the Middle East." Open Democracy, March 1, 2020. https://www.opendemocracy.net/en/north-africa-west-asia/bots-and-bans-social-media-and-regime-propaganda-in-the-middle-east/.

Hofheinz, Albrecht. "Arab Internet Use: Popular Trends and Public Impact." In *Arab Media and Political Renewal: Community, Legitimacy and Public Life*, edited by Naomi Sakr, 56–79. London: I.B. Tauris, 2007.

Holes, Clive. "Language and Identity in the Arabian Gulf." *Journal of Arabian Studies* 1, no. 2 (2011): 129–145.

Holland, Glesni. "The New Dawn: How the Rise of Fintech Is Transforming the Middle East." Tahawultech, August 3, 2018. https://www.tahawultech.com/features/fintech-middle-east/.

Hosea, Leana. "Libya Unrest: Inside Rebels' Media Centre in Benghazi." BBC News, April 15, 2011. https://www.bbc.com/news/world-africa-13092838.

Howard, Philip. *The Digital Origins of Dictatorship and Democracy: Information Technology and Political Islam.* Oxford: Oxford University Press, 2010.

Howard, Philip, and Muzammil Hussain. *Democracy's Fourth Wave? Digital Media and the Arab Spring.* Oxford: Oxford University Press, 2013.

Hoy, David Couzens. *The Time of Our Lives: A Critical History of Temporality.* Cambridge, MA: MIT Press, 2009.

HRinfo. "Implacable Adversaries: Arab Governments and the Internet." Arabic Network for Human Rights Information, 2006. http://anhri.net/wp-content/uploads/2019/05/Implacable-Adversaries.pdf.

Hroub, Khaled, ed. *Religious Broadcasting in the Middle East.* London: Hurst, 2012.

Hub71. "Mubadala Launches MENA Tech Investment Vehicles," October 21, 2019. https://hub71.com/whats-happening/articles/press-releases/mubadala-launches-mena-tech-investment-vehicles-us-150m-fund-of-funds-and-us-100m-direct-fund/.

Human Rights Watch. "If the Dead Could Speak: Mass Death and Torture in Syria's Detention Facilities," December 16, 2015. https://www.hrw.org/report/2015/12/16/if-dead-could-speak/mass-deaths-and-torture-syrias-detention-facilities.

Human Rights Watch. "The Internet in the Middle East and North Africa: A Cautious Start," June 1999. https://www.hrw.org/legacy/advocacy/internet/mena/int-mena.htm.

Hussain, Muzammil. "Digital Infrastructure Politics and Internet Freedom Stakeholders after the Arab Uprisings." *Journal of International Affairs* 68, no. 1 (2014): 37–56.

Hussein, Taha. "The Modern Renaissance of Arabic Literature." *World Literature* 63, no. 2 (1989): 249–256.

Hvidt, Martin. "Transformation of the Arab Gulf Economies into Knowledge Economies." Arab Center for Research and Policy Studies, 2015. https://www.dohainstitute.org/en/ResearchAndStudies/Pages/Transformation_of_the_Arab_Gulf_Economies_into_Knowledge_Economies_Motivational_Issues_Related_to_the_Tertiary_Education_S.aspx.

Iddins, Annemarie. "Mamfakinch: From Protest Slogan to Mediated Activism." *International Journal of Communication* 12 (2018): 3580–3599.

Index on Censorship. "Sudan Blacks Out Internet to Hide Brutal Suppression of Protests." IFEX, September 27, 2013. https://ifex.org/sudan-blacks-out-internet-to-hide-brutal-suppression-of-protests/.

Industry Development Agency. "The Egyptian Startup Ecosystem Report." Egyptian Ministry of Growth and Development, 2021. https://mcit.gov.eg/Upcont/Documents/Reports%20 and%20Documents_26102021000_Egyptian-Startup-Ecosystem-Report-2021.pdf.

Ingham, Edmund. "Top Cities for Starting Up in India." *Forbes*, December 6, 2015. https://www.forbes.com/sites/edmundingham/2015/12/06/indias-top-start-up-cities/?sh=24629 14a70d5.

International Crisis Group. "Algeria: Easing the Lockdown of the Hirak?," July 2020. https://www.crisisgroup.org/middle-east-north-africa/north-africa/algeria/217-algerie-vers-le-deconfinement-du-hirak.

International Data Corporation. "IoT Spending in the Middle East and Africa to See Double-Digit Growth over Coming Years." Zawya, August 1, 2019. https://www.zawya.com/mena/en/press-releases/story/IoT_spending_in_the_Middle_East__Africa_to_see_doubledigit_growth_over_coming_years-ZAWYA20190801102543/.

International Labour Organization. "Labour Migration," 2019. http://www.ilo.org/beirut/area sofwork/labour-migration/lang--en/index.htm.

International Trade Administration. "UAE: Country Commercial Guide." https://www.trade.gov/country-commercial-guides/united-arab-emirates-ecommerce.

Internet Society. "Enabling Digital Opportunities in the Middle East," October 27, 2017. https://www.internetsociety.org/resources/doc/2017/enabling-digital-opportunities-middle-east/.

Internet Society. "Middle East and North Africa Internet Infrastructure," 2019. https://www.internetsociety.org/wp-content/uploads/2020/09/Middle_East_North_Africa_Inter net_Infrastructure_2020-EN.pdf.

Internet World Stats. "Internet World Users by Language," 2020. https://www.internetworldstats.com/stats7.htm.

Investment Development Authority of Lebanon. "Sectors in Focus: ICT," July 23, 2023. http://investinlebanon.gov.lb/en/sectors_in_focus/ict.

Irby, Beverly, Nahed Abdelrahman, Barbara Polnick, and Julia Ballenger. *Women of Color in STEM: Navigating the Double Bind in Higher Education.* Charlotte, NC: Information Age, 2021.

Isherwood, Tom. "A New Direction or More of the Same? Political Blogging in Egypt." *Arab Media and Society* 6 (2008). https://www.arabmediasociety.com/a-new-direction-or-more-of-the-same/.

Isin, Engin, and Greg Nielsen. *Acts of Citizenship.* London: Zed , 2008.

Iskandar, Adel. "Media as Method in the Age of Arab Revolutions: Statism and Digital Contestation." In *The Oxford Handbook of Contemporary Middle Eastern and North African History*, edited by Amal Ghazal and Jens Hanssen, 342–364. Oxford: Oxford University Press, 2021.

Islamic Development Bank. "Youth Development Strategy 2020–2025," December 2019. https://www.isdb.org/sites/default/files/media/documents/2020-02/The%20IsDB%20Yo uth%20Development%20Strategy.pdf.

ITU. "Development Sector Measuring Digital Development Facts and Figures 2020." International Telecommunication Union, 2020. https://www.itu.int/en/ITU-D/Statistics/Documents/facts/FactsFigures2020.pdf.

ITU. "Generation Connect: Arab Youth Group." International Telecommunication Union, 2021. https://www.itu.int/en/ITU-D/Regional-Presence/ArabStates/Documents/events/Youth/GC-ARAB%20Priorities%20Document_Final.pdf.

ITU. "ICT Facts and Figures: The World in 2010." International Telecommunication Union, 2010. https://www.itu.int/en/ITU-D/Statistics/Documents/facts/ICTFactsFigures2010.pdf.

ITU. "ICT Facts and Figures: The World in 2015." International Telecommunication Union, 2015. https://www.itu.int/en/ITU-D/Statistics/Documents/facts/ICTFactsFigures2015.pdf.

ITU. "ICT Facts and Figures 2016." International Telecommunication Union, 2016. https://www.itu.int/en/ITU-D/Statistics/Documents/facts/ICTFactsFigures2016.pdf.

ITU. "Information Society Statistical Profiles 2009: Arab States." International Telecommunication Union, 2009. https://www.itu.int/pub/D-IND-RPM.AR-2009.

ITU. "International Bandwidth Usage." International Telecommunication Union, 2000. https://www.itu.int/itu-d/reports/statistics/2022/11/24/ff22-international-bandwidth-usage/.

ITU. "Internet for the Arab World." International Telecommunication Union, Telecommunication Development Bureau, October 2, 2000. http://www.itu.int/ITU-D/ict/papers/egypt2000/15-e.pdf.

ITU. "Internet Surge Slows, Leaving 2.7 Billion People Offline in 2022." International Telecommunication Union, September 16, 2022. https://www.itu.int/en/mediacentre/Pages/PR-2022-09-16-Internet-surge-slows.aspx.

ITU. "Measuring Digital Development: Fact and Figures 2019." International Telecommunication Union, 2019. https://www.itu.int/en/ITU-D/Statistics/Documents/facts/FactsFigures2019.pdf.

ITU. "Measuring Digital Development: Facts and Figures 2020." International Telecommunication Union, 2020. https://www.itu.int/en/ITU-D/Statistics/Documents/facts/FactsFigures2020.pdf.

ITU. "Measuring Digital Development: Facts and Figures 2021." International Telecommunication Union, 2021. https://www.itu.int/en/ITU-D/Statistics/Documents/facts/FactsFigures2021.pdf.

ITU. "Measuring Digital Development: Facts and Figures 2022." International Telecommunication Union, 2022. https://www.itu.int/hub/publication/d-ind-ict_mdd-2022/.

ITU. "Measuring the Information Society 2010." Information Telecommunication Union, 2010. https://www.itu.int/ITU-D/ict/publications/idi/material/2010/MIS_2010_without_annex_4-e.pdf.

ITU. "Measuring the Information Society Report 2017, Volume 1." International Telecommunication Union, 2017. https://www.itu.int/en/ITU-D/Statistics/Documents/publications/misr2017/MISR2017_Volume1.pdf.

ITU. "Measuring the Information Society Report 2018, Volume 2." International Telecommunication Union, 2018. https://www.itu.int/en/ITU-D/Statistics/Documents/publications/misr2018/MISR-2018-Vol-2-E.pdf.

Jacinto, Leela. "Can Hariri's 'Selfie Diplomacy' Boost His Chances in Lebanon's Upcoming Election?" France24, December 4, 2018. https://www.france24.com/en/20180412-lebanon-saudi-arabia-hariri-twitter-selfie-diplomacy-mbs.

Jafaar, Ali. "TV Execs Face New Threats: Saudi Cleric Issues Fatwa against Net Owners." *Variety* 412, no. 8 (2008): A16.

James, Laura. *Nasser at War: Arab Images of the Enemy*. New York: Palgrave Macmillan, 2006.

Jamieson, Kathleen. *Beyond the Double Bind: Women and Leadership*. New York: Oxford University Press, 1995.

Jasanoff, Sheila, and Sang-Hyun Kim. *Dreamscapes of Modernity: Sociotechnical Imaginaries and the Fabrication of Power*. Chicago: University of Chicago Press, 2015.

Jenkins, Henry. *Convergence Culture: Where Old and New Media Collide*. New York: New York University Press, 2008.

Jones, Calvert. "The Rhetoric of Self-Definition: Shaping a New Emirati Identity." In *Identity-Seekers: Nationhood and Nationalism in the Gulf Monarchies*, edited by Eleonora Ardemagni, 6–7. Milan: Italian Institute for International Political Studies, 2019. https://www.ispionline.it/it/pubblicazione/identity-seekers-nationhood-and-nationalism-gulf-monarchies-23076.

Jones, David, and Sofiane Sahraoui. *The Future of Labour Market Reform in the Gulf Region: Towards a Multi-Disciplinary, Evidence-Based and Practical Understanding*. Berlin: Gerlach Press, 2018.

Jones, Marc. *Digital Authoritarianism in the Middle East: Deception, Disinformation and Social Media*. Oxford: Oxford University Press, 2022.

Jones, Rory. "Google Plots New Europe-Asia Path." *Wall Street Journal*, November 4, 2020, A10.

Jones, Rory, and Drew FitzGerald. "Google Plans Fiber-Optic Network to Connect via Saudi Arabia and Israel for First Time." *Wall Street Journal*, November 23, 2022. https://www.wsj.com/articles/google-plans-fiber-optic-network-to-connect-via-saudi-arabia-and-israel-for-first-time-11606143590?mod=djemalertNEWS.

Kalaldeh, Farhan, and Jamal Al Homsi. "Jordan's Startup Economy: Assessing the Economic Contribution and Potential of Tech and Tech-Enabled Startups." Deutsche Gesellschaft für Internationale Zusammenarbeit (GIZ), May 2019. https://www.orange.jo/en/big/documents/startup_en.pdf.

Kalathil, Shanthi, and Taylor Boas. *Open Networks, Closed Regimes: The Impact of the Internet on Authoritarian Rule*. Washington, DC: Carnegie Endowment for International Peace, 2003.

Kanaan. https://kanaan.ps/en/Page/Index/1.

Kandaka. "Sudan Uprising: The Voice of a Woman Is a Revolution," April 11, 2019. https://kandaka.blog/2019/04/11/sudan-uprising-the-voice-of-a-woman-is-a-revolution/.

Karaki-Shelhoub, Zeinab. "Population ID Card Systems in the Middle East." In *Playing the Digital Card: Surveillance, Security and Identification in Global Perspective*, edited by Colin Bennett and David Lyon, 128–142. New York: Routledge, 2008.

Karasti, Helena, Karen Baker, and Florence Millerand. "Infrastructure Time: Long-Term Matters in Collaborative Development." *Computer Supported Cooperative Work* 19, no. 3 (2010): 377–415.

Karolak, Magdalena. "Civil Society and Web 2.0 Technology: Social Media in Bahrain." *Arab Media and Society* 14 (2012). https://www.arabmediasociety.com/civil-society-and-web-2-0-technology-social-media-in-bahrain.

Karombo, Tawanda. "Egyptian Startups Are Africa's New Venture Capital Darlings." Quartz Africa, July 2, 2021. https://qz.com/africa/2027988/egypt-attracts-startup-funding-after-banking-regulatory-changes/.

Kassab, Elizabeth Suzanne. *Contemporary Arab Thought: Cultural Critique in Comparative Perspective*. New York: Columbia University Press, 2009.

Kassir, Samir. *Being Arab*. London: Verso, 2013.

Katz, Claudio. *Dependency Theory After Fifty Years*. Translated by Stanley Malinowitz. Leiden: Brill, 2022.

Kavanaugh, Andrea. *The Social Control of Technology in North Africa: Information in the Global Economy*. Westport, CT: Praeger, 1998.

Kazan, Fayad. *Mass Media, Modernity, and Development: Arab States of the Gulf*. Westport, CT: Praeger, 1993.

Kemp, Geoffrey. *The East Moves West: India, China, and Asia's Growing Presence in the Middle East*. Washington, DC: Brookings Institution Press, 2012.

Kemp, Simon. "Digital 2020: Tunisia." Datareportal, February 18, 2020. https://datareportal.com/reports/digital-2020-tunisia.

Kemp, Simon. "Digital 2022: Saudi Arabia." Datareportal, February 9, 2022. https://datareportal.com/reports/digital-2022-saudi-arabia.

Kenner, David. "Arabic Facebook Launches." *Foreign Policy*, March 24, 2009. https://foreignpolicy.com/2009/03/24/arabic-facebook-launches/.

Kepel, Gilles. *Jihad: The Trail of Political Islam*. Cambridge, MA: Harvard University Press, 2002.

Kerr, Malcolm. "Arab Socialist Thought." *Journal of Contemporary History* 3, no. 3 (1968): 145–159.

Khader, Bishara. "The Social Impact of the Transfer of Technology to the Arab World." *Arab Studies Quarterly* 4, no. 3 (1982): 226–241.

Khaleej Times. "UAE: 'Demand for E-Books Grow Three-Fold Even as Piracy Concerns Remain High in Arab Markets,'" October 31, 2022. https://www.zawya.com/en/world/middle-east/uae-demand-for-e-books-grow-three-fold-even-as-piracy-concerns-remain-high-in-arab-markets-u8qwj5qp.

Khalidi, Rashid, Lisa Anderson, Muhammad Muslih, and Reeva Simon, eds. *The Origins of Arab Nationalism*. New York: Columbia University Press, 1991.

Khalifeh, Paul. "Pressing Issue: Lebanon's Print Media Is Dying." Middle East Eye, November 11, 2018. https://www.middleeasteye.net/news/pressing-issue-lebanons-print-media-dying.

Khalifi, Yousef. "The Challenges of Data." Smart Cities Report 2017, 6–8. https://issuu.com/theb igprojectme/docs/bigproject_smart_cities_2017.

Khalil, Joe F. "Modalities of Media Governance in the Arab World." In *Arab Media Moguls*, edited by Donatella Della Ratta, Naomi Sakr, and Jakob Skovgaard-Petersen, 13–30. London: I.B. Tauris, 2015.

Khalil, Joe F. "Turning Murders into Public Executions: Beheading Videos as Alternative Media." In *The Routledge Companion to Media and Activism*, edited by Graham Meilke, 232–240. New York: Routledge, 2018.

Khalil, Joe F. "Youth-Generated Media: A Case of Blogging and Arab Youth Cultural Politics." *Television & New Media* 14, no. 4 (2013): 338–350.

Khalil, Joe F., Gholam Khiabany, Tourya Guaaybess, and Blige Yesil, eds. *The Handbook of Media and Culture in the Middle East*. Hoboken, NJ: Wiley-Blackwell, 2023.

Khalil, Joe F., and Mohamed Zayani. "Deterritorialized Digital Capitalism and the Predicament of the Nation State: Netflix in Arabia." *Media, Culture & Society* 43, no. 2 (2021): 201–218.

Khalil, Joe F., and Mohamed Zayani. "Digitality and Debordered Spaces in the Era of Streaming: A Global South Perspective." *Television & New Media* 23, no. 2 (2022): 167–183.

Khalil, Joe F., and Mohamed Zayani. "Digitality and Music Streaming in the Middle East: Anghami and the Burgeoning Startup Culture." *International Journal of Communication* 16 (2022): 1532–1550.

Kamel, Dina. "Dubai Start-Ups' Funding Doubled in 2022 to $2 Billion." *The National*, June 18, 2023. https://tinyurl.com/34mes8nw.

Khamis, Sahar. "Cyber *Ummah*: The Internet and Muslim Communities." In *Handbook of Contemporary Islam and Muslim Lives*, edited by Mark Woodward and Ronald Lukens-Bull, 1–22. Cham, Switzerland: Springer, 2018. https://doi.org/10.1007/978-3-319-73653-2_69-1.

Khanfar, Waddah. "At Al Jazeera, We Saw the Arab Revolutions Coming. Why Didn't the West?" *Washington Post*, February 25, 2005. http://www.washingtonpost.com/wp-dyn/content/article/2011/02/25/AR2011022503177.html.

Khatib, Lina. "Social Media and Mobilization in the Arab Spring and Beyond." In *North African Politics: Change and Continuity*, edited by Yahia Zoubir and Gregory White, 114–127. London: Routledge, 2015.

Khorsheed, Mohammad. "Saudi Arabia: From Oil Kingdom to Knowledge-Based Economy." *Middle East Policy* 22, no. 3 (2015): 147–157.

King, Stephen. *Arab Winter: Democratic Consolidation, Civil War, and Radical Islamists*. Cambridge: Cambridge University Press, 2020.

Kirdar, Serra. *Education in the Arab World*. London: Bloomsbury Academic, 2017.

Kirk, Mimi. "Why Abu Dhabi Doubled Down on CCTV Surveillance." Bloomberg, July 21, 2016. https://www.citylab.com/life/2016/07/why-abu-dhabi-doubled-down-on-surveillance/492395/.

Knopová, Martina, and Eva Knopová. "The Third World War? In the Cyberspace." *Acta Informatica Pragensia* 3, no. 1 (2014): 23–32.

Kraft, Dina. "For Still-Stateless Palestinians, Cultural Life Serves as a Building Block." *Christian Science Monitor*, April 18, 2018. https://www.csmonitor.com/World/Middle-East/2018/0418/For-still-stateless-Palestinians-cultural-life-serves-as-a-building-block.

Kraidy, Marwan. *Hybridity, or the Cultural Logic of Globalization*. Philadelphia: Temple University Press, 2005.

Kraidy, Marwan. *The Naked Blogger of Cairo: Creative Insurgency in the Arab World*. Cambridge, MA: Harvard University Press, 2016.

Kraidy, Marwan. "Terror, Territoriality, Temporality: Hypermedia Events in the Age of Islamic State." *Television & New Media* 19, no. 2 (2018): 170–176.

Kraidy, Marwan. "The Project Image: Islamic State's Digital Visual Warfare and Global Network Affect." *Media, Culture & Society* 39, no. 8 (2017): 1194–1209.

Kraidy, Marwan. *Reality Television and Arab Politics: Contention in Public Life.* Cambridge: Cambridge University Press, 2010.

Kraidy, Marwan. "Saudi Arabia, Lebanon and the Changing Arab Information Order." *International Journal of Communication* 1, no. 1 (2007): 139–156.

Kraidy, Marwan, and Joe F. Khalil. *Arab Television Industries.* London: Palgrave Macmillan, 2009.

Kraidy, Marwan, and Marina Krikorian. "Mediating Islamic State." *International Journal of Communication* 14 (2020): 1762–1766. https://ijoc.org/index.php/ijoc/article/view/9854/3025.

Kreyenbroek, Philip, and Christine Allison. *Kurdish Culture and Identity.* London: Zed, 1996.

Kristeva, Julia. "In Quest of the Feminine: The Strange within Us." *Feminist Issues* 15, nos. 1–2 (1997): 72–90.

Kurzman, Charles. "Cross-Regional Approaches to Middle East Studies." *Middle East Studies Association Bulletin* 41, no. 1 (2007): 24–29.

Kushkush, Isma'il. "Sudan's Diaspora Has Played a Crucial Role in Supporting the Anti-Bashir Protests." Quartz Africa, April 11, 2019. https://qz.com/africa/1591956/sudans-diaspora-helped-bring-bashirs-end-near/.

LaMay, Craig. "Qatar's beIN Sports and Football Broadcasting in the Middle East." In *Football in the Middle East,* edited by Abdullah Al Arian, 303–322. London: Hurst, 2022.

Lamloum, Olfa. "Islamonline: Jeux et enjeux d'un média 'post-islamiste' déterritorialisé." In *Médias et islamisme,* edited by Olfa Lamloum, 45–62. Beirut: Presses de l'Institut Français du Proche-Orient, 2010.

Landorf, Brittany. "Female Reverberations Online: An Analysis of Tunisian, Egyptian, and Moroccan Female Cyberactivism during the Arab Spring." International Studies Honors Projects, Macalester University, 2014. https://digitalcommons.macalester.edu/intlstudies_honors/20.

Langton, James. "Dozens of Cyber Attacks Target UAE Government and Companies in January." *National,* February 19, 2018. https://www.thenational.ae/uae/dozens-of-cyber-attacks-target-uae-government-and-companies-in-january-1.705881.

Laroui, Abdallah. *Arabs and Historical Thought* [in Arabic]. Beirut: Dar Al Haqiqa, 1973.

Larsson, Göran. *Muslims and the New Media: Historical and Contemporary Debates.* London: Routledge, 2016.

Lawson, Fred. "The Political Economy of Rentierism in the Persian Gulf." In *Political Economy of the Persian Gulf,* edited by Mehran Kamrava, 13–38. London: Hurst, 2012.

Lee, Brian. "The Impact of Cyber Capabilities in the Syrian Civil War." *Small Wars Journal,* April 26, 2016. https://smallwarsjournal.com/jrnl/art/the-impact-of-cyber-capabilities-in-the-syrian-civil-war.

Lenze, Nele. *Politics and Digital Literature in the Middle East: Perspectives on Online Text and Context.* Cham, Switzerland: Palgrave Macmillan, 2019.

Leopardi, Francesco, and Massimiliano Trentin. "The International 'Debt Crisis' of the 1980s in the Middle East and North Africa." *Middle Eastern Studies* 58, no. 5 (2022): 699–711.

Lerner, Daniel. *The Passing of Traditional Society: Modernizing the Middle East.* Glencoe, IL: Free Press, 1958.

Levin, Ilya, and Dan Mamlok. "Culture and Society in the Digital Age." *Information* 12 (2021): 1–13.

Lightfoot, Michael. "Promoting the Knowledge Economy in the Arab World." *Sage Open* 1, no. 2 (October 2011). https://journals.sagepub.com/doi/full/10.1177/2158244011417457.

Lim, Merlyna. "Clicks, Cabs, and Coffee Houses: Social Media and Oppositional Movements in Egypt, 2004–11." *Journal of Communication* 62 (2012): 231–248.

Lim, Merlyna. "Unveiling Saudi Feminism(s): Historicization, Heterogeneity, and Corporeality in Women's Movements." *Canadian Journal of Communication* 43 (2018): 461–479.

Ling, Elizabeth. "Our Well-Being Is Paying for the Attention Economy." *Harvard Crimson*, September 30, 2022. https://www.thecrimson.com/article/2022/9/30/ling-attention-economy/.

Livingstone, Sonia, Dafna Lamish, Sun Lim, and Monica Blugar. "Global Perspectives on Children's Digital Opportunities: An Emerging Research and Policy Agenda." *Pediatrics* 140, no. 2 (2017): 137–141.

Lloyd, Catherine. "Transnational Mobilizations in Contexts of Violent Conflict: The Case of Solidarity with Women in Algeria." *Contemporary Politics* 5, no. 4 (1999): 365–377.

Lovink, Geert. *Networks without a Cause: A Critique of Social Media*. Cambridge: Polity, 2013.

Lunden, Ingrid. "Souq, Amazon of the Middle East, Raises $275M from Tiger and More at a $1B Valuation." TechCrunch, February 29, 2016. https://techcrunch.com/2016/02/29/souq-amazon-of-the-middle-east-raises-275m-from-tiger-and-more-reported-1b-valuation/.

Lunden, Ingrid, and Jon Russell. "Amazon to Acquire Souq, a Middle East Clone Once Valued at $1B, for $650M." TechCrunch, March 24, 2017. https://techcrunch.com/2017/03/23/amazon-to-acquire-souq-a-middle-east-clone-once-valued-at-1b-for-650m/.

Lynch, Marc. "Blogging the New Arab Public." *Arab Media and Society* 1 (2007). https://www.arabmediasociety.com/blogging-the-new-arab-public/.

Mabon, Simon. "Aiding Revolution? Wikileaks, Communication and the 'Arab Spring' in Egypt." *Third World Quarterly* 34, no. 10 (2013): 1834–1857.

MAGNiTT. "2021 MENA Venture Investment Report," January 2021. https://magnitt.com/research/2021-mena-venture-investment-report-50736.

MAGNiTT. "2021 MENA Venture Investor Ranking Report," February 2021. https://magnitt.com/research/2021-mena-venture-investor-ranking-report-50745.

MAGNiTT. "Emerging Venture Markets Report," January 2021. https://magnitt.com/research/2021-emerging-venture-markets-report-50737.

MAGNiTT. "FY2022 MENA Venture Investment Report," January 2023. https://magnitt.com/research/2022-mena-venture-investment-report-50849.

MAGNiTT. "MENA H1 2022 Venture Investment Report," July 2022. https://magnitt.com/research/H1-2022-MENA-venture-capital-report-50828.

MAGNiTT. "A Rundown of MENA's 3 IPOs in the Last 2 Years," March 10, 2021. https://magnitt.com/news/rundown-mena-ipos-52543?utm_source=socialmedia&utm_medium=Twitter&utm_campaign=Amp.

MAGNiTT. "Startup Fever: MENA Exits Reach $3 Billion over Five Years," June 21, 2017. https://magnitt.com/news/startup-fever-mena-exits-reach-3-billion-over-five-years-19321.

MAGNiTT. "Two Decades till Sunrise: The Evolution of VC in MENA," October 19, 2021. https://magnitt.com/news/the-evolution-of-vc-in-mena-52958?utm_source=daily&utm_medium=email&utm_campaign=Amp.

Maira, Sunaina. *Missing: Youth, Citizenship, and Empire after 9/11*. Durham, NC: Duke University Press, 2009.

Malecki, Edward, and Hu Wei. "A Wired World: The Evolving Geography of Submarine Cables and the Shift to Asia." *Annals of the Association of American Geographers* 99, no. 2 (2009): 360–382.

Manea, Elham. *The Arab State and Women's Rights: The Trap of Authoritarian Governance*. London: Routledge, 2014.

Mansell, Robin. *Imagining the Internet: Communication, Innovation, and Governance*. New York: Oxford University Press, 2012.

Marczak, Bill, John Scott-Railton, Noura Al Jizawi, Siena Anstis, and Ron Deibert. "The Great iPwn." Citizen Lab, December 20, 2020. https://citizenlab.ca/2020/12/the-great-ipwn-journalists-hacked-with-suspected-nso-group-imessage-zero-click-exploit/.

Margit, Maya. "UAE, Saudi Arabia, Turkey Posed to Lead Middle East Space Industry." *Jerusalem Post*, December 26, 2018. https://www.jpost.com/Middle-East/UAE-Saudi-Arabia-Turkey-posed-to-lead-Middle-East-space-industry-575528.

MarkMonitor. "BeoutQ Investigation," April 2019. https://docplayer.net/155798924-Beoutq-investigation-prepared-by-markmonitor-april-2019.html.

Martin, Justin, Ralph Martins, and Robb Wood. "Desire for Cultural Preservation as a Predictor of Support for Entertainment Media Censorship in Saudi Arabia, Qatar, and the United Arab Emirates." *International Journal of Communication* 10 (2016): 3400–3422.

Martinez, Angela, Lee Martin, and Susan Marlow. "Emancipation through Digital Entrepreneurship." *Organization* 25, no. 2 (2018): 585–608.

Marx, Willem. "Bassem Youssef: Egypt's Jon Stewart." *Bloomberg Businessweek*, March 29, 2012. https://www.bloomberg.com/news/articles/2012-03-29/bassem-youssef-egypts-jon-stew art#p1.

Masmoudi, Mustapha. "The Arab World and the Information Age: Promises and Challenges." In *The Information Revolution and the Arab World: Its Impacts on State and Society*, edited by Emirates Center for Strategic Studies and Research, 120–140. Abu Dhabi: ECSSR, 1998.

Masmoudi, Mustapha. "Le nouvel ordre mondial de l'information et les satellites de radiodiffu-sion directe." *Syracuse Journal of International Law and Commerce* 8, no. 2 (1981): 323–332. https://surface.syr.edu/jilc/vol8/iss2/3.

Mavridis, Nikolaos, Marina Katsaiti, Silvia Naef, and Abdullah Falasi. "Opinions and Attitudes toward Humanoid Robots in the Middle East." *AI & Society* 27 (2012): 517–534.

Mawlana, Hamid. "The Arab World and the Information Age: Promises and Challenges." In *The Information Revolution and the Arab World: Its Impact on State and Society*, edited by Emirates Center for Strategic Studies and Research, 107–119. Abu Dhabi: ECSSR, 1998.

Maxim, Bailey, ed. *The Colonial and Postcolonial Middle East*. New York: Britannica Educational, 2017.

Maximillian, Ashy. "Networked Communication and the Arab Spring." *New Media and Society* 18, no. 1 (2016): 99–116.

Mazzetti, Mark, Nicole Perlroth, and Ronen Bergman. "It Seemed Like a Popular Chat App. It's Secretly a Spy Tool." *New York Times*, December 22, 2019. https://www.nytimes.com/2019/12/22/us/politics/totok-app-uae.html.

MBC. "MBC Group Re-Launches Shahid.net, the Biggest Online TV Library in the Region," July 31, 2011. http://www.mbc.net/en/corporate/articles/MBC-Group-re-launches-Shahid-net,-the-biggest-online-TV-library-in-the-region.html.

Mbembe, Achille. *On the Postcolony*. Berkeley: University of California Press. 2001.

MBZUAI. "About Mohamed Bin Zayed University of Artificial Intelligence." https://mbzuai. ac.ae/about/.

McAnany, Emile. *Saving the World: A Brief History of Communication for Development*. Urbana-Champaign: University of Illinois Press, 2012.

McClure, Kristie. "On the Subject of Rights: Pluralism, Plurality and Political Identity." In *Dimensions of Radical Democracy: Pluralism, Citizenship, Pluralism*, edited by Chantal Mouffe, 108–127. New York: Verso, 1992.

McCormack, Derek. "Elemental Infrastructures for Atmospheric Media: On Stratospheric Variations, Value and the Commons." *Society and Space* 35, no. 3 (2017): 418–437.

McKernan, Bethan. "A Journey through the Past: Lost Music of the Palestinian Uprising Is Restored." *Guardian*, January 12, 2022. https://www.theguardian.com/world/2022/jan/12/a-journey-through-the-past-lost-music-of-the-palestinian-uprising-is-restored.

Meaker, Morgan. "Death by Spyware: How Surveillance Tech Is Helping Governments Stifle Dissent." World Politics Review, November 12, 2019. https://www.worldpoliticsreview.com/articles/28337/how-spyware-like-nso-pegasus-is-making-dissent-more-dangerous.

Mellor, Noha. *Arab Digital Journalism*. London: Routledge, 2022.

Mellor, Noha. "Bedouinization or Liberalization of Culture: The Paradox in the Saudi Monopoly of the Arab Media." In *Kingdom without Borders: Saudi Political, Religious, and Media Frontiers*, edited by Madawi Al Rasheed, 353–371. New York: Columbia University Press, 2008.

Mellor, Noha, Muhammad Ayish, Nabil Dajani, and Khalil Rinnawi, eds. *Arab Media Globalization and Emerging Media Industries*. Cambridge: Polity, 2011.

Melzer, E. J. "Gay Iraqi Laments Life after Invasion: Americans Form Gay Support Group in Baghdad." *Washington Blade*, August 19, 2005.

MENAbytes. "Careem Now Has One Million Captains Across Its Ride-Hailing Network in 14 Countries," September 2, 2018. https://www.menabytes.com/careem-captains-one-million/.

MENA Private Equity Association. "MENA Private Equity & Venture Capital Report 2015." https://www.difc.ae/events/mena-private-equity-and-venture-capital-report-2015/.

Menon, Vineetha. "DIC to Release Study of ME IT Sector." Arabian Business, October 16, 2008. https://www.arabianbusiness.com/industries/technology/dic-release-study-of-me-it-sector-85087.

Mernissi, Fatema. *Beyond the Veil: Male-Female Dynamics in Modern Muslim Society.* Bloomington: Indiana University Press, 1987.

Mernissi, Fatema. "The Satellite, the Prince, and Scheherazade: The Rise of Women as Communicators in Digital Islam." *Arab Media & Society* 12 (2004). https://www.arabmediasociety.com/the-satellite-the-prince-and-scheherazade-the-rise-of-women-as-communicators-in-digital-islam/.

Merolla, Daniela. "De la parole aux vidéos: Oralité, écriture et oralité médiatique dans la production culturelle amazigh." *Afrika Focus* 18, nos. 1–2 (2005): 33–57.

Metafora Productions. "Joe Show," 2016. https://metaforaproduction.com/portfolio-item/%D8%AC%D9%88-%D8%B4%D9%88/.

Middle East Eye. "EU States 'Approved Spy Equipment Sales to Egypt,'" February 26, 2016. https://www.middleeasteye.net/news/eu-states-approved-spy-equipment-sales-egypt.

Middle East Eye. "Google Plans Fibre-Optic Cable Linking Israel and Saudi Arabia," November 26, 2020. https://www.middleeasteye.net/news/google-israel-saudi-arabia-fiber-optic-cable-link-plans.

Middle East Eye. "Israeli Defense Companies Sign 'Historic' Deal with UAE Artificial Intelligence Firm," July 3, 2020. https://www.middleeasteye.net/news/israel-uae-defence-ai-companies-deal-signed.

Middle East Media. "Media Use by Platform," 2019. http://www.mideastmedia.org/survey/2019/chapter/media-use-by-platform/.

Middle East Media. "Media Use in the Middle East," 2019. www.mideastmedia.org/survey/2019/chapter/internet-use/.

Middle East Media. "Social Media," 2019. http://www.mideastmedia.org/survey/2019/chapter/social-media/#s336.

Mid East Information. "Anghami Gears Up for Ramadan with Great Opportunities in Content Generation," May 23, 2017. https://mid-east.info/anghami-gears-up-for-ramadan-with-great-opportunities-in-content-generation/.

Mihoub-Dramé, Samia. *Internet dans le monde arabe: Complexité d'une adoption.* Paris: L'Harmattan, 2005.

Miladi, Noureddine, and Noha Mellor, eds. *Routledge Handbook on Arab Media.* London: Routledge: 2020.

Miller, Rory. *Desert Kingdoms to Global Powers: The Rise of the Arab Gulf.* New Haven, CT: Yale University Press, 2016.

Miller, Rory, ed. *The Gulf Crisis: The View from Qatar.* Doha: HBKU University Press, 2018.

Miniaoui, Héla. *Economic Development in the Gulf Cooperation Council Countries: From Rentier States to Diversified Economies.* Singapore: Springer, 2020.

Mirgani, Suzi. "Introduction: Art and Cultural Production in the GCC." *Journal of Arabian Studies* 7, no. 1 (2017): 1–11.

Mirgani, Suzi. *Target Markets: International Terrorism Meets Global Capitalism in the Mall.* Bielefeld, Germany: Transcript, 2017.

Mishkhas, Abeer. "Saudi Arabia to Overturn Ban on Camera Phones." *Arab News*, December 17, 2004. https://www.arabnews.com/node/259698.

Mneimneh, Hassan. "The Gulf Crisis Is a Messaging Nightmare, with No Success in Sight." Fikra Forum, Washington Institute for Near East Policy, June 21, 2019. https://www.washingtoninstitute.org/policy-analysis/gulf-crisis-messaging-nightmare-no-success-sight.

Mohamedou, Mohammad-Mahmoud, ed. *State-Building in the Middle East and North Africa: One Hundred Years of Nationalism, Religion and Politics*. London: I.B. Tauris, 2021.

Mohsen, Nour. "Lebanon and Iraq: Two Distinct Demonstrations of Confessionalism's Failures to Manage Ethnic and Religious Pluralism." *Flux: International Relations Review* 11, no. 2 (2021): 39–49.

Momani, Bessma and Crystal Ennis. "Between Caution and Controversy: Lessons from the Gulf Arab States as (Re-)Emerging Donors." *Cambridge Review of International Affairs* 25, no. 4 (2012): 605–627.

Montague, Sarah. "The Baghdad Blogger Salam Pax." BBC Radio 4, September 9, 2003.

Moore-Gilbert, Kylie. "Mediated Mobilisation after the Arab Spring: How Online Activism Is Shaping Bahrain's Opposition." *Australian Journal of Political Science* 53, no. 1 (2018): 78–88.

Morozov, Evgeny. "Think Again: The Internet." *Foreign Policy*, May–June 2010. https://foreignpolicy.com/2010/04/26/think-again-the-internet/.

Mosco, Vincent. *The Digital Sublime: Myth, Power, and Cyberspace*. Cambridge, MA: MIT Press, 2004.

Moss, Dana. "The Ties That Bind: Internet Communication Technologies, Networked Authoritarianism, and 'Voice' in the Syrian Diaspora." *Globalizations* 15, no. 2 (2018): 265–282.

Mouchawar, Ronaldo. "Souq.com's CEO on Building an E-Commerce Powerhouse in the Middle East: Winning Trust in Regions Where Payments Are Made in Cash." *Harvard Business Review* 95, no. 5 (2017): 35–38.

Mouffe, Chantal, ed. *Dimensions of Radical Democracy: Pluralism, Citizenship, Community*. New York: Verso, 1992.

Muhammad, Fatima. "Saudi Arabia's E-Tail Laws Target Fraud, Protect Privacy." Zawya, October 26, 2019. https://www.zawya.com/en/legal/saudi-arabias-e-tail-laws-target-fraud-protect-privacy-hecrpr8m.

Mumford, Lewis. *Technics and Civilization*. Chicago: University of Chicago Press, [1934] 2020.

Murphy, Emma. "Problematizing Arab Youth: Generational Narratives of Systemic Failure." *Mediterranean Politics* 17, no. 1 (2012): 5–22.

Murphy, Emma, and Mahjoob Zweiri, eds. *The New Arab Media: Technology, Image and Perception*. Reading, UK: Ithaca, 2012.

Museum of the Future. https://museumofthefuture.ae/en.

Nabil, Yasmeen. "Investment in Saudi-Based Startups Record an All Time High in 2019." Wamda, January 29, 2020. https://www.wamda.com/2020/01/investment-saudi-based-startups-record-time-high-2019.

Nabil, Yasmeen. "W Ventures to Invest $50 Million in E-Sports Ecosystem." Wamda, October 30, 2019. https://www.wamda.com/2019/10/w-ventures-invest-50-million-e-sports-ecosystem.

Nagel, Caroline, and Lynn Staeheli. "ICT and Geographies of British Arab and Arab American Activism." *Global Networks* 10, no. 2 (2010): 262–281.

Nagle, John. *Multiculturalism's Double Bind: Creating Inclusivity, Cosmopolitanism and Difference*. New York: Routledge, 2016.

Naimy, Nadeem. *The Lebanese Prophets of New York*. Beirut: American University of Beirut Press, 1985.

Nair, Dinesh, and Matthew Martin. "Amazon in Talks to Buy Dubai's Souq.com in $1 Billion Deal." Bloomberg, November 24, 2016. https://www.bloomberg.com/news/articles/2016-11-24/amazon-said-in-talks-to-buy-dubai-s-souq-com-in-1-billion-deal.

Nakashima, Ellen, and Joby Warrick. "Stuxnet Was Work of U.S. and Israeli Experts, Officials Say." *Washington Post*, June 2, 2012. https://www.washingtonpost.com/world/national-security/stuxnet-was-work-of-us-and-israeli-experts-officials-say/2012/06/01/gJQAInEy6U_story.html.

Nanabhay, Mohamed, and Roxane Farmanfarmaian. "From Spectacle to Spectacular: How Physical Space, Social Media and Mainstream Broadcast Amplified the Public Sphere in Egypt's 'Revolution.'" *Journal of North African Studies* 16, no. 4 (2011): 573–603.

Nasrallah, Tawfiq. "Sheikh Mohammed bin Rashid: Innovate or Risk Extinction." *Gulf News*, September 17, 2021. https://gulfnews.com/uae/sheikh-mohammed-bin-rashid-innovate-or-risk-extinction-1.1631889156131.

National. "UAE Unveils Coder Training Campaign with Tech Giants Google and Amazon." *National*, July 10, 2021. https://www.thenationalnews.com/uae/2021/07/10/uae-unveils-programmer-training-campaign-with-tech-giants-google-and-amazon/.

Navarria, Giovanni. "E-Government: Who Controls the Controllers?" Open Democracy, February 9, 2006. https://www.opendemocracy.net/media-edemocracy/egovernment_3 254.jsp.

Neate, Rupert. "Rupert Murdoch: Gulf Should Lift Media Restrictions." *Telegraph*, March 9, 2010. https://www.telegraph.co.uk/finance/newsbysector/mediatechnologyandtelecoms/7408 728/Rupert-Murdoch-Gulf-should-lift-media-restrictions.html.

Negroponte, Nicholas. *Being Digital*. New York: Alfred A. Knopf, 1995.

Newcombe, Tod. "The United Arab Emirates: A Rising Star in E-Government." Information Policy, May 4, 2014. https://www.i-policy.org/2014/05/the-united-arab-emirates-a-rising-star-in-e-government.html.

Newsom, Victoria, Catherine Cassara, and Lara Lengel. "Discourses on Technology Policy in the Middle East and North Africa: Gender Mainstreaming vs. Local Knowledge." *Communication Studies* 62, no. 1 (2011): 74–89.

Norris, Pippa. "Preaching to the Converted? Pluralism, Participation and Party Websites." *Party Politics* 9, no. 10 (2003): 21–45.

Northlet, Jessica. "Imagining a New Political Space: The Power of Youth and Peaceful Protest in Algeria." *Idees* 51, 2020. https://revistaidees.cat/en/imagining-a-new-political-space-the-power-of-youth-and-peaceful-protest-in-algeria/.

Ntloko, Khalipha. "A Data-Driven Analysis: The Future of eSports in the Middle East." Meltwater, August 28, 2020. https://www.meltwater.com/en/blog/data-driven-analysis-the-future-of-esports-in-the-middle-east.

Odeh, Layan, and Matthew Martin. "Uber's Mideast Addition Careem Offers Bus Hailing to Pilgrims." Bloomberg, May 14, 2019. https://www.bloomberg.com/news/articles/2019-05-14/uber-s-middle-east-unit-starts-bus-service-in-saudi-arabia.

Odell, Joe. "Inside the Dark Web of the UAE's Surveillance State." Middle East Eye, March 1, 2018. http://www.middleeasteye.net/columns/uae-surveillance-state-1032283790.

O'Donovan, Nick. *Pursuing the Knowledge Economy: A Sympathetic History of High-Skill, High-Wage Hubris*. Newcastle, UK: Agenda, 2022.

OECD. "Empowering Women in the Digital Age," March 14, 2018. https://www.oecd.org/scie nce/empowering-women-in-the-digital-age-brochure.pdf.

Office of the Minister of State for Administrative Reform. "Lebanon Digital Transformation Strategy." Republic of Lebanon, 2018. http://studies.gov.lb/Sectors/Information-Com munications-Technology-Media/2018/IT-18-1?lang=en-us.

Ojanperä, Sanna, Mark Graham, and Matthew Zook. "The Digital Knowledge Economy Index: Mapping Content Production." *Journal of Development Studies* 55, no. 12 (2019): 2626–2643.

Ojo, Adegboyega, Edward Curry, Tomasz Janowski, and Zamira Dzhusupova. "Designing Next-Generation Smart City Initiatives: The SCID Framework." In *Transforming City Governments for Successful Smart Cities*, edited by Manuel Pedro Rodríguez-Bolívar, 43–67. Cham, Switzerland: Springer, 2015.

Oledzki, Jerzy. "Polish Perspectives on the New Information Order." *Journal of International Affairs* 35, no. 2 (1981): 155–164.

Omar, Noha. "Innovation and Economic Performance in MENA Region." *Review of Economics and Political Science* 4, no. 2 (2019): 158–175.

O'Mara, Margaret. *The Code: Silicon Valley and the Remaking of America*. New York: Penguin, 2019.

O'Reilly, Tim. "What Is Web 2.0," September 30, 2005. https://www.oreilly.com/pub/a/web2/ archive/what-is-web-20.html.

Ortiz-Ospina, Esteban. "The Rise of Social Media." Our World in Data, September 18, 2019. https://ourworldindata.org/rise-of-social-media.

Oruc, Firat, ed. *Sites of Pluralism: Community Politics in the Middle East.* New York: Oxford University Press, 2019.

Osman, Nadda. "'Blackface' Arab Stars Spark Backlash over Tasteless Solidarity with US Protests." Middle East Eye, June 3, 2020. https://www.middleeasteye.net/news/arab-influencers-under-fire-blackface-solidarity-blacklivesmatter.

Otterbeck, Jonas. "Wahhabi Ideology of Social Control versus a New Publicness in Saudi Arabia." *Contemporary Islam* 6 (2012): 341–353.

Ouaras, Karim. "Tagging in Algeria: Graffiti as Aesthetic Claim and Protest." *African Studies* 23, nos. 1–2 (2018): 173–190.

Owen, Roger. "The Arab Economies in the 1970s." *Middle East Report* 100 (1981). https://merip.org/1981/11/the-arab-economies-in-the-1970s/.

Owen, Taylor. *Disruptive Power: The Crisis of the State in the Digital Age.* Oxford: Oxford University Press, 2005.

Oxford Business Group. "Strategies to Transform Jordan into a Digital Economy and Leading ICT Regional Centre," 2018. https://oxfordbusinessgroup.com/overview/major-contributor-strategies-target-transformation-digital-economy-and-leading-regional-centre.

Pace, Jonathan. "The Concept of Digital Capitalism." *Communication Theory* 28 (2018): 254–269.

Pack, Howard. "Asian Successes vs. Middle Eastern Failures: The Role of Technology Transfer in Economic Development." *Issues* 24, no. 3 (2008). https://issues.org/pack/.

Pagliery, Jose. "The Inside Story of the Biggest Hack in History." CNN Business, 2015. https://money.cnn.com/2015/08/05/technology/aramco-hack/index.html.

Pahuja, Raj. "The Global Rise of eSports and the Importance of Being Aware of Local Laws in Order to Be Successful in the Middle East." Al Tamimi & Co., September 2017. https://www.tamimi.com/law-update-articles/global-rise-esports-importance-aware-local-laws-order-successful-middle-east/.

Palestinian Museum. https://www.palmuseum.org/.

Palestinian National Internet Naming Authority. "Promote Palestine." https://www.pnina.ps/.

Paracha, Zubair. "Anghami Commits $3 Million Worth of Free Audio Ads for Small Businesses on Its Music Stream Service." MENAbytes, April 20, 2020. https://www.menabytes.com/anghami-free-ads/.

Paracha, Zubair. "Arabic Audiobook Startup Kitab Sawti Gets Acquired by Storytel." MENAbytes, July 8, 2020. https://www.menabytes.com/kitab-sawti-storytel/.

Paracha, Zubair. "Mubadala Launches $150 Million Fund of Funds and $100 Million Direct Fund, to Invest in Startups in MENA." MENAbytes, October 21, 2019. https://www.menabytes.com/mubadala-mena/.

Paragi, Beáta. *Foreign Aid in the Middle East: In Search of Peace and Democracy.* London: I.B. Tauris, 2019.

Parcero, Osiris, and James Ryan. "Becoming a Knowledge Economy." *Journal of the Knowledge Economy* 8, no. 4 (2017): 1146–1173.

Paul, Katie. "Chairman of Saudi Media Group MBC Allowed to Travel to Dubai." Reuters, May 29, 2018. https://www.reuters.com/article/saudi-arrests-mbc-idUSL5N1SZ25S.

Pax, Salam. *Salam Pax: The Clandestine Diary of an Ordinary Iraqi.* New York: Grove, 2003.

Pellicer, Miquel, and Eva Wegner. "Quantitative Research in MENA Political Science." In *Political Science Research in the Middle East and North Africa: Methodological and Ethical Challenges,* edited by Janine Clark and Francesco Cavatorta, 187–196. Oxford: Oxford University Press, 2018.

Pelton, Joseph, and John Howkins. *Satellites International.* New York: Stockton, 1998.

Pepe, Teresa. *Blogging from Egypt: Digital Literature, 2005–2016.* Edinburgh: Edinburgh University Press, 2019.

Perlmutter, David. *Blogwars.* Oxford: Oxford University Press, 2008.

Perlroth, Nicole. "Hacking Group Claims N.S.A. Infiltrated Mideast Banking System." *New York Times*, April 16, 2017. https://www.nytimes.com/2017/04/15/us/shadow-brokers-nsa-hack-middle-east.html.

Perlroth, Nicole. "In Cyber Attack on Saudi Firm, U.S. Sees Iran Fighting Back." *New York Times*, October 24, 2012. https://www.nytimes.com/2012/10/24/business/global/cyberattack-on-saudi-oil-firm-disquiets-us.html.

Phillips, Angela. *Journalism in Context: Practice and Theory for the Digital Age.* New York: Routledge, 2005.

Philo, Chris, and Kate Swanson. "Afterword: Global Portraits and Local Snapshots." In *Telling Young Lives: Portraits of Global Youth*, edited by Craig Jeffrey and Jane Dyson, 193–208. Philadelphia: Temple University Press, 2008.

Piracy Monitor. "beoutQ: Notorious Pirate Is Down, but Its Echo Reverberates," May 6, 2020. https://piracymonitor.org/the-impact-of-beoutq-piracy-on-bein-media/.

Plantin, Jean-Christophe, and Aswin Punathambekar. "Digital Media Infrastructures: Pipes, Platforms, and Politics." *Media, Culture & Society* 41, no. 2 (2019): 163–174.

Platt, Gordon. "GCC Mall Culture Meets the Future." *Global Finance*, July–August 2017. https://www.gfmag.com/magazine/julyaugust-2017/gcc-mall-culture-meets-future.

Pollock, David. *The Arab Street? Public Opinion in the Arab World.* Washington, DC: Washington Institute for Near Eastern Policy, 1992.

Pormann, Peter. "The Arab 'Cultural Awakening (*Nahda*),' 1870–1950, and the Classical Tradition." *International Journal of the Classical Tradition* 13, no. 1 (2006): 3–20.

Prashad, Vijay. *Arab Spring, Libyan Winter.* Oakland, CA: AK Press, 2012.

Pressman, Jeremy. "Power without Influence: The Bush Administration's Foreign Policy Failure in the Middle East." *International Security* 33, no. 4 (2009): 149–179.

Pupic, Tamara. "In the Pursuit of Greatness: Instabeat Founder Hind Hobeika." Entrepreneur Middle East, November 19, 2019. https://www.entrepreneur.com/article/342524.

PwC. "MENA Entertainment and Media Outlook 2020–2024," March 2021. https://www.pwc.com/m1/en/publications/documents/mena-entertainment-media-outlook-2020-2024.pdf.

PwC. "US$320 Billion by 2030? The Potential Impact of AI in the Middle East," 2018. https://www.pwc.com/m1/en/publications/documents/economic-potential-ai-middle-east.pdf.

PwC. "What Doctor? Why AI and Robotics Will Define New Health," June 2017. https://www.pwc.com/gx/en/industries/healthcare/publications/ai-robotics-new-health/ai-robotics-new-health.pdf.

Qatar News Agency. "4th Arab Digital Content Forum Concluded in Doha." *Gulf Times*, October 7, 2020. https://www.gulf-times.com/story/674770/4th-Arab-Digital-Content-Forum-concluded-in-Doha.

Qatar News Agency. "Qatar 2022 Hayya Card," November 13, 2022. https://www.qna.org.qa/en/News-Area/Special-News/2022-11/13/0052-qatar-2022-hayya-card-exclusive-gateway-to-fifa-world-cup-qatar-2022.

Queen Rania Foundation. "Resources for Early Childhood Development." https://www.qrf.org/en/educational-resources/resources-early-childhood-development.

Qui, Winston. "Google's Blue-Raman Cable to Create New Eurasia Route through Israel." Submarine Cable Networks, April 15, 2020. https://www.submarinenetworks.com/en/systems/asia-europe-africa/blue-raman/google-s-blue-raman-cable-creates-new-route-across-israel.

Radcliffe, Damian. "AI in the Middle East: Here's What You Need to Know." ZDNet, August 20, 2020. https://www.zdnet.com/article/ai-in-the-middle-east-heres-what-you-need-to-know/.

Radcliffe, Damian. "COVID Hit Startups Badly, but Something Surprising Is Happening." ZDNet, November 19, 2020. https://www.zdnet.com/article/covid-hit-startups-badly-but-something-surprising-is-happening/.

Radcliffe, Damian. "E-Government in the GCC Countries: Promises and Impediments." In *Digital Middle East: State and Society in the Middle East*, edited by Mohamed Zayani, 239–260. Oxford: Oxford University Press, 2018.

Radcliffe, Damian. "Skype Banned, WhatsApp Blocked: What's Middle East's Problem with Messenger Apps?" ZDNet, December 11, 2017. https://www.zdnet.com/article/skype-ban ned-whatsapp-blocked-whats-middle-easts-problem-with-messenger-apps/.

Radsch, Courtney. "Core to Commonplace: The Evolution of Egypt's Blogosphere." *Arab Media and Society* 6 (September 2008). https://www.arabmediasociety.com/core-to-commonpl ace-the-evolution-of-egypts-blogosphere/.

Radsch, Courtney. "Treating the Internet as the Enemy in the Middle East." Committee to Protect Journalists, April 27, 2015. https://cpj.org/2015/04/attacks-on-the-press-treating-inter net-as-enemy-in-middle-east.php.

Radwan, Rawan. "Why China Is a Natural Partner for Saudi Arabia in Its Quest to Become a Tech Innovation Leader." *Arab News*, December 7, 2002. https://www.arabnews.com/node/ 2212481/saudi-arabia.

Rahmani, Naeemah. "Children Internet Addiction: A Digital Crime" [in Arabic]. *Journal of Heritage* 12 (2014): 69–80. https://platform.almanhal.com/Files/2/46573.

Ramady, Mohamed, ed. *The Political Economy of Wasta: Use and Abuse of Social Capital Networking*. Cham, Switzerland: Springer, 2016.

Rannard, Georgina. "Saudi Wastes No Time to Rap at the Wheel." BBC News, June 29, 2018. https://www.bbc.com/news/world-middle-east-44659099?ocid=socialflow_twitter.

Raz, Daniella. "The Arab World's Digital Divide." Arab Barometer, December 25, 2020. https:// www.arabbarometer.org/2020/09/the-mena-digital-divide/.

Refai, Deena. "Tahrir Tech." *Cairo Review of Global Affairs* 13 (2014). https://www.thecairorev iew.com/midan/tahrir-tech/.

Regier, Terry, and Muhammad Khalidi. "The Arab Street: Tracking a Political Metaphor." *Middle East Journal* 63, no. 1 (2009): 11–29.

Renard, Amélie Le. "The Politics of Unveiling Saudi Women: Between Postcolonial Fantasies and the Surveillance State." Jadaliyya, December 15, 2014. https://www.jadaliyya.com/Details/ 31570.

Renard, Amélie Le. "Young Urban Saudi Women's Transgressions of Official Rules and the Production of a New Social Group." *Journal of Middle East Women's Studies* 9, no. 3 (2013): 108–135.

Reporters without Borders. "Syria: Annual Report 2007." http://www.rsf.org/article.php3?id_arti cle=20777.

Reynolds, Dwight. *The Cambridge Companion to Modern Arab Culture*. Cambridge: Cambridge University Press, 2015.

Rheingold, Howard. *The Virtual Community: Homesteading on the Electronic Frontier*. New York: Addison-Wesley, 1993.

Riegert, Kristina. "Understanding Popular Arab Bloggers: From Public Spheres to Cultural Citizens." *International Journal of Communication* 9 (2015): 458–477. https://ijoc.org/ index.php/ijoc/article/view/2627.

Riegert, Kristina, and Gail Ramsay. "Activists, Individualists, and Comics: The Counter-Publicness of Lebanese Blogs." *Television and New Media* 14, no. 4 (2012): 286–303.

Right, Mindy. "Most-Followed Politicians on Twitter, 2019." *CEO World Magazine*, June 23, 2019. https://ceoworld.biz/2019/06/23/most-followed-politicians-on-twitter-2019/.

Rinnawi, Khalil. "Imagined Coherence: Transnational Media and the Arab Diaspora in Europe." In *Media Evolution on the Eve of the Arab Spring*, edited by Leila Hudson, Adel Iskandar, and Mimi Kirk, 209–220. New York: Palgrave Macmillan, 2014.

Rist, Gilbert, and Patrick Camiller. *The History of Development: From Western Origins to Global Faith*. London: Zed Books, 2019.

Robinson, Melia. "Here's Why Israel Could Be the Next Silicon Valley." Business Insider, June 14, 2016. https://www.businessinsider.com/why-israel-could-be-the-next-silicon-valley-2016-6.

Rolfe, Brett. "Building an Electronic Repertoire of Contention." *Social Movement Studies* 4, no. 1 (2005): 65–74.

Romm, Robin, ed. *Double Bind: Women on Ambition*. New York: Liveright, 2017.

Rossel, Pierre, and Matthias Finger. "Conceptualizing E-Governance." In *Proceedings of the First International Conference on Theory and Practice of Electronic Governance (ICEGOV '07)*, 399–407. New York: Association for Computing Machinery, 2007. https://doi.org/10.1145/1328057.1328141.

Rossel, Pierre, and Matthias Finger. "Conceptualizing E-Governance." *Management* (2007): 399–407.

Rottenburg, Richard, Oulimata Gueye, Julien McHardy, and Philipp Ziegler, eds. *Digital Imaginaries. African Positions beyond the Binary*. Bielefeld, Germany: Kerber, 2021.

Rudner, Martin. "'Electronic Jihad': The Internet as Al Qaeda's Catalyst for Global Terror." *Studies in Conflict and Terrorism* 40, no. 1 (2017): 10–23.

Rushdi, Duqah, and Anthony Yazitzis. "Middle East Fintech Study." Deloitte, June 2020. https://www2.deloitte.com/xe/en/pages/financial-services/articles/dme-fintech-study.html.

Saad, Sabrine, Stéphane Bazan, and Christophe Varin. "Asymmetric Cyber-Warfare between Israel and Hezbollah: The Web as a New Strategic Battlefield." Proceedings of the ACM Web Science Conference, June 2011. https://pdfs.semanticscholar.org/1656/20de2a4d7c37bf46064036c9704f757bfc52.pdf.

Sabbagh, Karim, Mohamad Mourad, Wassim Kabbara, Ramez Shehadi, and Hatem Samman. "Understanding the Arab Digital Generation." Wamda, October 10, 2012. https://www.wamda.com/2012/10/understanding-the-arab-digital-generation-report.

Sabry, Tarik. "On Historicism, the Aporia of Time and the Arab Revolutions." *Middle East Journal of Culture and Communication* 5, no. 1 (2012): 80–85.

Sabry, Tarik, and Joe F. Khalil, eds. *Culture, Time and Publics in the Arab World: Media Public Space and Temporality in the Middle East*. London: I.B. Tauris, 2019.

Sabry, Tarik, and Nisrine Mansour. *Children and Screen Media in Changing Arab Contexts*. Cham, Switzerland: Palgrave Pivot, 2019.

Saeed, Khaldoun, and Hazem Badr. "Google Launches 'Abtal Al Internet' Security Program for Children." *Asharq Al Awsat*, October 2, 2018. https://english.aawsat.com/home/article/1413676/google-launches-%E2%80%98abtal-al-internet%E2%80%99-security-program-children.

Said, Edward W. *Orientalism*. New York: Vintage, 1979.

Sakr, Naomi. *Satellite Realms: Transnational Television, Globalization and the Middle East*. London: I.B. Tauris, 2001.

Sakr, Naomi. "Satellite Television and Development in the Middle East." *Middle East Report* 210 (1999). https://www.merip.org/mer/mer210/satellite-television-development-middle-east.

Sanger, David, and Mark Mazzetti. "U.S. Had Cyberattack Plan if Iran Nuclear Dispute Led to Conflict." *New York Times*, February 16, 2016. https://www.nytimes.com/2016/02/17/world/middleeast/us-had-cyberattack-planned-if-iran-nuclear-negotiations-failed.html.

Sardar, Ziauddin. *Science and Technology in the Middle East*. London: Longman, 1982.

Sardarizadeh, Shayan. "Facebook Removes 'Fake' UAE, Egypt Accounts for Paid Disinformation Operation." BBC Monitoring, October 7, 2019. https://monitoring.bbc.co.uk/product/c2015157.

Satter, Raphael, and Christopher Bing. "'Mercenary' Hacker Group Runs Rampant in Middle East." Reuters, October 7, 2020. https://www.reuters.com/article/blackberry-cyber-mercenary-hackers-idINL1N2GQ21K.

Saudi Ministry of Economy and Planning. "Saudi Arabia's Ninth Development Plan, 2010–2014." https://www.mep.gov.sa/DocumentsLibrary/NinthDevelopmentPlan/Ninth%20Development%20Plan%20-%20Chapter%204%20-%20National%20Economy%20Under%20The%20Ninth%20Development%20Plan.pdf.

Schanzer, Jonathan. "Yemen's War on Terror." *Orbis* 48, no. 3 (2004): 517–531.

Schanzer, Jonathan, and Steven Miller. *Facebook Fatwa: Saudi Clerics, Wahhabi Islam, and Social Media*. Washington, DC: FDD, 2012.

Schiller, Daniel. *Digital Capitalism: Networking the Global Market System*. Cambridge, MA: MIT Press, 2000.

Schiwietz, Christine. *American Higher Education Goes Global*. Austin: Lioncrest, 2022.

Schleiner, Anne-Marie. *Transnational Play: Piracy, Urban Art, and Mobile Games*. Amsterdam: Amsterdam University Press, 2000.

Schleusener, Luke. "From Blog to Street: The Bahraini Public Sphere in Transition." *Arab Media and Society* 1 (2007). https://www.arabmediasociety.com/from-blog-to-street-the-bahra ini-public-sphere-in-transition/.

Schroeder, Christopher. "How Hind Hobeika Created the Google Glass of Swim Goggles." *Fast Company*, August 27, 2013. https://www.fastcompany.com/3016356/how-hind-hobeika-created-the-google-glass-of-swim-goggles.

Segal, Aaron. "The Middle East: What Money Can't Buy." In *Learning by Doing: Science and Technology in the Developing World*, edited by Aaron Segal, 83–105. New York: Routledge, 1987.

Seib, Philip. "Public Diplomacy and the Media in the Middle East." In *Bullets and Bulletins*, edited by Mohamed Zayani and Suzi Mirgani, 179–198. New York: Oxford University Press, 2016.

Seib, Philip, ed. *Toward a New Public Diplomacy: Redirecting U.S. Foreign Policy*. New York: Palgrave Macmillan, 2009.

Seib, Philip. "US Public Diplomacy and the Terrorism Challenge." *The Hague Journal of Diplomacy* 14 (2019): 154–168.

Senft, Theresa. "Microcelebrity and the Branded Self." In *A Companion to New Media Dynamics*, edited by John Hartley, Jean Burgess, and Axel Bruns, 346–354. Malden, MA: Wiley, 2013.

Serrano, Sofia. "10 Startups Join the First 'Google for Startups Accelerator' in MENA." Campaign Middle East, February 11, 2021. https://campaignme.com/10-startups-join-the-first-goo gle-for-startups-accelerator-in-mena/.

Sexton, Michael, and Eliza Campbell, eds. *Cyber War and Cyber Peace in the Middle East: Digital Conflict in the Cradle of Civilization*. London: I.B. Tauris, 2022.

Shafiee, Katayoun. "Science and Technology Studies (STS), Modern Middle East History, and the Infrastructural Turn." *History Compass* 17, no. 2 (2019). https://doi.org/10.1111/hic3.12598.

Shah, Hemant. *The Production of Modernization: Daniel Lerner, Mass Media, and the Passing of Traditional Society*. Philadelphia: Temple University Press, 2011.

Shapiro, Bee. "Is Huda Kattan the Most Influential Beauty Blogger in the World?" *New York Times*, March 20, 2017. https://www.nytimes.com/2017/03/20/fashion/is-huda-kattan-the-kim-kardashian-west-of-beauty-bloggers.html.

Shareef, Sami. *Arab Satellites: A Critical Overview* [in Arabic]. Cairo: Dar Ennahda Al Arabiya, 2004.

Shaver, Lea, and Nagla Rizk, eds. *Access to Knowledge in Egypt: New Research on Intellectual Property, Innovation and Development*. London: Bloomsbury, 2010.

Shehabat, Ahmad. "The Social Media Cyber-War: The Unfolding Events in the Syrian Revolution." *Global Media Journal* 6, no. 2 (2012). http://www.hca.westernsydney.edu.au/gmjau/arch ive/v6_2012_2/ahmad_shehabat%20_RA.html.

Shiblak, Abbas. "Arabia's Bedoon." In *Statelessness and Citizenship: A Comparative Study on the Benefits of Nationality*, edited by Brad Blitzand and Maureen Lynch, 172–193. Cheltenham, UK: Edward Elgar, 2011.

Shirky, Clay. *Here Comes Everybody: The Power of Organizing without Organizations*. New York: Penguin, 2011.

Shirky, Clay. "The Political Power of Social Media." *Foreign Affairs*, January–February 2010. https://www.foreignaffairs.com/articles/2010-12-20/political-power-social-media.

Shishkina, Alisa, and Leonid Issaev. "Internet Censorship in Arab Countries: Religious and Moral Aspects." *Religions* 9, no. 11 (2018): 358.

Shuqum, Raied. "E-Commerce a Fast-Growing Trend in the Middle East." *Arab Weekly*, May 22, 2015. https://thearabweekly.com/e-commerce-fast-growing-trend-arab-world.

Siapera, Eugenia. "Minority Activism on the Web: Between Deliberative Democracy and Multiculturalism." *Journal of Ethnic and Migration Studies* 31, no. 3 (2005): 499–519.

Sidani, Yusuf, and Jon Thornberry. "Nepotism in the Arab World: An Institutional Theory Perspective." *Business Ethics Quarterly* 23, no. 1 (2013): 69–96.

Silva, Marco. "Algeria Protests: How Disinformation Spread on Social Media." BBC News, September 16, 2019. https://www.bbc.com/news/blogs-trending-49679634.

Silverman, Craig, Jane Lytvynenko, and William Kung. "Disinformation for Hire: How a New Breed of PR Firms Is Selling Lies Online." Buzzfeed News, January 6, 2020. https://www.buzzfeednews.com/article/craigsilverman/disinformation-for-hire-black-pr-firms.

Silverstone, Roger. "What's New about New Media? Introduction." *New Media & Society* 1, no. 1 (1999): 10–12.

Simon, Andrew. *Media of the Masses: Cassette Culture in Modern Egypt.* Stanford, CA: Stanford University Press, 2022.

Singer, Hans. "The 1980s: A Lost Decade." In *Growth and External Debt Management,* edited by Hans Singer and Soumitra Sharma, 46–56. London: Palgrave Macmillan, 1989.

Šisler, Vit. "Digital Arabs: Representation in Video Games." *European Journal of Cultural Studies* 11, no. 2 (2008): 203–220.

Smidi, Adam, and Shahin, Saif. "Social Media and Social Mobilisation in the Middle East: A Survey of Research on the Arab Spring." *India Quarterly* 73, no. 2 (2017): 196–209.

Smith, Matt. "The Middle East's Other Revolution: Tech Trends from Morocco to Oman." *Wired,* January 23, 2022. https://wired.me/technology/middle-east-technology-trends-from-morocco-to-oman/.

Smith, Sophie. "Digital Transformation in the GCC." Euro-Gulf Information Centre, 2020. https://www.egic.info/digital-transformation-in-the-gcc.

Society.Culture.Lebanon Conference. "Towards a New Lebanon," 1995. http://www.lebanon.com/scl/.

Soliman, Mohammed. "COVID-19 and the Digital Landscape in the Gulf." Middle East Institute, May 13, 2020. https://www.mei.edu/publications/covid-19-and-digital-landscape-gulf.

Soliman, Mohammed. "How Tech Is Cementing the UAE-Israel Alliance." Middle East Institute, May 11, 2021. https://mei.edu/publications/how-tech-cementing-uae-israel-alliance.

Soliman, Mohammed. "The Gulf has a 5G Conundrum and Open RAN is the Key to its Tech Sovereignty." Middle East Institute, January 12, 2022. https://www.mei.edu/publications/gulf-has-5g-conundrum-and-open-ran-key-its-tech-sovereignty.

Sosale, Sujatha. "Toward a Critical Genealogy of Communication, Development and Social Change." In *New Frontiers in International Communication Theory,* edited by Mehdi Semati, 33–54. Oxford: Rowman & Littlefield, 2004.

Soyres, François de, Mohamed Abdel Jelil, Caroline Cerruti, and Leah Kiwara. "What Kenya's Mobile Money Success Could Mean for the Arab World." World Bank, October 3, 2018. https://www.worldbank.org/en/news/feature/2018/10/03/what-kenya-s-mobile-money-success-could-mean-for-the-arab-world.

Spivak, Gayatri. *An Aesthetic Education in the Era of Globalization.* Cambridge, MA: Harvard University Press, 2013.

Springborg, Robert. "Globalization and Its Discontents in the MENA Region." *Middle East Policy* 23, no. 2 (2016): 146–160.

Springer, Paul. *Cyber Warfare.* Santa Barbara, CA: ABC-CLIO, 2015.

Sreberny, Annabelle. *Small Media, Big Revolution.* Minneapolis: University of Minnesota Press, 1994.

Sreberny, Annabelle. "Women's Digital Activism in a Changing Middle East." *International Journal of Middle East Studies* 47, no. 2 (2015): 357–361.

Sreberney, Annabelle, and Gholam Kiabany. *Blogistan: The Internet and Politics in Iran.* London: I.B. Tauris, 2010.

Stalder, Felix. *The Digital Condition.* Translated by Valentine Pakis. Cambridge: Polity, 2018.

Star, Susan, and Geoffery Bowker. "How to Infrastructure." In *Handbook of New Media*, edited by Sonia Livingstone and Leah Lievrouw, 151–162. London: SAGE, 2002.

Starosielski, Nicole. *The Undersea Network*. Durham, NC: Duke University Press, 2015.

Stassen, Murray. "After Previously Being Exclusively Available on Deezer in MENA, Warner-Backed Rotana Music Signs Strategic Partnership with Anghami." Music Business Worldwide, April 6, 2022. https://www.musicbusinessworldwide.com/after-previously-being-exclusiv ely-available-on-deezer-in-mena-warner-backed-rotana-music-signs-strategic-partnership-with-anghami/.

Stassen, Murray. "Why Anghami, with over 1M Paying Users, Doesn't Feel Threatened by Spotify in the Middle East." Music Business Worldwide, March 5, 2019. https://www.musicbusine ssworldwide.com/anghami-with-over-1m-paying-users-doesnt-feel-threatened-by-spotify-in-the-middle-east/.

Statista. "Expected Share of Internet of Things Use Case Spending in the Middle East and North Africa in 2021, by Sector," November 16, 2020. https://www.statista.com/statistics/1181 170/mena-share-of-iot-use-cases-spending-by-sector/.

Statista. "Leading Countries Based on Number of Twitter Users as of January 2022." https://www. statista.com/statistics/242606/number-of-active-twitter-users-in-selected-countries/.

Statista. "Most Used Social Media Platforms in Saudi Arabia in 2022." https://www.statista.com/ statistics/1318233/saudi-arabia-most-used-social-media-platforms-by-share-of-users/.

Statista. "Number of Online Stores and Platforms in Saudi Arabia from 2018–2021," June 13, 2022. https://www.statista.com/statistics/1311861/saudi-arabia-number-of-online-stores-and-platforms/.

Statista. "Share of Internet Users Who Are Single Online Daters Worldwide as of Q4 in 2019." https://www.statista.com/statistics/1199389/share-of-single-online-daters-worldwide/.

Steel, Griet. "Navigating (Im)Mobility: Female Entrepreneurship and Social Media in Khartoum." *Africa* 87, no. 2 (2017): 233–252.

Steinmueller, Edward. "ICTs and the Possibility for Leapfrogging by Developed Countries." *International Labor Review* 140, no. 2 (2001): 193–210.

Stetter, Stephan. *The Middle East and Globalization: Encounters and Horizons*. New York: Palgrave Macmillan, 2012.

Stevens, Paul. "The Political Ways of Paradox." *English Literary Renaissance* 26, no. 2 (1996): 203–224.

Su, Alice. "How One Syrian Fought to the Death for a Free Internet." *Wired*, September 27, 2017. https://www.wired.com/story/how-one-syrian-fought-to-the-death-for-a-free-internet/.

Sullivan, Kevin. "Saudi Youth Use Cellphone Savvy to Outwit the Sentries of Romance." *Washington Post*, August 2, 2006, A01.

Sun, Rivera. "Blue Revolution: Kuwaiti Women Gain Suffrage." CounterPunch, May 12, 2016. https://www.counterpunch.org/2016/05/12/blue-revolution-kuwaiti-women-gain-suffrage/.

Tadros, Mahfouz. "The Arab Gulf States and the Knowledge Economy: Challenges and Opportunities." Arab Gulf States Institute in Washington, Policy Paper no. 6, July 14, 2015. https://agsiw.org/wp-content/uploads/2015/07/Tadros_Knowledge-Economy_Rev1.pdf.

Tantawi, Olfa. "'Modern' Preachers: Strategies and Mixed Discourses." In *Religious Broadcasting in the Middle East*, edited by Khaled Hroub, 103–125. London: Hurst, 2012.

Tartaglione, Nancy. "Jon Stewart Bids Farewell to Egyptian Satire as Pal Bassem Youssef's Show Cancelled." Deadline, June 3, 2014. https://deadline.com/2014/06/jon-stewart-farewell-to-egyptian-satire-bassem-youssef-show-cancelled-pressure-video-739390/.

Tawil-Souri, Helga. "Digital Occupation: Gaza's High-Tech Enclosure." *Journal of Palestine Studies* 41, no. 2 (2012): 27–43.

Tayie, Samy. "Children and Mass Media in the Arab World: A Second Level Analysis." In *Empowerment through Media Education: An Intercultural Dialogue*, edited by Ulla Carlsson, Samy Tayie, Geneviève Delaunay, and José Tornero, 67–88. Gothenburg: International

Clearinghouse on Children, Youth and Media, 2008. http://norden.diva-portal.org/smash/get/diva2:1534775/FULLTEXT01.pdf.

Taylor, Charles. *Modern Social Imaginaries*. Durham, NC: Duke University Press, 2003.

Tech Plugged. "Anghami, the First Platform to Hit over 10 Billion Streams Milestone in MENA in 2019," December 19, 2019. https://techplugged.com/anghami-the-first-platform-to-hit-over-10-billion-streams-milestone-in-mena-in-2019/.

Therwath, Ingrid. "Cyber-Hindutva: Hindu Nationalism, the Diaspora and the Web." *Social Science Information* 51, no. 4 (2012): 551–577.

Thieux, Laurence. "Les réseaux sociaux: Une arme à double tranchant pour les mouvements sociaux et leur lutte contre le 'pouvoir' en Algérie." European Institute of the Mediterranean, Barcelona, 2020. https://www.iemed.org/publication/les-reseaux-sociaux-une-arme-a-double-tranchant-pour-les-mouvements-sociaux-et-leur-lutte-contre-le-pouvoir-en-algerie/.

Third, Amanda, and Kai-Ti Kao. "ICT Leapfrogging Policy and Development in the Third World." In *Encyclopedia of Information Ethics and Security*, edited by Marian Quigley, 326–343. Hershey, PA: IGI Global, 2007.

Thomas, Pradip. "Development Communication and Social Change in Historical Context." In *The Handbook of Development Communication and Social Change*, edited by Karin Wilkins, Thomas Tufte, and Rafael Obregon, 7–19. Chichester: John Wiley, 2014.

Thompson, John. *The Media and Modernity: A Social Theory of the Media*. Stanford: Stanford University Press, 1995.

Thompson, Mark. *Being Young, Saudi, and Male: Identity and Politics in a Globalized Kingdom*. Cambridge: Cambridge University Press, 2019.

Tilly, Charles. *The Contentious French: Four Centuries of Popular Struggle*. Cambridge, MA: Harvard University Press, 1986.

Tilly, Charles. *Regimes and Repertoires*. Chicago: University of Chicago Press, 2006.

TIMEP. "Export of Surveillance to Mena Countries." Tahrir Institute for Middle East Policy, October 23, 2019. https://timep.org/reports-briefings/timep-brief-export-of-surveillance-to-mena-countries.

TIMEP. "Use of Surveillance Technology in MENA." Tahrir Institute for Middle East Policy, October 23, 2019. https://timep.org/reports-briefings/timep-brief-use-of-surveillance-technology-in-mena/.

Tkacheva, Olesya, Lowell Schwartz, Martin Libicki, Julie Taylor, Jeffrey Martini, and Caroline Baxter. *Internet Freedom and Political Space*. Washington, DC: RAND, 2013.

Tok, Evren, Jason McSparren, Maha Al Merekhi, Hanaa Elghaish, and Fatema Al Mohammad. "Crafting Smart Cities in the Gulf Region: A Comparison of Masdar and Lusail." In *Handbook of Research on Digital Media and Creative Technologies*, edited by Dew Harrison, 448–460. Hershey, PA: IGI Global, 2015.

Toukan, Hanan. "The Palestinian Museum." *Radical Philosophy* 2, no. 3 (2018): 10–22. https://www.radicalphilosophy.com/article/the-palestinian-museum#fnref6.

Trade Arabia. "Data Security 'Biggest Challenge for GCC Companies.'" Zawya, December 16, 2019. https://www.zawya.com/mena/en/business/storyData_security_biggest_challenge_for_GCC_companies_survey-SNG_162331285.

Treré, Emiliano. *Hybrid Media Activism: Ecologies, Imaginaries, Algorithms*. London: Routledge, 2019.

Tucker, Judith, and Miriam Lowi. "Saudi Arabia's Reforms Expand the Space for Women, but Still Deny Them a Voice of Their Own." *Washington Post*, August 11, 2018. https://www.washingtonpost.com/news/democracy-post/wp/2018/08/11/saudi-arabias-reforms-expand-the-space-for-women-but-still-deny-them-a-voice-of-their-own/?utm_term=.4f6b88eb6160.

UAE Government Portal. "UAE Centennial 2071," 2021. https://u.ae/en/about-the-uae/strategies-initiatives-and-awards/strategies-plans-and-visions/innovation-and-future-shaping/uae-centennial-2071.

UAE Government Portal. "UAE Strategy for Artificial Intelligence," 2017. https://u.ae/en/about-the-uae/strategies-initiatives-and-awards/strategies-plans-and-visions/government-services-and-digital-transformation/uae-strategy-for-artificial-intelligence.

Ulrich, Brian. "Historicizing Arab Blogs." *Arab Media and Society* 8 (2009). https://www.arabm ediasociety.com/historicizing-arab-blogs-reflections-on-the-transmission-of-ideas-and-info rmation-in-middle-eastern-history.

UN. "Gender Mainstreaming." https://www.unwomen.org/en/how-we-work/un-system-coord ination/gender-mainstreaming.

UN. "E-Government Survey 2020." https://publicadministration.un.org/egovkb/en-us/Repo rts/UN-E-Government-Survey-2020.

UN. "Sustainable Development Goals." https://www.un.org/sustainabledevelopment/sustaina ble-development-goals/.

UNCTAD. "ICT Policy Review: National E-Commerce Strategy for Egypt." UN Conference on Trade and Development, 2017. https://unctad.org/system/files/official-document/dtlsti ct2017d3_en.pdf.

UNCTAD. "The UNCTAD B2C E-Commerce Index 2020." United Nations Conference on Trade and Development, 2020. https://unctad.org/system/files/official-document/tn_unctad_ ict4d17_en.pdf.

UNDP. "Arab Human Development Report 2016: Youth and the Prospects for Human Development in Changing Reality." UN Development Programme, November 2016. https://hdr.undp.org/content/arab-human-development-report-2016-youth-and-prospe cts-human-development-changing-reality.

UNDP and MBRF. "Global Knowledge Index 2021." https://www.undp.org/sites/g/files/zskgke 326/files/migration/arabstates/GKI-Report-2021---CPs-3_Full_compressed.pdf.

UNESCO. "Information and Communication Technology (ICT) in Education in Five Arab States." UN Development Program, April 2013. http://uis.unesco.org/sites/default/files/ documents/information-and-communication-technology-ict-in-education-in-five-arab-sta tes-a-comparative-analysis-of-ict-integration-and-e-readiness-in-schools-en_0.pdf.

UN Habitat. "Egypt's Clean Fuels Initiative." https://unhabitat.org/sites/default/files/downl oad-manager-files/Module%206%20-%20Annexure%20E%20case%20study%20Ca iro.pdf.

Uniacke, Robert. "Authoritarianism in the Information Age: State Branding, Depoliticizing and 'De-Civilizing' of Online Civil Society." *British Journal of Middle Eastern Studies* 48, no. 5 (2021): 979–999.

UNICEF. "Children in a Digital World." 2017. https://www.unicef.org/media/48601/file.

UNICEF. "How Many Children and Young People Have Internet Access at Home? Estimating Digital Connectivity during the COVID-19 Pandemic," 2020. https://data.unicef.org/ resources/children-and-young-people-internet-access-at-home-during-covid19/.

UNICEF. "MENA Generation 2030," 2019. https://www.unicef.org/mena/media/4141/file/ MENA-Gen2030.pdf.

Vaast, Melanie. "What Are the Opportunities in the MENA E-Commerce Market." E-Commerce Nation, February 27, 2017. https://www.ecommerce-nation.com/opportunities-mena-ecommerce-market/.

Vacca, John. *Guide to Wireless Network Security*. New York: Springer, 2006.

Valladeres, Carolina. "How We Started the Arab World's Biggest Music Service." BBC News, January 30, 2017. https://www.bbc.com/news/business-38664037.

Vallor, Shannon, ed. *The Oxford Handbook of Philosophy of Technology*. New York: Oxford University Press, 2022.

Van Dijck, José, Thomas Poell, and Martijn de Waal. *The Platform Society: Public Values in a Connective World*. New York: Oxford University Press, 2018.

Vein, Chris. "Why Increasing Digital Arabic Content Is Key for Global Development." *Guardian*, April 28, 2014. http://www.theguardian.com/media-network/media-network-blog/2014/ apr/28/global-development-digital-arabic-content.

Vodafone. "Middle East Barometer Report 2019." https://www.vodafone.qa/en/business/ media/document/1551489531555/vodafone-iot-middle-east-barometer-2019-final.pdf.

Wagner, Ben. "Push-Button Autocracy in Tunisia: Analyzing the Role of Internet Infrastructure, Institutions and International Markets in Creating a Tunisian Censorship Regime." *Telecommunications Policy* 32, no. 6 (2012): 484–492.

WAM. "Dh500,000 Fine If You Use Fraud IP in UAE." Emirates 24/7, July 22, 2016. https://www.emirates247.com/news/emirates/dh500-000-fine-if-you-use-fraud-ip-in-uae-2016-07-22-1.636441.

Wamda. "Enhancing Access: Assessing the Funding Landscape for MENA's Sartups," October 2014. https://www.wamda.com/research/pdf/enhancing-access.

Ward, Robert, and Dankwart Rustow. *Political Modernization in Japan and Turkey*. Princeton, NJ: Princeton University Press, 1964.

Warf, Barney, and Peter Vincent. "Multiple Geographies of the Arab Internet." *Area* 39, no. 1 (2007): 83–96.

Warner, Kelsey. "Crown Prince of Abu Dhabi Unveils One of Middle East's Biggest Defence Groups." *National*, November 5, 2019. https://www.thenational.ae/uae/government/crown-prince-of-abu-dhabi-unveils-one-of-middle-east-s-biggest-defence-groups-1.933512.

Watanabe, Lisa. "Gulf States' Engagement in North Africa: The Role of Foreign Aid." In *The Small Gulf States: Foreign and Security Policies before and after the Arab Spring*, edited by Jean-Marc Rickli and Khalid Almezaini, 168–181. London: Routledge, 2017.

Watts, Clint. *Messing with the Enemy: Surviving in a Social Media World of Hackers, Terrorists, Russians and Fake News*. New York: HarperCollins, 2018.

Weimann, Gabriel. "Terrorist Migration to the Dark Web." *Perspectives on Terrorism* 10, no. 3 (2016): 40–44.

Weldali, Maria. "Awqaf Ministry Opens New Technological Channel for Giving." *Jordan Times*, November 7, 2019. http://www.jordantimes.com/news/local/awqaf-ministry-opens-new-technological-channel-giving.

Wendel, Samuel. "Dubai Launches Region's First E-Commerce Free Zone." Forbes Middle East, October 29, 2017. https://www.forbesmiddleeast.com/en/dubai-launches-regions-first-e-commerce-free-zone/.

Westall, Sylvia, and Angus McDowall. "Saudi Arabia's Rulers Adapt Message for Social Media Age." Reuters, May 24, 2016. https://www.reuters.com/article/us-saudi-socialmedia-idUSKCN0YF1P0.

Wheeler, Deborah. *Digital Resistance in the Middle East: New Media Activism in Everyday Life*. Edinburgh: Edinburgh University Press, 2017.

Wheeler, Deborah. "Empowering Publics: Information Technology and Democratization in the Arab World—Lessons from Internet Cafés and Beyond." Oxford Internet Institute, Research Report 11, no. 1, July 2006. https://papers.ssrn.com/sol3/papers.cfm?abstract_id=1308527.

Wheeler, Deborah. "Empowerment Zones: Women, Internet Cafés and Life Transformations in Egypt." *Information Technologies and International Development* 4, no. 2 (2007): 89–104.

Wheeler, Deborah. *The Internet in the Middle East: Global Expectations and Local Imaginations in Kuwait*. Albany: State University of New York Press, 2006.

Wheeler, Deborah. "Saudi Women Driving Change? Rebranding, Resistance, and the Kingdom of Change." *The Journal of the Middle East and Africa* 11, no. 1 (2020): 87–109.

Wilkins, Karin. "Considering 'Traditional Society' in the Middle East: Learning Lerner All Over Again." *Journal of Middle East Media* 6 (2010). https://jmem.gsu.edu/files/2014/08/JMEM-2010_ENG_Wilkins.pdf.

Wilkins, Karin. "Development and Modernization in the Middle East." In *The Handbook of Media and Culture in the Middle East*, edited by Joe F. Khalil, Gholam Khiabany, Tourya Guaaybess, and Blige Yesil, 30–36. Hoboken, NJ: Wiley-Blackwell, 2023.

Wilkins, Karin. *Prisms of Prejudice: Mediating the Middle East from the United States*. Oakland: University of California Press, 2021.

Wilkins, Karin, and Bella Mody. "Reshaping Development Communication: Developing Communication and Communicating Development." *Communication Theory* 11, no. 4 (2001): 385–396.

Wilson, Mark, and Kenneth Corey. "The Role of ICT in Arab Spring Movements." *Netcom* 26, nos. 3–4 (2012): 343–356.

Winkler, Carol, and Kareem Damanhoury. *Proto-State Media System: The Digital Rise of Al Qaeda and ISIS*. New York: Oxford University Press, 2022.

Winston, Brian. *Media Technology and Society: From the Telegraph to the Internet*. London: Routledge, 1998.

Wiseman, Alexander, and Emily Anderson. "ICT Integrated Education and National Innovation Systems in the Gulf Cooperation Council Countries." *Computers and Education* 59, no. 2 (2012): 607–618.

Women to Drive Movement. https://oct26driving.com/.

Woodhams, Samuel. "Digital Authoritarianism Is Rising in the Middle East." Foreign Policy In Focus, August 20, 2019. https://fpif.org/digital-authoritarianism-is-rising-in-the-middle-east/.

World Bank. *Building Knowledge Economies*. Washington, DC: World Bank, 2007. https://elibrary. worldbank.org/doi/abs/10.1596/978-0-8213-6957-9.

World Bank. "Individuals Using the Internet (% of Population): Arab World." World Bank Data, 2021. https://data.worldbank.org/indicator/IT.NET.USER.ZS?most_recent_value_desc= true&locations=1A.

World Bank. "Individuals Using the Internet (% of Population): Syrian Arab Republic." World Bank Data, 2020. https://data.worldbank.org/indicator/IT.NET.USER.ZS?locations=SY.

World Bank. "Labor Force Participation Rate, Female." World Bank Data, 2021. https://data. worldbank.org/indicator/SL.TLF.CACT.FE.ZS.

World Bank, "Literacy Rate, Adult Total (% of People Ages 15 and Above): Middle East and North Africa." World Bank Data, 2020. https://data.worldbank.org/indicator/SE.ADT.LITR. ZS?locations=ZQ.

World Bank. "Research and Development Expenditure (% of GDP)." World Bank Data, 2014. https://data.worldbank.org/indicator/GB.XPD.RSDV.GD.ZS.

World Bank. "School Enrollment, Tertiary (% Gross)—Middle East & North Africa." World Bank Data, 2018. https://data.worldbank.org/indicator/SE.TER.ENRR?locations=ZQ&most_ recent_value_desc=false.

World Bank. "Transforming Arab Economies: Traveling the Knowledge and Innovation Road." World Bank, CMI, EIB, and ISESCO, 2013. https://documents1.worldbank.org/curated/ en/664441468059651205/pdf/827360ESW0v10P00Box379869B00PUBLIC0.pdf.

World Economic Forum. "Digital Policy Playbook 2017: Approaches to National Digital Governance," September 2017. http://www3.weforum.org/docs/White_Paper_Digital_ Policy_Playbook_Approaches_National_Digital_Governance_report_2017.pdf.

World Economic Forum. "Global Gender Gap Report 2022." https://www3.weforum.org/docs/ WEF_GGGR_2022.pdf.

Worrall, James. *International Institutions of the Middle East: The GCC, Arab League and Arab Maghreb Union*. London: Routledge, 2017.

Wyne, Jamil. "Country Insights: Exploring Trends and Challenges to Scale for Startups in Egypt, Jordan, Lebanon and the UAE." Wamda Research Lab, September 2015. http://backend. wamda.com/api/v1/downloads/publications/country-insights.

Yamamoto, Tatsuya. "The Current Situation of ICT Development in the Middle East and ICT Support Policies: The Case of Syrian Arab Republic." *Systemics, Cybernetics and Informatics* 2, no. 2 (2004): 51–55.

Yangyue, Liu. *Competitive Political Regime and Internet Control: Case Studies of Malaysia, Thailand and Indonesia*. Newcastle, UK: Cambridge Scholars, 2015.

Yil-Kaitala, Kirsi. "Revolution 2.0 in Egypt: Pushing for Change, Foreign Influences in a Popular Revolt." *Journal of Political Marketing* 13 (2014): 127–151.

Yin, J. K. "The Electronic Intifada: The Palestinian Online Resistance in the Second Intifada." *Journal of Information Warfare* 18, no. 1 (2009): 1–19.

YouGov and Bayt. "The Skills Gap in the Middle East and North Africa: A Real Problem or a Mere Trifle?," 2016. https://d25d2506sfb94s.cloudfront.net/r/17/The%20Skills%20Gap%20 in%20MENA%20WhitePaper%202016.pdf.

Youmans, William. *An Unlikely Audience: Al Jazeera's Struggle in America*. New York: Oxford University Press, 2017.

Younes, George. "A Generic Five-Stage Model for the Implementation of Mobile Government." *Review of Information and Communication Technology for Development in the Arab Region* 21 (2014): 44–46. https://www.unescwa.org/publications/information-communications-tec hnology-development-21st-issue.

Youngs, Gillian. "Digital Globalization and Democracy: The Territorial Walls Come Tumbling Down." *Development* 54, no. 2 (2011): 147–149.

Youssef, Nouran. "'FinxAr': Fintech Index to Track the Development of the Financial Technology Industry in the Arab World" [in Arabic]. Arab Monetary Fund, April 2021. https://www. amf.org.ae/sites/default/files/publications/2021-12/index-modern-financial-technolog ies-arab-countries.pdf.

Youssif, Tarik. "Development, Growth and Policy Reform in the Middle East and North Africa since 1950." *Journal of Economic Perspective* 18, no. 3 (2004): 91–115.

Zaatar, Mariam, and Ahmad Bodada. "Digital Media and the Construction of Digital Education in the Arab World: Smartphone as a Model" [in Arabic]. *Arab Journal for Media and Youth Culture* 3, no 12 (2020): 33–46. https://platform.almanhal.com/Reader/Article/ 141495.

Zaharna, Rhonda. *Battles to Bridges: US Strategic Communication and Public Diplomacy After 9/11*. New York: Palgrave Macmillan, 2010.

Zahidi, Saadia. *Fifty Million Rising: The New Generation of Working Women Transforming the Muslim World*. New York: Nation, 2018.

Zahlan, Antoine. *Technology Transfer and Change in the Arab World*. New York: Pergamon, 1978.

Zakaria, Norhayati. "From the Souk to the Cyber-Souk: Acculturating to E-Commerce in the MENA Region." In *Digital Middle East: State and Society in the Information Age*, edited by Mohamed Zayani, 143–166. Oxford: Oxford University Press, 2018.

Zanini, Michele, and Sean Edwards. "The Networking of Terror in the Information Age." In *Networks and Netwars: The Future of Terror, Crime, and Militancy*, edited by John Arquilla and David Ronfeldt, 29–60. Santa Monica, CA: RAND, 2001.

Zanoyan, Vahan. "After the Oil Boom: The Holiday Ends in the Gulf." *Foreign Affairs* 74, no. 6 (1995): 2–7.

Zawya. "Careem Bot is Now Helping People in Iraq Book Rides via WhatsApp," June 30, 2009. https://www.zawya.com/en/press-release/careem-bot-is-now-helping-people-in-iraq-book-rides-via-whatsapp-ul37fa3d.

Zawya. "Dubai Internet City Launches 'GoFreelance' to Attract International, Local Tech Talent," November 21, 2018. https://www.zawya.com/mena/en/economy/story/Dubai_Internet_ City_launches_GoFreelance_to_attract_international_local_tech_talent-WAM201811 21112856199.

Zawya. "Dubai Internet City Partners Secure over $2.12Bln in Investment since Its Launch," March 6, 2018. https://www.zawya.com/mena/en/companies/story/Dubai_Internet_ City_partners_secure_over_212bln_in_investment_since_its_launch-ZAWYA2018030 6111919.

Zawya. "Dubai Internet City Welcomes 10th Innovation Centre," November 9, 2017. https:// www.zawya.com/en/press-release/dubai-internet-city-welcomes-10th-innovation-centre-az0ko3gu.

Zawya. "Enterprises in the UAE/KSA Are Leaving IoT Devices Vulnerable to Cybersecurity Threats," October 3, 2019. https://www.zawya.com/en/press-release/enterprises-in-the-uae-and-ksa-are-leaving-iot-devices-vulnerable-to-cybersecurity-threats-finds-ncipher-saywdww4.

Zawya. "Gaming Giant Tencent Games Picks Dubai for MENA Headquarters," June 25, 2019. https://www.zawya.com/mena/en/business/story/Gaming_giant_Tencent_Games_ picks_Dubai_for_MENA_headquarters-SNG_147692182.

Zawya. "Kingdom Accounts for Middle East & Africa's Highest Cosmetics & Beauty Products Consumption," March 10, 2022. https://www.zawya.com/en/press-release/companies-news/kingdom-accounts-for-middle-east-and-africas-highest-cosmetics-and-beauty-produ cts-consumption-bqavl0we.

Zawya. "Landmark Group Launches E-Commerce Site for Centrepoint in Kuwait," October 31, 2019. https://www.zawya.com/en/press-release/landmark-group-launches-e-commerce-site-for-centrepoint-in-kuwait-hbhm1ycg.

Zawya. "MBC Launches New Version of Its Streaming Platform Shahid from Dubai," January 16, 2020. https://www.zawya.com/mena/en/press-releases/story/MBC_launches_new_version_of_its_streaming_platform_Shahid_from_Dubai_the_Capital_of_Arab_Media-ZAWYA20200116153622/.

Zawya. "Strong GCC Consumer Optimism Underlines Opportunities for E-Commerce & Tourism," December 10, 2019. https://www.zawya.com/en/press-release/strong-gcc-consumer-optimism-underlines-opportunities-for-e-commerce-amp-tourism-gvnfkkm4.

Zayani, Mohamed, ed. *A Fledgling Democracy: Tunisia in the Aftermath of the Arab Uprisings.* New York: Oxford University Press, 2022.

Zayani, Mohamed. "Courting and Containing the Arab Street: Arab Public Opinion, the Middle East and U.S. Public Diplomacy." *Arab Studies Quarterly* 30, no. 2 (2008): 45–64.

Zayani, Mohamed. "Digital Journalism, Social Media Platforms and Audience Engagement: The Case of AJ+." *Digital Journalism* 9, no. 1 (2021): 24–41.

Zayani, Mohamed, ed. *Digital Middle East: State and Society in the Middle East.* New York: Oxford University Press, 2018.

Zayani, Mohamed. *Networked Publics and Digital Contention: The Politics of Everyday Life in Tunisia.* Oxford: Oxford University Press, 2015.

Zayani, Mohamed. "Social Movements in the Digital Age: Change and Stasis in the Middle East." In *IEMed Mediterranean Yearbook: Social Movements, Digital Transformations, and Changes in the Mediterranean Region*, 23–29. Barcelona: European Institute of the Mediterranean, 2019.

Zayani, Mohamed. "Transnational Media, Regional Politics and State Security." *British Journal of Middle East Studies* 39, no. 3 (2012): 307–327.

Zayani, Mohamed, and Suzi Mirgani, eds. *Bullets and Bulletins: Politics and the Media in the Wake of the Arab Uprisings.* New York: Oxford University Press, 2016.

Zetter, Kim. "Meet 'Flame,' the Massive Spy Malware Infiltrating Iranian Computers." *Wired*, May 28, 2012. https://www.wired.com/2012/05/flame/.

Zetter, Kim. "The NSA Acknowledges What We All Feared: Iran Learns from US Cyberattacks." *Wired*, February 15, 2015. https://www.wired.com/2015/02/nsa-acknowledges-feared-iran-learns-us-cyberattacks/.

Zhuo, Xiaolin, Barry Wellman, and Justine Yu. "Egypt: The First Internet Revolt?" *Peace Magazine* 27, no. 3 (2011): 6. http://peacemagazine.org/archive/v27n3p06.htm.

Index

Fourth Industrial Revolution, 34, 38–39
France 24, 19

gaming, 142–45
Generation Alpha, 200
Generation Z, 200
Ghonim, Wael, 21, 95
Girls of Riyadh (novel), 180–81
globalization, 18–19, 32
Global North, 224–25
Global South, 17, 22, 35–36, 221–22, 224–25
Google
  Abtal Al Internet (Internet Heroes), 197–98
  artificial intelligence and, 166–67
  BERT, 166–67
  blogs, 82–83, 89
  circumventing censorship and, 104
  cloud computing and, 167
  innovation hubs, 62
  podcasts, 147–48
  search engines, 137
  submarine cables, 33
Google Arts and Culture, 188
Google for Startups Accelerator, 158
Grindr, 207–8
Group of 77, 17. *See also* Non-Aligned
  Movement (NAM)
Gulf Cooperation Council (GCC), 12–13, 38,
  46, 95–96
Gulf Crisis, 114–15
Gulf Information Technology Exhibition
  (GITEX), 166–67
Gulf War, 80, 135

Habib, Elie, 163
hacking, 105–6, 111
hashtag, 221
HBO, 151
healthcare, 36, 150–51
hegemony, 17, 19, 41, 58–59, 84–85
heritage, 188–89, 191–92
Hobeika, Hind, 173–74
Huawei, 32, 165–66
Huda Beauty, 204, 219–20. *See also* Kattan, Huda
hydrocarbon industry, 124, 131
hypermedia, 186, 214

IBM, 135, 167
Ibn Sina (Avicenna), 166–67
identification technology, 109–10
imaginaries, 20–22
imagined community, Middle East as, 14–15
imperialism, 16–17, 26
incubation, 127, 155–56
India, 170
Indian Ocean, 41
Indian subcontinent, 63–64

industrialization, 36–37
influencers
  e-commerce and, 153–54
  realty television, 214–15
  social media, 213–16, 218
information and communication technologies
  (ICTs). *See specific topic*
Information Revolution, 55–57
infrastructure
  generally, 23–25
  Arab uprisings, impact of, 40–41
  artificial intelligence, 36
  autocracy and, 20–21, 38
  China, dependence on for, 32–33
  fiber optics, 20, 29, 31–32
  fintech, 35–36, 168
  healthcare, 36
  internet penetration, 30–32
  leapfrogging, 34–37
  local capacity, developing, 36–37
  local digital networks, shift to, 68
  mobile telephony, 34–36
  national versus regional nature of, 20–21
  neutrality, lack of, 68–69
  personal computers, 31
  predigital era, in, 57–58
  satellite technology, 26–29, 35
  state control over, 58–65, 102–3
  state policy and, 20–21
  submarine cables, 20, 29–30
  telecommunications, 34–36
  variation between countries, 67–68
infrastructure studies, 23–24
innovation initiatives, 62
Instabeat, 173–74
instability of Middle East, 13–14
Instagram
  activism on, 219–20
  statistics of usage, 205–6
  women and, 179, 212–13
integrated digital service providers (IDSPs), 150
international bandwidth usage, 47–48
International Media Support (IMS), 140
International Telecommunication Union (ITU)
  Arab Regional Television Development
    Conference, 56
  digital gender gap statistics, 48
  digital literacy statistics, 49–50
  national digital strategies and, 51
  women and internet usage, on, 202
internet freedom fallacy, 64–65
Internet of Things (IoT), 152, 166–70
internet penetration. *See also specific country*
  infrastructure and, 30–32
  rankings generally, 46–50
Internet Relay Chats (IRCs), 77–78
Internews, 140